MW00770066

Human Technological Enhancement and Theological Anthropology

Victoria Lorrimar explores anthropologies of co-creation as a theological response to the questions posed by technologically enhanced humans, a prospect that is disturbing to some, but compelling for many. The central-ity of the imagination for moral reasoning, attested in recent scholarship on the imagination, offers a fruitful starting point for a theological engage-ment with these envisioned technological futures. Lorrimar approaches the topic under the purview of a doctrine of creation that affirms a rela-tionship between human and divine creativity. Traditionally, theological treatments of creativity have been almost exclusively applied to artis-tic endeavours. Here, Lorrimar breaks new ground by extending such theological accounts to include technology, and uniting them with the strengths of scientific accounts of co-creation. She draws on metaphor studies and cognitive sciences, as well as literary studies, to develop an account of human creativity in relation to divine creativity, which is then applied to various enhancement scenarios.

VICTORIA LORRIMAR is Lecturer in Systematic Theology at Trin-ity College Queensland (Australian College of Theology) and Honorary Research Fellow at the University of Queensland.

VICTORIA LORRIMAR
Trinity College Queensland

Human Technological Enhancement and Theological Anthropology

CAMBRIDGE
UNIVERSITY PRESS

CAMBRIDGE
UNIVERSITY PRESS

University Printing House, Cambridge CB2 8BS, United Kingdom

One Liberty Plaza, 20th Floor, New York, NY 10006, USA

477 Williamstown Road, Port Melbourne, VIC 3207, Australia

314–321, 3rd Floor, Plot 3, Splendor Forum, Jasola District Centre,
New Delhi – 110025, India

103 Penang Road, #05–06/07, Visioncrest Commercial, Singapore 238467

Cambridge University Press is part of the University of Cambridge.

It furthers the University's mission by disseminating knowledge in the pursuit of
education, learning, and research at the highest international levels of excellence.

www.cambridge.org
Information on this title: www.cambridge.org/9781316515020
DOI: 10.1017/9781009091824

© Cambridge University Press 2022

First published 2022

A catalogue record for this publication is available from the British Library.

ISBN 978-1-316-51502-0 Hardback

Contents

Acknowledgements   *page* ix
List of Abbreviations   xi

Introduction   1

I   Understanding the Challenges

1 Visions of Human Enhancement   11
What Is Transhumanism?   11
The Novelty of Human Enhancement?   20
Imagining Prospective Technologies   25
Conclusion   39

2 Human Creativity and a Doctrine of Creation   40
'Playing God'   40
The Relationship Between Divine and Human
   Creativity   43
The Scope of Creativity: Technology as a Creative
   Enterprise   56
Creativity and Fallenness   61
Conclusion   62

II   Responding Theologically to Human Enhancement

3 Humans as 'Created Co-creators'   67
The Created Co-creator in Context   67

Theological Coherency   97
The Created Co-creator as a Response to Human
    Enhancement Issues   114
Conclusion   133

4 **Co-creation Theology and the Imagination**   135
Imagination and Epistemology   135
Why the Imaginative Deficit in Hefner?   145
Retrieving the Imagination   154
Conclusion   168

5 **Humans as 'Sub-creators'**   171
Tolkien's Sub-creation   172
Sub-creation and Reality   181
Sub-creation as a Response to Human Enhancement
    Issues   200
Tolkien's Sub-creation vs. Hefner's Co-creation   201
Tolkien and Technology   203
Conclusion   214

III   **Seeking a Synthesis**

6 **Engaging Human Enhancement Theologically:**
   A New Model of Human Creativity   217
Overcoming Dichotomies of Thought in Co-creation
    Theologies   218
A Vision of Moral Co-creation   224
Conclusion   266

7 **Engaging Human Enhancement Theologically:**
   A Productive Approach   267
Applying the Proposal   270
Conclusion   290

Conclusion   295
Future Direction   298

Bibliography   303
Index   341

Acknowledgements

This project highlights the expansive capacity of the human imagination, yet I cannot imagine an alternate future in which I could have completed it without the support of so many wonderful people.

Alister McGrath supervised the doctoral research that developed into this book and I appreciated his guidance throughout. My thinking benefitted enormously from conversations with Michael Burdett as well as his generosity in including me in a research symposium in Oxford in July 2017 related to his grant 'Creaturehood and Deification in an Age of Biotechnological Enhancement'. As a part-time researcher on this grant, I am also thankful to the John Templeton Foundation for their support, and the collaborations with Michael and other project participants that resulted.

I cannot name all members of the theological community in Oxford who contributed to my formation as a scholar and my overall well-being, but special mention goes to Peter Gent, Oliver Keenan, Elizabeth Li, Megan Loumagne, Kirsten Mackerras, Bethany Sollereder, Tobias Tan and Bill Wood.

I am grateful to the FJ Church Overseas Scholarship Trust for providing support according to Fred Church's original bequest for tuition costs during my three years in Oxford. In the same vein, the generosity of donor John Ford through Oriel College's scholarship in science and theology provided both much-appreciated financial support and the opportunity to be part of Oriel's wonderful community.

My long association with Vose Seminary in Perth, Western Australia, where I completed my Master of Divinity, has been formative for my research and teaching. Michael Parsons was my first teacher in theology and ethics; his unassuming knowledge and gentle wisdom has profoundly shaped my own practice in scholarship, teaching and faith even now. His successor, Michael O'Neil, encouraged me to pursue further studies in theology, and the college allowed me to try my hand at teaching. I have been strengthened by the friendship and mentoring of these faithful witnesses.

Since 2018 I've been privileged to be part of the faculty at Trinity College Queensland. The staff and students have graciously accompanied me as I've tried to figure out the two new roles of teaching and mothering in that time, and I'm thankful for their patience and confidence.

Finally, I would not have produced this work were it not for my parents, who have always encouraged me, and the steady support and adventurous spirit of my husband, Rodney.

List of Abbreviations

The major works of Hefner are abbreviated as follows:

THB   *Technology and Human Becoming* (2003)
THF   *The Human Factor: Evolution, Culture, Religion* (1993)

The major works of Tolkien are abbreviated as follows:

FR   *The Fellowship of the Ring* (1966)
LBN   'Leaf by Niggle' (2001)
Letters   *The Letters of J. R. R. Tolkien* (1981)
LOTR   *The Lord of the Rings* (refers to the whole series)
OFS   *On Fairy-Stories* (2001)
RK   *The Return of the King* (1966)
Silmarillion   *The Silmarillion* (1977)
TT   *The Two Towers* (1966)

Full publication information for each is provided in the bibliography; publication year corresponds to the particular editions consulted.

Introduction

Imagining the Future

For decades, science fiction has captured the imagination concerning our future relationship with technology, and the ways in which it might alter our very nature. We are captivated by narratives of 'technocultures' and human enhancement despite the often dystopic character of such works. For the most part, these possibilities remained firmly in the domain of fiction. Increasingly, however, advances in genetics, robotics, information and nanotechnologies (GRIN) are bringing the fantasies of science fiction writers closer to reality. Ethical questions concerning human genetic modification are no longer merely idle speculations, but pressing concerns, with the development of CRISPR/Cas9 technology in 2014 rendering precise gene-editing solutions within reach.[1] IBM supercomputer Deep Blue's landmark defeat of world chess champion Garry Kasparov in 1997 was superseded by the even more impressive victory of computer program AlphaGo over professional human player Lee Sedol at the complex Chinese strategy board game Go in 2016, injecting new vigour into speculations over the future of artificial intelligence (AI).

Enthusiasm for enhancement technologies reaches its zenith in the transhumanist movement, gaining prominence in academic, commercial and popular spheres. Transhumanists advocate for a deliberate programme of human enhancement ranging from

---

[1] Feng Zhang, Yan Wen and Xiong Guo. 'CRISPR/Cas9 for Genome Editing: Progress, Implications and Challenges', *Human Molecular Genetics* 23 (2014).

radical life extension to cognitive enhancement and even moral enhancement. Despite significant technological advances, many transhumanist visions of future human existence *still* read like science fiction, e.g. the proposal that we may one (not too far off) day scan a human brain and replicate its functionality on a silicon substrate.[2]

The relationship between transhumanism and science fiction bears exploring, however – not only have the visions and aspirations of many technological innovators been inspired by their own reading of science fiction, but many of these professionals have themselves written in the genre. Science fiction as a medium may reflect our understanding of what it means to be human, particularly as it responds to technological possibilities. Take the 2013 film, *Her*, directed by Spike Jonze. We are introduced to lonely Theodore Twombly, who finds friendship and ultimately enters into a romantic relationship with a 'female' AI operating system. Theodore's humanity is not diminished by this encounter with AI, rather much of his emotional dysfunction is healed through the relationship. Despite her non-biological nature, the operating system is essentially attributed a human identity.

Films like *Her*, and the older *A.I.*, demonstrate that our understanding of what makes us human extends beyond our biological makeup. We are moving towards a more fluid notion of human nature as the boundaries between the natural and artificial are blurred. N. Katherine Hayles contends that we are unavoidably posthuman – our technological dependencies and relationships render us cyborgs.[3] We have seen a proliferation of neologisms defining our species in terms of its technological nature – *Homo faber* and 'technosapien' are two which come to mind.

[2] Hans Moravec, *Mind Children: The Future of Robot and Human Intelligence* (Cambridge, MA: Harvard University Press, 1988).
[3] N. Katherine Hayles, *How We Became Posthuman: Virtual Bodies in Cybernetics, Literature, and Informatics* (Chicago, IL: University of Chicago Press, 1999).

The challenges of ever-progressing technology and associated narratives of the future prompt many theological questions. What place does technology have in our understanding of creation, anthropology, soteriology and eschatology? The Christian church is often perceived as standing in opposition to prospective technological enhancements, with the notion of 'playing God' familiar in public discourse. We associate the use of technology to enhance human capabilities with the Greek myth of Prometheus, a Titan who stole fire from the gods and gifted it to humanity. For the most part this myth is deployed as a warning against hubris (hence Mary Shelley gave her novel *Frankenstein* the subtitle of *The Modern Prometheus*), reinforcing the bounds of human creaturehood.

Yet there is a trajectory in Christian thought that can be offset against these objections. Notions of creaturely finitude exist in tension with celebrations of human freedom and creativity. From the Renaissance humanist thinkers who extolled the unique creativity of humans among the creation and their capacity to determine their own nature, to the 'Noosphere', or collective consciousness, that Pierre Teilhard de Chardin imagined humanity is evolving towards, the malleability of human nature and the freedom to alter it have been championed by particular individuals or groups.

Since the time of the Renaissance, the claims for human artistry have grown more audacious, but a biblical exploration suggests that we may properly locate human creativity within an overarching doctrine of creation. Our understanding of creativity is further informed by the field of creativity studies, which, generally, highlights both novelty and value as important dimensions, and theological analogies concerning creativity are important background to the central questions of this research. While the majority of scholarship around human creativity concentrates on the arts for its subject, the chief contention of this work is that *technology* is a legitimate element of human making and therefore may be fruitfully engaged through the lens of human creativity.

Those theologians who have approached technological progress with degrees of optimism tend towards understandings of
humans as co-creators with God. The notion of co-creation also
has historical roots, however recent accounts rely increasingly on
scientific arguments as well as theological. Philip Hefner's theological anthropology of the 'created co-creator' arguably represents
the most sustained attempt at a scientifically engaged theology of
co-creation, understanding humans as products of biocultural evolution with both agency and responsibility for accomplishing God's
purposes for the whole creation.[4] Hefner's model has been formative for certain accounts of theological anthropology, particularly
as theologians consider the relationship between continuing creation and the eschatological future. Co-creation theologies are often
central in theological engagements with emerging technologies that
allow us to manipulate both human and non-human nature.[5]

The technological nature of transhumanist visions invites, even
requires, a corresponding engagement with technology on the part
of theologians who would respond to transhumanism, or human
enhancement more generally. The imaginative dimension of transhumanism, particularly evident in its relationship with science
fiction, also suggests that the imagination ought to receive attention in theological responses to the movement.[6] This study owes its
timeliness to a confluence of developments in theology, cognitive

---

[4] Philip Hefner, *The Human Factor: Evolution, Culture, Religion* (Minneapolis, MN:
Fortress Press, 1993).

[5] Ted Peters, for example, builds on Hefner's understanding of co-creation in his own
articulation of future-oriented human freedom (*Playing God? Genetic Determinism
and Human Freedom*, 2nd edn (New York: Routledge, 2003), 125). Ron Cole-Turner
highlights the co-creative agency of humans in his cautiously optimistic response to
human genetic enhancement ('Biotechnology and the Religion-Science Discussion',
In *The Oxford Handbook of Religion and Science*, ed. Philip Clayton (Oxford: Oxford
University Press, 2008), 942–943).

[6] Michael Burdett, in a recent assessment of the historical and contemporary
landscape of the science and religion field, laments the neglect of the imagination in
science and religion scholarship (Michael Burdett, 'Assessing the Field of Science
and Religion: Advice from the Next Generation', *Zygon* 52, no. 3 (2017), 760).

science and literary studies. Particular currents of thought in these fields are brought into conversation with theological anthropologies developed in the area of science and religion. Graham Ward describes the imagination as the thread that brings together theology, literature and philosophy. Essential to theology, 'exploring the divine is always an exploration of the imagination or that store of images which the imagination stirs into patterns and narratives'.[7] Though often overlooked, the imagination occupies an equally important place in scientific enquiry.

The imagination's importance is attested in various scientific, philosophical and theological sources. The excesses of Romanticism notwithstanding, there is renewed interest in the imagination's capacity to illuminate truths inaccessible to the senses or abstracted reason. Independent programmes of scholarship are calling greater attention to the role of the imagination in scientific investigation, and to its importance for theological construction. When it comes to accounting for human imagination, the science and religion field has yet to catch up with developments in the separate disciplines of theology and of science.

Jeanine Thweatt-Bates expresses the hope that theologians might participate in the construction of the 'posthuman'.[8] This book aims at such participation, offering a much-needed evaluation of existing theological resources for constructive engagement with enhancement technologies, and suggestions for the enrichment of such resources. With renewed attention to the imagination, a scientifically oriented theology of co-creation might be rehabilitated for a robust contribution to human enhancement discourse.

In exploring a theological anthropology of humans as co-creators with God, this book focuses on epistemological concerns as they intersect with the discernment of appropriate human

---

7 Graham Ward, *Unbelievable: Why We Believe and Why We Don't* (London: I. B. Tauris, 2014), 200–203.

8 Jeanine Thweatt-Bates, *Cyborg Selves: A Theological Anthropology of the Posthuman* (Surrey: Ashgate Publishing, 2012), 8.

action. While an epistemological focus identifies pertinent critiques of the theological anthropologies considered here, it has its limitations also. The noetic effects of sin, particularly for the imagination as an emphasis of this study, are only gestured towards but have clear implications for both discernment and practical application when it comes to humans acting as co-creators. Human activity is grounded within a soteriology that extends far beyond epistemology, and the discussion of co-creation here is situated within an (assumed) orthodox understanding of salvation as effected by God, and not by us.

Views of human creativity can easily fall prey to anthropological conceits. In a theological discussion of creation and redemption, our preoccupation with the human experience may cause us to forget that we are located within the broader context of creatureliness. This work treats its central questions, therefore, within an overarching theological understanding that resists human exceptionalism, a theme that will be considered at the margins of this work.

To make the case for an imaginative, scientifically informed theology of co-creation, this study is divided into three parts. Part I establishes the foundations of the study, introducing the philosophical and theological questions posed by human technological enhancement. Chapter 1 surveys representative enhancements envisioned by transhumanists and other enhancement advocates and explores their imaginative reach into the public sphere, particularly through the medium of science fiction. Chapter 2 highlights the tendency towards a negative Christian evaluation of technological enhancement as 'playing God', and explores the relationship between human creativity and divine creation in terms of its biblical foundations, historical development, insights from the field of creativity studies and the contributions of select theological accounts. Part II introduces the major theological interlocutors for the study. Hefner's created co-creator model is taken as a starting point, engaging as it does with scientific insights, and is interrogated in terms of the scientific methodology he adopts and the usefulness of his framework for reflecting on human technological enhancement (Chapter 3). Identifying an imaginative deficit in Hefner's approach, Chapter 4 reviews the epistemological importance accorded to the imagination in select scientific and theological discourse. J. R. R. Tolkien's proposal of humans as 'sub-creators' is introduced as an imaginative corrective to Hefner's approach, and evaluated for its ability to address technological questions (Chapter 5). Can the scientifically grounded notion of human creativity developed in light of real-world concerns be united with a more literary approach to human creativity that draws on the imagination to both inspire human action and caution against overstepping limits? Part III gives an affirmative answer to this question, locating a synthesis and extension of the relative strengths of Hefner's and Tolkien's understanding of human creativity in the interstices of contemporary theology, cognitive science and literature studies. Studies in metaphor, phenomenology and posthumanism are incorporated into a preliminary sketch of a constructive theology of co-creation that can engage with transhumanist visions of a technologically enhanced humanity. Chapter 6 draws on these additional disciplines in mapping the terrain of an imaginative, scientifically informed theological anthropology, which is then applied to several human enhancement scenarios in Chapter 7 to demonstrate its utility.

Preliminary versions of sections from the third chapter of this work were published as 'The Scientific Character of the Created Co-Creator', *Zygon* 52, no. 3 (2017): 726–746; 'Are Scientific Research Programmes Applicable to Theology? On Philip Hefner's Use of Lakatos', *Theology and Science* 15, no. 2 (2017): 188–202; and 'Human Uniqueness and Technology: Are We Co-Creators with God?' in *Issues in Science and Theology: Are We Special?*, ed. M. Fuller, D. Evers, A. Runehov and K. Saether (New York: Springer, 2018). Sections from the first and final chapters were published together in 'Human Flourishing, Joy, and the Prospect of Radical Life Extension', *The Expository Times* 129, no. 12 (2018): 554–561.

The goal of this book is to deepen our understanding of human creativity from a theological perspective, and to resource Christian theology (and more broadly the church) for reflecting on the possibilities for enhancing human capabilities through (plausible or far-fetched) technologies.

Part I | Understanding the Challenges

1 | Visions of Human Enhancement

What Is Transhumanism?

Transhumanism is a movement that promotes the enhancement of the human condition through advancing technologies such as genetic engineering, nanotechnology and AI.[1] It seeks the evolution of intelligent life beyond the human, both its form and limitations.[2] Complete liberation from the constraints of natural evolution is the ultimate vision of transhumanism.[3]

Nick Bostrom, on behalf of the World Transhumanist Association, formally defines the movement as follows:

(1) The intellectual and cultural movement that affirms the possibility and desirability of fundamentally improving the human condition through applied reason, especially by developing and making

[1] Nick Bostrom and Michael Depaul, 'Transhumanist Values', *Journal of Philosophical Research* 30 (2005), 3. The term 'transhumanism' is often used interchangeably with 'posthumanism'. 'Transhumanism' will generally be used here, as 'posthumanism' can also refer to a school of thought that rejects humanism and the Enlightenment emphasis on the individual (Stuart Sim, 'Posthumanism', In *The Routledge Companion to Postmodernism*, ed. Stuart Sim (London: Routledge, 2012), 1). The work will still draw upon resources that use the term 'posthumanism' in an equivalent sense to 'transhumanism'. For example, Brent Waters uses the term 'posthumanism' in speaking about technological enhancement of human being (*From Human to Posthuman: Christian Theology and Technology in a Postmodern World* (Aldershot: Ashgate Publishing, 2006)).

[2] Anders Sandberg, 'Transhumanism and the Meaning of Life', In *Religion and Transhumanism: The Unknown Future of Human Enhancement*, ed. Calvin Mercer and Tracy Trothen (Santa Barbara, CA: Praeger Publishers, 2015), 3.

[3] *Ibid.*, 9.

widely available technologies to eliminate aging and to greatly enhance human intellectual, physical, and psychological capacities. (2) The study of the ramifications, promises, and potential dangers of technologies that will enable us to overcome fundamental human limitations, and the related study of the ethical matters involved in developing and using such technologies.[4]

Transhumanism is not homogenous, however. Anders Sandberg highlights three separate strands of transhumanism, aiming for the enhancement of the individual, the betterment of humanity or the achievement of life potential for the universe.[5] Accepting that the movement has its own diversity, this work will focus on several major themes within transhumanism as they are advanced by representative thinkers. The specific technologies involved are less relevant here than the ways in which the future of humanity is envisioned.

Furthermore, transhumanism is not only concerned with the technological enhancement of the human person but is bound up in a greater vision for the transformation of human society.[6] James Hughes, bioethicist and transhumanist, contends that 'we cannot imagine the grandeur of transhuman civilisation', in much the same way that the present civilisation transcends that of our Paleolithic ancestors.[7] Hughes' affirmation of the transhumanist approach is driven by both positive and negative motivations. On the one hand, fear of becoming the 'ensnared victims' of the

[4] Nick Bostrom, 'The Transhumanist FAQ: A General Introduction (Version 2.1)', *World Transhumanist Association*, 2003, www.nickbostrom.com/views/transhum anist.pdf, 4.
[5] Sandberg, 'Transhumanism and the Meaning of Life', 4.
[6] Stephen Garner, 'Christian Theology and Transhumanism: The 'Created Co-creator' and Bioethical Principles', In *Religion and Transhumanism: The Unknown Future of Human Enhancement*, ed. Calvin Mercer and Tracy Trothen (Santa Barbara, CA: Praeger Publishers, 2015), 229.
[7] James Hughes, 'The Big Questions: What Comes after Homo Sapiens?' 70–72 www.newscientist.com/article/mg19225780-076-the-big-questions-what-comes-after-homo-sapiens/, 71.

'exponentially growing web of machines' requires us to embrace transhumanism and remain ahead of the 'singularity'.[8] On the other hand, transhumanism represents the Enlightenment's positive vision at its zenith, the means by which we might create once and for all a 'single tolerant democratic society'.[9] For transhumanists, human enhancement is the route to a good life.

Acknowledging that transhumanism as a philosophy considers the technological enhancement of human characteristics in a holistic sense, particular aspects of human enhancement will be examined as examples: hedonic recalibration, radical life extension, mind-uploading and moral enhancement. With the exception of mind-uploading, perhaps, these enhancements may be endorsed to varying degrees by those who do not identify as transhumanist – transhumanism simply sits at the extreme end of advocacy for employing technology in aid of human enhancement. The examples given are by no means exhaustive – a range of cognitive and physical enhancements proposed and envisioned would fall outside of the categories represented. Nor are particular technologies or enhancements in focus; what follows is merely a brief survey of what enhancement might entail before the questions are treated in a more general sense.

Radical Life Extension

Humanity as a whole has sought immortality as far back as we can ascertain through literature. From at least the time of the ancient Sumerian *Epic of Gilgamesh* onward, ideas of immortality have captivated the human imagination, taking different shape as technology develops.

Radical life extension is a growing area of research (and funding).[10] Transhumanist Aubrey de Grey and colleagues envision

---

[8] *Ibid.*, 71.

[9] *Ibid.*, 71.

[10] For one example of serious engagement with anti-ageing research, see Google's company Calico: www.calicolabs.com/.

what they term 'engineered negligible senescence', proposing to prevent ageing by targeting the biomolecular processes associated with progressive loss of vitality on an individual basis.[11] A combination of gene therapy, exercise and growth factor supplementation can counter age-related cell loss, while genetically engineered muscle might negate a decline in hormone secretion.[12] The logic of the philosophical Ship of Theseus is applied (as the ship voyaged, each plank was replaced one at a time so that the ship was perpetually replenished) to biological cells.[13] Life extension in an enhancement context is not merely a lengthened life (which could include prolonged senescence), but a slowing down or reversal of the ageing process that also increases health and quality of life.[14]

De Grey personally hopes to reach 'longevity escape velocity' (or 'actuarial escape velocity'), living long enough to benefit from rejuvenation therapies and thus stay ahead of the ageing curve.[15] He calls for policy measures that will prioritise such research, highlighting the elimination of retirement benefits as an economic incentive, and considers thousand-year lifespans to be attainable.[16] Bostrom represents death in fable form as an evil tyrant of a dragon, which must be killed.[17] Of course, a negative view of death alone does not equal transhumanism, except where combined with advocacy for radical life extension. Michael Hauskeller makes the

---

[11] For a summary of de Grey and colleagues' proposal for 'engineering negligible senescence', see Aubrey de Grey et al., 'Time to Talk SENS: Critiquing the Immutability of Human Aging', *Annals of the New York Academy of Sciences* 959 (2002).

[12] *Ibid.*, 456.

[13] Larry Temkin, 'Is Living Longer Living Better?' in *Enhancing Human Capacities*, ed. Julian Savulescu, Ruud ter Meulen and Guy Kahane (Chichester: Wiley-Blackwell, 2011), 352.

[14] Gaia Barazzetti and Massimo Reichlin. 'Life Extension and Personal Identity', in *Enhancing Human Capacities*, ed. Julian Savulescu, Ruud ter Meulen and Guy Kahane (Chichester: Wiley-Blackwell, 2011), 398.

[15] Aubrey de Grey, 'Escape Velocity: Why the Prospect of Extreme Human Life Extension Matters Now'. *PLOS Biology* 2, nos. 723–726 (2004).

[16] *Ibid.*

[17] Nick Bostrom, 'The Fable of the Dragon Tyrant', *Journal of Medical Ethics* 31 (2005).

valid point that a wish to avoid death can be held simultaneously with a reluctance to live forever, even if both desires cannot be achieved together.[18]

Hedonic Recalibration

Another dimension of human enhancement is the notion of 'hedonic recalibration'. David Pearce argues that pain and suffering can be entirely removed from our experience through pharmaceutical and genetic intervention, promoting an abolitionist project seeking the annihilation of pain in all sentient life (beginning with humans).[19] Pearce terms his online manifesto to abolish suffering 'The Hedonist Imperative', revealing some of the philosophical underpinnings of the project. In this vision of enhanced human life, well-being is genetically programmed.[20]

Though largely in agreement with Pearce, Bostrom emphasises a more positive concept of the good life i.e. a life that is marked not only by the absence of suffering but by an abundance of 'good' feelings. He offers the following appeal in favour of increasing both the quality and the length of life:

> Have you ever been so happy that you felt like melting into tears? Has there been a moment in your life of such depth and sublimity that the rest of existence seemed like dull, gray slumber from which you had only just woken up? It is so easy to forget how good things can be when they are at their best. But on those occasions when we do remember – whether it comes from the total fulfillment of being immersed in creative work or from the tender ecstasy of reciprocated love – then we realize just how valuable every single minute of existence can be, when it is this good. And you might have thought to yourself, 'It ought to be like this always. Why can't this last forever?'

---

[18] Michael Hauskeller, *Better Humans? Understanding the Enhancement Project* (New York: Routledge, 2013), 90.

[19] David Pearce, 'The Abolitionist Project', 2007, www.abolitionist.com/.

[20] Bostrom, 'The Transhumanist FAQ', 44.

Well, maybe – just maybe – it could.[21]

We might ask how the engineering of positive affect envisioned here connects with a deeper sense of meaning or purpose. Sandberg describes efforts to construct and articulate 'pure transhumanist concepts of meaning'.[22] The notion of extropianism (synonymous with transhumanism) was developed and disseminated by the Extropy Institute in the early 1990s – an institution that has shaped much of contemporary transhumanism. Transhumanist advocate Max More uses 'meaning' in a psychological sense (as opposed to teleological or ethical) in his claim that extropianism provides 'an inspiring and uplifting meaning and direction to our lives, while remaining flexible and firmly founded in science, reason, and the boundless search for improvement'.[23]

Greg Wadley presents mood enhancement as a characteristic of existing technologies and investigates the ways in which digital technologies are used to improve mood.[24] He argues that emerging technologies such as wearable devices that induce transcranial direct current stimulation operate in similar ways to many pharmaceutical mood interventions and represent an alternative option for regulating and enhancing mood.[25]

Moral Enhancement

Others would identify human morality as a target for enhancement through technology. Defining moral enhancement is especially tricky; Harris Wiseman offers a working rendition of moral enhancement as 'some technological or pharmacological means of affecting the biological aspects of moral functioning, to boost

---

[21] *Ibid.*, 34.

[22] Sandberg, 'Transhumanism and the Meaning of Life', 6.

[23] More, Max. 'The Extropian Principles 2.5', *Extropy* 11 (1993); Sandberg, 'Transhumanism and the Meaning of Life', 7.

[24] Greg Wadley, 'Mood-Enhancing Technology', in *Proceedings of the 28th Australian Conference on Computer-Human Interaction* (New York: ACM, 2016).

[25] *Ibid.*, 327.

what is desirable, or remove what is problematic'.[26] Aimed generally at the psychological and affective functioning of people, moral enhancement shares much in common with the mood enhancement proposals discussed in the previous section.

Ingmar Persson and Julian Savulescu call for the use of biomedical means of moral enhancement, focusing especially on the development and application of psychopharmaceuticals to this end.[27] As traditional approaches to moral education have had only limited success, argue Savulescu and Persson, global environmental catastrophe can only be avoided through biomedical means of moral enhancement.[28] Essentially, they argue that the human psychology and morality that has developed through evolutionary pressures is no longer fit for purpose in the advanced technological and populous societies most people inhabit today.[29] Moral enhancement is not merely desirable, in this view, but imperative to keep up with the likely effects of cognitive enhancement.[30] Through drug treatment and genetic engineering, we might speed up the 'motivational internalisation of moral doctrines'.[31] Increasing oxytocin levels, for example, may increase trust and other pro-social behaviours.[32] Similarly, increasing serotonin levels through the use of selective serotonin reuptake inhibitors (SSRIs) can reduce aggression and

---

[26] Harris Wiseman, *The Myth of the Moral Brain: The Limits of Moral Enhancement* (Cambridge, MA: MIT Press, 2016), 6.

[27] Ingmar Persson and Julian Savulescu, 'Unfit for the Future? Human Nature, Scientific Progress, and the Need for Moral Enhancement', in *Enhancing Human Capacities*, ed. Julian Savulescu, Ruud ter Meulen and Guy Kahane (Chichester: Wiley-Blackwell, 2011), 498.

[28] Ingmar Persson and Julian Savulescu, *Unfit for the Future: The Need for Moral Enhancement* (Oxford: Oxford University Press, 2012), 9–10.

[29] Persson and Savulescu, 'Unfit for the Future?' 486.

[30] Ingmar Persson and Julian Savulescu, 'The Perils of Cognitive Enhancement and the Urgent Imperative to Enhance the Moral Character of Humanity', *Journal of Applied Philosophy* 25, no. 3 (2008). Note that they interpret cognitive enhancement loosely to include the use of external aids such as supercomputers.

[31] Persson and Savulescu, *Unfit for the Future*, 107.

[32] *Ibid.*, 119.

increase cooperation.[33] More generally, moral enhancement should target dispositions related to altruism and justice.[34] Robin Hanson makes a related argument that we should use (unspecified) brain augmentation techniques to increase transparency, reduce self-deception and thus encourage a 'truth-orientation'.[35]

As a natural extension of the imperative to enhance our own moral sensibility, Savulescu further contends that we should harness our growing ability to manipulate human genes to deliberately engineer 'ethically better children'.[36] Again, this is motivated by a somewhat utilitarian argument in support of future generations. For the most part, proposals for moral enhancement are tentative in nature, acknowledging the intricate relationships between positive and negative emotions and the difficulty of achieving specific enhancements. Moral enhancement is a fraught subject; the judging of what is 'moral' is complicated; however, advocates contend that the technological engineering of greater morality is a worthy pursuit given the challenges before humanity and the positive outcomes that could be realised.

Mind-Uploading

At the more radical end of transhumanist proposals is the notion of 'mind-uploading'. Hans Moravec, former director of robotics at Carnegie-Mellon University and developer of advanced robots for both NASA and the military, was the first scientist to popularise the idea of living perpetually via a digital substrate. In his 1988 work *Mind Children*, he envisioned a procedure in which the entirety of the information encoded within the neurons of a human brain

---

[33] Persson and Savulescu, 'Unfit for the Future?' 499

[34] Persson and Savulescu, 'The Perils of Cognitive Enhancement', 169.

[35] Robin Hanson, 'Enhancing Our Truth Orientation', in *Human Enhancement*, ed. by Nick Bostrom and Julian Savulescu (Oxford: Oxford University Press, 2009).

[36] Julian Savulescu, 'The Maverick: 'It's Our Duty to Have Designer Babies', 2012, www.readersdigest.co.uk/magazine/readers-digest-main/themaverick-its-our-duty-to-have-designer-babies; cf. Julian Savulescu, 'Procreative Beneficence: Why We Should Select the Best Children', *Bioethics* 15 (2001).

could be read, copied and uploaded to a computer.[37] Rather than a radical extension of biological life, this approach seeks immortality through software existence.

Moravec captures the prevailing attitude towards the body taken by proponents of mind-uploading. He defines human being as

> The *pattern* and the *process* going on in my head and body, not the machinery supporting that process. If the process is preserved, I am preserved. The rest is mere jelly.[38]

This vision relies on a material understanding of the self, thus allowing replication on a computer model, and it is common for 'uploaders' to use the language of information technology in describing the human brain.[39]

Ray Kurzweil considers mind-uploading to be a likely scenario, picturing a point in the future at which 'we will have effectively uploaded ourselves, albeit gradually, never quite noticing the transfer'.[40] Apart from increased longevity, mind-uploading also pursues the goal of greater intelligence through escaping the limitations of the biological, degenerating brain. Personal identity and memories can be 'backed up', and the uploaded mind would benefit from running on a more efficient 'compiler'.[41]

This is only a brief foray into the types of technological enhancements envisioned, which cover lifespan, happiness, morality and intelligence. While there are specific discourses, including critique, surrounding each particular type of enhancement,

---

[37] Moravec, *Mind Children*, 109.

[38] Moravec, *Mind Children*, 117.

[39] See, for example, Ralph Merkle, 'Uploading: Transferring Consciousness from Brain to Computer', *Extropy: The Journal of Transhumanist Thought* 11 (1993).

[40] Ray Kurzweil, *The Singularity Is Near: When Humans Transcend Biology* (London: Penguin Books, 2005), 202.

[41] Randal Koene, 'Uploading to Substrate-Independent Minds', In *The Transhumanist Reader: Classical and Contemporary Essays on the Science, Technology, and Philosophy of the Human Future*, ed. Max More and Natasha Vita-More (Oxford: Wiley & Sons, 2013), 147–148.

this work is concerned not with ethics at a casuistry level, but with the general project of enhancing human characteristics through technology, and its theological import. Additionally, human enhancement is not necessarily given a blanket endorsement by its proponents but is nuanced in the support it receives; Savulescu and Persson, for example, argue strongly against research into increased longevity in their advocacy of moral bioenhancement.[42] Bostrom and Hughes both focus more on the motivating effect of existential risks in their own arguments for a transhumanist position; while generally positive towards human enhancement, their approbation of particular augmentations is less clear.

The Novelty of Human Enhancement?

Many of the objections levelled at enhancement technologies frame them as a new and unprecedented threat in human history, requiring urgent action. Leon Kass describes the biotechnological revolution as 'not the old crude power to kill the creature made in God's image, but the new science-based power to remake him after our own fantasies'.[43]

Just how novel are these transhumanist visions of the future? Gerhold Becker similarly asks:

Has biotech just opened a new chapter in the long history of the scientific conquest of nature, or has it effectively closed the old volume and begun to write the first lines of an entirely different story? … Can we utilize its potential and carry on with our familiar worldviews and religious interpretations of the world, or is biotechnology in itself some sort of new ideology which challenges our traditional place in nature? Is it endowing us with the creative powers of

[42] Persson and Savulescu, *Unfit for the Future*, 131.
[43] Leon Kass, 'Ageless Bodies, Happy Souls: Biotechnology and the Pursuit of Perfection', *The New Atlantis* 1 (2003), 10.

God, or rather reducing us and the mystery of life to mere genetic components at the molecular level?[44]

Peter Medawar, in his essay 'The Genetic Improvement of Man', contends that the notion of improving humanity in some way 'must be pretty well coeval with human speculative thought'.[45] He distinguishes three major categories of future visions when it comes to human improvement: Olympian, Arcadian and Utopian. The Olympian vision holds that humans can become like gods, achieving moral perfection though spiritual insight and discipline. Olympians direct their improving gaze upwards or inwards, according to Medawar. The Arcadian, however, directs their gaze back in time, towards an ancient Golden Age. Improvement takes the form of a natural innocence, where progress is eschewed and peace is the goal. The Utopian looks neither inwards nor backwards in their quest for improvement but always forwards, believing that human improvement comes through mastery of the physical environment and new creation.[46] Speaking of utopia in a more general sense, Mark Coeckelbergh argues instead that utopian thinking often looks backward and forward at the same time in its vision of an alternative society.[47]

Bostrom acknowledges the historical continuity of the transhumanist movement as well, describing it as a progression from early myths of immortality such as the *Epic of Gilgamesh*.[48] He traces the roots of transhumanism to the 'rational humanism' arising

---

[44] Gerhold Becker, 'Biotechnology: The New Ethical Frontier: An Introduction', in *Changing Nature's Course: The Ethical Challenge of Biotechnology*, ed. Gerhold Becker (Hong Kong: Hong Kong University Press, 1996), 5.

[45] P. B. Medawar, 'The Genetic Improvement of Man', in *The Hope of Progress* (London: Methuen & Co., 1972), 69.

[46] Medawar, 'The Genetic Improvement of Man', 69–70.

[47] He gives the example of William Morris' *News from Nowhere* (Mark Coeckelbergh, *New Romantic Cyborgs: Romanticism, Information Technology, and the End of the Machine* (Cambridge, MA: MIT Press, 2017), 58.

[48] Nick Bostrom, 'A History of Transhumanist Thought', *Journal of Evolution and Technology* 14, no. 1 (2005), 1–4.

from the convergence of Renaissance humanism with Enlightenment scientific and critical reasoning.[49] We might, therefore, locate transhumanism as the latest instalment of a historical trajectory emphasising human dominion over nature, as well as the malleability of human nature, and the freedom and responsibility of humans to improve their capabilities. Renaissance humanist thinkers extolled the unique creativity of humans among the creation and their capacity to determine their own nature. Francis Bacon, the 'father of modern science', extended the vision of Italian humanists by uniting the idea of dominion over nature with the promise of modern empirical science. The introduction of evolutionary theory after Darwin provided additional resources to this trajectory – human malleability now encompassed the biological nature as well.

We need to consider the claims, promises and fears associated with transhumanism within this larger history that has understood human nature to be malleable and sought to improve it. As Medawar reminds us, before the transhumanism of today properly emerged it has long been within our means to influence human biological nature on a large scale through selective breeding and culling, and there are plenty of non-scientific means of corrupting human moral nature. Similarly, technology has been bound up in human evolution in various degrees. Medawar suggests that the 'proxy evolution of humans beings through exosomatic instruments has contributed more to our biological success that the conventional evolution of our own, or endosomatic, organs'.[50] We may be alarmed at the greater risk posed by more recent scientific advances, but they are by no means entirely new.[51]

---

[49] Bostrom, 'The Transhumanist FAQ', 39–40.

[50] P. B. Medawar, 'Technology and Evolution', in *Pluto's Republic* (Oxford: Oxford University Press, 1982), 185.

[51] P. B. Medawar, 'Science and the Sanctity of Life', in *The Hope of Progress* (London: Methuen & Co., 1972), 87–88.

Transhumanism as a Religious Narrative

On the surface, transhumanism appears to represent the height of a 'scientistic' confidence in human capabilities, the 'progress' narrative taken to its ultimate conclusion. Yet, in many respects, transhumanist expectations for the future resemble religious ones. Ron Cole-Turner provides an interesting comparison of the visions held by some transhumanists, specifically with respect to the technological singularity, with the apocalyptic future described by several popular evangelical Christians.[52] Robert Geraci agrees, arguing that 'the sacred categories of Jewish and Christian apocalyptic traditions have thoroughly penetrated the futuristic musings of important researchers in robotics and artificial intelligence'.[53]

The resemblance between Christian eschatology and transhumanism must not be overstated, however. Superficially, the respective futures in which transhumanists and Christians place their hope share some similarities – immortality, a removal of suffering, etc. Christians and transhumanists generally share the expectation that the future will differ markedly from the present.[54] But there are some key differences between the two worldviews. While technology is credited with achieving human transcendence in transhumanist thought, for Christians this transformation can only be brought about through the work of divine grace.[55] Furthermore, technology's promise of control over the self may be set against religion's requirement to surrender the self.[56]

Brent Waters summarises this adjusted understanding of transhumanism well:

---

[52] Ronald Cole-Turner, 'The Singularity and the Rapture: Transhumanist and Popular Christian Views of the Future', *Zygon* 47, no. 4 (2012).

[53] Robert Geraci, *Apocalyptic AI: Visions of Heaven in Robotics, Artificial Intelligence, and Virtual Reality* (New York: Oxford University Press, 2010), 7.

[54] Cole-Turner, 'The Singularity and the Rapture', 792.

[55] Ronald Cole-Turner, 'Going beyond the Human: Christians and Other Transhumanists', *Theology and Science* 13, no. 2 (2015), 154–155.

[56] Cole-Turner, 'Biotechnology', 941.

The prospect of becoming posthuman is *not* a profane, postmodern alternative to a modern paradigm, mired and encumbered by primitive and un-exorcized religious beliefs. Rather, posthuman discourse represents idiosyncratic religious sentiments that have been forged in postmodern and historicist rhetoric which retains, albeit in a highly eclectic structure, a providential and progressive grammar. Posthumanism is *not* a postmodern alternative to lingering religious beliefs, but is itself a contending postmodern religion.[57]

Bostrom contends, nevertheless, that transhumanism is able to serve some of the same functions that have traditionally been fulfilled by religion: offering a greater vision and a sense of purpose.[58] Transhumanists reject supernaturalism and 'irreducible spiritual phenomena', however, as they 'prefer to derive their understanding of the world from rational modes of enquiry'.[59] Former evangelical Christian Meghan O'Gieblyn lends weight to the understanding of transhumanism as a religious substitute, recounting her own disillusionment with Christian faith and discovery of transhumanist philosophy as a satisfying alternative.

Transhumanism offered a vision of redemption without the thorny problems of divine justice. It was an evolutionary approach to eschatology, one in which humanity took it upon itself to bring about the final glorification of the body and could not be blamed if the path to redemption was messy or inefficient.[60]

As we shall see, thinking of transhumanism in religious terms is helpful in formulating a Christian response to the challenges presented by the movement. We would do well, however, to

---

[57] Waters, *From Human to Posthuman*, 79.

[58] Bostrom, 'The Transhumanist FAQ', 46.

[59] *Ibid.*, 46.

[60] Meghan O'Gieblyn, 'God in the Machine: My Strange Journey into Transhumanism', *The Guardian*, www.theguardian.com/technology/2017/apr/18/god-in-the-machine-my-strange-journey-into-transhumanism.

heed Thweatt-Bates' warning against drawing parallels too quickly between transhumanism and religion, without taking the former on its own terms, as this is likely to prematurely forestall dialogue.[61] As such, the relationship between human enhancement and the popular imagination is considered next, before looking at the more particular ways in which Christian theology has responded to these prospective enhancements.

Imagining Prospective Technologies

Science Fiction and Technology

For many, narratives of 'technocultures' and human enhancement are reminiscent of science fiction, and often dismissed for this reason. The relationship between transhumanism and science fiction is worth exploring, however – not only have the visions and aspirations of many technological innovators been inspired by their own reading of science fiction, but many of these professionals have themselves written in the genre.

So, what exactly is science fiction? A good starting point is Kingsley Amis' description:

> Science fiction is that class of prose narrative treating of a situation that could not arise in the world we know, but which is hypothesised on the basis of some innovation in science or technology, or pseudo-science or pseudo-technology, whether human or extra-terrestrial in origin.[62]

As J. M. Van der Laan points out, however, much of science fiction deals with science and technology scenarios that *could* plausibly arise, or are visible on the horizon. He points to the example of Ray Bradbury, who was in the process of imagining the 'seashells'

---

[61] Thweatt-Bates, *Cyborg Selves*, 61.

[62] Kingsley Amis, *New Maps of Hell: A Survey of Science Fiction* (New York: Arno Press, 1975), 18.

(thimble-sized radios) that one of his characters places in her ears to listen to audio in *Fahrenheit 451*, only to see a passer-by wearing earbuds (a technology which he had not yet encountered).[63] This is an example of science fiction 'dramatiz[ing] for us how the present has already been invaded by the future'.[64]

Margaret Atwood distinguishes between science fiction proper and speculative fiction, arguing that the former 'denotes books with things in them we can't yet do or begin to do, talking beings we can never meet, and places we can't go', while the latter 'employs the means already more or less to hand, and takes place on Planet Earth'.[65] A more general definition is offered in *The Encyclopedia of Science Fiction*: 'SF [science fiction] proper requires a consciousness of the scientific outlook, and it probably also requires a sense of the possibilities of change, whether social or technological.'[66] The diversity of science fiction literature renders a more precise definition unlikely, and this serves as a guiding demarcation for the genre.

Examining the purposes and functions of science fiction is more fruitful than attempting to define it. In his comprehensive *History of Science Fiction*, Adam Roberts labels the majority of science fiction written in the nineteenth and twentieth centuries as 'extrapolated technology fiction'.[67] Well-known science fiction writer Ursula Le Guin explains the role of science fiction in contemplating possible futures. 'The future is a safe, sterile laboratory for

---

[63] J. M. van der Laan, 'Editor's Notes: Science, Technology, and Science Fiction', *Bulletin of Science Technology & Society* 30, no. 4 (2010), 234. Van der Laan actually draws this example from Amis, *New Maps of Hell*, 112.

[64] Veronica Hollinger, 'Science Fiction and Postmodernism', in *A Companion to Science Fiction*, ed. D. Seed (Malden, MA: Blackwell, 2005), 246.

[65] Margaret Atwood, '*The Handmaid's Tale* and *Oryx and Crake* in Context', *PMLA: Publications of the Modern Language Association of America* 119, no. 3 (2004), 513.

[66] Brian Stableford, John Clute and Peter Nicholls. 'History of SF', In *The Encyclopedia of Science Fiction* (New York: St. Martin's Press, 1993), 567.

[67] Adam Roberts, *The History of Science Fiction* (Basingstoke: Palgrave Macmillan, 2007), 4.

trying out ideas in, a means of thinking about reality.'[68] Samuel R. Delaney offers a similar view, arguing that science fiction 'is training for thinking about the actual changes – sometimes catastrophic, often confusing – that the real world funnels at us year after year'.[69]

Jacques Ellul, philosopher and critic of technology, reflects an alternative view of science fiction: that it actually serves as an adaptation mechanism, portraying extreme and unacceptable uses of technology to foster complacence with the current state of technology.[70] 'Since technology is nothing like what it has been shown to be, it strikes us as perfectly acceptable and reassuring. We take refuge in the real technological society in order to escape the fiction that was presented as the true technology.'[71] While Ellul's concerns over the adjustment and compensation effects of science fiction may be an unintended by-product of the genre (he does not consider this a deliberate intention of sci-fi creators),[72] science fiction is written for a range of purposes, from pure escapist entertainment to serious speculation over aspects of the technological future.

Science fiction inspires and influences many technologists, this connection is well attested.[73] Reportedly, the invention of the

---

[68] As quoted in Eileen Gunn, 'How America's Leading Science Fiction Authors Are Shaping Your Future', *Smithsonian Magazine*, www.smithsonianmag.com/arts-culture/how-americas-leading-science-fiction-authors-are-shaping-your-future-180951169/.

[69] As quoted in Gunn, 'Science Fiction Shaping Your Future'.

[70] Jacques Ellul, *The Technological System*, Trans. J. Neugroschel (New York: Continuum, 1980), 112.

[71] *Ibid.*, 112. Richard Stivers picks up on Ellul's point, reading much of contemporary science fiction as compensating for bleak reality, even as he highlights important exceptions such as Aldous Huxley's *Brave New World* ('Our Brave New World Today', *Bulletin of Science Technology & Society* 30, no. 4 (2010), 251).

[72] Van der Laan also offers the corrective that this may be true of *bad* science fiction, and, even more so, of bad science fiction uncritically read or viewed. Well-crafted science fiction can encourage critical reflection, creating 'a little crack in the technological system where freedom can be experienced' ('Editor's Notes', 238).

[73] See, for example, Robert Bly, *The Science in Science Fiction: Eighty-Three SF Predictions That Became Scientific Reality* (Dallas, TX: BenBella, 2005); Mark Brake and Neil Hook, *Different Engines: How Science Drives Fiction and Fiction Drives*

mobile phone in the 1970s was inspired by the handheld communication devices in the original *Star Trek* series.[74] Geoffrey Landis is a prolific science fiction writer who also works as a scientist for NASA. Charles Sheffield wrote a large corpus of science fiction alongside his significant position as Chief Scientist for a satellite data processing company that consulted for NASA. Arthur C. Clarke, perhaps best known for his *2001: A Space Odyssey* novel, was a mathematician and physicist who proposed a method of conducting telecommunications relays via geostationary satellites – so important for the field that the geosynchronous orbit around the equator is known officially as the Clarke Orbit.[75] Cryonics founder Robert Ettinger wrote a short story in which a wealthy magnate is refrigerated and later resurrected long before he produced his scientific treatise on the subject.[76]

Cory Doctorow explains the phenomenon of 'design fiction' – the commissioning of 'what-if' stories by corporations to consider the potential marketability for technological products.[77] Elsewhere, he argues that 'science fiction does something better than predict the future: it *influences* it'.[78] The connection between science fiction and industry has a long pedigree, as highlighted by the

Science (London: Macmillan, 2008); Thomas Disch, *The Dreams Our Stuff Is Made Of: How Science Fiction Conquered the World* (New York: Simon & Schuster, 1998); William Shatner and Chip Walter. *I'm Working On That: A Trek from Science Fiction to Science Fact* (New York: Pocket, 2002).

[74] Paul Davies, 'Putting the Science in Fiction', *Cosmos*. https://cosmosmagazine.com/the-future/putting-science-fiction.

[75] Arthur C. Clarke, 'Extra-Terrestrial Relays: Can Rocket Stations Give World–Wide Radio Coverage?', *Wireless World*.

[76] Robert Ettinger, 'The Penultimate Trump', *Startling Stories* 17, no. 1 (1948); Robert Ettinger, *The Prospect of Immortality* (New York: Doubleday, 1964), 388.

[77] Interviewed in Gunn, 'Science Fiction Shaping Your Future'.

[78] Cory Doctorow, 'I've Created a Monster! (And So Can You)', in *Frankenstein, or the Modern Prometheus: Annotated for Scientists, Engineers, and Creators of All Kinds*, ed. David Guston, Ed Finn and Jason Robert (Cambridge, MA: MIT Press, 2017), 209, emphasis original.

aerospace industry's use of futurist science fiction imagery in their early advertisements.[79]

It is not only the space exploration industry that profits from fictional speculations, computer scientist Mark Pesce makes the bold (if slightly hyperbolic) claim that 'The recent history of hard science fiction has been *the* deciding influence on the direction of software development. ... To the degree they [sci-fi writers] are successful in "infecting" the hacker community with the beauty of their ideas, they can expect to see those ideas brought to life.'[80]

The nexus between science fiction and technological development is more recently illustrated in Project Hieroglyph, an online project initiated by the Center for Science and the Imagination at Arizona State University. The project offers 'a space for writers, scientists, artists and engineers to collaborate on creative, ambitious visions of our near future'.[81] An anthology produced by the project in 2014, collating fictional visions of the near future based on contemporary science and technology, was recognised by the Association of Professional Futurists for its contribution to futurist studies.[82] The project grew out of a desire to re-brand science fiction away from the dystopic tendencies of the genre and instead focus on constructive, optimistic and achievable depictions of the future.[83] Michael Solana expresses similar hopes for the ability of science fiction to influence perceptions of technology in a more positive way, calling upon writers to tell more optimistic stories.

---

[79] See, for example, the work of science fiction illustrator Arthur Radebaugh, who also illustrated several advertisements for aerospace company Bohn.

[80] Mark Pesce, 'Magic Mirror: The Novel as a Software Development Platform', *MIT Communications Forum*, http://web.mit.edu/comm-forum/papers/pesce.html.

[81] Center for Science and the Imagination, Arizona State University, 'Project Hieroglyph', http://csi.asu.edu/project-hieroglyph/page/2/.

[82] Joey Eschrich, 'Hieroglyph Anthology Earns Futurist Award', *Center for Science and the Imagination, ASU*, http://csi.asu.edu/press/news/hieroglyph-anthology-earns-futurist-award/.

[83] Debbie Siegelbaum, 'Project Hieroglyph: Fighting Society's Dystopian Future', *BBC News*, www.bbc.co.uk/news/magazine-28974943.

Our dystopian obsession has grown up in our nightmares as a true monster, which can only be countered by something truly beautiful. Simply, we need a hero. Our fears are demons in our fiction placing our utopia at risk, but we must not run from them. We must stand up and defeat them. Artificial intelligence, longevity therapy, biotechnology, nuclear energy – it is in our power to create a brilliant world, but we must tell ourselves a story where our tools empower us to do it. To every young writer out there obsessed with genre, consider our slowly coalescing counterculture, and wonder what side of this you're standing on. ... The time is fit for us to dream again.[84]

In yet another indicator of the importance of science fiction for technological inspiration, writer Neil Gaiman shares an anecdote from the first ever state-sponsored science fiction conference in China in 2007. Upon asking a government official why China had shifted away from their previous disapproval and discouragement of science fiction and associated conventions, he received the following response:

Oh, you know for years we've been making wonderful things. We make your iPods. We make phones. We make them better than anybody else, but we don't come up with any of these ideas. You bring us things and then we make them. So we went on a tour of America talking to people at Microsoft, at Google, at Apple, and we asked them a lot of questions about themselves, just the people working there. And we discovered that they all read science fiction when they were teenagers. So we think maybe it's a good thing.[85]

[84] Michael Solana, 'Stop Writing Dystopian Sci-Fi: It's Making Us All Fear Technology', *Wired*, www.wired.com/2014/08/stop-writing-dystopian-sci-fiits-making-us-all-fear-technology/.

[85] As cited in Neil Gaiman, 'The Pornography of Genre, or the Genre of Pornography', in *The View from the Cheap Seats: Selected Non-Fiction* (London: Headline Publishing, 2016), 41.

Students at the Massachusetts Institute of Technology (MIT) have in recent years been able to take a class entitled 'Science Fiction to Science Fabrication', which involves reading selected science fiction works, creating functional prototypes inspired by the readings, and then reflecting on the social implications of such technologies.[86] Science fiction is taken seriously as a source for fuelling imagination and innovation, at least by the technology industry.

This is not surprising, when we consider the monetary aspect. Robert Geraci argues for a strong link between popular science works, which share much in common with some forms of science fiction, and research funding.

> The value of the apocalyptic imagination lies in its power to create excitement in the lay public and government funding agencies. Pop science in general, and Apocalyptic AI in particular, is a – sometimes conscious, sometimes unconscious – strategy for the acquisition of cultural prestige, especially as such prestige is measured in financial support.[87]

Others challenge the degree to which science fiction impacts proper scientific work, with physicist Freeman Dyson stating that 'science is my territory, but science fiction is the landscape of my dreams'.[88] Certainly, we should resist a simplistic approach that draws direct associations between fictional imaginings and complex technological developments. Colin Milburn offers a more nuanced account of modification processes at work between fiction and science, suggesting we might consider the relationship of scientists to science fiction as akin to 'fan practice' (even if not all individual scientists are sci-fi fans).[89] Examples include

---

[86] Gunn, 'Science Fiction Shaping Your Future'.

[87] Geraci, *Apocalyptic AI*, 3.

[88] Freeman Dyson, *Imagined Worlds* (Cambridge, MA: Harvard University Press, 1997), 9.

[89] Colin Milburn, 'Modifiable Futures: Science Fiction at the Bench', *Isis* 101 (2010), 561.

the transformation optics and electromagnetic cloaking research inspired by fictional invisibility technologies in the *Fantastic Four* comics, *Star Trek* series and Harry Potter novels (despite the latter being fantasy, rather than sci-fi) – while the ideas are inspired by fiction, extensive modifications are required to produce a scientifically viable approximation.[90] The denial of any science fiction influence by some scientists is particularly revelatory – insisting on the absolute autonomy of scientific thought from broader cultural influences.[91] Instead, Milburn contends, scientists consume culture like any other but additionally possess the resources necessary for modifying science fiction ideas into usable science.[92]

We must not overstate the mutual influences of science and science fiction. Science fiction writers are neither prophets nor clairvoyant, and professional science is more than the 'fulfillment of literary dreams, diligently turning fantasies into reality'.[93] There is a degree of overlap between science fiction, however, and the speculations often included at the end of research papers and grant proposals that ruminate on the potential implications of current research.[94] Many non-fiction works relating to science are highly speculative in nature, ranging from J. B. S. Haldane's *Daedalus* to Kurzweil's *The Singularity Is Near*. Milburn highlights the engagement in many non-fiction texts with science fiction in the development of theoretical arguments.[95] Joshua Raulerson describes a narrowing speculative feedback loop of the 'hyperreal' in which techno-utopian and fringe science movements assert 'a vision of Singularity that increasingly recognizes little if any meaningful distinction whatsoever between its fictive and nonfictive representations, reading both science fiction and futurist nonfiction as scripts

---

[90] Milburn, 'Modifiable Futures', 567.

[91] *Ibid.*, 263.

[92] *Ibid.*, 565.

[93] *Ibid.*, 561.

[94] *Ibid.*, 568.

[95] Colin Milburn, 'Posthumanism', in *The Oxford Handbook of Science Fiction*, ed. Rob Latham (Oxford: Oxford University Press, 2014), 529.

for a redemptive future they await with the oracular self-assurance of the devout'.[96] Given this complex relationship, Milburn makes the valid call for a study of science fiction within the history of science discipline, taking historiographical concerns seriously.[97] This will require a cross-disciplinary effort, drawing on methodologies from literary and cultural studies in addition to those of history of science. He summarises the contemporary state:

> As historians and cultural theorists of science, we are becoming increasingly attentive to the powerful role that scientific specula-tion, technological forecasting, and promissory futures play in the development of science and to how futurological narratives and road maps function as scripts in the everyday routine of laboratory protocols.[98]

Artificial intelligence researchers are also attending to the importance of imagination. The company DeepMind asserts that 'if our algorithms are to develop equally sophisticated behaviours, they too must have the capability to "imagine" and reason about the future. Beyond that they must be able to construct a plan using this knowledge.'[99] Imagination is recognised as a central dimen-sion of human cognition, an idea that later chapters of this work will explore. Kurzweil goes beyond science fiction as a source of inspiration to the imaginative realm of fantasy fiction even, claim-ing in reference to J. K. Rowling's Harry Potter series that 'these tales may be imaginary, but they are not unreasonable visions of our world as it will exist only a few decades from now. Essen-tially all of the Potter "magic" will be realized through [Kurzweil's proposed] technologies.'[100]

---

[96] Joshua Raulerson, *Singularities: Technoculture, Transhumanism, and Science Fiction in the 21st Century* (Liverpool: Liverpool University Press, 2013), 5.

[97] Milburn, 'Modifiable Futures', 561.

[98] *Ibid.*, 568.

[99] DeepMind. 'Agents that Imagine and Plan', https://deepmind.com/blog/agents-imagine-and-plan/.

[100] Kurzweil, *The Singularity Is Near*, 35.

While these reflections focus on the role of speculative or science fiction in inspiring technological development, another important function of the genre is to consider the implications of particular technologies. Clark Miller and Ira Bennett, both scientists involved in public policy, argue that science fiction is a form of truth-telling, providing us with an 'imagined sense of what tomorrow's forms of life might look like', and shaping the public imagination through its mode of narrative storytelling.[101] They call for science fiction to be integrated into more rational approaches to technology assessment.[102]

Science Fiction and Expectations of the Future

Perhaps even more apparent than its influence on technological innovation is the way that science fiction impacts everyday expectations of what the future will be like. Even financial service professionals (not the first profession that comes to mind when you think of science fiction) draw on works of science fiction to consider the future of their field and employment more generally.[103]

Sherryl Vint highlights the contemporary dimension of science fiction – while it often addresses the future it also interrogates current anxieties concerning the future.[104] Geraci offers related insights from his experience in the online virtual reality game *Second Life*, through which he investigated the visions of and hopes for the future among aficionados of the game.[105]

Science fiction, according to media theorist Scott Bukatman, 'frequently posits a reconception of the human and the ability

---

[101] Clark Miller and Ira Bennett. 'Thinking Longer Term About Technology: Is There Value in Science Fiction-Inspired Approaches to Constructing Futures?', *Science and Public Policy* 35, no. 8 (2008), 600.

[102] *Ibid.*, 604.

[103] Richard Weber, 'Where No One Has Gone Before: When Science Fiction Inspires Technology', *Journal of Financial Service Professionals* 70, no. 4 (2016).

[104] Sherryl Vint, *Bodies of Tomorrow: Technology, Subjectivity, Science Fiction* (Toronto: University of Toronto Press, 2007), 22.

[105] Geraci, *Apocalyptic AI*, 3.

to interface with the new terminal experience'.[106] Similarly, Scott Midson construes the technological explorations in science fiction to be a 'way to usefully begin to rethink how we see ourselves in relation to technologies in ways that do not prefigure the (ideal) human through practices of exclusion'.[107]

Human Enhancement in Science Fiction

All transhumanists accept the premise of much contemporary science fiction – that humanity will converge with the technology it has produced.[108] Indeed, Bostrom attests science fiction's capacity to provoke reflection on the future of human evolution.[109] Science fiction is a particularly suitable medium for exploring posthuman questions, as it allows us to imagine bodies and selves other than they are at present, it is 'a discourse defined by its ability to estrange our commonplace perceptions of reality'.[110] Science fiction not only reflects or illustrates theoretical models of the posthuman but also allows models of 'possible future selves' to be put forward and identified with by readers.[111] Milburn takes this a step further, intimating that science fiction itself may function as part of a posthumanisation process – 'reading science fiction might turn you posthuman'.[112] Posthumanist discourse is a hybrid, according to Milburn, 'mashing together scientific concepts, sociological extrapolations, and SF scenarios'.[113]

So, how might this relate to human enhancement technologies particularly? A very brief survey is offered here of the same

---

[106] Scott Bukatman, *Terminal Identity: The Virtual Subject in Post/Machine Science Fiction* (Durham, NC: Duke University Press, 1993), 118.

[107] Scott Midson, *Cyborg Theology: Humans, Technology and God* (London: I. B. Taurus, 2018), 111.

[108] Michael Burdett, *Eschatology and the Technological Future* (New York: Routledge, 2015), 81.

[109] Bostrom, 'The Transhumanist FAQ', 40.

[110] Vint, *Bodies of Tomorrow*, 19.

[111] *Ibid.*, 20.

[112] Milburn, 'Posthumanism', 525.

[113] *Ibid.*, 533.

themes of human enhancement identified with respect to transhumanist visions of the future, with examples of their representation in science fiction.[114] Further examples will be highlighted in a later section, as we consider how science fiction might inform theological reflection on human enhancement.

In terms of radical life extension, we might look to Robert Heinlein's character Lazarus Long. Featuring in a number of Heinlein's works,[115] Long lives for over two thousand years as a result of both selective breeding and rejuvenation therapies. Generally, Long and his family are represented positively, though there are political conflicts surrounding an incorrect notion that they possess and are withholding anti-ageing therapies from the wider population. Bruce Sterling's *Holy Fire* (1997), on the other hand, imagines a future in which life-extension technology has taken hold more broadly, and senior citizens have opened an insurmountable gap over younger generations when it comes to wealth and political control.

The cyperpunk genre often explores what it means to be human and depicts examples of what may be considered transhumans. Seminal works such as William Gibson's *Neuromancer* (1984) and Neil Stephenson's *Snow Crash* (1992) convey a certain indeterminacy when it comes to human nature and show how intertwined a human being is with technology. M. Keith Booker and Anne-Marie Thomas argue that 'Cyberpunk not only calls into question what it means to be human, but also suggests that the posthuman is an

---

[114] A more comprehensive survey of science fiction as it engages transhumanist ideas is provided by Burdett, *Eschatology and the Technological Future*. Christina Bieber Lake suggested only a few years ago that visions of the transhumanist future have been insufficiently 'fleshed out' in fiction and locates this as a problem more broadly associated with utopian writing – the impossibility of imagining perfection (Christina Bieber Lake, *Prophets of the Posthuman: American Fiction, Biotechnology, and the Ethics of Personhood* (Notre Dame, IN: University of Notre Dame Press, 2013), 169).

[115] The first of which is Robert Heinlein, *Methuselah's Children* (New York: Gnome Press, 1958).

inevitable consequence of the dissolution of boundaries between human and machine. ... Cyberpunk is a fictional attempt to grapple with the realities of our postmodern condition.'[116]

When Case, the protagonist in *Neuromancer*, dismisses the biological body, unaugmented and disconnected from cyberspace, as 'meat',[117] he sounds a lot like certain transhumanists.[118] Mark Dery sums up this attitude to the flesh characterised by cyberpunk fiction and mind-uploading proponents: 'It's the body's job to be a symbol of detestable putridity in the eyes of an information society characterized by an exaltation of mind and a contempt for matter, most of all the body – that aging, earth-bound relic of Darwinian evolution that Net junkies refer to as meat.'[119] This disdain for the body is reflected not only in depictions of bodily augmentation, but also in more extreme fictional mind-uploading scenarios. Richard Stallman writes a short story that might even be read as a utopia, in which a human gradually shifts more of his existence onto a virtual platform as his relationship with a virtual 'soul mate' progresses, only to experience a fuller joy than he could ever have imagined once the upload is complete.[120]

Of course, not all fictional explorations of enhancement themes are positive as to the outcomes. Robert Sawyer imagines a scenario in which an individual undergoes a non-destructive mind-uploading process, only to end up in identity crisis as both his biological and 'artificial' self claim to be more genuine.[121] James Tiptree Jr's Hugo award-winning novella, 'The Girl Who

---

[116] M. Keith Booker and Anne-Marie Thomas, *The Science Fiction Handbook* (Chichester: Wiley-Blackwell, 2009), 110.

[117] William Gibson, *Neuromancer* (New York: Ace Books, 1984), 6.

[118] Compare this with the previously cited comment from Moravec that the body, apart from its information systems, is 'mere jelly' (Moravec, *Mind Children*, 117).

[119] Mark Dery, *The Pyrotechnic Insanitarium: American Culture on the Brink* (New York: Grove Press, 1999), 142.

[120] Richard Stallman, 'Made for You', 2012, https://ieet.org/index.php/IEET2/more/stallman20121228.

[121] Robert Sawyer, *Mindscan* (New York: Tor, 2005).

Was Plugged In', features the protagonist P. Burke, a physically deformed teenage girl who is given the chance to realise her dreams of physical perfection and attendant celebrity by escaping her body to become a 'Remote'.[122] With her own brain 'plugged in' she is able to control a beautiful body, grown intentionally without a brain, employed by corporate interests to use her celebrity to promote their products ('remote' bodies are preferred for the job as they are more easily controlled than the unpredictable stars of reality).

Philip K. Dick satirises the idea of hedonic recalibration in his acclaimed *Do Androids Dream of Electric Sheep?* (1968). The novel opens with a humorous vignette concerning the 'Penfield mood organ', which allows its users to dial up such specific moods as 'awareness of the manifold possibilities open to me in the future' and 'acknowledgment of husband's superior wisdom in all matters'.[123] Protagonist Rick Deckard argues with his wife over her deliberate programming of despair using the device. 'But then I realized how unhealthy it was, sensing the absence of life, not just in this building but everywhere, and not reacting – do you see? I guess you don't. But that used to be considered a sign of mental illness; they called it "absence of appropriate affect".'[124] Similarly, the fictional soma in Aldous Huxley's *Brave New World* (1932) induces a state of content apathy and reflects some of the more alarming aspects of mood 'enhancement' and its potential for control via distraction.

Greg Egan's short story 'Axiomatic' envisions the possibility of neural implants and modifiers that can affect morality,[125] a technology (albeit different in the details) that Savulescu advocates for strongly. In Egan's tale, however, this technology is not used to

---

[122] James Tiptree Jr, 'The Girl Who Was Plugged in', in *Her Smoke Rose Up Forever* (San Francisco, CA: Tachyon Publications, 2004).

[123] Philip K. Dick, *Do Androids Dream of Electric Sheep?* (New York: Ballantine Books, 1996), 4, 6.

[124] *Ibid.*, 5.

[125] Greg Egan, 'Axiomatic', in *Axiomatic* (London: Millennium, 1995).

enhance superior moral impulses, but rather to override existing moral 'squeamishness' in committing vengeful murder. Again the question of motive and power when it comes to the agents using technology is raised.

Conclusion

The technological enhancement of human characteristics is imagined in diverse ways, both in the proposals of transhumanist advocates and in the futures sketched out by science fiction writers. Enhancement proposals target all aspects of human being – intellectual, emotional, physical and even spiritual. These prospective technologies imagine a radically altered existence for humans, or even the emergence of a new successor species of human making. The possibility of engineering such changes to our own existence has unavoidable implications for theological anthropology, and the activity of enhancement through technology will be considered from a theological perspective in subsequent chapters.

2 | Human Creativity and a Doctrine of Creation

Questions surrounding human enhancement present new opportunities for theologians to engage in cross-disciplinary reflection on many of the 'big questions', and to recover a place for God in public discourse. What is our purpose? What constitutes the good life? Do we determine our own destiny? And of particular interest to this research: what is our role in ongoing creation? Cole-Turner speaks for many when he raises the following questions:

> Can theology – that communal process by which the church's faith seeks to understand – can theology aim at understanding technology? Can we put the words God and technology together in any kind of meaningful sentence? Can theology guess what God is doing in today's technology? Or by our silence do we leave it utterly godless? Can we have a theology of technology that comprehends, gives meaning to, dares to influence the direction and set limits to this explosion of new powers?[1]

'Playing God'

Many would answer Cole-Turner's question with a steadfast 'No!', human enhancement proposals having largely been opposed by religious adherents. The charge of 'playing God' is often levelled in Christian circles at the prospect of deliberately using

---

[1] Ronald Cole-Turner, 'Science, Technology, and Mission', in *The Local Church in a Global Era: Reflections for a New Century*, ed. Max L. Stackhouse, Tim Dearborn and Scott Paeth (Grand Rapids, MI: Eerdmans, 2000), 101.

technologies to alter, and particularly to enhance, human characteristics.[2] These enhancement proposals transgress the boundary
between Creator and creation. A Pew research study conducted
in 2016, for example, showed a stronger rejection of hypothetical
enhancements among individuals with higher religious commitment (predominantly Christian) than those with lower religious
commitment or none, on the grounds that they were 'meddling
with nature' and 'cross[ing] a line we should not cross'.[3] Revealing more general perceptions, the popular publication *Christianity Today* published the results with the sensationalist headline 'Christians to Science: Leave Our Bodies How God Made
Them'.[4]

The genetic aspect of human enhancement has been particularly contentious among Christian ethicists. The advent of human
germline modification technologies has alerted some to the danger
of altering our genetic code so far that human nature is compro-
mised in some (often undefined) way. Yet Cole-Turner, concerned
with the public perception of religious views on this topic, challenges what he considers to be the widespread assumption that all
or most religious scholars are opposed to germline modification,
asserting that 'nearly all the official statements of religious bodies leave the door open on the question of the morality of genetic
modification of human offspring'.[5] He surveys the general (but not

---

[2] The term 'playing God', of course, is most strongly associated with Paul Ramsey
(*Fabricated Man: The Ethics of Genetic Control* (New Haven, CT: Yale University
Press, 1970), 138).

[3] Pew Research Center, 'US Public Wary of Biomedical Technologies to "Enhance"
Human Abilities', July 2016. The overall results, regardless of religious conviction,
still indicated a wariness of enhancement; however, the opposition was significantly
higher when correlated with religion.

[4] Sarah Eekhoff Zylstra, 'Christians to Science: Leave Our Bodies How God Made
Them', *Christianity Today*, 26 July 2016, https://www.christianitytoday.com/news/
2016/july/christians-science-leave-bodies-alone-pew-human-enhancement.html.

[5] Ronald Cole-Turner, 'Religion and the Question of Human Germline Modification',
in *Design and Destiny: Jewish and Christian Perspectives on Human Germline
Modification*, ed. Ronald Cole-Turner (Cambridge, MA: MIT Press, 2008), 8.

insurmountable in his view) misgivings held by certain religious bodies over the use of genetic modification, grouping them in a list of four main concerns: (1) safety, (2) the protection of embryos, (3) social and economic justice concerns and (4) a preference for therapy over enhancement.[6]

Despite the evidence he provides, however, many Christian ethicists writing on the subject would still rule out human germline modification even for therapeutic purposes alone. Gilbert Meilaender offers a good example of a commonly held position in Christian ethics with respect to germ cell therapy. In his argument that this technology is beyond the bounds of human finitude, he cites C. S. Lewis' warnings in *The Abolition of Man* against humans gaining too much control over nature.[7] Michael Banner, though he does not deliver a final opinion, expresses his concerns over the use of genetic modification even in non-human animals, questioning whether the practice is consistent with the Christian doctrine of creation.[8] Even in the secular sphere, a number of philosophers, scientists and other thinkers have expressed reservations over the use of such technologies, and their future consequences for humanity.[9]

Of those theologians who do permit human germline modification, the vast majority argue that it should be limited to therapeutic applications, rejecting its use for enhancement purposes (concern four above). Cole-Turner is willing to go a little further than this, endorsing the use of germline modification for human

---

[6] Ronald Cole-Turner, 'Religion, Genetics and the Future', in *Design and Destiny: Jewish and Christian Perspectives on Human Germline Modification*, ed. Ronald Cole-Turner (Cambridge, MA: MIT Press, 2008), 201.

[7] Gilbert Meilaender, *Bioethics* (Grand Rapids, MI: Eerdmans, 2013), 43.

[8] Michael Banner, *Christian Ethics and Contemporary Moral Problems* (Cambridge: Cambridge University Press, 1999), 224.

[9] A near consensus among scientists expresses ethical reservations over the genetic modification of germ cells, although this view is beginning to change (Paul G. McDonough, 'The Ethics of Somatic and Germline Gene Therapy', *Annals of the New York Academy of Sciences* 816, no. 1 (1997), 381).

enhancement with a few limitations.[10] Cole-Turner's acceptance of genetic enhancements is somewhat pragmatic; he acknowledges the often-blurred boundary between therapy and enhancement and the likelihood that one will easily lead to the other.[11]

Christians have written against human enhancement more broadly as well: Bill McKibben, addressing a more general audience, not only rejects genetic engineering even for therapeutic purposes but argues against any kind of enhancement on the basis that it undermines the givenness of life and the joy that is often won through struggle (he opens his book by describing the running of a marathon, the epitome of both the strength and the frailty of human being that he believes future generations will no longer get to experience).[12]

Willem Drees argues that the charge of 'playing God' is generally rooted in fear, as new technologies shift the boundary between what we accept as given and what we can affect through our own action. 'We accuse others of playing God when they have moved what was beyond our powers to our side of the boundary.'[13] Acknowledging these fears, we may nevertheless ask whether there are resources in Christian theology to indicate or permit a more open, less reactionary response to the prospect of enhancing human abilities through technology.

The Relationship Between Divine and Human Creativity

Before we attempt a specific 'theology of technology', we might fruitfully begin our theological reflections on the prospect of

---

[10] Cole-Turner, 'Biotechnology', 937.

[11] Cole-Turner, 'Religion, Genetics and the Future', 210–211. He does warn, however, that attempts to distinguish between therapy and enhancement are not merely anthropological in nature, but theological (ibid., 213).

[12] Bill McKibben, Enough: Genetic Engineering and the End of Human Nature (London: Bloomsbury Publishing, 2004), 1–3.

[13] Willem Drees, 'Playing God? Yes!' Religion in the Light of Technology', Zygon 37, no. 3 (2002), 651.

'enhancing' ourselves with the doctrine of creation. The charge of 'playing God' commonly levelled at enhancement technologies by religious objectors orients us to the central question: how does human creativity relate to divine? Do sharp demarcations between the creative work of God and the scope of human action exist that would affirm a 'playing God' prohibition, or are there parallels between human and divine creativity that might legitimise these technological endeavours?

For a long time, the semantic scope of 'creation' rejected the possibility of such parallels and served to underscore the radical otherness of God. Trevor Hart charts the historical shift which saw the notion of *creare* extended from its previous preserve of God alone to human artistry.[14] 'Creation proper' may still apply solely to the work of God in certain instances, but the idea of creation more generally has expanded in scope.[15] In view of this semantic shift, the question of whether humans might appropriately be considered to 'create' is the starting point for Hart's exploration of human making.

Hart returns to the biblical account with a summary of the lexical terms in the Hebrew Scriptures, demonstrating the complexity of Hebrew language of creation beyond the more restricted use of *bārā'*.[16] The verb *yatsar*, for example, used in Genesis 2:7 to describe God's fashioning of the human from the earth and in Genesis 2:18 to describe his forming of other animals also, is used of human activity as well (e.g. Isaiah 29:16, Habbakuk 2:18). The term and its cognates invoke strong connotations for us with art and craftsmanship, referring to the work of the potter (likely connected to the 'lumps of clay' that made up the raw materials in Genesis 2:7) and the woodcarver.[17] He sketches out the biblical portrayal of God

---

[14] Trevor Hart, *Making Good: Creation, Creativity, and Artistry* (Waco, TX: Baylor University Press, 2014), 2.

[15] *Ibid.*, 5.

[16] *Ibid.*, 5–6.

[17] Hart provides a more detailed account of these biblical uses, including some translational variations that impact the imagery of Genesis 2:7 (*ibid.*, 31–33). See also

as artist and contends that we might situate human making within a theology of creation, rather than relegating it to the more distant doctrines of preservation, providence or redemption. 'Viewing creation as a project divinely begun and established, yet one that is handed over to us with "more to be made of it yet" and inviting our responsible participation in the making, affords a fruitful perspective on the matter.'[18] Colin Gunton represents creation in a similar fashion, though he orients his work around a doctrine of God rather than human making.[19] To illustrate the place of human artistry in this collaboration as it unfolds in scripture, Hart draws on the examples of Noah crafting the ark and the building of the tabernacle.[20]

Having established the biblical contours of the divine artist metaphor, Hart tracks the metaphor's divergence from its humble origins in scripture to an ultimate reversal: by the time of the Enlightenment 'human artistry was pictured now in terms of God's artistry rather than vice versa'.[21] While the classic and mediaeval understanding of *ars* encompassed human productivity more generally, modern Western notions of 'the arts' are far more limited.[22] At the same time, they are more audacious, with the notion of art as faithful mimesis giving way gradually through the Renaissance and the Romantic era to the idea of the artist or poet as 'creator'.[23]

We can see this shift in thinking beyond the realm of art too. Humanist thinkers in the Italian Renaissance accorded great

---

B. Otzen, 'Yatsar', in *Theological Dictionary of the Old Testament*, ed. G. Johannes Botterweck and Helmer Ringgren (Grand Rapids, MI: Eerdmans, 1990).

[18] Hart, *Making Good*, 8.

[19] Colin Gunton, *The Triune Creator: A Historical and Systematic Study* (Grand Rapids, MI: Eerdmans, 1998), 89.

[20] Hart, *Making Good*, 40.

[21] *Ibid.*, 28.

[22] *Ibid.*, 153.

[23] Hart gives a detailed account of this shift, focusing primarily on the development of visual art, in chapter 8 of *Making Good*. He nuances the simplistic descriptions often offered by cautioning that the Renaissance period at least was still generally characterised by a view of art as respective mimesis, even as it accorded greater significance to transformation (*Ibid.*, 162).

significance to the creative ability and agency of humans in the world. In 1486, Giovanni Pico della Mirandola pronounced his *Oration on the Dignity of Man*, which outlined the exalted status and creative freedom of humankind. While non-human animals were given specific forms or natures by God, according to Pico, the human is made according to an 'indeterminate image' in order that humans might define themselves.[24] God's address to humans captures the essence of this humanist manifesto.

> I have placed you at the very center of the world, so that from that vantage point you may with greater ease glance round about you on all that the world contains. We have made you a creature neither of heaven nor of earth, neither mortal nor immortal, in order that you may, as the free and proud shaper of your own being, fashion yourself in the form you may prefer. It will be in your power to descend to the lower, brutish forms of life; you will be able, through your own decision, to rise again to the superior orders whose life is divine.[25]

This ascription of creative dominion to humans is a prominent feature in Italian humanist thought.[26] Charles Trinkaus describes 'an important new concept of man as actor, creator, shaper of nature and history'.[27] Humans possess these qualities because they are made in God's image and likeness.[28] The emphasis on human ingenuity appears to be linked with the Renaissance exultation of humanity's artistic and technological achievements and potential.[29] Giannozzo Manetti writes, for example,

[24] Giovanni Pico della Mirandola, *Oration on the Dignity of Man*, trans. A. Robert Caponigri (Chicago, IL: Henry Regnery Co., 1956), 4.

[25] Pico della Mirandola, *Oration on the Dignity of Man*, 7–8.

[26] Charles Trinkaus, *In Our Image and Likeness: Humanity and Divinity in Italian Humanist Thought* (Notre Dame, IN: University of Notre Dame Press, 1995), 248, 482–485.

[27] *Ibid.*, 248.

[28] *Ibid.*, 248.

[29] Richard Bauckham, *Living with Other Creatures: Green Exegesis and Theology* (Waco, TX: Baylor University Press, 2011), 44.

After that first, new and rude creation of the world, everything seems to have been discovered, constructed and completed by us out of some singular and outstanding acuteness of the human mind ... The world and all its beauties seems to have been first invented and established by Almighty God for the use of man, and afterwards gratefully received by man and rendered much more beautiful, much more ornate and far more refined.[30]

According to Manetti, humans are second creators of a world that is 'superimposed on the original divine creation of the natural world'.[31]

Manetti's near contemporary, Marsilio Ficino, expressed similar ideas, stating rather cryptically that 'human arts make on their own whatever nature itself makes: it is as if we were not her slaves but her rivals'.[32] Humans are imitators of divine creativity, and 'perfect all the works of lower nature, correcting and emending them'.[33] Ficino also included the Greek notion of *techne* along with the more traditional arts in his description of human creativity.[34] Surrounded by the fruits and promise of the burgeoning industry in Renaissance Florence, Ficino concluded in light of humanity's evident mastery over the world that the human 'acts as the vicar of God, since he inhabits all the elements and cultivates all'.[35] Together these Renaissance thinkers offer an early theology of creation that includes creaturely activity, though obviously with less of a biological dimension to the fashioning of human nature than the approaches that will feature in the current work.

---

[30] Giannozzo Manetti, *De dignitate et excellentia hominis*, ed. Elizabeth Leonard (Patavii: In Aedibus Antenoreis, 1974), as quoted by Trinkaus, *In Our Image and Likeness*, 247.

[31] Trinkaus, *In Our Image and Likeness*, 247.

[32] Marsilio Ficino, *Platonic Theology*, ed. James Hankin and William Bowen, trans. Michael Allen, vol. IV. (Cambridge, MA: Harvard University Press, 2004), XIII:3.

[33] *Ibid.*

[34] J. M. Cocking, *Imagination: A Study in the History of Ideas*, ed. Penelope Murray (London: Routledge, 1991), 172.

[35] Ficino, *Theologica platonica*, vol. II, 225; trans. Trinkaus, *In Our Image and Likeness*, 483.

We can trace, therefore, a growing propensity to focus on human creativity that pulls away from the stricter constraints it possessed in earlier thought. This escape trajectory continued through the incorporation of a dominion narrative more focused on the superiority of human creativity over that which was beneath it, rather than its subservient relationship to the divine. Francis Bacon, the Enlightenment thinker often referred to as the 'father of modern science', exemplifies a greater tradition that came to see nature as something to be mastered, a subject of human dominion. Bacon's position is captured in some of his most well-known lines: 'Man by the fall fell at the same time from his state of innocency and from his dominion over creation. Both of these losses can in this life be in some part repaired; the former by religion and faith, the latter by arts and sciences.'[36] For Bacon, the human task was to recover human dominion over nature in its fullest, an aim that manifests in the title of his incomplete masterpiece *The Great Instauration*. This view prompted statements laden in tones of mastery such as 'I am come in very truth leading you to Nature with all her children to bind her to your service and make her your slave'.[37] Bacon extended the vision of Italian humanists by uniting the idea of dominion with the promise of modern empirical science.[38] The new style of thinking epitomised by Bacon, however, was not only scientific but generally optimistic concerning the expansion of human knowledge. The seventeenth century was an age of utopian thought, though the older utopias differed from those of today by referring to contemporary societies, rather than future imaginings.[39] Thus, the frontispiece to *The Great Instauration* depicts ships freely

[36] Bacon Francis, '*Novum Organon* 12.52', in *The Works of Francis Bacon*, ed. James Spedding, Robert Ellis and Douglas Heath (London: Longman, 1858), IV: 247–248.
[37] Francis Bacon, 'The Masculine Birth of Time', in *The Philosophy of Francis Bacon: An Essay on Its Development from 1603–1609*, ed. Benjamin Farrington. (Liverpool: Liverpool University Press, 1964), 62.
[38] Bauckham, *Living with Other Creatures*, 50.
[39] P. B. Medawar, 'On "The Effecting of All Things Possible"', in *The Hope of Progress* (London: Methuen & Co., 1972), 127.

passing the pillars of Hercules that guard the Straits of Gibraltar (previously thought to mark the end of the known world), and *plus ultra* was the motto taken up by Bacon's followers.[40] This emphasis on dominion came to be enmeshed within theological understandings of creation, as 'creation' found its way into the vocabulary used for human activities. Hart summarises of the reversal this effected:

> Like the artist, it had always been understood, God (albeit in his own 'divine' way) fashioned a world with great skill and wisdom, producing something good and pleasing and for the identifiable benefit of all concerned. Like God, it now came increasingly to be held, the artist (albeit in his own 'creaturely' way) was concerned to call something radically novel and unprecedented into existence rather than merely replicating or imitating an object to order from a given design or template – something that was the product of his own personal and inner vision rather than the dictates of any external circumstance, something in the fashioning of which he might properly expect by the exercise of his will and power to transcend the limits ordinarily supposed to belong to his chosen materials, and something the result of which was intended first for his own personal delight and satisfaction before that of others.[41]

This does not mean, however, that it is inappropriate to speak of humans as genuinely 'creative'. Drawing on support from the likes of Walter Brueggemann, Terence Fretheim and Jürgen Moltmann, Hart concludes that 'at various key points in the story of God's creative fashioning of a world fit for his own indwelling with us, divine artistry actively solicits a corresponding creaturely creativity, apart from which the project cannot and will not come to fruition.'[42]

But Hart takes pains to orient the sense in which we might think of human artistry as genuine creativity to an earlier understanding

[40] *Ibid.*, 122.
[41] Hart, *Making Good*, 189–190.
[42] *Ibid.*, 37.

of what artistry entails. *Craftmanship*, as we understand it now, is in some ways a more helpful term.[43] God is the master craftsman, with humans analogous to the apprentice in the master's workshop. In such an analogy, 'the existence of certain established limits or boundaries is to the fore: there are considerations of authority and obedience to be observed, traditional ways of working with which faith must be kept, accepted standards of excellence to be acknowledged and pursued'.[44] Within this context, though, genuine freedom and ingenuity operates, nurtured and schooled within the Master's domain.[45] Rather than forming order out of chaos by human innovation, as artistry has come to be understood, the artist works within the divinely ordered cosmos.[46] The 'otherness' of God must not be undermined in the analogy of human creativity to divine;[47] this is taken as a foundational commitment that underpins the exploration of human creativity in the present work.

Understanding Human Creativity

Creativity Studies

Always acknowledging the alterity of God, the parallels between God's creative work and our own may be illuminated by examining the mechanics and nuances of human creativity as a concept. This is the task of the burgeoning field of creativity studies, which highlights the interdisciplinarity of its purview.

---

[43] A full genealogy and semantic treatment of 'art', 'craft' (and 'technology', introduced later) is not offered here, as all are treated as aspects of human making involving creativity. Hart reminds us that the relegation of art to the realm of recreation and play, as opposed to useful work, is a product of modern theory, and 'art' and 'craft' were essentially equivalent terms prior to the Renaissance (*Ibid.*, 21–22).

[44] Hart, *Making Good*, 43.

[45] *Ibid.*, 43.

[46] *Ibid.*, 197.

[47] *Ibid.*, 214.

Whereas Hart focuses on the shifting understanding of human artistry as creativity, physicist David Bohm takes a broader perspective. Exploring the relevant etymologies, he illustrates how science, art and technology all have their origins in a sense of what is 'fitting', and spring from the same basic human impulse.[48] Gilles Deleuze and Felix Guattari similarly contend that creation can occur across the intersecting planes of philosophy, art and science, the rich overlapping of which leads to an inevitable degree of unpredictability.[49] Margaret Boden goes even further in her demonstration of the breadth of creativity, not only considering human creativity in science and technology, but also raising the possibility of machine creativity.[50] The extent of human creativity has been described in a recent popular work, *The Runaway Species*, which draws parallels between the ingenuity of NASA engineers in addressing mechanical emergencies during the Apollo 13 mission and the innovative artistic works of Picasso.[51]

Rob Pope's expansive study *Creativity: Theory, History, Practice* considers the ramifications of industrialisation for the language of creativity, and the associated Marxist shift to the vocabulary of 'production'.[52] A more recently renewed interest in creativity is traced through its increased emphasis on efficiency and results, rather than exploration.[53] Though Pope does not treat the relationship between divine and human creation from the perspective of a Christian world view, he does draw links more

[48] David Bohm, *On Creativity* (London: Routledge, 2003), 80–86.
[49] Gilles Deleuze and Felix Guattari, *What Is Philosophy?*, trans. Graham Burchell and Hugh Tomlinson (London: Verso, 1994), 163–199.
[50] Margaret Boden, *The Creative Mind: Myths and Mechanisms* (London: Routledge, 2004), 7–12, 277–304.
[51] Anthony Brandt and David Eagleman, *The Runaway Species: How Human Creativity Remakes the World* (Edinburgh: Canongate Books, 2017).
[52] Rob Pope, *Creativity: Theory, History, Practice* (Abingdon: Routledge, 2005), 7–8.
[53] *Ibid.*, 26–27.

generally between religious creation myths and human creativity,[54] and his emphasis on the importance of metaphor and language resonates with themes picked up later in the present work.

Other contributions from the field of creativity studies focus more on defining and describing the mechanics of creativity, rather than the intellectual history of its usage. Creativity involves discovering possibilities in the world (natural and social), and then bringing them into being.[55] Novelty features in definitions of creativity – Boden, for example, permits the term 'creative' to properly apply only to radically original ideas.[56] Nor is creativity homogenous – Boden describes creativity in terms of novel recombinations, as well as explorations and transformations of conceptual spaces.[57] Typologies that distinguish nuances of creativity are proffered, from Boden's *P-creativity* vs *H-creativity* (differentiating between the psychologically and historically creative) to James Kaufman and Ronald Beghetto's 'Four C Model' that delineates creativity by degree, generality and professionalism.[58] The multiplicity of typologies, though each may provide certain insights, is testament to the wide-ranging use of the concept and its interest across disciplines.

While much scholarship in creativity studies focuses on the mechanics of how creativity works, Lee Martin and Nick Wilson highlight the origin of novelty as crucial for a proper understanding of creativity.[59] Pope discusses the effect of the present 'crisis of subjectivity' to surround our understanding of creativity's

---

54 See especially *ibid.*, chapter 5.
55 Lee Martin and Nick Wilson, 'Defining Creativity with Discovery', *Creativity Research Journal* 29, no. 4 (2017), 420.
56 Boden, *The Creative Mind*, 51.
57 *Ibid.*, 4.
58 *Ibid.*, 43–49; James Kaufman and Ronald Beghetto, 'Beyond Big and Little: The Four C Model of Creativity', *Review of General Psychology* 13, no. 1 (2009).
59 Martin and Wilson, 'Defining Creativity', 418.

source of inspiration with uncertainty.[60] This is where theological accounts make a valuable contribution: human creative novelty has its origins in the divine.[61] Research has also suggested a positive correlation between awe and creative insight,[62] another finding that coheres with a divine dimension to creativity.

Creativity studies also recognise a value dimension to creativity – the products of genuine creativity must be evaluated as 'good' by a community consensus.[63] When Robert Weisberg argued for the exclusion of value judgements in deeming something 'creative', objections were raised by creativity studies scholars.[64] Again this validates a connection between creativity and morality, and fits well with a theistic explanation for making such a connection.

Bringing together the consensus of much of the creativity studies field, and aligned with the changing understanding of creativity traced from its biblical origins through a Renaissance expansion of scope, Boden's description of creativity as 'the ability to come

---

[60] Pope, *Creativity*, 18; cf. Timothy Clark, *The Theory of Inspiration: Composition as a Crisis of Subjectivity in Romantic and Post-Romantic Writing* (Manchester: Manchester University Press, 1997).

[61] Martin and Wilson do not claim a theistic rationale, though it would render their assertions about creativity novelty more coherent.

[62] Alice Cirico et al., 'Awe Enhances Creative Thinking: An Experimental Study', *Creativity Research Journal* 30, no. 2 (2018).

[63] Mark Runco and Garrett Jaeger. 'The Standard Definition of Creativity', *Creativity Research Journal* 24, no. 1 (2012). Runco identifies a mutual benefit between the culture of a community and the creativity of those within it (*Creativity: Theories and Themes: Research, Development, and Practice* (London: Academic Press, 2014), 222). Interestingly, moral value as an essential characteristic of creativity is more strongly articulated in Eastern perceptions than Western ones, a phenomenon that is perhaps linked with the increased focus on utility in the West already discussed (Weihua Niu and Robert Sternberg, 'Contemporary Studies on the Concept of Creativity: The East and the Western', *Journal of Creative Behavior* 36 (2002)).

[64] Robert Weisberg, 'On the Usefulness of "Value" in the Definition of Creativity', *Creativity Research Journal* 27 (2015); cf. David Harrington, 'On the Usefulness of "Value" in the Definition of Creativity: A Commentary', *Creativity Research Journal* 30, no. 1 (2018).

up with ideas and artefacts that are *new, surprising and valuable*' serves as a helpful definition for the present purpose.[65] Furthermore, Boden highlights the universality of human creativity – while expert knowledge is often involved, we all possess creative power to some degree, grounded in our 'ordinary human abilities'.[66] Understanding the relationship of this human capacity to the divine work of creation requires further theological resources, to which we will now turn.

A Theological Understanding

Hart synthesises these insights from creativity studies into a theological account, construing creativity as a gift to which the recipient can imaginatively respond and hand on in turn (i.e. it becomes a part of the tradition).[67] Many artists attest to this sensibility of having received a gift, and the limits and responsibilities thus entailed.[68] Hart cites Tolkien's sense of creativity as uncovering meaning that is given, arguing that such meaning 'can be traced directly to the ultimate provenance of all human artistry in the primordial plenitude of God's own creative work'.[69] Tolkien's theology of sub-creation will be treated comprehensively later in this work.

Theological accounts offered by the likes of Jacques Maritain and Dorothy Sayers, scholars contemporaneous with Tolkien, reinforce the theological significance of human making and its proper place within a doctrine of creation. Maritain describes the creativity of the artist as a development of divine creation, a work

---

[65] Boden, *The Creative Mind*, 1, emphasis original.

[66] *Ibid.*, 22.

[67] Hart, *Making Good*, 250–251. Hart is directly quoting Todd Lubart, 'Creativity Across Cultures', in *Handbook of Creativity*, ed. Robert Sternberg (Cambridge: Cambridge University Press, 1999), 339.

[68] Hart, *Making Good*, 262.

[69] *Ibid.*, 265.

proceeding from the whole soul which bears the image of God.[70] Though he distinguishes the creation of God (who is able to truly generate another substance through divine utterance) and human works of creating (which can only ever be signs), Maritain nevertheless grounds the dignity of art in his assertion that it 'realizes in act one of the fundamental aspects of the ontological likeness of our soul with God'.[71] Sayers, too, locates human creativity in our being made in the image of a triune Creator.[72] She articulates a trinitarian anthropology first through a character in her play *The Zeal of Thy House*, an analogy that she then unpacks in *The Mind of the Maker*.[73] 'Every work of creation is threefold', she writes, 'an earthly trinity to match the heavenly'.[74] Human creativity is broken down into the Creative Idea, the Creative Energy and the Creative Power, analogous of the Father, Word and Holy Spirit, respectively.[75] Charles Raven had previously drawn a trinitarian analogy with the human artist, outlining:

> The artist's will which purposes to create the picture and the impulse which prepares pigments and canvas is God the Father ... the artist's conception of the complete picture, his cartoon of the grand design ... is God the Son ... the artist's energy, the vital and creative activity whereby is produced upon the canvas of matter the

[70] Jacques Maritain, *Art and Scholasticism and the Frontiers of Poetry*, trans. J. Evans. (New York: C. Scribner's Sons, 1962), 122.

[71] *Ibid.*, 122.

[72] Dorothy Sayers, 'Vocation in Work', in *A Christian Basis for the Post-War World*, ed. A. E. Baker (London: SCM Press, 1942), 90.

[73] Dorothy Sayers, *Four Sacred Plays* (London: Victor Gollancz, (1948); Dorothy Sayers, *The Mind of the Maker* (New York: HarperCollins, 1987).

[74] Sayers, *Four Sacred Plays*, 103.

[75] *Ibid.*, 103. The orthodoxy and sufficiency of her treatment of the Trinity is beyond the present scope here; however, the cautions of Karen Kilby (among others) against projecting human ideals onto the immanent Trinity bears remembering (Kilby, 'Perichoresis and Projection: Problems with Social Doctrines of the Trinity', *New Blackfriars* 81, no. 957 (2000)).

perfect image which the will has planned and the vision conceived is God the Holy Spirit.[76]

These trinitarian comparisons underscore a relationship between human creativity and the work of God as Creator.[77] Though he does not address the trinitarian aspect, Robert Miner derives a similar conclusion from his study of Aquinas' account of human making (particularly in terms of art) and its relation to divine creation.

> Because Aquinas does not imagine human making to occur within a desacralized, sheerly human territory, but understands it rather as a mode of participation in the divine, it may be said that human construction acquires a significance that is difficult for modern secular perspectives to appreciate. It becomes a privileged site where God speaks through the creature, the agent of divine providence.[78]

To locate human creativity and an associated theological anthropology within an overarching doctrine of creation is thus warranted.

The Scope of Creativity: Technology as a Creative Enterprise

Hart, like the theologians discussed above, treats human creativity primarily in terms of artistic enterprise, though he acknowledges its broader application to other human activities. Affirming that only God bestows existence upon the creaturely, he includes in the rubric of creation biblically attested activities that require our participation for creation's completion: 'planning, making, shaping,

---

[76] As cited in Frederick Dillistone, *Charles Raven: Naturalist, Historian, Theologian* (Grand Rapids, MI: Eerdmans, 1975), 87.

[77] This project has continued into contemporary scholarship, see, for example, Brian Horne, 'Art: A Trinitarian Imperative', in *Trinitarian Theology Today: Essays on Divine Being and Act*, ed. Christoph Schwöbel (Edinburgh: T. & T. Clark, 1995).

[78] Robert Miner, *Truth in the Making: Creativity Knowledge in Theology and Philosophy* (London: Routledge, 2013), 18.

forming, developing, and so on'.[79] The chief contention of the present work is that *technology*, and specifically the development of technologies for enhancing human capacities, falls within the scope of this creaturely contribution to creation. Furthermore, technology, as a domain of human creativity, can benefit from the insights of the field of creativity studies, and the theological reflections on creativity and the imagination that have concentrated more on the arts to date.

Of course, it is not a new development to treat technology as a mode of creativity. Pope draws our attention to the corporatisation of 'creativity' in technological programmes of this century; its wedding to neoliberal politics.[80] A prime example is Kimberley Seltzer's and Tom Bentley's *The Creative Age: Knowledge and Skills for the New Economy*, which outlines a goal-oriented and problem-solving approach to creativity bearing little resemblance to the understanding of creativity articulated above.[81] In what follows, technology will be considered in light of the more comprehensive scope of creativity described thus far, and within a theological framework. The decision to ground this theological treatment of human enhancement technology within a doctrine of creation and theology of human creativity garners support from a long history of identifying humans as 'co-creators' with God. The 'corresponding creaturely creativity' which God conscripts into the broader project of creation, according to Hart, finds (albeit perhaps indirect) precedents and allies in the thought of certain individuals and movements to which we will now turn.

Co-creation and Science

In addition to the arts, we find correlations between human and divine creativity in the sciences. Mary Midgley explores the impact

79 Hart, *Making Good*, 83.
80 Pope, *Creativity*, 26.
81 Kimberley Seltzer and Tom Bentley, *The Creative Age: Knowledge and Skills for the New Economy* (Buckingham: Demos, 1999); cf. Pope, *Creativity*, 26.

of the dominion rhetoric associated with human creativity on later conceptions of science. 'It is notorious that Bacon regularly described scientific activity in oddly savage imagery, incorporating violent conquest as a central part of his original myth of scientific supremacy.'[82] Humans are not merely to guide the course of nature with a gentle hand, but to 'storm and occupy her castles and strongholds and extend the bounds of human empire'.[83] This rhetoric resurfaced in the 1981 encyclical *Laborem exercens*, issued by Pope John Paul II, focused on the significance of human work. Technology is named as an ally as 'man in a sense continues to develop [the Creator's] activity',[84] praised as 'the fruit of the work of the human intellect and a historical confirmation of man's dominion over nature'.[85] We can see the co-creation metaphor implicit in the thought of French Jesuit priest, philosopher and palaeontologist Pierre Teilhard de Chardin, who famously described humans as 'evolution become aware of itself'.[86] While Teilhard was not very well received in his own time, there has been a recent resurgence of interest in his work as theologians engage with contemporary evolutionary theory.[87] Teilhard conceived of biological and cultural history advancing towards what he termed the 'Noosphere', the 'thinking envelope of the Earth' – a collective consciousness that encompasses the entire planet.[88] Technology is integral to the Noosphere, and Teilhard envisioned that it might one day be used to enhance individual human

---

[82] Mary Midgley, *Science and Poetry* (London: Routledge, 2001), 41.

[83] Francis Bacon, 'Of the Dignity and Advancement of Learning', in *The Works of Francis Bacon*, ed. James Spedding, Robert Ellis and Douglas Heath (New York: Garrett Press, 1860), 372–373.

[84] John Paul II, *Laborem exercens* (Rome: Vatican, 1981). §5.

[85] *Ibid.*, §5.

[86] Pierre Teilhard de Chardin, *The Phenomenon of Man*, trans. Bernard Wall (New York, NY: Harper & Row, 1961), 220; he derives this idea from Julian Huxley, 'Transhumanism', in *New Bottles for New Wine* (London: Chatto & Windus, 1957).

[87] For example, Pope Francis cited Teilhard in the 2015 encyclical *Laudato si'*.

[88] Pierre Teilhard de Chardin, *The Future of Man*, trans. Norman Denny (London: Collins, 1964), 132.

beings.[89] For Teilhard, humanity's evolution is driving and being pulled (by God) towards the 'Omega Point', culminating in the 'Ultra-Human' who is drawn into union with the cosmic Christ.[90]

Arthur Peacocke, both an Anglican priest and a trained biochemist, also names humans as co-creators. Writing mainly in response to ecological concerns, he argues that through the evolutionary process humans now represent a medium for divine creativity. 'To be co-creator with the 'living God' who always actualizes in his creation new possibilities, previously unimagined humanly speaking, is to be prepared always to adjust creatively and deliberately to the changes necessary for God's purposes to be fulfilled'.[91] Peacocke echoes Teilhard in the description of humans as creation conscious of itself.[92] Exploring the creative potential displayed in technological ingenuity, Peacocke contends that 'man now has, at his present stage of intellectual, cultural, and social evolution, the opportunity of consciously becoming co-creator and co-worker with God in his work on Earth, and perhaps even a little beyond Earth.'[93]

Though he uses the term 're-creation' instead of 'co-creation', Jesuit philosopher W. Norris Clarke also foregrounds technology in the human task 'to recreate the world that has been given him, malleable and plastic under his fingers, to be transformed by his own initiative and artistic inventiveness'.[94] The end result is an expression of something new, reflecting both the divine and the human images.[95]

---

[89] Pierre Teilhard de Chardin, *Activation of Energy*, trans. Renè Hague. (London: Collins, 1970), 160.

[90] Teilhard de Chardin, *The Future of Man*, 276–305.

[91] Arthur Peacocke, *Creation and the World of Science: The Bampton Lectures 1978* (Oxford: Clarendon Press, 1979), 316.

[92] *Ibid.*, 301.

[93] *Ibid.*, 304.

[94] W. Norris Clarke, 'Technology and Man: A Christian Vision', *Technology and Culture* 3, no. 4 (1962), 427–428.

[95] *Ibid.*, 428.

Of course, many accounts of humans as agents of creation focus on non-human creation as the object of the creative work and human mastery, and not all would extend the scope of co-creation to include humans as its object. But we also see the notion that human 'nature' is to some degree within our power to alter. Extending Hart's treatment of human making to the prospect of human enhancement technologies is therefore warranted, and potentially very fruitful.

As Peter Scott argues, theologians must reckon with 'the technological factor' today. Scott calls for a reconstruction of theological anthropology that does justice to humanity's place in a technological society.[96] This is the task of the present work, particularly as theological anthropology informs our views on using technology to enhance human capacities. Furthermore, the exploration of human enhancement issues demands a consideration of technology itself, and the place it occupies in human activity. Yet technology is a very broad category. Stephen Kline surveys the different uses of the term 'technology', highlighting its ambiguity.[97] He arrives as the composite meaning of 'sociotechnical systems of manufacture and use', arguing that this pattern has been used by humans and their evolutionary ancestors for the past 2 million years to extend their capabilities.[98] 'Technology' in the sense that Kline uses it, therefore, is not solely the product of a 'high-tech age' but has affected our evolutionary path,[99] and this will be adopted as a working definition for this treatment of technology within the human enhancement context.

A theological anthropology that is able to engage human enhancement questions must also be commensurate with scientific

[96] Peter Scott, 'The Technological Factor: Redemption, Nature, and the Image of God', *Zygon* 35, no. 2 (2000), 371.
[97] Stephen Kline, 'What Is Technology?' *Bulletin of Science Technology & Society* 5, no. 3 (1985).
[98] *Ibid.*, 217.
[99] *Ibid.*, 217.

insights. This opens broader questions of the relationship between science and theology which can only partially be explored here but are the focus of a growing field of study. Suffice it to say that human enhancement proposals are founded on the understanding that contemporary humans are the product of a long and complicated evolutionary process, an assertion that has implications for traditional Christian doctrines such as creation and the *imago Dei*. In developing a theological anthropology that can address questions pertinent to human enhancement, Hart's understanding of human creativity must be expanded to accommodate our evolutionary history.

The understanding of humans as co-creators is well attested in Christian thought and is taken as a natural starting point in exploring whether the prospect of enhancing human abilities with technology might be compatible with orthodox Christianity. To determine whether such a position might gain traction in dialogue with human enhancement concerns, the present work will explore in detail what is arguably the most sustained account of humans as co-creators in recent time that incorporates scientific perspectives: Philip Hefner's 'created co-creator' model of theological anthropology. Hefner's work will be examined in terms of the way he perceives and frames the relationship between science and theology, the place accorded to both technology and creativity in his theological anthropology, contextualised in evolutionary history, and whether his proposals are able to engage transhumanist visions of the future in a robust manner.

Creativity and Fallenness

Though claiming too much for human creativity at the expense of its subordination to divine creation has already been cautioned against, a further limitation must be registered. To what extent is human creativity impacted by the systemic reality of sin? A hamartiology is beyond the present scope, nevertheless human creativity is exercised only within the confines of a fallen world. Hart makes the relevant point, though, that

> epistemological undecidability (the unavailability of pure presence, unmediated meaning, or absolute certainty) is arguably part of what makes us morally responsible beings at all and calls forth from us imaginative and 'creative' responses to situations rather than excusing our failure to engage in initiatives designed to pursue and promote the good, the true, and the beautiful.[100]

Our freedom may not be unbounded, but this does not preclude our making significant creative contributions to the world and future that God is bringing about.

Just as the technological nature of transhumanist visions calls forth a corresponding engagement with technology by theologians who would respond to transhumanism, so also the imaginative dimension of transhumanism, particularly evident in its relationship with science fiction, dictates that the imagination ought to receive greater attention in theological responses. In particular, the imagination's role in epistemology and communication of knowledge warrants exploration in this context. Furthermore, theological engagement with human enhancement proposals will need to promote a robust ethic and vision of human flourishing that can sustain virtue in a technological environment. Later chapters will offer further reflection on the epistemic limitations that impinge on moral discernment.

Conclusion

Theologically we can support an analogy between human and divine creation. Insights from the field of creativity studies are compatible with the notion that human creativity is connected

---

[100] Hart, *Making Good*, 240.

to God's creative work, and the treatment of human creativity within a broader doctrine of creation makes sense on the basis of this relationship. This theological understanding has led to the description of humans as co-creators with God, particularly in connection to the sciences. Building on Hart's compelling case for correspondence between human and divine creativity within the artistic realm, we now turn to the field of science and religion for Hefner's account of co-creation, more specifically directed to technological activity, to determine its utility as theologians engage with the challenges surrounding human technological enhancement.

Part II | Responding Theologically to Human Enhancement

3 | Humans as 'Created Co-creators'

The Created Co-creator in Context

Philip Hefner offers a contemporary theology of co-creation with his 'created co-creator' metaphor for understanding human creativity, drawing heavily on scientific methodology in the process. While the history of co-creation theology is important for understanding Hefner's particular representation of the concept, it forms only part of the context in which we must locate his thought. A history of interacting with natural scientists and an interest in fostering dialogue between science (particularly evolutionary biology) and theological enquiry are evident in his work and thus shape his conclusions concerning human creativity.

The Theological Task

Hefner's understanding of the theological task illuminates his created co-creator model and associated reframing of certain doctrines. Early in his career, Hefner defines the task of theology as follows:

> Theology stands under a double responsibility – to preserve the Christianness of its statements while at the same time speaking relevantly to the situations in which it finds itself. Theology must, therefore, recapitulate its essential Christian character in every present moment so as to be genuinely alive, Christianly speaking, within the circumstances which its environment sets before it.[1]

[1] Philip Hefner, *Faith and the Vitalities of History* (New York: Harper & Row, 1966), 183.

For Hefner, the particular circumstances set before him include the evolutionary account of human origins. He aims to provide 'a theological anthropology in the light of the natural sciences',[2] calling on theologians to 'reconsider how scientific knowledge and revealed theology can interact, so that they may inform human life more wisely in an age of science and technology'.[3] Hefner writes in response to what he perceives to be a global crisis brought about by poor human choices, both wilful and unwitting.[4] Furthermore, he identifies an intellectual dissonance, claiming that:

> although science and technology are more clearly a premise of our continued existence than ever before, signs are everywhere that people are dissatisfied with the thesis of secularization, which holds that religion and metaphysics are vestiges of our human infancy that will be supplanted by scientific knowledge. We desire a religion and metaphysics that work for us as we seek meaning in our present situation.[5]

His understanding of the natural world as 'God's greatest project' leads Hefner to claim that 'theology is not on track unless it can interpret the traditions of the religious communities as revelation about the natural order'.[6] He is even more blunt in his assertion that 'theology as explanation is dead unless it learns to integrate within itself elements of scientific understandings that undergird explanation for our time in history'.[7] While he does not offer a detailed account of how he understands the relationship between theology and science, Hefner does reject an overly simplistic identification of science with the 'what?' questions and religion with the 'why?' questions. He summarises his own position as follows:

---

[2] Hefner, THF, xiii.
[3] Philip Hefner, 'Sociobiology, Ethics and Theology', Zygon 19 (1984), 190.
[4] Hefner, THF, 4.
[5] Hefner, THF, 10.
[6] Ibid., 75.
[7] Ibid., 219. Note that this comment is in response to contemporary claims of religious naturalists.

science sets forth the description of the teleonomic structures and processes of nature, including human nature, while religion, through myth and ritual, speaks of the way in which those structures and processes are to be interpreted and the specific directions they are to take within the parameters of what they are capable of.[8]

According to Hefner, his major work on the created co-creator was written to answer the central question: 'Just who are we human beings and what are we here for?'[9]

The Lakatosian Research Programme

A logical starting point for understanding Hefner's model is his own summary of his core claim.

Human beings are God's created co-creators whose purpose is to be the agency, acting in freedom, to birth the future that is most wholesome for the nature that has birthed us – the nature that is not only our own genetic heritage, but also the entire human community and the evolutionary and ecological reality in which and to which we belong. Exercising this agency is said to be God's will for humans.[10]

This passage is the main source referenced with respect to Hefner on co-creation. Hefner situates this claim, however, within a whole framework of ideas that seeks to express and reinterpret traditional theological concepts through the application of a particular methodology for the progression of scientific knowledge. Hefner's created co-creator model is usually abstracted from his thought in its entirety and treated as a self-sufficient concept;[11] yet

[8] *Ibid.*, 213. He avoids the NOMA approach, however, with a subsequent claim that science may offer hermeneutical insights, and religion may add to our knowledge of teleonomy.

[9] *Ibid.*, 4.

[10] Hefner, *THF*, 27.

[11] Elaine Graham, 'Bioethics after Posthumanism: Natural Law, Communicative Action and the Problem of Self-Design', *Ecotheology* 9, no. 2 (2004), 194–195.

a real engagement with Hefner on co-creation should also give consideration to the 'hypotheses' he extrapolates from his portrayal of humans as created co-creators, and the accompanying reinterpretation of the traditional doctrines of God, sin and evil.

At first glance, Hefner's major work *The Human Factor* bears little resemblance to most theological monographs. Given his stated objective to integrate science and theology in his exposition of human nature, it is not surprising that his account borrows much from scientific methodology. For Hefner, scientific formulations become relevant to theology when theologians seek to articulate explanations of general human experience that transcend the religious tradition.[12] He goes even further to say that theological statements must 'observe the [scientific] canons of dealing with a wide range of data, falsifiability, and fruitfulness' to convey truth successfully beyond their particular religious tradition.[13]

In his own efforts to express theological concepts in a manner commensurate with scientific theory, Hefner is particularly indebted to Imre Lakatos' model of scientific research programmes. A Hungarian philosopher of science and contemporary of Karl Popper and Thomas Kuhn, Lakatos' understanding of scientific knowledge acquisition attempts a corrective to both Popper and Kuhn. In place of Kuhn's understanding of scientific reasoning in terms of *successive* paradigms, Lakatos instead sees *competing* research programmes.[14] He criticises Kuhn's subjection of scientific belief to non-rational standards of acceptance,[15] and he seeks to

---

[12] Philip Hefner, 'Theology's Truth and Scientific Formulation', *Zygon* 23, no. 1 (1988), 264.

[13] Hefner, 'Theology's Truth', 264.

[14] Nancey Murphy, *Theology in an Age of Scientific Reasoning* (Ithaca, NY: Cornell University Press, 1990), 59.

[15] Lakatos charges Kuhn with reducing scientific revolution to 'a matter for mob psychology' and denying any role to rationality in the process (*The Methodology of Scientific Research Programmes*, ed. John Worrall and Gregory Currie, vol. I (Cambridge: Cambridge University Press, 1978), 91; cf. Thomas Kuhn, 'Logic of Discovery or Psychology of Research?' in *Criticism and the Growth of Knowledge*, ed.

improve on Popper's theory of falsification by acknowledging that counter-instances are not always decisive for the abandonment of a scientific hypothesis.[16] Rather, a theory is falsified and replaced when a new theory arises that has greater explanatory power and can account for novel facts.[17]

The Lakatosian research programme has several components. At its heart is what Lakatos terms the 'hard core' – the basic idea.[18] Generally, the nature of the claims in the hard core means that it cannot be directly falsified or verified – it is '"irrefutable" by the methodological decision of its proponents'.[19] The veracity of such claims, however, can be indirectly upheld or impugned through the testing of associated 'auxiliary hypotheses'.[20] These take the form of 'observational' hypotheses which may change in response to observed anomalies; they can be adjusted in response to counter-instances and thus 'bear the brunt of tests' in service to the hard core.[21]

Characteristic of the Lakatosian research programme is the articulation of a set of methodological rules: the *negative heuristic* 'tell us what paths of research to avoid' while the *positive heuristic* tell us 'what paths to pursue'.[22] In a bona fide research programme, the auxiliary hypotheses must be formulated in accordance with the positive heuristic, i.e. they must represent an increase of knowledge.[23] The negative heuristic forbids the application of a *modus tollens* form of argumentation to the hard

Imre Lakatos and Alan Musgrave (Amsterdam: North-Holland Publishing Co., 1970)).

[16] Lakatos, *Methodology of Scientific Research Programmes*, 4, 92.

[17] *Ibid.*, 31–33.

[18] Hefner equates the 'hard core' with Kuhn's concept of the 'paradigm' ('Theology's Truth', 270).

[19] Lakatos, *Methodology of Scientific Research Programmes*, 48.

[20] *Ibid.*, 48.

[21] *Ibid.*, 48.

[22] *Ibid.*, 47.

[23] *Ibid.*, 95.

core itself, instead redirecting the burden of proof to the 'protective belt' of auxiliary hypotheses.[24] These hypotheses can then be reformulated in response to falsifying data, while the hard core remains intact. As Nancey Murphy, another adopter of Lakatosian methodology, points out, a certain 'dogmatism' is required for scientific progress – the negative heuristic allows space for a theory to be fully developed instead of prematurely discarded.[25] In Lakatos' adroit phrase, the scientist through observation may 'be encouraged by Nature's *yes*, but not discouraged by its *no*'.[26]

The key evaluative criteria of a scientific proposal for Lakatos is its fruitfulness in generating new insights.[27] A research programme is eventually discarded if it is judged to be degenerative (i.e. no longer producing new ideas) and waning in influence rather than progressive.[28] According to Lakatos this renders the shift between a degenerating research programme to a progressive one a rational shift, as opposed to the irrational paradigm shift proposed by Kuhn.[29]

Hefner is explicit about his borrowing from philosophies of science and the way he translates these insights into the theological context. He does acknowledge that a scientific methodology is not immediately applicable to theology without some kind of transformation.[30] Rather than importing Popper's or Lakatos' models wholesale, he suggests 'that they be adapted heuristically rather than literally, endorsing the suggestions that theological theories should be referred to the world of possible experience, and that it is

---

[24] *Ibid.*, 48.
[25] Murphy, *Theology in an Age of Scientific Reasoning*, 60.
[26] Lakatos, *Methodology of Scientific Research Programmes*, 50n.
[27] That is, its 'heuristic power' (*ibid.*, 52).
[28] Lakatos, *Methodology of Scientific Research Programmes*, 48. Of course, the same criticism that Lakatos levels at Kuhn may be applied here – the determination of a programme's fruitfulness is subjective and is therefore arguably as non-rational as the Kuhnian paradigm shift. The point at which a degenerative programme is judged to be no longer capable of becoming progressive again is not obvious to discern.
[29] *Ibid.*, 91–92.
[30] Hefner, *THF*, 23.

desirable to discern what a possible theory negates as well as what it affirms'.[31] One example of modification is Hefner's extension of a research programme's production of new 'facts', a criterion for fruitfulness within the Lakatosian framework, to include new interpretations of existing knowledge.[32]

Theological statements differ from scientific statements in the precision of empirical content and predictive ability.[33] Obviously, theological statements must make some reference to God. For this reason Hefner rejects Popper's model of falsification in favour of Lakatos' refinement. While the concept of 'God' itself is not falsifiable, a notion of the divine may reside in the 'hard core' of the Lakatosian framework, shielded from direct falsification by the 'protective belt' of auxiliary hypotheses yet also testable on these same grounds.[34]

Hefner does acknowledge the challenges inherent in applying even a modified scientific framework to theology – particularly the lack of consensus (within or outside the theological community) concerning the falsifiability of theological ideas.[35] Additionally, the notion of fruitfulness as an evaluative measure may meet some resistance within the theological community, which has traditionally concerned itself with what is right and true.[36] With this context established, however, Hefner sets out to construct theological proposals that conform to the structure of a scientific research programme and its requirements of falsifiability (i.e. potential falsifiers and permissible conditions can be identified with respect to the claims he places in the hard core).[37] Furthermore, the theological task requires that 'theological statements will be used

---

[31] Ibid., 24.
[32] Hefner, 'Theology's Truth', 270.
[33] Ibid., 269.
[34] Hefner, 'Theology's Truth', 269.
[35] Hefner, THF, 25.
[36] Ibid., 26. A more developed account of the relationship between fruitfulness and truth may go some way to answering such resistance.
[37] Ibid., 25.

in theory-construction that conforms to the criteria of falsifiability and fruitfulness', as part of theology's 'explanatory function for general human experience'.[38]

Hefner is not the only, or even the first, theologian to find the Lakatosian structure valuable for theological explanation. Early in her career, Murphy adopted a Lakatosian framework in areas of her work (and Hefner owes much to Murphy's interpretation of Lakatos); however, she later rejected Lakatos' model in favour of Alasdair MacIntyre's understanding of rationality.[39] Robert Russell values the work of Imre Lakatos for theological thought,[40] while Karl Peters,[41] Philip Clayton,[42] and Gregory Peterson all engage with the model in their theological writings.[43] Hefner argues that a Lakatosian framework can also be applied to Wolfhart Pannenberg's theology, and Pannenberg accepts this characterisation of his work.[44]

The validity of Hefner's adoption of a Lakatosian framework for theological explanation depends on the acceptability of Lakatos' model itself (does it provide an adequate account of the progression of scientific knowledge?) as well as the epistemological rigour of Lakatos' criterion of fruitfulness. Both questions are outside the

[38] Hefner, 'Theology's Truth', 268.
[39] Murphy, *Theology in an Age of Scientific Reasoning*; Nancey Murphy and Warren Brown, *Did My Neurons Make Me Do It? Philosophical and Neurobiological Perspectives on Moral Responsibility and Free Will* (Oxford: Oxford University Press, 2007); Hefner, *THF*, 23.
[40] Robert Russell, 'Cosmology from Alpha to Omega: Response to Reviews', *Zygon* 45, no. 1 (2010), 238.
[41] Karl Peters, 'Empirical Theology in Light of Science', *Zygon* 27, no. 3 (1992).
[42] Philip Clayton, *Explanation from Physics to Theology: An Essay in Rationality and Religion* (New Haven, CT: Yale University Press, 1989).
[43] Gregory Peterson, 'The Scientific Status of Theology: Imre Lakatos, Method and Demarcation', *Perspectives in Science and Christian Faith* 50 (1988).
[44] Hefner's characterisation, and Pannenberg's acceptance, occurred via a written dialogue in *Zygon* (Philip Hefner, 'The Role of Science in Pannenberg's Theological Thinking', *Zygon* 24, no. 2 (1989), 146–148; Wolfhart Pannenberg, 'Theological Appropriation of Scientific Understandings: Response to Hefner, Wicken, Eaves, and Tipler', *Zygon* 24, no. 2 (1989), 258–259).

present scope, relying on detailed philosophical argumentation, however, they have been explored elsewhere by the author.[45]

The Created Co-creator Model

Acknowledging potential vulnerabilities in Hefner's dependence on Lakatos, let us allow for now that a Lakatosian framework is a reasonable choice for formulating theological statements. What follows is a detailed exposition of Hefner's created co-creator model within the structure of a Lakatosian research programme. As Hefner insists that the protective belt of hypotheses are empirically testable, the scientific testability and evidential support for each hypothesis will be briefly evaluated. Though Hefner often uses the term 'science' in generic ways, the scope here will largely concern insights from evolutionary biology and evolutionary psychology in particular (and climatology to a lesser extent) as most relevant to Hefner's claims.

Hefner's oft-cited statement on the subject of the created co-creator functions as the hard core of his proposal within the Lakatosian framework.[46]

Human beings are God's created co-creators whose purpose is to be the agency, acting in freedom, to birth the future that is most wholesome for the nature that has birthed us – the nature that is not only our own genetic heritage, but also the entire human community and the evolutionary and ecological reality in which and to which we belong. Exercising this agency is said to be God's will for humans.[47]

[45] Victoria Lorrimar, 'Are Scientific Research Programmes Applicable to Theology? On Philip Hefner's Use of Lakatos', *Theology and Science* 15, no. 2 (2017).

[46] While Hefner articulated earlier models of the created co-creator, this study considers the model elaborated in *THF* in 1993 to be the most comprehensive and representative of Hefner's mature thought on the concept.

[47] Hefner, *THF*, 27.

Having provided this empirical description of human nature, Hefner proceeds to articulate a theological theory within a Lakatosian framework intended to explain the empirical description and form part of the normative grammar of Christian faith.[48] Building on the core claim stated above, he elaborates on the 'theological theory' by breaking down its essential aspects into 'core elements', identifying 'auxiliary hypotheses' associated with each that can be tested for their fruitfulness and thus support the core of his proposal.

Core Element 1

The first 'core element' is as follows: 'The human being is created by God to be a co-creator in the creation that God has brought into being and for which God has purposes'. He summarises this in the more recognised term 'created co-creator'. The adjective 'created' denotes the 'conditionedness' of human beings, both as located within an ecosystem and as recipients of a genetic nature that is bestowed on the individual rather than chosen.[49] Humans did not place themselves within the evolutionary process and thus are not superior to any other creatures within the same ecosystem.[50] Rather, humans are characterised by a sense of belonging among all creatures.[51]

'Co-creator', on the other hand, emphasises the freedom of humans to make decisions and construct contextualising narratives in which these decisions are made.[52] Hefner considers co-creation

---

[48] *Ibid.*, 32.
[49] Hefner points out that even genetic engineering does not prevent individuals from receiving a genome that they did not choose themselves (Hefner, *THF*, 36).
[50] *Ibid.*, 36.
[51] Philip Hefner, 'The Foundations of Belonging in a Christian Worldview', in *Belonging and Alienation: Religious Foundations for the Human Future*, ed. Philip Hefner and Widick Schroeder (Chicago, IL: Centre for the Scientific Study of Religion, 1976), 163.
[52] Hefner, *THF*, 38.

a distinctive quality of humans, though he warns against its application in service to anthropocentric ends.[53] Yet the co-creator remains contingent on God as creator and is creative in a derivative sense.[54]

Hefner assigns several auxiliary hypotheses to the understanding of humans as created co-creators. The first of these concerns 'teleonomy', the apparent purposefulness of structures and processes in biological systems (unlike 'teleology', teleonomy does not ascribe purposefulness to human or divine intent). While Hefner believes that *teleological* claims about nature can only be asserted on the basis of faith, *teleonomic* responses to certain biological structures and processes can be discerned empirically.[55] He argues for a teleonomic axiom that hypothesises the purpose and meaning of something based on its structure.[56] Theologically, Hefner argues for a version of natural law theology by grounding this teleonomic axiom in God's creative action.[57] Both naturalistic and theological perspectives 'would conclude that nature is all we possess as the chief source for understanding what the world is about'.[58] He formulates the testable hypothesis as follows:

Hypothesis 1

Integral to *Homo sapiens* and its evolutionary history are certain structures and processes, the requirements for whose functioning may be said to constitute, at least in a tentative way, goals and purposes for human life.[59]

Hefner preempts challenges to this hypothesis on the basis of the naturalistic fallacy, arguing that the teleonomic axiom does not

---

53 *Ibid.*, 38–39.
54 *Ibid.*, 39.
55 *Ibid.*, 39.
56 Hefner, *THF*, 40.
57 *Ibid.*, 40.
58 *Ibid.*, 40.
59 *Ibid.*, 40.

involve crass, unreflective moves from is to ought but, rather, speaks in tentative and careful ways of both the possibility and the necessity to make such moves.[60]

According to Hefner, this hypothesis is testable in the same way that all descriptions of structures and processes can be evaluated for their accuracy and adequacy.[61] The meaning and purpose of creatures must be continuous with the equipment with which they are endowed. Humans are equipped with 'self-awareness, decision-making, action, and self-assessment based on the reception of complex feedbacks [sic]' – Hefner argues that this natural equipment is a good fit for the purpose of the created co-creator,[62] and it is this fit that can be subjected to testing.

Hefner speaks in terms of kinship, citing nucleotide sequence comparisons and comparative morphological studies as evidence for human continuity with processes applicable to the 'whole of nature',[63] and the ecological model as empirical support for the natural structures in which humans live.[64] Plenty of scientific studies support the continuity of human morphology with that of other species. Until it was superseded by molecular analyses, comparative morphology (comparing observable characteristics between species) was the major tool underpinning the construction of phylogenies (branched diagrams representing the order in which a groups of species share a common ancestor).[65] Entire 'trees of life' are built through the identification of homologous structures in two separate species derived from a common ancestor. Advances in molecular analyses have only added to what was already inferred from the cruder morphological comparisons.[66]

---

[60] Ibid., 58.

[61] Ibid., 41.

[62] Ibid., 58–59.

[63] Hefner, THF, 65.

[64] Ibid., 65.

[65] Mark Ridley, Evolution, 3rd edn (Oxford: Blackwell Publishers, 2004), 425.

[66] A good summary of these developments can be found in Jaume Bertranpetit and Francesc Calafell, 'Genome Views on Human Evolution', in Evolution: From

The notion that structure implies function is also well attested in scientific thought. In molecular biology, for example, functional protein studies infer information about the putative function of a protein based on structural elements and the underlying DNA sequence. Among its many applications, this principle underpins the prediction of transmembrane proteins through the identification of coding regions for hydrophilic protein segments (i.e. segments able to cross a membrane) using the entire genome sequence of an organism.[67] As many similar examples could be offered, Hefner can reasonably claim that this first hypothesis receives some support from available scientific evidence.

Yet there is a difference between inferring function from structure and Hefner's more ambitious claim that purposes and goals can be constituted by natural structures and processes. Scientists would generally balk at extrapolating a larger purpose or goal from the structure of an organism. The debate surrounding teleology in the natural sciences was well under way at the time of Hefner's writing, and continues today.[68]

While Hefner does use the term 'teleonomy' in place of teleology, it is questionable whether the created co-creator function can be extrapolated from teleonomic notions alone. Some would argue that all uses of the term teleonomy are thinly veiled teleological statements. Though tongue-in-cheek, a little truth can be found in David Hull's quip:

Haldane [in the 1930s] can be found remarking, 'Teleology is like a mistress to a biologist: he cannot live without her but he's unwilling

---

Molecules to Ecosystems, ed. Andrés Moya and Enrique Font (Oxford: Oxford University Press, 2004).

[67] Anders Krogh et al., 'Predicting Transmembrane Protein Topology with a Hidden Markov Model: Application to Complete Genomes', *Journal of Molecular Biology* 305 (2001).

[68] Pier Luigi Luisi provides a helpful summary of this debate (*The Emergence of Life: From Chemical Origins to Synthetic Biology* (Cambridge: Cambridge University Press, 2016), 244).

to be seen with her in public.' Today the mistress has become a lawfully wedded wife. Biologists no longer feel obligated to apologize for their use of teleological language; they flaunt it. The only concession which they make to its disreputable past is to rename it 'teleonomy'.[69]

We can find sustained attempts to reconcile contemporary science with the notion of teleology, such as Terrence Deacon's account of emergence that rejects substance dualism in favour of property dualism.[70] While Hefner's choice to use teleonomic language is certainly more palatable to many scientists, the validity of defining the human as co-creator on this basis is debatable. Therefore, while parts of this hypothesis are supported by scientific conclusions, in its entirety it makes claims potentially beyond the reach of scientific discovery.

The second auxiliary hypothesis is closely related to the first:

Hypothesis 2

The meaning and purpose of human beings are conceived in terms of their placement within natural processes and their contribution to those same processes.[71]

Nature is the 'progenitor' of Homo sapiens and thus gives insight into human purpose, with humans defined as 'the diviner[s] of ultimate meanings within the natural processes'.[72] The ultimate purpose of humans is not to build up the human community, or even to serve God, but rather to serve the whole creation. 'The direction God-ward leads us reflexively to nature.'[73]

---

[69] David Hull, 'Philosophy and Biology', in *Philosophy of Science: Contemporary Philosophy: A New Survey*, ed. Guttorm Fløistad (The Hague: Nijhoff, 1982).

[70] Terrence Deacon, *Incomplete Nature: How Mind Emerged from Matter* (New York: Norton, 2012).

[71] Hefner, *THF*, 41.

[72] *Ibid.*, 73.

[73] *Ibid.*, 60.

In testing this hypothesis, 'nonhuman nature may provide clues to the character and purpose of human being', and the consequences of certain human behaviours (wholesome or destructive) towards the rest of nature are taken into account.[74] In some ways this is an expansion of the first hypothesis, considering human function in light of not only its own structures but also the structure of the entire natural order in which it is embedded. If assuming a goal or purpose based on an organism's biological structure is problematic for some, assuming a purpose beyond the organism's own requirements to those of other species is even less plausible to those who would reject teleological arguments. The problems associated with scientifically supporting the teleological claims of the first hypothesis thus apply to this hypothesis as well.

To argue that human behaviour has consequences for the rest of nature is straightforward enough – such a claim would be more or less universally accepted. We can even say, as mentioned above, that it is in our best interests to act in ways that are wholesome for the rest of nature. But does it necessarily follow that the purpose of human being is therefore to act beneficially for the whole of nature? How do we understand situations in which judgement is required over which aspect of nature to prioritise, i.e. when interests are in competition? This shifts this hypothesis into the speculative realm, and if Hefner is to properly avoid challenges on the basis of the naturalistic fallacy, then his proposal must retain its tentative nature. This claim cannot be sustained or rejected on the basis of scientific insights alone.

A pragmatic criterion for truth emerges with the second hypothesis and leads to the third:

Hypothesis 3

A concept of 'wholesomeness' is both unavoidable and useful as a criterion governing the behaviour of human beings within their

74 *Ibid.*, 41.

natural ambience, as they consider what their contribution to nature should be.[75]

Though it appears an ambiguous criterion, Hefner suggests that a definition of wholesomeness can be arrived at via consensus.[76] Hefner describes the criteria for this hypothesis as pragmatic, arguing that human action will have to be 'empirically discernible as in some way beneficial'.[77] Indeed, the assertion that humans should act to benefit nature is hardly objectionable. Many examples of humans acting in opposition to this goal could be provided however, Hefner is not hypothesising that all action must be beneficial, only that wholesomeness is an appropriate criterion for action.

It makes logical sense that in the context of an ecosystem, where the harming of one participant is detrimental to all, it is in the interests of humans that their action towards the rest of nature should be wholesome. This goes for all participants, however, not only those capable of conscious reflection. Such a statement does not necessarily constitute a hypothesis or merit a place in a scientific research programme. Nor does Hefner's stated means of validation with respect to this particular hypothesis: consensus. Scientific consensus has been incorrect at various points in history and this is likely to continue (hence the requirement for ongoing research and the construction of sophisticated philosophies of theory acceptance and change). If granted the status of a hypothesis, however, we might ask how the wholesomeness criterion could be falsified? By identifying a different criterion that serves equally well? The difficulty of articulating a means of falsification is another indication that the hypothesis is not adequately formulated. In this case, it appears that Hefner is stretching the understanding of what constitutes a hypothesis. His claim that wholesomeness should govern

---

[75] Hefner, *THF*, 42.
[76] *Ibid.*, 42.
[77] *Ibid.*, 61.

human behaviour towards the rest of nature is reasonable, but not significant when it comes to the scientific validation of his model.

As these first three hypotheses establish that nature is the domain for human purpose, Hefner proposes a fourth hypothesis concerned with this special status accorded to the natural order:

Hypothesis 4

Nature is the medium through which the world, including human beings, receives knowledge, as well as grace. If God is brought into the discussion, then nature is the medium of divine knowledge and grace.[78]

In this Hefner follows the urging of Joseph Sittler, who emphasised that human history only transpires within the larger context of natural history.[79] Hefner further argues that the human mind must also be perceived as an entity of nature, citing representations of the mind's emergence in the context of evolutionary epistemology.[80]

In his location of human meaning and purpose within the natural order, Hefner challenges what he considers to be the dominant understanding of our relationship to nature.

Instead of relatedness and kinship, [prevailing symbol systems] speak of our responsibility for nature as its stewards or masters, and of the possibilities nature presents to us for exercising our creative abilities and propensities to reshape it, to make it conform to us and serve us. In the main, humans have symbolized their work upon nature as furthering its development and improving it, thus placing

[78] Hefner, THF, 42.
[79] Ibid., 58; cf. Joseph Sittler, 'The Sittler Speeches', in Center for the Study of Campus Ministry Yearbook, ed. Phil Schroeder (Valparaiso, IN: Valparaiso University Press, 1978), 31–32.
[80] Hefner, THF, 61; cf. Karl Peters, 'Religion and an Evolutionary Theory of Knowledge', Zygon 17 (1982), 392–393; Robert Richards, Darwin and the Emergence of Evolutionary Theories of Mind and Behavior (Chicago, IL: University of Chicago Press, 1987), 574–593.

the weight of the good on the side of *doing unto* nature rather than accepting a place *within* it.[81]

Rather, nature is 'God's great project' – we must resist instrumentalising non-human nature and instead recognise that our task concerns the most wholesome future for all of nature.[82]

Hefner construes this hypothesis as a truism yet contends that it can be tested by determining the plausibility of statements about knowledge or grace derived from nature in light of our understandings of human nature.[83] This leads to the question of whether plausibility is an appropriate scientific criterion. Certainly, the claim that all knowledge that humans can obtain is mediated through nature is unobjectionable – scientists would be in agreement with this. The human brain is a natural entity and the medium by which we acquire knowledge.[84]

Hefner does not stop with the mediation of knowledge, however, but also hypothesises that nature mediates grace. What he means by grace is not immediately clear, especially as he distinguishes between grace and divine grace. Regardless of his meaning, the inclusion of divine grace in his statement puts the burden of proof (if he wishes his hypothesis to be scientifically sound) on the existence of divine grace. This is a claim that might be situated within the hard core but does not belong in the protective belt of a Lakatosian research programme. As it stands, therefore, this hypothesis again makes claims that extend beyond the purview of scientific verification.

Core Element 2

Hefner identifies a second core element to his thesis that humans are created co-creators:

---

[81] Hefner, *THF*, 67, emphasis original.

[82] *Ibid.*, 74.

[83] *Ibid.*, 42, 61.

[84] The citations Hefner gives for the natural status of the mind offer scientific support for this. See footnote 80 on p. 83.

> The conditioning matrix that has produced the human being – the evolutionary process – is God's process of bringing into being a creature who represents the creation's zone of a new stage of freedom and who therefore is crucial for the emergence of a free creation.[85]

Hefner reduces this statement to the challenge of 'interpreting the evolutionary process as the work of God' – a major challenge, in his view, for the contemporary theologian.[86] Natural selection processes in particular raise questions of theodicy that Hefner addresses later in the volume.[87] The emphasis here is on the freedom that emerges from the evolutionary matrix. For Hefner, the unavoidability of human freedom is almost tautological, which only makes sense when he goes on to define freedom not primarily in terms of liberty or ability to shape the world but rather as a 'condition of existence'.[88] Despite their apparent negation of each other, freedom and determinism are dialectical for Hefner – 'freedom requires the structure of determinism for its becoming' and the 'causal context' is enabled by freedom 'to persist in new and different ways'.[89] Insight from the field of epigenetics 'clarifies how a deterministic biological system can favour the emergence of freedom'.[90] While freedom and determinism can exist in conflict, producing fear, we are constantly seeking situations in which they are consonant with respect to our human destiny.[91]

Associated with the conditioning matrix core element are a further two auxiliary hypotheses.

[85] Hefner, *THF*, 42.
[86] *Ibid.*, 42.
[87] *Ibid.*, 271.
[88] *Ibid.*, 97.
[89] Hefner, *THF*, 115.
[90] *Ibid.*, 116.
[91] *Ibid.*, 117, 121.

Hypothesis 5

Freedom characterizes human existence as the condition in which humans have no choice but to act and to construct the narratives and symbols that contextualize that action. Such contextualization provides justification, explanation, and norms for guiding and assessing the action. This condition is intrinsic to the evolutionary processes at the level of *Homo sapiens*.[92]

The testability of this hypothesis is linked to its utility for understanding humans and their relationship with nature (including other humans). Hefner gives two examples to make his case: the choice of whether to prolong a parent's life using medical intervention, and the development and implication of environmental policies that require assigning comparative values to different forms of life. Both instances require not only human decision but also the construction of stories that justify such decisions (like instructions to honour our parents and to serve as stewards to the creation).[93] With respect to the latter, the centrality of narrative construction to the human mind is well attested in the human sciences. Karl Peters, to use one of the examples put forward by Hefner, highlights the constructivist element of the human central nervous system – the ability to construct contextualising narratives has enabled humans to evolve as they have.[94] Hefner also cites neuroscientist William Calvin in his argument that the brain's capacity to observe and interpret information through the constructing of meaningful narratives is crucial for survival.[95] More recently this is supported by social psychologist Jonathan Haidt, who argues that the human mind is essentially a story processor.[96]

[92] *Ibid.*, 45.
[93] *Ibid.*, 98.
[94] Karl Peters, 'Humanity in Nature: Conserving Yet Creating', *Zygon* 24 (1989).
[95] William Calvin, *The Cerebral Symphony: Seashore Reflections on the Structure of Consciousness* (New York: Bantam Press, 1989).
[96] Jonathan Haidt, *The Righteous Mind: Why Good People Are Divided by Politics and Religion* (New York: Vintage Books, 2013), 287.

The question of freedom is more complex. Scientifically speaking, Hefner points us to Theodosius Dobzhansky's exploration of genetically determined phenotype plasticity and the explanation this offers for the emergence of freedom within an evolutionary framework.[97] He cites the more recent (at the time of his writing) work of Rodney Holmes and Terrence Deacon as an extension of Dobzhansky's insight.[98] More recently, Moczek et al. have connected phenotypic plasticity with evolutionary innovation.[99] This should not be equated with freedom, however, as Moczek et al. struggle to reconcile the apparent paradox between the Darwinian notion that every new trait is somehow derived from an old one, and the existence of complex novel traits.[100] The language of freedom, and an understanding of how it fits within processes of evolution, again reaches beyond the explanatory capacity of science, though such an understanding may be compatible with scientific knowledge.

The second hypothesis attached to this core element reiterates one of the central ideas in Hefner's core claim.

Hypothesis 6

Homo sapiens is a two-natured creature, a symbiosis of genes and culture.[101]

97 Hefner, *THF*, 99; cf. Theodosius Dobzhansky, *The Biological Basis of Human Freedom*. (New York: Columbia University Press, 1956), 68.

98 Terrence Deacon, 'Brain-Language Co-Evolution', in *The Evolution of Human Languages*, ed. John Hawkins and Murray Gell-Mann (Reading, MA: Addison-Wesley, 1992); Rodney Holmes, 'Did *Homo Religiosus* Emerge from the Evolution of the Brain?', *Insights: The Magazine of the Chicago Centre for Religion and Science* 3 (1991).

99 Armin P. Moczek et al., 'The Role of Developmental Plasticity in Evolutionary Innovation', *Proceedings of the Royal Society B: Biological Sciences* 278, no. 1719 (2011), 2705.

100 Moczek et al., 'The Role of Developmental Plasticity in Evolutionary Innovation', 2705.

101 Hefner, *THF*, 45.

We see here the beginnings of an idea that is prominent in Hefner's theological anthropology – human beings are the product of 'biocultural' evolution. This is a natural process in which our genetic and cultural heritages combine to produce free agents that are now capable of shaping future evolution.[102] Hefner describes this 'two-natured character' of humans as follows:

> *Homo sapiens* is itself a nodal point wherein two streams of information come together and co-exist. The one stream is inherited genetic information, the other is cultural information. Both of these streams come together in the central nervous system. Since they have coevolved and coadapted together, they are one reality, not two.[103]

Hefner acknowledges the difficulty in adequately describing the relationship between genes and culture; however, he supports the symbiosis model proposed by Ralph Burhoe.[104] He also commends Gerd Theissen's interpretation of biblical faith through the lens of Burhoe's model as a proposal for cultural evolution that transcends certain biological constraints.[105] Furthermore, Hefner argues that this complex gene-culture symbiosis that is the contemporary human has emerged from a deterministic evolutionary process as truly free – a freedom 'rooted in the genetically controlled adaptive plasticity of the human phenotype'.[106] Yet this freedom exists in tension with conditions that are 'suitable for the

---

[102] *Ibid.*, 28–29.

[103] *Ibid.*, 29. This understanding is not original to Hefner, and here he draws heavily on the work of Timothy Goldsmith (*The Biological Roots of Human Nature: Forging Links Between Evolution and Behavior* (New York: Oxford University Press, 1991)).

[104] Hefner, *THF*, 30; cf. Ralph Burhoe, 'Religion's Role in Human Evolution: The Missing Link Between Ape-Man's Selfish Genes and Civilized Altruism', *Zygon* 14 (1979).

[105] Hefner, *THF*, 30; cf. Gerd Theissen, *Biblical Faith: An Evolutionary Approach* (Philadelphia, PA: Fortress Press, 1985).

[106] Hefner, *THF*, 30. On this point Hefner refers us to Dobzhansky, *The Biological Basis of Human Freedom*.

THE CREATED CO-CREATOR IN CONTEXT

emergence of values', reinforced through the evolutionary context in which they were fashioned.[107] The two-natured character of human beings is antithetical to dualism, contends Hefner, as both streams of information have emerged from the one process of nature.[108]

Hefner suggests that this hypothesis is tested and supported by a large body of relevant scientific literature. When it comes to testing, this is possibly the most straightforward of Hefner's hypotheses. A wealth of studies demonstrate the influence of cultural factors on our biological function and vice versa. Cultural food options tend to conform to preferences influenced by genetically predisposed nutritional requirements – which explains why many prefer the taste of foods high in sugar, fat and salt. Conventional evolutionary theory has been expanded to include the phenomenon known as 'niche construction' – the ability of organisms to modify sources of natural selection within their environment. According to Laland et al., 'culture amplifies the capacity of human beings' for niche construction.[109] Lactose digestion is an oft-cited example, with genetic mutations producing lactase persistence beyond weaning increasingly distributed among particular populations since the beginning of animal domestication.[110]

Similarly, the cultural activity of yam cultivation in West Africa has been associated with an increased occurrence of the sickle cell anaemia gene in the local population, offering protection against the higher risk of malaria that comes with yam cultivation. Laland et al. do point out, however, that this is not direct causation by the

---

[107] Hefner, *THF*, 31.
[108] *Ibid.*, 102.
[109] Kevin Laland, John Odling-Smee and Marcus Feldman, 'Niche Construction, Biological Evolution, and Cultural Change'. *Behavioral and Brain Sciences* 23 (2000), 131.
[110] Pascale Gerbault et al., 'Evolution of Lactase Persistence: An Example of Human Niche Construction', *Philosophical Transactions of the Royal Society B: Biological Sciences* 366 (2011), 863.

cultural variable but rather that the ecological variable of standing water is exerting selection pressure. They propose a particular model of gene-culture coevolution in which 'instead of being exclusively responsible for allowing us to codirect our own evolution, in contrast to what happens in every other species, culture now becomes merely the principal way in which we humans do the same thing that most other species do'.[111] Molecular signatures likely generated by cultural selection pressures have been identified in the human genome, with calls for cross-disciplinary studies to illuminate further the evolutionary relationship between genes and culture.[112] More recently, insights from the field of epigenetics (which was in its infancy at the time of *The Human Factor*'s publication, and therefore it is unsurprising that Hefner only briefly mentions it) have improved our evolutionary models and afforded a place to environmental factors (some of which are cultural) in inheritable characteristics.[113] Novel patterns of brain waves have emerged since the increased usage of smartphones and other handheld internet devices; we can only speculate as to whether and how soon such changes will be reflected in the genome.[114] Therefore, although there are more nuanced understandings available, it does seem evident that Hefner's hypothesis concerning the human as a gene-culture symbiont is supported by scientific accounts of coevolution.

[111] Laland, Odling-Smee and Feldman, 'Niche Construction, Biological Evolution, and Cultural Change', 137.
[112] Kevin Laland, John Odling-Smee and Sean Myles. 'How Culture Shaped the Human Genome: Bringing Genetics and the Human Sciences Together', *Nature Reviews Genetics* 11 (2010), 146.
[113] Michael Skinner, 'Environmental Epigenetics and a Unified Theory of the Molecular Aspects of Evolution: A Neo-Lamarckian Concept that Facilitates Neo-Darwinian Evolution'. *Genome Biology and Evolution* 7, no. 5 (2015).
[114] Mari Swingle, *I-Minds: How Cell Phones, Computers, Gaming, and Social Media Are Changing Our Brains, Our Behavior, and the Evolution of our Species* (Gabriola, BC: New Society Publishers, 2016), 63.

Core Element 3

The final core element that Hefner outlines within the created co-creator hard core elaborates on the freedom that exists in tension with conditionedness.

> The freedom that marks the created co-creator and its culture is an instrumentality of God for enabling the creation (consisting of the evolutionary past of genetic and cultural inheritance as well as the contemporary ecosystem) to participate in the intentional fulfillment of God's purposes.[115]

This freedom is itself chosen by the creation and means that the world is defined not by its past or present but rather by what it is becoming.[116] The understanding of freedom is therefore eschatological. When it comes to the participation of the creation in God's purposes, and the human role in this, Hefner understands the doctrine of the *imago Dei* to mean that 'humans can be the vehicle for grace toward the creation'.[117] Associated with this core element are three further auxiliary hypotheses.

Hypothesis 7

> The challenge that culture poses to human being can be stated thus: Culture is a system of information that humans must construct so as to adequately serve the three tasks of interpreting the world in which humans live, guiding human behavior, and interfacing with the physico-biogenetic cultural systems that constitute the environment in which we live.[118]

This hypothesis carries a great deal of weight for the entire theory according to Hefner.[119] He points out that 'whatever the human

[115] Hefner, *THF*, 45.
[116] *Ibid.*, 46.
[117] *Ibid.*, 238.
[118] Hefner, *THF*, 48.
[119] *Ibid.*, 49.

being acts out culturally fully implicates the genetic and ecosys-tem symbionts'.[120] Yet 'culture is also always seeking to stretch genes and ecosystem in order to fulfill what seems from the cultural perspective to be desirable and useful novel ends.'[121]

Hefner again refers us to the scientific literature for the testing of this hypothesis, arguing that neuroscientific evidence 'supports the notion that our biogenetic equipment as human beings is built to sustain the formation of culture'.[122] He gives the example of the comparatively premature birth of human offspring compared with other species; the skull continues to grow long after birth to develop the neurological equipment necessary for culture.[123]

A potential falsifier for this hypothesis would be the existence of a group of humans with no identifiable culture, who are still able to carry out Hefner's identified tasks of interpretation, guidance of behaviour and interaction with the environment. No known example exists, which appears to support the hypothesis. Yet the hypothesis is constituted by multiple claims. The claim that culture is constructed by humans is well attested by the scientific litera-ture. Popper, for example, distinguished the cultural world – 'the products of the human mind' – from the physical world.[124]

The purpose of culture is less straightforward. Anthropologist Clifford Geertz would agree with Hefner, defining culture as 'the fabric of meaning in terms of which humans interpret their experi-ence and guide their action'.[125] Psychological explorations of cul-ture have spoken of its function as an evolutionary adaptation.[126]

---

[120] *Ibid.*, 47.

[121] *Ibid.*, 47.

[122] *Ibid.*, 163. This he relates back to the previous hypothesis that humans are gene-culture symbionts.

[123] *Ibid.*, 163–164.

[124] Karl Popper, *Objective Knowledge: An Evolutionary Approach* (Oxford: Clarendon Press, 1972), chapter 4.

[125] Clifford Geertz, *The Interpretation of Cultures: Selected Essays* (New York: Basic Books, 1973), 144–145.

[126] See, for example, Jerome Barkow, Leda Cosmides and John Tooby, *The Adapted Mind: Evolutionary Psychology and the Generation of Culture* (Oxford: Oxford

While scientific research into the purpose of culture remains fairly scant (and this largely seems to be carried out in the life sciences, garnering less interest among physical scientists), further developments in the field may support Hefner's hypothesis, to the extent that its claims can be considered scientific ones. At the very least, it has not been falsified by existing scientific data.

Hypothesis 8

We now live in a condition that may be termed technological civilization. This condition is characterized by the fact that human decision has conditioned virtually all of the planetary physico-biogenetic systems, so that human decision is the critical factor in the continued functioning of the planet's systems.[127]

Essentially, all natural systems are now affected by the human cultural overlay – there are no longer any locations completely untouched by human decision.[128] Again, human freedom is emphasised in this hypothesis. The created co-creator is the agent in technological civilisation, recognising it to be the form of the natural world 'commensurate with their particular epoch in evolutionary history'.[129]

There are two parts to this hypothesis – the pervasion of technology globally and the critical role accorded to humans for the planet's future. With respect to the first, there is strong scientific corroboration for what Hefner describes as the cultural overlay of natural systems. The beginning of the millennium saw a coordinated effort to consider the present environmental conditions at the global level, with the United Nations Environment Program reporting the pervasive impact of human activity on the natural

University Press, 1992); Darrin R. Lehman, Chi-yue Chiu and Mark Schaller, 'Psychology and Culture', *Annual Review of Psychology* 55, no. 1 (2004), 691.

[127] Hefner, *THF*, 49.
[128] *Ibid.*, 153.
[129] Hefner, *THF*, 155.

environment.[130] More recent reports from the Intergovernmental Panel on Climate Change (IPCC), which reviews, evaluates and synthesises the latest scientific research on climate change, offer a sobering assessment of the vulnerability of natural systems – largely as a result of human activity.[131]

The second part of the hypothesis concerns the centrality of humans for determining the planet's future. Again, many scientists would agree with Hefner's premise. The plethora of international climate conventions and agreements, as well as growing research into sustainable technologies, suggests that the majority of scientists and policy developers at least operate under the assumption that human action plays a critical role. Sociobiologist E. O. Wilson recently published a desperate plea for humans to exercise their decisive capacity to avert global environmental catastrophe.[132] Sir John Houghton, atmospheric physicist and previous chair of the IPCC, urges us to take our environmental stewardship responsibilities seriously as we consider the impact of our actions now and in the future.[133]

Hefner's identification of the current global situation as a technological civilisation, in which human decision is decisive, is expressed in neutral terms. It could be argued, however, that the way to foster the wholesomeness of non-human creation is to reduce the impact of human activity on the rest of nature. We see this frequently today in the language of environmental advocacy groups calling for a reduction in our 'ecological footprint' – this framing of the problem is more helpful than simply drawing attention to the centrality of human agency.

---

[130] United Nations Environment Program, *Global Environment Outlook 2000* (London: Earthscan, 2000).

[131] Intergovernmental Panel on Climate Change, *Climate Change 2014: Impacts, Adaptation, and Vulnerability* (Cambridge: Cambridge University Press, 2014).

[132] Edward O. Wilson, *Half-Earth: Our Planet's Fight for Life* (New York: Liveright Publishing, 2016).

[133] John T. Houghton, *Global Warming: The Complete Briefing* (Cambridge: Cambridge University Press, 2015), 357.

Whether this hypothesis makes sense of novel facts, a key idea of the Lakatosian model, or merely explains data already available to Hefner at the time of writing is another question.[134] As it continues to be corroborated by up-to-date research in the interaction of technology and the environment, however, this hypothesis may be considered validated by scientific knowledge.

Hypothesis 9

Myth and ritual are critical components of the cultural system of information and guidance. They are marked in linguistic form by declarative or imperative discourse, and their concepts are vastly underdetermined by the data of evidence. In light of human evolutionary history, these marks were necessary if culture was to serve its evolutionary function.[135]

In this final hypothesis, Hefner elaborates on the role of myth and ritual, speculating that they are the chief carriers of cultural information that both motivates and interprets human behaviour beyond the purely physiological.[136] In agreement with Paul Ricoeur he affirms the intrinsic meaning of myth and ritual,[137] describing their relation to each other, and to praxis: 'myth portrays reality, ritual presents symbolically the action that reality requires, while praxis translates the ritual into ordinary, everyday living'.[138] He considers fruitful Julian Jaynes' proposal that over three thousand years ago the human mind functioned bicamerally, with the informed right hemisphere of the brain 'speaking' commands to the left (such commands were heard and interpreted as the voice of

---

134 Here, Murphy's critique of Hefner's 'fuzzy' interpretation of novel facts becomes relevant (Nancey Murphy, 'From Critical Realism to a Methodological Approach: Response to Robbins, Van Huyssteen, and Hefner', *Zygon* 23, no. 3 (1988), 289).

135 Hefner, *THF*, 49.

136 *Ibid.*, 149.

137 *Ibid.*, 151.

138 *Ibid.*, 156.

the gods).[139] Though he resists a completely adaptationist account of myth and ritual, he considers them facilitators for imprinting information.[140]

Hefner suggests that this last hypothesis is highly speculative and 'has no possibility of being tested in a scientific manner'.[141] However, it can be scrutinised for blatant scientific errors.[142] Hefner concedes that we have no conclusive evidence when it comes to the evolutionary origins of ritual or myth, suggesting they are underdetermined by data.[143] The non-scientific nature of this hypothesis does not invalidate its potential fruitfulness, but it does not comply with Hefner's stated aim of articulating falsifiable hypotheses.[144] Perhaps the inability of this hypothesis to be properly tested lies with the contemporary human stance towards the nature and reality of myth. Hefner traces the history of how humans have understood myth, from a premodern position of naive realism, through the Enlightenment debunking of myth using critical reason, to the simultaneous deconstruction and affirmation of myth – 'we believe in myth under the conditions of *irony*'.[145]

Hefner does cite research suggesting that the human central nervous system has 'mythopoeic requirements' (Wilson's phrase) for ordering the information at its disposal.[146] A more explicit scientific proposal is offered by Jaynes, which Hefner approves but

[139] *Ibid.*, 163; cf. Julian Jaynes, *The Origin of Consciousness in the Breakdown of the Bicameral Mind* (Boston, MA: Houghton Mifflin, 1977).
[140] Hefner, *THF*, 171–172; cf. John Pfeiffer, *The Creative Explosion: An Enquiry into the Origins of Art and Religion* (Ithaca, NY: Cornell University Press, 1982), 227–228; Mihaly Csikszentmihalyi, *Tomorrow's Mind* (San Francisco, CA: HarperCollins, 1993).
[141] Hefner, *THF*, 49.
[142] *Ibid.*, 49.
[143] *Ibid.*, 159, 202.
[144] *Ibid.*, 25.
[145] *Ibid.*, 187, emphasis original.
[146] *Ibid.*, 185. The works cited by Hefner include Charles Laughlin, John McManus and Eugene d'Aquili, *Brain, Symbol and Experience: Toward a Neurophenomenology of Human Consciousness* (New York: Columbia University Press, 1990); Edward O. Wilson, *On Human Nature* (Cambridge, MA: Harvard University Press, 1978).

also acknowledges to be speculative (and eccentric). With respect to Jaynes' theory of bicameral brain functioning, the scientific jury is still out. The theory has been controversial since its inception; however, it has been suggested that neuroimaging studies support Jaynes' hypothesis.[147]

The underdetermination of myth represents no problems for Hefner with respect to its unfalsifiability – the very nature and function of myth in evolutionary history requires action prior to the gathering of data that could support or falsify it.[148] Hefner does point out, however, that this hypothesis rejects the possibility that humans could have survived this long without the information provided by myth and ritual.[149] A potential falsifier may therefore be the existence of human culture that does not possess any form of myth or ritual – and no examples have been discovered thus far. Despite this, the inability to specify how this hypothesis might be corroborated scientifically suggests that Hefner's characterisation of it as speculative and non-scientific holds.

Theological Coherency

A sign of a successful research programme according to Lakatos is its ability to generate novel insights. As part of his positive heuristic Hefner reformulates several traditional Christian doctrines in accordance with contemporary scientific knowledge, and these are worth examining before we come to an evaluation of Hefner's proposal in terms of a Lakatosian framework. Hefner's revisions of the doctrines of God, sin and evil are of particular relevance to a treatment of human creativity within a theology of creation.

---

[147] Leo Sher, 'Neuroimaging, Auditory Hallucinations, and the Bicameral Mind', *Journal of Psychiatry and Neuroscience* 25, no. 3 (2000), 240.

[148] Hefner, *THF*, 204.

[149] *Ibid.*, 267.

Doctrine of God

Contending that our present concepts of God are conditioned by past understandings of nature that are no longer considered scientifically valid,[150] Hefner proposes a model of God that takes into account more recent scientific insights into nature. He follows Paul Tillich's conception of God as the 'name for that which concerns us ultimately',[151] and draws parallels between the function of the term *God* and the function of metaphysics in the work of Alfred North Whitehead.[152] *God* has a threefold meaning: 'objective reality, transforming experience, and internal mental construct'.[153]

Hefner's understanding of God carries over into his view of how we should speak about God. 'God-talk should be viewed as expressing something about our experience of a world that is scientifically understood.'[154] 'God-talk', for Hefner, becomes a tool for speaking of ultimate reality. He reads the Sermon on the Mount as an example of Jesus using the tool of God-talk to establish the coherence of human experience in the world, presenting a vision for human life 'fully in accord with the fundamental nature of reality'.[155]

While Hefner locates himself within the Christian tradition, and is largely happy to operate within that sphere, he takes a universalist approach to other religions, pointing out that they have 'stood the same test of history and selection as Christianity has'.[156] He also articulates what he considers the scientific equivalent of the Christian notion of God's prior love for the creation:

---

[150] Hefner, *THF*, 82.
[151] *Ibid.*, 32; cf. Paul Tillich, *Systematic Theology*, vol. I (Chicago, IL: University of Chicago Press, 1951), 211f.
[152] Hefner, *THF*, 91.
[153] *Ibid.*, 91.
[154] *Ibid.*, 81.
[155] *Ibid.*, 86.
[156] *Ibid.*, 194.

The reality system of nature in which we live is itself basically an ambience in which we truly belong, an ambience that has brought us into being, and that enables us to fulfill the purposes for which we were brought into being. The central reality that undergirds all of our concrete experience and to which we continually seek to adapt is disposed toward us in a way that we can interpret as graciousness and beneficent support.[157]

Hefner's understanding of the Trinity, which he describes as 'an authentic attempt to engage in world-view construction on the basis of Christian faith',[158] is informed by process thought. He concludes from the doctrine of the Trinity that 'Christian theology has wanted to make the career of God and that of the world inseparable'.[159] Hefner diverges from traditional understandings of the work of the Trinity in ascribing the work of both creation and redemption exclusively to the Second Person.[160] In this respect, his grounding of human creativity in the doctrine of the *imago Dei* differs significantly from Sayers' and Maritain's trinitarian approaches treated in the previous chapter.

Sin and Evil

An understanding of humans as 'created co-creators' leads Hefner to an interpretation of sin that is also at odds with traditional notions. Hefner displays an apparent aversion to the term 'sin'. He refers to 'the confusion and out-of-kilteredness between humans and the rest of nature',[161] reading the imagery of Genesis as a myth that expresses this state.[162] Certainly Hefner rejects some notions concerning sin, such as a historical first pair and fall and the

---

[157] *Ibid.*
[158] *Ibid.*, 234; cf. Hefner, 'The Foundations of Belonging'.
[159] *Ibid.*, 169.
[160] *Ibid.*
[161] *Ibid.*, 67.
[162] *Ibid.*, 68.

transmission of sin via concupiscence,[163] favouring instead 'traditions that speak of intrinsic infallibility and weakness in the very
constitution of *Homo sapiens*'.[164] He is also sceptical of concepts
of original sinlessness, arguing that the 'symbol of primeval bless-
edness in the garden' indicates a grounding of human being in
ultimate reality, a consequence of it being created by God.[165]

Hefner follows the likes of Ralph Burhoe and Donald Campbell in his understanding of original sin as 'the inherent conflict
within us between the information inherited from our prehuman
evolutionary past that governs our genetic constitution and the
cultural information that our brains make possible'.[166] 'The origin of the myths, philosophy, and theology of sin and evil, lies in
the primordial human reading of the world and our place in it.
Their importance lies in their being part of viable information systems that not only served human understanding, but also human
survival'.[167] This language comes close to suggesting that religion
is an evolutionary adaptation. Hefner understands the traditional
theological concepts of the fall and original sin to be 'mythic renditions' of the biologically grounded sense of discrepancy between
the prehuman components of our central nervous system and the
more recently developed higher functions.[168] He similarly locates
our sense of guilt in the denial of our primitive motivators (which
tend to be connected with pleasure responses).[169] He refers to the
'turmoil' that may result when the two natures of the human are not

---

[163] *Ibid.*, 139–140.
[164] *Ibid.*, 225.
[165] *Ibid.*, 240.
[166] *Ibid.*, 68; cf. Ralph Burhoe, *Toward a Scientific Theology* (Belfast: Christian Journals, 1981), 65, 201–28; Donald Campbell, 'The Conflict Between Social and Biological Evolution and the Concept of Original Sin', *Zygon* 10 (1975); Donald Campbell, 'On the Conflicts Between Biological and Social Evolution and Between Psychology and Moral Tradition', *Zygon* 11 (1976).
[167] Hefner, *THF*, 125.
[168] Hefner, *THF*, 132.
[169] *Ibid.*, 133.

in harmony,[170] drawing on Burhoe's description of the 'divided will at war with itself – a living hell – in those brains when and where culturetype and genotype are not suitably coadapted'.[171] Guilt is a human predisposition 'because of the broad range of evolutionarily originated information that it carries within it, whose expectations it cannot or will not fulfill'.[172]

The understanding of evil undergoes a similar modification at the hands of Hefner's research programme. Hefner attributes the *incurvatus in se* of the tradition to the susceptibility of humans and human culture to deception over the true nature of reality.[173] While Hefner does not include it in his own Lakatosian explication of the 'created co-creator', he suggests that John Hick's proposal that 'evil is the unavoidable accompaniment of the kind of natural system that is required if freedom and personhood are to emerge' serves as an additional auxiliary hypothesis.[174] Though Hefner relegates theodicy to the hard core of his programme, he identifies a starting point for testing in Hick's work.[175] The understanding of evil, for Hefner, is a major point on which any world view must stand or fall.[176]

A discussion of sin and evil naturally directs us to the topic of morality. Hefner often uses the term 'error' in conjunction with the failure of humans to fulfill our task as created co-creator. He singles humans out from other creatures for our capacity to negotiate the natural laws as we observe them, yet acknowledges that 'we are more negotiators, we have not understood what proposals we ought to make.'[177]

[170] *Ibid.*, 118.
[171] *Ibid.*; cf. Burhoe, *Toward a Scientific Theology*, 126.
[172] Hefner, *THF*, 240.
[173] *Ibid.*, 240.
[174] *Ibid.*, 271; cf. John Hick, 'An Irenaean Theodicy', in *Encountering Evil*, ed. Stephen Davis (Atlanta, GA: John Knox, 1981).
[175] Hefner, *THF*, 271.
[176] Hefner, 'The Foundations of Belonging', 166.
[177] Hefner, *THF*, 67.

Hefner accepts the view that morality is grounded in our evolutionary history.[178] 'Prehuman components are active within us ... still engaged in the ongoing struggle to learn how to function in a way that is appropriate to their human context.'[179] Values and morality emerged along with freedom.[180] The imposition of cultural obligations, through the establishment of social contracts, allows us to counter the impulses of our 'selfish' genes.[181]

He equates the love command of the Judeo-Christian tradition with the trans-kin altruism described by Ralph Burhoe – beneficent behaviour towards others even though they may not be genetically related.[182] Yet theology, in Hefner's view, suggests that the scientific explanations for altruism are inadequate by themselves; we need alternative means for grounding the value of altruism in the fundamental reality.[183] These means are provided through religious myths.[184] The biblical references containing the imperative to love the other (Mathew 5:43–38; 22:37–40; John 13:34) are interpreted by Hefner as assertions that love (which includes, but extends beyond, altruism) is intrinsic to human nature, grounded in 'the way things are' by the contextualising Christian narrative from which the love command is derived.[185] Scientific claims are integrated into his argument, thus 'the assumption that the emergence of natural structures and processes is not in vain is [Hefner's] way of affirming God and also showing what difference it makes to introduce God into the discussion'.[186]

178 Ibid., 178.
179 Ibid., 179; cf. Anthony Stevens, Archetypes: A Natural History of the Self (New York: Morrow, 1983), 267–271.
180 Hefner, THF, 179–180.
181 Ibid., 181–182. Hefner, as well as the thinkers he draws from, is responding to the notion of the selfish gene as articulated by Richard Dawkins.
182 Ibid., 197.
183 Hefner does articulate a form of moral realism, grounding values in 'the fundamental character of reality' (ibid., 188).
184 Hefner, THF, 197.
185 Ibid., 207–208.
186 Ibid., 59.

Hefner's treatment of the doctrine of God, and of sin, is not articulated explicitly for the purpose of locating human creativity within a broader doctrine of creation. His work is not incompatible with such a move; however, he has very much focused on incorporating knowledge of human evolutionary history into his theological anthropology, rather than attempting a theological justification of the way in which human creating resembles the divine.

How Lakatosian is the Created Co-creator Model?

Having examined Hefner's created co-creator more closely, and its implications for certain doctrines, we now return to the methodological framework that undergirds his model. How faithful is his theological construction to the Lakatosian structure he aims to employ?

Hefner concedes the difficulty of defining falsification in a theological context.[187] In many instances, he would replace the stricter scientific notion of falsification with the softer criteria of amenability to public discussion.[188] He acknowledges his own 'methodological opaqueness', which he considers a product of his context – while writing *The Human Factor* he was working both in the instruction of Lutheran ordinands and in academic engagement with many working in scientific disciplines.[189] Robert Russell, writing more generally on the theological appropriation of Lakatosian methodology, suggests that 'Theological explanations are subject to validation not by verificationist/foundationalist standards, but by intersubjective testability and universalizability, as performed by the disciplinary community.'[190] While this does offer a helpful redefinition of theory validation within the theological context, it is not clear that Hefner adopted any such view, and Russell's

---

[187] *Ibid.*, 25.
[188] *Ibid.*, 24.
[189] Hefner, *THF*, xvi.
[190] Robert Russell, 'Ian Barbour's Methodological Breakthrough: Creating the "Bridge" Between Science and Theology', *Theology and Science* 15, no. 1 (2017), 33.

own reconfiguration comes several decades after the peak period of theological engagement with Lakatosian methodology.

At the close of *The Human Factor*, Hefner offers his own evaluation of how successful the created co-creator model is as a Lakatosian research programme. He identifies a number of novel facts associated with his model, including the referral of human meaning to nature, the emphasis on teleonomy when it comes to humans, the inclusion of the biocultural evolutionary model into his theological anthropology, more complex conceptualisations of freedom and determinism, the integration of technology into evolution and human nature, the conceptual role afforded to myth and ritual within culture, and the identification of evil and theodicy as potential falsifiers.[191] He also considers his doctrinal reinterpretations to comprise novel facts, including the relation of nature to grace, the purpose of human existence, and his definitions of atonement, justification and original sin.[192]

Whether any of Hefner's doctrinal reinterpretations are truly novel is questionable, though they of course meet his definition of novel. The present work has considered only a few of Hefner's theological commitments, although it is likely that his reframing of certain doctrines falls outside what is generally considered theologically orthodox. There appears to be a dissonance between some of Hefner's theological conclusions and his claim that one of the responsibilities of theology is to 'preserve the Christianness of its statements'.[193] A probing of other doctrinal implications is likely to yield further questions concerning the theological significance of Hefner's created co-creator model; however, such an investigation is beyond the scope of this work.

---

[191] Hefner, *THF*, 268–271. It bears reminding that much of this depends on Hefner's redefinition and expansion of Lakatos' concept of novel facts, which Murphy questioned (as mentioned above).

[192] *Ibid.*, 272–275.

[193] Hefner, *Faith and the Vitalities of History*, 183. Quite what he means by 'Christianness' is unclear.

THEOLOGICAL COHERENCY

When it comes to scientific corroboration, several of Hefner's auxiliary hypotheses do appear to hold up against scientific knowledge that has arisen since Hefner's formulation. Though comparative morphology is not a new discipline, the discovery of the polymerase chain reaction (PCR) technique for the amplification of DNA in the 1990s has allowed the extension of morphological studies to include traits at the molecular level.[194] Along with increasingly sophisticated bioinformatic tools, this has made a vast difference to the field of phylogenetics, which maps the relationships and evolutionary history of the various species. These developments have only confirmed Hefner's argument in the first auxiliary hypothesis that humans will exhibit continuity with the rest of nature in the realm of structures and processes.[195] Similar arguments could be made for the ongoing corroboration of Hefner's hypothesis concerning the interplay of culture and genes and the predisposition of the human mind towards narrative construction.

As argued in the previous section, however, not all of Hefner's hypotheses are scientifically valid. Of the nine hypotheses put forward by Hefner, only three could be considered falsifiable by scientific data (hypotheses 6, 7 and 8). The remaining hypotheses all make claims extending beyond that which could be scientifically falsified – Hefner himself points out that his last hypothesis is incapable of being subjected to scientific testing.[196] Though the three hypotheses formulated sufficiently to be

194 Rafael Zardoya and Axel Meyer, 'Molecular Evidence on the Origin of and the Phylogenetic Relationships Among the Major Groups of Vertebrates', in *Evolution: From Molecules to Ecosystems*, ed. Andrés Moya and Enrique Font (Oxford: Oxford University Press, 2004), 209–210. See, for example, Thierry Backeljau et al., 'Random Amplified Polymorphic DNA (RAPD) and Parsimony Methods', *Cladistics* 11 (1995). Note that molecular analyses are distinct from comparative morphology in that they do not concern observable characteristics (Ridley, *Evolution*, 425).
195 Hefner does mention nucleotide sequence comparisons, but the technology has advanced considerably since publication in 1993 (Hefner, *THF*, 65).
196 *Ibid.*, 49.

scientifically falsifiable appear to be supported by current scientific knowledge, this hardly constitutes a successful Lakatosian research programme. Within the assumptions of the Lakatosian framework, the majority of Hefner's auxiliary hypotheses would require substantial reconfiguration (and it is questionable whether this is even possible) to reasonably protect his hard core.

But should a successful Lakatosian research programme be the goal? Perhaps in claiming scientific falsifiability for his theological statements, Hefner does theology (and epistemology more generally) a disservice. His many caveats notwithstanding, Hefner appears to have bought into the modernist privileging of scientific explanation above all other aspects of knowing. Peter Hacker expresses the problem well:

> Every source of truth is also unavoidably a source of falsehood, from which its own canons of reasoning and confirmation attempt to protect it. But it can also become a source of conceptual confusion, and consequently of forms of intellectual myth-making, against which it is typically powerless. Scientism, the illicit extension of the methods and categories of science beyond their legitimate domain, is one such form, and the conception of the unity of the sciences and the methodological homogeneity of the natural sciences and of humanistic studies one such myth. It is the task of philosophy to defend us against such illusions of reason.[197]

The intent to explain theology in scientific terms is vulnerable to Hacker's 'illusions of reason'. Yet is Hefner really so unaware of this danger? He acknowledges the limits to science, especially in later works. For example, he writes that 'science must learn from religion that even though the ships that science builds are huge and impressive, the sea is even bigger and rougher'.[198] He insists that

---

[197] Peter Hacker, *Wittgenstein: Connections and Controversies* (New York: Oxford University Press, 2001), 73.
[198] Philip Hefner, 'Spiritual Transformation and Healing: An Encounter with the Sacred', in *Spiritual Transformation and Healing: Anthropological, Theological,*

science can raise questions which cannot themselves be resolved using scientific reasoning.[199] It seems that the critique offered of Lakatos earlier, that his model does not sufficiently account for the contextual character of scientific enquiry, does not then apply to Hefner, or at least not to the same extent. Revisiting his epistemological commitments, Hefner allows that knowledge is conditioned, pointing out that 'we can neither understand nor participate in the ongoing life of faith and theology apart from the mediation of social reality'.[200] Ultimately Hefner acknowledges the limitations of methodology, his verdict approaching the poetic: 'Like a twig caught in the raging current of a storm-roiled river, the fruits of the method are more in the realm of hope than of certainty.'[201]

Despite the methodological insufficiencies in Hefner's approach to scientific knowledge, his created co-creator model is largely compatible with the findings of contemporary science. Perhaps Hefner's transgression is not that he reduces theology to scientific explanations, but rather that he gives the impression that such a move can be performed. Hefner's model is actually far richer than a scientific account alone could provide. He makes claims about human nature and reality that, while not contravened by scientific knowledge, are not evident without recourse to non-scientific sources of knowledge. That Hefner misrepresents his work is unlikely a conscious deception, and we can reasonably attribute to him the best of intentions in the project of harmonising theology and science. Ultimately, however, we can learn from Hefner's example that theology suffers when scholars attempt to reduce it to scientific explanations. The methodological strictures of the sciences that allow them to perform scientific tasks so successfully also

Neuroscientific, and Clinical Perspectives, ed. Joan Koss-Chioino and Philip Hefner (Oxford: Altamira Press, 2006), 130.
199 Hefner, THF, 147.
200 Philip Hefner, 'The Cultural Significance of Jesus' Death as Sacrifice', Journal of Religion 60, no. 4 (1980), 427.
201 Hefner, THF, 152.

prevent them from offering a complete anthropology. As Peterson contends, 'a full, genuine (theological) anthropology must necessarily take the soteriological risk, to which the sciences can only incompletely contribute'.[202] It is the fundamental commitments concerning ultimate reality that allow Hefner's model to make sense of insights from the natural world.

This critique does not negate the potential value of the created co-creator metaphor when deliberating the use of technology. An affirmation of the extra-scientific metaphysical commitments involved may give the position more worth in the eyes of many theologians (and scientists!), and the scientific commensurability of many elements recommends the model for communication in a pluralistic context. Such a synthesis of scientific and theological content provides a far more convincing response than an account derived from either scientific sources or sources more traditional for theological construction (e.g. scripture) alone. Hefner does appear to have shifted in his views over time, referring a decade later to the created co-creator as a 'diagnostic idea' that 'interprets ordinary existence'.[203] He is content to summarise his construction as 'the common experience that we are able to do things that are novel; that we are able to change the world around us and the world within us in ways that seem important and desirable'.[204]

Hefner's model may also be refined and nuanced if combined with more recent developments in the area. Deacon's account of emergence has already been offered as a more robust attempt to understand human freedom and self-awareness in a non-reductionist framework. In recent years, Hefner has engaged with the scholarship of Donna Haraway. He suggests that Haraway's cyborg and the created co-creator are sibling images. Even then,

---

[202] Gregory Peterson, 'The Created Co-creator: What It Is and What It Is Not', *Zygon* 39, no. 4 (2004), 839.

[203] Philip Hefner, 'The Created Co-creator Meets Cyborg', www.metanexus.net/essay/created-co-creator-meets-cyborg, 1.

[204] *Ibid.*, 2.

however, Hefner still insists on reducing createdness to 'kinship with the processes that have created us'.[205] This sits in uneasy tension with his contention that 'we cannot avoid the question of God, because we create as if it matters'.[206] In his most developed exposition of the created co-creator, Hefner appears reluctant to bring his own theological convictions into his understanding of anthropology and the human future, yet ultimately cannot avoid doing so. More recently, looking back over his career in science and religion, Hefner offers an updated conception of the theologian's task: they are to reflect on findings of scientific research.[207] Viewed through the lens of Hefner's later thought as to how science and religion relate to one another, which no longer includes reference to a criterion of falsification or to Lakatosian philosophy of science, many of the methodological concerns raised here with respect to Hefner's earlier work are alleviated.[208]

Co-creation and Technology

Garner believes Hefner's model is a useful starting point for engaging with transhumanism, particularly in light of the technological agency it accords to humans.[209] Hefner himself writes explicitly on transhumanism in a short article, though he mainly addresses more pervasive ideas of enhancement rather than the more extreme transhumanist philosophies.[210] His own understanding of how co-creation relates to human enhancement is perhaps best represented in his reflections on the imagery of God knitting together the unborn in the mother's womb in Psalm 139, in conjunction with his own personal experience of physical impairment. The psalm

---

[205] Philip Hefner, 'Human Being: Questioning and Being Questioned', *Zygon* 39, no. 4 (2004), 5.
[206] *Ibid.*, 7.
[207] Philip Hefner, 'Life in Religion-and-Science', *Theology and Science* 13, no. 1 (2015), 11.
[208] Hefner, 'Life in Religion-and-Science'.
[209] Garner, 'Christian Theology and Transhumanism', 230–231.
[210] Philip Hefner, 'The Animal that Aspires to be an Angel: The Challenge of Transhumanism', *Dialog* 48, no. 2 (2009).

expresses my personal faith, and yet I am glad to have that knitting undone and redone, through the very human instrumentality of knowledge, skill, and ingenuity. I do not consider that original knitting to be sacrosanct in its details; it is not my unrevisable destiny – destiny, yes, but capable of editing and revision by human hands. One might even say that [transhumanism] partners with the God of psalm 139.[211]

As the present research concerns the use and validity of human enhancement technologies, it is worth exploring further the place Hefner affords to technology within his framework. Alluded to briefly in his eighth auxiliary hypothesis, Hefner contends that technology is a phase of cultural evolution and locates it within evolutionary processes.[212] He thus refuses a dualism between nature and technology (or, by implication, nature and culture). Instead, technology is linked with both freedom and decision, a natural part of 'the evolutionary process-become-aware itself'.[213] Technology is therefore a form of nature and we must interpret its purpose by referring to the natural order from which it emerged.[214] In later work he reaffirms his view that neither culture nor technology are ontologically distinct from nature. 'Nature has produced humans, and since it has decreed that they are cultural creatures, their nature is culture-nature. Technology, the product of culture, comes to be natural to humans.'[215]

As technology is rolled into culture in Hefner's work, it also worth revisiting what Hefner means by the term culture (discussed especially in his seventh auxiliary hypothesis). In Hefner's words, 'culture is defined as learned and taught patterns of behavior, together with the symbol systems that contextualize and interpret

---

[211] *Ibid.*, 161.
[212] Hefner, *THF*, 49.
[213] *Ibid.* Here we see echoes of Teilhard and Huxley.
[214] *Ibid.*, 154.
[215] Hefner, 'The Created Co-creator Meets Cyborg', 5.

the behavior'.[216] Yet he speaks of culture as if it has an agency of its own, i.e. it creates new conditions that bring about the stretching of genes and the ecosystem.[217] It is by culture that we 'create the world views and mores that literally put our worlds together and tell us where we fit'.[218] Culture is 'the primary instrument by which humans act upon the rest of nature'.[219] It is culture that allows for important brain learning to be 'inherited' by subsequent generations, thus, rendering human learning uniquely cumulative among animals.[220]

In conjunction with this conception of nature and culture, Hefner's understanding of human freedom and its place in ultimate reality prompts him to define technology as 'an expression of the fundamental self-transcending reality of God'.[221] He perceives of technology as sacramental, arguing that 'technological restlessness is a means of grace'.[222] This extends his notion that each person is a sacrament, 'an earthy human body living on the cusp of transcendence'.[223] He affirms Teilhard's mystic vision of the sacramental nature of the planet (which *is* the body of Christ) and human participation in this reality, suggesting that the use of technology is central to such participation.[224]

---

[216] Philip Hefner, 'Biocultural Evolution and the Created Co-creator', in *Science and Theology: The New Consonance*, ed. Ted Peters (Boulder, CO: Westview Press, 1998), 175.

[217] Hefner, *THF*, 47.

[218] *Ibid.*, 65.

[219] *Ibid.*, 67.

[220] *Ibid.*, 109.

[221] Philip Hefner, *Technology and Human Becoming* (Minneapolis, MN: Fortress Press, 2003), 87.

[222] *Ibid.*, 86. Hefner cites the well-known line from Augustine's *Confessions*, 'You have created us for union with yourself, and our hearts are restless until we find our rest in you' in support of his argument that restlessness is the medium by which we attain union with God (*ibid.*, 86; cf. Augustine, *Confessions*, i.i.1).

[223] Philip Hefner, 'Nature, Mystery and God', in *Our Bodies Are Selves*, ed. Philip Hefner, Ann Milliken Pederson and Susan Barreto (Eugene, OR: Cascade Books, 2015), 153.

[224] *Ibid.*, 153; cf. Pierre Teilhard de Chardin, 'Mass on the World', in *Hymn of the Universe*, trans. Gerald Vann (New York: Harper & Row, 1965).

According to Hefner, technology serves as a mirror, reflecting back to us our human desires.[225] It reveals our finitude, frailty and mortality, as well as our desire to overcome these limitations.[226] 'Simply by being there, technology of all kinds expresses the truth that we need technical assistance in order to become who and what we want to be, because our finitude does not carry us as far as we want to go.'[227]

Hefner is clear that technological development, including the ethical challenges that often accompany it, is one of the means by which we exercise our agency as created co-creators.[228] This co-creative agency is not afforded to us as a means to advance our own self-interested ends, however. Rather, we are to exercise this freedom (or 'stretching activity') to realise God's divine purposes for all creation.[229] And for Hefner this appears to be a natural human instinct – 'We are restless if we cannot change the world around us and within us in ways that we think are better.'[230]

Hefner takes a functional approach to the *imago Dei*, arguing that we represent God's freedom, love and intentionality when we act as created co-creators.[231] Others have explicitly connected the use of technology with the doctrine of the *imago Dei*,[232] however, Hefner takes this a step further by suggesting that technology itself, as a new phase of evolution, can serve as a vessel for the image of God.[233]

---

[225] Hefner, *Technology and Human Becoming*, 34.
[226] *Ibid.*, 35.
[227] *Ibid.*, 35.
[228] Hefner, *THF*, 121.
[229] *Ibid.*, 48.
[230] Hefner, 'The Created Co-creator Meets Cyborg'.
[231] Philip Hefner, 'Biocultural Evolution: A Clue to the Meaning of Nature', in *Evolutionary and Molecular Biology: Scientific Perspectives on Divine Action*, ed. Robert J. Russell, William R. Stoeger and Francisco J. Ayala (Vatican Observatory and Berkeley, CA: Vatican Observatory & CTNS, 1998), 347.
[232] See, for example, Stephen V. Monsma, *Responsible Technology: A Christian Perspective* (Grand Rapids, MI: Eerdmans, 1986), 19.
[233] Hefner, *THF*, 77.

Paul Tillich speaks of the three major functions of human life: self-integration (the incorporation of new experiences into the self), self-transcendence (the stretch towards the infinite) and self-creation (the use of language and technology in the creation of culture).[234] He also declares the technological city to be God's creation, through the intermediary of human creativity.[235] Technology is also spoken of theologically in the context of both human freedom and human responsibility. Stephen Monsma defines technology as 'a distinct human cultural activity in which human beings exercise freedom and responsibility to God by forming and transforming the natural creation, with the aid of tools and procedures, for practical ends and purposes'.[236]

Assigning technological ingenuity to the realm of co-creation, or the status of humans as the *imago Dei*, does not mean that it is always employed for positive ends. Jason Roberts captures this well: 'As products of *Homo sapiens'* ethically ambivalent biocultural nature, whatever "cures" we create are true *pharmakoi* – potentially both poison and remedy.'[237] Though Hefner accepts the risks associated with the human mandate for co-creation, he believes humans are required to act regardless. He describes the technological crisis as a 'challenge to our self-awareness and our efforts to discern human purpose in the most adequate way'.[238] Even so, science and technology constitute the 'medium through which we will express the future of life on earth'.[239] Technology is not merely

---

[234] Paul Tillich, *Systematic Theology*, vol. III (Welwyn: James Nisbet & Co., 1964), 32–34, 61–66.

[235] Paul Tillich, 'The Technological City as Symbol', in *The Spiritual Situation in Our Technological Society*, ed. J. Mark Thomas and D. Ric Thomas (Macon, GA: Mercer University Press, 1988).

[236] Monsma, *Responsible Technology*, 19.

[237] Jason Roberts, '"Fill and Subdue?" Imaging God in New Social and Ecological Contexts', *Zygon* 50, no. 1 (2015), 60.

[238] Hefner, *THF*, 49.

[239] Ibid., 105.

external to us, it shapes our self-image in complex ways. Furthermore, the very existence and possibilities of technology should motivate us to 'face up to the necessity of decisions and their complexity' with respect to the planet's future.[240] 'Technology speaks powerfully of a sense that leaving nature in its prehuman state is somehow a betrayal of human genius.'[241] The tension between the ambivalence of technology and the moral imperative to find technological solutions will be picked up again in later sections, as adoptions and extensions of Hefner's model are explored.

The Created Co-creator as a Response to Human Enhancement Issues

Acknowledging the potential refinements to Hefner's 'created co-creator' model identified in the previous section, let us consider its usefulness as a theological response to transhumanism, and related questions of human enhancement. For a theology of human creativity to successfully engage these questions, it must offer both an openness to dialogue with scientific and technological thought and a robust account of the human imagination (as argued in the previous chapter).

The Theological Application of the Created Co-creator to Biotechnological Issues

Hefner's created co-creator metaphor has been incorporated into the work of several contemporary theologians addressing questions related to human enhancement.

As a Christian ethicist, Ronald Cole-Turner argues from a position that locates the notion of human transformation within Christian thought. He draws upon the popular maxim, dating back to Irenaeus but reiterated by many others, that 'God becomes like

---

[240] *Ibid.*, 105.
[241] *Ibid.*, 70.

CREATED CO-CREATOR AND HUMAN ENHANCEMENT

us so we might be made like God.'[242] Cole-Turner compels us to
see that technology use is bound up with our theological understanding of humanity.[243] We must ground our deliberations over
the value and implementation of human enhancement technologies within a greater theological vision.[244] For Cole-Turner, that
vision is of a humanity created in God's image, being redeemed
and transformed in Christ by grace.[245]

Concerning the ethics of certain biotechnologies, Cole-Turner
challenges the use of the phrase 'playing God' and its implication
that 'creation is completed, static and fixed in place by God'.[246] He
draws upon scientific accounts of progress in nature, an idea that
he claims grew out of the Christian view of history.[247] He attributes
to nature, both human and non-human, a moral ambiguity that
is currently unresolved.[248] However, human nature is dynamic,
driven by the purpose of glorifying God.[249]

Within his understanding of creation as continually evolving,
Cole-Turner subscribes to the notion that humans are 'co-creators'
with God. Acknowledging the problems inherent in the term

[242] Ronald Cole-Turner, 'Introduction: The Transhumanist Challenge', in
*Transhumanism and Transcendence: Christian Hope in an Age of Technological
Enhancement*, ed. Ronald Cole-Turner (Washington, DC: Georgetown University
Press, 2011), 5. Cf. Irenaeus. 'Against Heresies', in *Ante-Nicene Fathers*, ed. Alexander
Roberts and James Donaldson, vol. I (Peabody, MA: Hendrickson Publishers, 2004),
v. Cole-Turner's appropriation of Irenaeus' phrase warrants fuller explanation
elsewhere. He does not appear to do justice to Irenaeus' original meaning, which
likely concerns adoption more than human creativity. For a helpful account of
theosis in Irenaeus, see B. C. Blackwell, *Christosis: Pauline Soteriology in Light of
Deification in Irenaeus and Cyril of Alexandria*, trans. J. E. Steely (Tübingen: Mohr
Siebeck, 2011).
[243] Cole-Turner, 'Religion, Genetics and the Future', 6.
[244] Cole-Turner, 'Introduction', 6.
[245] *Ibid.*, 6.
[246] Cole-Turner, 'Biotechnology', 942.
[247] Ronald Cole-Turner, *The New Genesis: Theology and the Genetic Revolution*
(Louisville, KY: Westminster John Knox Press, 1993), 55.
[248] *Ibid.*, 59.
[249] *Ibid.*, 62.

'co-creation' by itself,[250] Cole-Turner follows Hefner's lead in adopting the modified 'created co-creator' construction.[251] While acknowledging our creatureliness, Cole-Turner describes a vision that 'through biotechnology we can accompany God's own continuing creative work, which because of technology can operate now at a wholly new level.'[252]

Cole-Turner's understanding of what it means for humans to be co-creators is further revealed in the reservations he expresses over the phrase 'playing God'. He challenges the implication that modifying nature with technology is illegitimate, linking this to a fallacious understanding of nature as static.[253] He also rejects the view that some aspects of creation (he gives the example of the human embryo) are granted a special status and treated as 'wholly off limits to technology'.[254] This is consistent with Cole-Turner's early argument that the gene is not the 'exclusive realm of divine grace and creativity' and that treating DNA as sacred is therefore arbitrary.[255] He points out that genomic research has not lived up to initial expectations – to date it has proven difficult or impossible in the overwhelming majority of cases to predict functionality from genomic sequence.[256]

In tension with the understanding of humans as co-creators, Cole-Turner affirms that 'human beings are creatures whose meaning and destiny are only understood in relation to the Creator'.[257] He also suggests, however, that a greater knowledge of human biology and genetic engineering might actually provide insight into

---

[250] The major problem, of course, being that it suggests God and humanity are on an equal footing as partners in creation (Cole-Turner, 'Biotechnology', 942).
[251] Ibid., 943.
[252] Ibid., 942.
[253] Cole-Turner, 'Biotechnology', 942.
[254] Ibid., 942.
[255] Cole-Turner, The New Genesis, 45.
[256] Ronald Cole-Turner, 'Synthetic Biology: Theological Questions about Biological Engineering', in Without Nature? A New Condition for Theology, ed. David Albertson and Cabell King (New York: Fordham University Press, 2010), 144.
[257] Cole-Turner, 'Religion, Genetics and the Future', 213.

the constraints (e.g. physical and chemical) under which God creates.[258] Human nature, therefore, reveals something of its creator. Cole-Turner is clear when it comes to the goal of human enhancement technology. For Christians, the only objective can be 'to transform the person in the direction of the new creation in Jesus Christ'.[259] While Cole-Turner is open to the use of human enhancement technologies as a part of this transformation, his enthusiasm is not unqualified. He warns that 'a new self through prayer is not the same as a new self through technology'.[260] With this caveat, he does concede that religious means of self-modification and technological means can complement each other.[261] However, technology must not be established as a rival god, rather it serves as a tool to further the purposes of the true God and to ultimately glorify God.[262] Furthermore, Cole-Turner is sceptical when it comes to human moral reasoning, acknowledging the tension between good intentions and flawed human nature.[263] This understanding leads him to limit the application of germline modification on the basis of motive: only those uses which spring from compassion, and do not promote injustice, are acceptable.[264]

Cole-Turner's final position towards human technological enhancement can be summarised in the test he prescribes for such technologies: 'The central theological question raised by

258 Cole-Turner, 'Synthetic Biology', 150.
259 Ronald Cole-Turner, ed., *Transhumanism and Transcendence: Christian Hope in an Age of Technological Enhancement* (Washington, DC: Georgetown University Press, 2011), 10.
260 Cole-Turner, 'Biotechnology', 941.
261 Ibid., 941.
262 Ibid.; Cole-Turner, *The New Genesis*, 51.
263 Ronald Cole-Turner, 'Human Limits: Theological Perspectives on Germ-Line Modification', in *Designing Our Descendants: The Promises and Perils of Genetic Modifications*, ed. Audrey Chapman and Mark Frankel (Baltimore, MD: John Hopkins University Press, 2003), 192–193.
264 Ibid., 193.

technologies that modify humans is whether they serve the purposes of God in creating and renewing or redeeming the creation.'[265]

This statement captures the difficulty of addressing human enhancement from a theological perspective more generally. Cole-Turner does not elaborate on the 'purposes of God' here, and there is a degree of dissonance between the probable future he describes as a result of using technologies for human enhancement, and a Christian vision of redemption. 'Technologized people will be feared as dangerous, envied as superhumans, shunned as anomalies and followed as great leaders.'[266] He paints this picture as part of a call for theologians to engage with the issues that technological progress is rendering inevitable; certainly, there is further reflection to be done to consider this particular vision of the future against eschatological hope.

Perhaps the most interesting current in Cole-Turner's thought is his identification of transhumanist visions of the future as not completely dissimilar to those of many Christians. It is this shared impulse for transcendence, this common imagination of a transformed humanity, that holds the promise of a way forward in the dialogue between science and theology over genetic enhancement technologies and the future. While theological perspectives on human dignity and worth shape responses to particular technologies, the existence and prospect of such technologies must also challenge and inform a theological understanding of what it means to be human. Cole-Turner is interested in both sides of this debate and issues a particularly pertinent challenge for theologians considering the place of technology in our transformation and redemption – 'Is this simply a case of Christians needing to update their repertoire of the modalities of grace?'[267]

---

[265] Cole-Turner, 'Religion, Genetics and the Future', 213.
[266] *Ibid.*, 221. We do not have to look far to find parallel visions in science fiction.
[267] Cole-Turner, 'Introduction', 9.

CREATED CO-CREATOR AND HUMAN ENHANCEMENT

Cole-Turner's affirmative answer to this question springs from his understanding of human creativity, developed in part through an interaction with Hefner's work. While Cole-Turner does draw significantly on Hefner, his representation of co-creation looks very different. Hefner begins with a scientific methodology and a consideration of evolutionary history, concluding that *Homo sapiens* has emerged from the evolutionary process as a biocultural organism with the capacity to shape its own future evolution. Cole-Turner writes as a Christian theologian first and grounds his understanding of co-creation firmly within the theological landscape of creation and redemption. For Cole-Turner, humans partner with God in creative and redemptive work at the invitation of God,[268] whereas Hefner sees this activity as an evolved freedom, which in turn is an instrumentality of God.[269]

Another scholar who builds on the work of Hefner is Ted Peters, who differs from Hefner in identifying as a systematic theologian. Whereas Hefner attempts to articulate theology in scientific terms, Peters sees his own task as a 'response theology' – 'a form of intellectual discourse that responds theologically to issues prompted by public debate over scientific matters'.[270]

Similarly, Peters argues that humans cannot help but use technology – it is fundamental to our nature. 'Human creativity is ambiguous. We are condemned to be creative. We cannot avoid it. The human being is a tool maker and a tool user. We are *homo faber*. We cannot be human without being technological.'[271] The use of technology in service of 'neighbour love' or beneficence, according to Peters, means 'we are playing human in a free and

---

[268] Cole-Turner, *The New Genesis*, 11.
[269] Hefner, *THF*, 32.
[270] Peters, *Playing God?*, xv. Peters does describe his approach as the borrowing of 'methods of inquiry from the natural sciences' for use in 'theological research programs', but arguably his work is still more explicitly theological than Hefner aims to be in *THF* (*ibid.*, xvi).
[271] Ted Peters, *Science, Theology and Ethics* (Aldershot: Ashgate Publishing, 2003), 222.

responsible way'.[272] By employing our creativity and ingenuity to devise new ways of improving ourselves, provided it is in service of the flourishing of all creation, we are not 'playing God' but rather acting in a way that is fundamentally human. 'To seek a better future is to "play human" as God intends us to.'[273]

Peters is pragmatic when it comes to the likelihood of human enhancement technologies being employed in the future, arguing that 'The task before us is to be good stewards of the advance of genetic science and technology so that it contributes to human welfare without creating new injustices.'[274] Our 'ethical mandate' concerns the purpose to which we direct our creativity and the seriousness with which we approach our creative responsibilities.[275] 'To influence our own evolutionary development is to invoke human creativity, to exercise the freedom that makes self-determination possible – in this case, the human race as a totality is the self doing the determining.'[276]

While Hefner attempts to convey his message in terms acceptable to a naturalist position, Peters argues that a theological perspective is essential to understand our place in nature.[277] For Peters, the resurrection of Christ is central to the debate on human enhancement.[278] Though he questions projects which attempt to provide a vision of human nature without recourse to theological statements, he does acknowledge the value in demonstrating the compatibility of scientific and theological anthropologies.[279]

Peters summarises the difficulty of distinguishing between human and divine creativity well.

---

[272] Peters, *Playing God?*, 27.
[273] *Ibid.*, 146.
[274] *Ibid.*, 2.
[275] *Ibid.*, 16.
[276] *Ibid.*, 20.
[277] *Ibid.*, 21.
[278] *Ibid.*, 63.
[279] *Ibid.*, 51.

Theologically, just how sound is it to separate so sharply between what God creates and what human invention creates? If we make such a distinction, then how do we identify what God creates? Should we presume that something found in nature that has not yet been touched by human technology constitutes a divine creation? Does it mean that as soon as human creativity alters its natural state that it leaves the realm of divine creation and enters the realm of human creation? Does it mean that God creates only part of reality and that human technology creates a different part?[280]

Peter sees in Hefner's created co-creator proposal a two-dimensional understanding of creation that is able to address this problem of situating human creativity. Despite the analogous relationship between human and divine creativity, Peters resists attempts to equate one with the other. Peterson, describing Peters' understanding of the created co-creator metaphor, suggests that it 'stands both as an encouragement to create and as a warning against utopian hubris'.[281] The doctrines of *creatio ex nihilo* and *creatio continua* are key – everything that exists is a result of God's creative act.[282] Peters contends:

One might even include evolutionary history in the story of God's ongoing creative work. One might further include the evolutionary development of the human genome with its resulting intelligence and creativity – as an additional chapter in the story of nature. At this point divine creativity and human creativity enjoy some overlap. They are not sharply separated.

For Peters, God's creative activity is best understood as the giving of a future to the world.[283] An ethics of co-creation therefore

---

280 Peters, *Playing God?*, 124.
281 Peterson, 'The Created Co-creator', 233.
282 Peters, *Playing God?*, 125.
283 *Ibid.*, 146.

demands of us that we envision a better future.[284] Peters concludes from this that we should at least 'keep the door open' for human technological enhancement.[285] With such a future-oriented theology of creation, we are better equipped to consider the challenges of enhancing human beings through technology.[286] Finally, Peters reminds us that human power and divine power are not in competition – ascribing creative agency to humans does not diminish divine creativity in any way.[287]

Usefulness of the Created Co-creator Designation

Hefner's account aims to synthesise evolutionary insights with a theological perspective on human creativity. But how helpful is the co-creator metaphor ultimately for explaining our role in creation? The scope of responses to Hefner's work, and differing interpretations of his thought, suggests that the co-creator designation, even when qualified with the 'created' modifier, is of limited utility. The versatility in its application points to an inherent ambiguity. It can be employed on the one hand to elevate humans to almost divine status in their creative activity,[288] or understood as a close synonym for human stewardship of God's creation.[289]

Anna Case-Winters raises a similar question, suggesting that Hefner's created co-creator does not differ fundamentally from the notion of stewardship. This is by no means the prevailing view, however, with Paul Jersild, for example, arguing that stewardship and co-creation are very different concepts.[290] Peterson argues that 'the deceitfully diminutive *co-* is in some ways the

---

[284] *Ibid.*, 146.
[285] *Ibid.*, 146.
[286] *Ibid.*, 157.
[287] *Ibid.*, 208.
[288] Stephen Garner, 'Transhumanism and the *imago Dei*: Narratives of Apprehension and Hope' (PhD diss., University of Auckland, 2006), 200.
[289] Anna Case-Winters, 'Rethinking the Image of God', *Zygon* 39, no. 4 (2004), 821.
[290] Paul Jersild, *Spirit Ethics: Scripture and the Moral Life* (Minneapolis, MN: Fortress Press, 2000), 167–70.

most radical and least appreciated part of Hefner's project', interpreting the prefix to mean that 'we are as much in control or responsible for creation as God is'.[291] This lack of consensus serves only to highlight the term's ambiguity. Interlocutors of Hefner's have offered their own terminology as a substitute for the created co-creator. Peterson, for example, suggests 'creative creatures' as a more suitable alternative,[292] while Burdett corrects to 'created intra-creator' (interpreting Hefner's model within a strong trinitarian and Christological framework).[293]

Hefner does acknowledge the vulnerability of the term 'co-creator' to criticism, as well as the proposals for alternative terms. He rejects alternatives and affirms 'co-creator', however, as he believes that only the latter does justice to the dual nature of humans and the polarity that comes of being created yet also co-creator.[294] He suggests that, though a dangerous concept at risk of being misconstrued, the risk is unavoidable if we are to fulfil the anthropological task in light of current global challenges.[295]

Acknowledging the potential for misinterpretation, 'co-creation' will be employed as a theological term that ascribes a role to humans in ongoing creation, albeit one that is both distinct from and subordinate to God's work of creation. It may be contrasted with a notion of humans as merely vehicles or passive recipients of God's creation. An understanding of humans as co-creators asserts that 'rearranging matter, supercreating, and bringing new possibilities into existence, are basic to human nature'.[296]

---

[291] Peterson, 'The Created Co-creator', 829.
[292] James Peterson, *Genetic Turning Points: The Ethics of Human Genetic Intervention* (Grand Rapids, MI: Eerdmans, 2001), 55.
[293] Burdett, *Eschatology and the Technological Future*, 244n.
[294] Hefner, *THF*, 37, 39.
[295] Ibid., 237.
[296] Hefner, *Technology and Human Becoming*, 81.

The Limits of Co-creation

Aside from its susceptibility to misinterpretation, it is also unclear from Hefner's exposition of the created co-creator just how we are to determine whether our co-creative activity is aligned with divine purposes. The goal is not to articulate a foolproof set of rules for arbitrating whether a particular action is appropriate co-creative activity or not – this would reduce the question to a simple deontological ethic, which has proven generally insufficient and unsatisfactory in addressing moral quandaries. Yet if we *are* created co-creators, then we must be equipped in some way to judge our creative endeavours. A stronger sense of limits and the discernment process would be helpful.

Peterson questions how the freedom of the created co-creator is to be used and calls for the development of an appropriate ethic to support the anthropological claims made by Hefner.[297] The 'wholesome future' Hefner refers to, the birthing of which is the goal of human co-creative activity, needs to be filled out, however Hefner has little to say on this.[298]

Proponents of co-creation are not blind to the difficulties surrounding the discernment of appropriate creative action, however. Peacocke sets out the problem eloquently:

> The exploration which is science and its progeny, technology, might then come to be seen as an aspect of the fulfilment of man's personal and social development in co-operation with the God who all the time is creating the new. Man would then, through his science and technology, be exploring with God the creative possibilities within the universe God has brought into being. This is to see man as co-explorer with God. But these themes, of co-creation and co-exploration, imply intelligent participation by man in God's

[297] Peterson, 'The Created Co-creator', 839.
[298] *Ibid.*, 837.

work of creation. And for that God's meaning has to be discerned.[299]

Hefner is certainly aware of the ambivalence of the created co-creator and its ability to act according to the divine will. Tying this quality ultimately to human freedom, he writes:

There is unmistakeable grace mediated through the co-creator's technological accomplishments ... Evolution itself will be the instrument of God's judgment and grace with respect to this work of the co-creator. If humans survive, they alone will bear the responsibility for the future and they alone will be able to seize the opportunities to actualize the possibilities for grace that are contained within it.[300]

More recently he speaks anew of the 'ambivalent double vision that sees both danger and possibility', acknowledging this as a challenge for the way in which we create.[301] Hefner also suggests there are limits to co-creation in his rejection of an infinite malleability to human nature.[302] Rather, 'there are structures to which we are beholden for our very nature ... which can be repudiated or ignored only at our peril.'[303] As humans, we are to actively seek the bounds that define us.[304] Yet we do not have autonomous power when it comes to co-creation, and the power that we do have stems from God's prevenient action.

[God] unleashed the process of evolution and it has come to this – a species with the capacity for self-awareness and ecosystem-defining power and responsibility. This we share with God himself, since this defining power and responsibility are his. By his grace, he has

[299] Peacocke, *Creation and the World of Science*, 306.
[300] Hefner, *THF*, 250.
[301] Hefner, 'The Created Co-creator Meets Cyborg', 5.
[302] Hefner, 'The Foundations of Belonging', 162.
[303] *Ibid.*, 163.
[304] *Ibid.*, 171.

determined, or at least permitted, that his creator-power of defining, naming, and using shall be advanced and carried out through
the agency of *Homo sapiens*.[305]

Peters also acknowledges the dangers inherent in human creativity, the tension that exists between the ability to enhance human
freedom and improve the world on the one hand and inflict suffering through either ignorance or malicious intent on the other.[306] A
major critique he offers of transhumanism is its failure 'to operate with an anthropology that is realistic regarding the human
proclivity to turn good into evil'.[307] Cole-Turner is even more cautious than Hefner in this respect. While he does ultimately support
some form of co-creation as an explanation for human creative
participation, he expresses reservations with the metaphor. These
chiefly concern the issue of discerning the divine will for human
co-creative activity.[308] Cole-Turner is less optimistic than Hefner
in his assessment of the human capacity for discernment. This may
be because Cole-Turner takes the effects of sin far more seriously
than Hefner, whose account of sin reduces it largely to the tension
between the biological drives remnant of our evolutionary past and
the impulses that spring from our sociocultural nature.[309]

As mentioned above, Cole-Turner does hint that gains in scientific knowledge may illuminate constraints to creativity.[310] It is
unclear whether he extends this to human creativity as well or
would restrict it to divine creativity. Even assuming the former,

---

[305] *Ibid.*, 176.

[306] Peters, *Playing God?*, 59.

[307] Ted Peters, 'CRISPR, the Precautionary Principle, and Bioethics', *Theology and
Science* 13, no. 3 (2015), 131.

[308] Ronald Cole-Turner, 'Is Genetic Engineering Co-creation?' *Theology Today* 44, no. 3
(1987), 345; Cole-Turner, *The New Genesis*, 101; Cole-Turner, 'Human Limits',
192–193. Hefner's qualifier of 'created' goes a long way to easing Cole-Turner's
concerns with respect to co-creation, however, and allows him to finally adopt the
metaphor for his own use (Cole-Turner, 'Biotechnology', 942–943).

[309] Hefner, *THF*, 131–132.

[310] Cole-Turner, 'Synthetic Biology', 150.

however, we are left with only an impression that limits to human co-creation exist, but no constructive means for determining their nature. We are to 'place our work and our powers in the service of a creator who is still creating a future not yet determined';[311] how we might go about this task is less plain. He offers the motives of those creating as a criterion for judgement;[312] however, it does not necessarily follow that good intentions produce outcomes aligned with the divine purpose for creation.

Cole-Turner takes pains to emphasise that human works are subsumed under the divine: 'Does technology play any role in *what a gracious God is doing* to carry forward to completion this great project known as creation?'[313] Elsewhere, he implores us to consider that 'our technology can and should be seen as instruments in the creator's hands, by which God will continue to sculpt Adam's clay'.[314] He avoids ascribing a concrete sense of agency to humans despite his final affirmation of their status as created co-creators, prompting the question of whether the metaphor adequately conveys his stance on human creativity. While Cole-Turner clearly affirms technology as a modality of divine grace, he is less certain regarding the extent to which the responsibility for human technological enhancement is delegated to humans. His equivocation on this matter further reinforces the ambiguous nature of the term co-creation; at the very least it seems to set up a false dichotomy between human agency and divine will in creation. He often falls back on the more widely used language of 'partnership' when

---

[311] Cole-Turner, 'Is Genetic Engineering Co-creation?', 349.
[312] Cole-Turner, 'Human Limits', 193.
[313] Cole-Turner, 'Going Beyond the Human', 155, emphasis added.
[314] Ronald Cole-Turner, 'Toward a Theology for the Age of Biotechnology', in *Beyond Cloning: Religion and the Remaking of Humanity*, ed. Ronald Cole-Turner (Harrisburg, PA: Trinity Press International, 2001), 150. Despite his lack of capitalisation for 'creator' in this passage, it is clear from the context that he is referring to God, and not to humans.

it comes to human creativity, linking it explicitly with our use of technology.[315]

It is clear from these accounts that the created co-creator should not be understood to mean that God has handed over God's creative agency to humans, or that humans are in any way equal to God in their creativity. The existence of limits is affirmed by all of the theologians examined here. Having established that such limits exist, however, the problem of discernment remains. How are we to discover such limits as we go about our creative work, particularly as we are faced with global crises that prompt us to act?

In one sense, Cole-Turner comes closer to Hefner in prescribing a practical limit to human technological intervention. He argues that we can define a genetic defect as 'that which causes a condition comparable to those which evoked the compassion of Jesus of Nazareth and which is therefore disclosed as contrary to the purposes of God.'[316] If we can imagine that Jesus would have healed, then we should do the same if we are able. Certainly, this is a more tangible approach towards defining limits than Hefner provides, and an idea worth exploring elsewhere; however, it still places the responsibility of discernment with the fallible human intellect. Additionally, this principle may validate many therapeutic applications of genetic manipulation but is of little utility when it comes to enhancement. Of more use, perhaps, is Cole-Turner's argument that we must accord noetic priority to theological insights concerning redemption over scientific observations of nature;[317] however, this point raises a different set of hermeneutical difficulties for discerning divine purpose.

Roberts aims for more a concrete defining of the boundaries to co-creation, articulating four guiding principles for future created co-creation. These principles are (1) the distinction between our biocultural and eschatological futures, (2) an understanding

[315] Cole-Turner, *The New Genesis*, 100.
[316] *Ibid.*, 91.
[317] *Ibid.*, 102.

of humans and the good works they do as both wholly natural and mediators of grace, (3) a resistance to the transhumanist view that death ought to be defeated and (4) an acknowledgement that human freedom is finite and fallible.[318] With the exception of the third principle perhaps, none of Robert's articulated guidelines offer pragmatic advice – in fact, the final guideline is really just a reaffirmation of human limitation. Instead, Roberts offers overarching statements such as 'while humanity's biocultural and eschatological futures ought not to be conflated, the effort we exert toward our biocultural future *may* matter in "the end"'.[319] Garner takes a slightly different approach, suggesting that the created co-creator might be employed effectively to ethical questions in conjunction with the bioethical principles of autonomy, nonmaleficence, beneficence and justice.[320] Like Roberts' proposal, these principles operate at a broader level. How might we develop these general principles to aid us as we consider various technological options and deliberate over the best course of action?

The Role of the Imagination for the Created Co-creator

Although Hefner does not consider the role of the imagination for the work of the created co-creator, he does recognize its importance in elucidating the concept. *The Human Factor* is filled with references to poetry that illuminate his conclusions concerning human nature. In *Technology and Human Becoming*, he draws on both poetry and visual artwork to illustrate human attitudes towards technology.[321] He at least perceives the explanatory power of fiction and art, though he does not engage the imagination

---

318 Roberts, 'Fill and Subdue?', 57–59.
319 *Ibid.*, 57, emphasis added.
320 Garner, 'Christian Theology and Transhumanism'. Garner derives these principles from the programmatic work of bioethics, Tom Beauchamp and James Childress, *Principles of Biomedical Ethics* (New York: Oxford University Press, 2001).
321 Hefner, *Technology and Human Becoming*, 1–2, 89.

beyond the purpose of illustration. More recently, he calls for a greater imaginative component in our response to contemporary challenges.

> We are the storytellers of nature, the ones whose ecological niche includes articulating nature's project. In this, we join the work of the poets. It may well be that not only has evolution entered the stage of morality and spirituality, but also the phase of poetry, in which imaginative frameworks of meaning that can interpret nature are essential for nature's continued life.[322]

This appears to be a reversal of Hefner's earlier view, expressed in *The Human Factor*, that the role of artists in creating new mythic proposals is secondary to that of preachers, politicians and business/technology entrepreneurs.[323] Perhaps Hefner's created co-creator would look different if he were developing it today. In his later reflections on technology, Hefner suggested that 'technology emerges from our freedom to imagine what does not exist and to believe in what is not actual'.[324] He celebrates a number of scientific achievements, from the codebreaking work of Alan Turing and his contemporaries to the discovery of DNA and the completion of the Human Genome Project, emphasising the narratives that underpinned these endeavours.[325] Hefner points out in his most recent discussion of technology that imagining alternative worlds, and acting on those imaginings, comes naturally to humans.[326] It is fair to say that Hefner's appreciation of imagination and its importance has grown over the course of his career, as he later connects the imagination more explicitly with the work of

---

[322] Philip Hefner, 'A Fuller Concept of Evolution: Big Bang to Spirit', *Zygon* 47, no. 2 (2012), 307.

[323] Hefner, *THF*, 214.

[324] Hefner, *Technology and Human Becoming*, 60.

[325] *Ibid.*, 60–63.

[326] Philip Hefner, 'The Human Journey', in *Our Bodies Are Selves*, ed. Philip Hefner, Ann Milliken Pederson and Susan Barreto (Eugene, OR: Cascade Books, 2015), 134.

the created co-creator.[327] In our role as co-creators we create both new worlds with our technology, and the meaning and purpose of those new worlds.[328] Yet Hefner identifies a reluctance on the part of many to acknowledge the centrality of imagination and story for human existence.

> Most of the people who are known today for their mastery of the dense facts of the world – scientist, engineers, policymakers, and the like – do not cotton to the idea that their work is dependent on imagination and story. Most religious believers share this skepticism about story. Most of the scientists and religious people I know share a dislike for the word *postmodern* precisely because they wish to fence off fact from story.[329]

Like Hefner, Cole-Turner gives an account of human creativity that emphasises rationality. They presume some kind of epistemic access to the principles that guide co-creation (even if they cannot articulate the nature of this access and express caution) but do not offer a plausible means for attaining such knowledge. Their concept of human creativity is more promising for theological engagement with the scientific challenges of our times than a fearful Christian response to technological advances, but still privileges the role of reason at the expense of the imagination. It is possible that this elevation of reason can be traced back to Hefner's choice of a Lakatosian model in the first place – Lakatos was above all else a rationalist.[330] In Hefner's modification of Lakatos' work, and in Cole-Turner's adaptation of Hefner's model, the central place of reason has been preserved. This is not to say that the locatedness of humans and the associated epistemic limitations are not acknowledged – Hefner writes that 'reason does not

327 Hefner, *THF*, 78.
328 *Ibid.*, 77–78.
329 Hefner, *Technology and Human Becoming*, 68.
330 Paul Feyerabend, Robert Cohen and Marx Wartofsky, eds., *Essays in Memory of Imre Lakatos*, 458–491 (Dordrecht: D. Reidel Publishing, 1976), preface.

have the capability of climbing some hill to get an overview of all there is'.[331] Yet reason is still the means by which we probe into the depths of nature to encounter truth, even if that truth is only partial.[332]

Despite not developing an imaginative component in his work, Cole-Turner does recognise the importance of such resources. He draws an interesting parallel between the transition to an agricultural way of life depicted in Genesis and the current impending transition to a society that relies on genetic engineering technologies.[333] Both transitions, he argues, are theological as well as technological, with the prospect of genetic engineering reopening the question of the human place in nature by giving us the power to create.[334] Most interesting, however, is the response he suggests to these challenges: 'What we need today is a sustained effort at theological and poetic imagination that will yield texts and liturgies for the new age. We need visions and images that will sustain and restrain us as we define ourselves in the future.'[335] Peters, too, acknowledges the importance of imagination for co-creation. He ties our ability to imagine alternate futures, our desire to create something new 'according to a vision of a better reality', to the freedom we have in the future given to us by God.[336] This leads us to one of the major questions posed in the present study – what if using and engaging the imagination was considered instrumental in theological construction, not just illustration? Incorporating the imagination in constructing narratives of the future, even a future which features technological enhancement, may go some way to reconciling the dissonance previously identified between the tentative endorsement of enhancement technologies by certain

[331] Hefner, THF, 79–80.
[332] Ibid., 81.
[333] Cole-Turner, 'Is Genetic Engineering Co-creation?', 343.
[334] Ibid., 338–339.
[335] Ibid., 343.
[336] Peters, Playing God?, 204.

theologians and the bleak future envisioned as a likely outcome of such activity.

Conclusion

Hefner's understanding of the human as created co-creator is located within a long tradition of co-creation theologies, and his particular model contributes enormously to contemporary accounts that explicitly address questions of human technological enhancement.

Hefner's dependence on a Lakatosian research programme methodology, while rendering his own explanation of co-creation unique, is potentially problematic in light of critiques of Lakatos that have yet to be successfully dismissed. The results of Hefner's articulation of the created co-creator using the structure of a Lakatosian research programme are also questionable. Many of the auxiliary hypotheses he proposes are not as falsifiable as he would have us believe. On the whole, however, Hefner's model appears to be compatible with the findings of contemporary science, albeit not always presented in a strictly scientific format. If Hefner's model is instead viewed as one that encompasses more than just a scientific approach to anthropology, and Hefner's stated objective to frame it in purely scientific terms is forgiven, then we may have the beginnings of a response to the challenges proposed by transhumanism and related developments.

For Hefner's model also has many strengths. It offers a theological anthropology that takes scientific insights seriously in its construction and is open to engagement with contemporary questions surrounding technology. The adaptation of the created co-creator metaphor by theologians currently writing in response to biotechnological and bioethical concerns is a testament to its usefulness as a starting point in this growing area of study. As theologians venture further into the territory of human enhancement, their reflections will be strengthened by the appreciation for the insights of evolutionary biology, genetics and cognitive sciences modelled by Hefner.[337]

Acknowledging the weaknesses in Hefner's model, namely its overemphasis on rationality and neglect of the imagination, the following chapters will consider the role accorded to the imagination in philosophical, theological and scientific schools of thought, and the potential for enriching Hefner's anthropology with more imaginative perspectives on human creativity.

[337] Hefner's proposal was selected as the focus of the present work as his approach centres on the subject of human creativity and theological anthropology, whereas Peters' work is more oriented to eschatology and Cole-Turner's to specific ethical concerns.

4 | Co-creation Theology and the Imagination

The imagination takes a central place in both transhumanist visions of the future and the technological innovation needed for these projects of human enhancement. A theological response will require attending to the imagination also; however, this is an underdeveloped aspect of Hefner's theological anthropology. Several potential explanations for this lack are located in both his theological heritage and the science and religion field more generally, and the importance of the imagination (particularly as it applies to human creativity) in the separate disciplines of theology and science is attested. The renewed interest in the imaginative dimensions of knowing and believing suggests that a more imaginative theology of human creativity may better engage human enhancement questions.

Imagination and Epistemology

Defining the Imagination

In Chapter 2, the case was made that technology might properly be considered an element of human creativity. Creativity and imagination overlap somewhat semantically and conceptually, with Rob Pope contending that the recent focus on the notion of creativity has encroached upon some of the territory that belongs properly to imagination.[1] Hart describes the overlap between the two with a degree of hesitation, allowing that:

---

[1] Pope, *Creativity*, 14.

it is difficult to suppose other than that the two notions are naturally rather than unnaturally yoked, and if by no means all that is imaginative is 'creative' in the sense we have now begun to associate with this term (nothing is more imaginative than a torture chamber), perhaps it is safe to suggest, nonetheless, that all that is creative is necessarily imaginative.[2]

On the basis of such a distinction, a closer treatment of the imagination in the context of human creativity may direct us more helpfully in our moral assessment of what constitutes good co-creative activity, remembering that creativity itself is usually judged on the basis of value in some way.[3] In the same way that creativity is fundamental to our 'otherness' from God, Hart argues that imagination is an epistemic necessity of our creaturely reality if we are to know anything of God.[4]

We will consider the imagination as a broader concept before turning to its place in a theology of human creativity in the next chapter. The first difficulty we run into is the fact that imagination is notoriously difficult to define. Richard Kearney highlights the necessity of defining the imagination in relation to its genealogy: 'We need to recall what imagination was *then* in order to understand imagination *now*.'[5] With this caveat, the current scope will be limited to more recent understandings of the imagination but generally operates in alignment with James Engell's exposition locating the origin of current understandings of the imagination in the eighteenth century.[6]

Kearney compares the imagination to Augustine's observation of time – 'we think we know what it is but when asked we realize we

[2] Hart, *Making Good*, 94.
[3] See page 53.
[4] Hart, *Making Good*, 13.
[5] Richard Kearney, *The Wake of Imagination: Toward a Postmodern Culture* (London: Routledge, 1994), 17.
[6] See James Engell, *The Creative Imagination: Enlightenment to Romanticism* (Cambridge, MA: Harvard University Press, 1981).

don't'.[7] Kendall Walton describes the term imagination as 'serving as a placeholder for a notion yet to be fully clarified'.[8] Indeed, the character of imagination itself renders it difficult to define. James K. A. Smith likens it to an intuition that 'eludes propositional articulation' and cites Charles Taylor's assertion that the imagination 'can never be adequately expressed in the form of explicit doctrines'.[9] The imagination is an affective faculty that attempts to make meaning of the world.[10] Smith does attempt to give a more concrete definition, however, describing the imagination as a 'quasi-faculty whereby we construe the world on a precognitive level, on a register that is fundamentally *aesthetic* because it is so closely tied to the *body*'.[11] Smith adopts a heuristic use for the imagination that names 'a kind of faculty by which we navigate and make sense of our world, but in ways and on a register that flies below the radar of conscious reflection',[12] a working definition that is useful for the present purpose. Similarly, Hart allows the reality of what imagination does to 'shape our definition for us', rather than offering a neat description.[13]

Acknowledging the lack of consensus when it comes to definition, and the heterogeneity inherent in the concept of imagination, let us turn to the way it is described by some thinkers in the context

---

7 Richard Kearney, *Poetics of Imaginings: Modern to Postmodern* (Edinburgh: Edinburgh University Press, 1998), 1.

8 Kendall Walton, *Mimesis as Make-Believe: On the Foundation of the Representational Arts* (Cambridge, MA: Harvard University Press, 1990), 21.

9 James K. A. Smith, *Desiring the Kingdom: Worship, Worldview, and Cultural Formation* (Grand Rapids, MI: Baker Academic, 2009), cf. Charles Taylor, *Modern Social Imaginaries*, (Durham, NC: Duke University Press, 2004), 25.

10 Smith, *Desiring the Kingdom*, 66.

11 James K. A. Smith, *Imagining the Kingdom: How Worship Works* (Grand Rapids, MI: Baker Academic, 2013), 17, emphasis original. The linking here of the imagination to embodiment is especially important for the human enhancement debate and its implications for human bodies.

12 *Ibid.*, 19.

13 Trevor Hart, 'The Glory of Imagination and the Imagination of Glory', In *Called to Hope: Perspectives on Life to Come*, ed. John Colwell (Carlisle: Paternoster Press, 2000), 226.

of epistemology.[14] Historically, the imagination has had both its enthusiasts and its critics concerning its contribution to human understanding, and both may give us insight into the way it is employed today.

The Romantic Imagination

When it comes to questions of rationality and imagination, truth and knowing, we immediately encounter the nineteenth-century Romantic movement. The Romantic tradition was in part a reaction against the 'desiccating rationalism' which emptied the natural world of wonder and joy.[15] According to Malcolm Guite, Enlightenment philosophers essentially divorced the imagination from reason.[16] This view is represented well in David Hume's assertion that 'nothing is more dangerous to reason than the flights of the imagination'.[17] Instead, Romantic poets championed the imagination and its connection to ultimate reality – Nigel Rapport describes this swing to imaginative insights as a 'redemptive mission'.[18] Romanticism was not restricted to poetry, rather M. H. Abrams declares it a 'comprehensive intellectual tendency' that encompassed philosophy in addition to literature and had a substantial

---

[14] Indeed, Williamson argues that it is inappropriate to begin an inquiry into the imagination with a definition, as this is to risk prejudging the results (Timothy Williamson, 'Knowing by Imagining', in *Knowledge Through Imagination*, ed. Amy Kind and Peter Kung (Oxford: Oxford University Press, 2016), 113).

[15] Alister McGrath, *Re-imagining Nature: The Promise of a Christian Natural Theology* (Hoboken, NJ: Wiley-Blackwell, 2016), 48.

[16] Malcolm Guite, *Faith, Hope and Poetry: Theology and the Poetic Imagination* (Farnham: Ashgate Publishing, 2012) 145.

[17] David Hume, *A Treatise on Human Nature*, ed. L. A. Selby-Bigge (Oxford: Clarendon Press, 1888), 267. This is not to paint Hume as a rationalist, arguing as he did that reason should be subject to the passions (*ibid.*, 415).

[18] Nigel Rapport, '"Imagination Is the Barest Reality": On the Universal Human Imagining of the World', in *Reflections on Imagination: Human Capacity and Ethnographic Method*, ed. Mark Harris and Nigel Rapport (Farnham: Ashgate, 2015), 3.

impact on political and social changes in both England and Germany in its time.[19] John Keats, writing about one of his own poems, described it in correspondence as 'a regular stepping of the Imagination towards a Truth'.[20] Douglas Hedley, in reference to Wordsworth, suggests 'the poet's imaginative capacity is dependent upon the ability to penetrate truths obscured by the more narrow constraints of physical science and to envisage the hidden shape of reality'.[21]

In his famous defence of poetry, written in 1821, Shelley reverses earlier understandings of the relationship between reason and the imagination: 'Reason is to the imagination as the instrument to the agent, as the body to the spirit, as the shadow to the substance.'[22] After defining poetry as the exercise of the imagination, Shelley speaks exultantly of the imaginative faculty:

> Poets are the hierophants of an unapprehended inspiration; the mirrors of the gigantic shadows which futurity casts upon the present; the words which express what they understand not; the trumpets which sing to battle; and feel not what they inspire; the influence which is moved not, but moves. Poets are the unacknowledged legislators of the world.[23]

Poet and literary critic Charles Baudelaire exalts the imagination as the 'queen of truth'.[24] For thinkers like Keats and John

---

[19] M. H. Abrams, *Natural Supernaturalism: Tradition and Revolution in Romantic Literature* (New York: W. W. Norton & Co., 1971), 11.

[20] Letter to Taylor, January 1818 (cited in Medawar, 'The Genetic Improvement of Man', 43).

[21] Douglas Hedley, 'Austin Farrer's Shaping Spirit of Imagination', in *Scripture Metaphysics and Poetry: Austin Farrer's The Glass of Vision with Critical Commentary*, ed. Robert MacSwain (London: Routledge, 2016), 204.

[22] Percy Bysshe Shelley, 'A Defense of Poetry', in *Political Tracts of Wordsworth, Coleridge and Shelley*, ed. R. J. White (Cambridge: Cambridge University Press, 1953), 199.

[23] *Ibid.*, 206.

[24] Charles Baudelaire, *Baudelaire as a Literary Critic*, trans. Francis Hyslop Jr University Park, PA: Pennsylvania State University Press, 1964), 182.

Henry Newman, suggests Avis, the imagination was 'the power that kindles insight into reality'.[25] Alison Milbank describes the Romantic project as using the imagination to 'awaken in the reader this feeling of homesickness for the truth'.[26]

Arguably the most important Romantic thinker when it comes to the imagination, however, is Samuel Taylor Coleridge. Coleridge spoke of the imagination as 'the speculative reason ... the power by which we produce, or aim to produce, unity, necessity and universality in all our knowledge by means of principles *a priori*'.[27] He famously distinguished the primary imagination – 'a repetition in the finite mind of the eternal act of creation in the infinite I AM' – with the secondary imagination, in which human creativity consists of an echo of the primary imagination, allowing us to 're-create'.[28] Christian socialism founder F. D. Maurice, who acknowledged a significant debt to Coleridge in his own work, wrote that language may be 'streaked with the light of truths just rising above the horizon'.[29]

The Romantic movement had its excesses, however, when it came to its elevation of imagination. In Romantic thought the imagination came to be considered the 'central human faculty', promising wholeness and redemption.[30] Arguably, many of the

---

[25] Paul Avis, *God and the Creative Imagination: Metaphor, Symbol and Myth in Religion and Theology* (London: Routledge, 1999), 8.

[26] Alison Milbank, 'Apologetics and the Imagination: Making Strange', in *Imaginative Apologetics: Theology, Philosophy and the Catholic Tradition*, ed. Andrew Davison (London: SCM Press, 2011), 33.

[27] Samuel Taylor Coleridge, *Biographia Literaria*, ed. George Watson (London: Dent, 1965), 160.

[28] Coleridge, *Biographia Literaria*, 167.

[29] F. D. Maurice, *Subscription No Bondage, Or the Practical Advantages Afforded by the Thirty-Nine Articles as Guides in All the Branches of Academical Education* (Oxford: J. H. Parker, 1835), 40. For a discussion of Coleridge's influence on Maurice, see Graham Neville, *Coleridge and Liberal Religious Thought: Romanticism, Science and Theological Tradition* (London: Tauris, 2010), 56.

[30] David Gouwens, *Kierkegaard's Dialectic of the Imagination* (New York: Peter Lang, 1989), 16.

Romantic poets saw the imagination as antithetical to reason. According to Medawar, this view saw 'the pathway of Reason being long and winding and stopping short of the summit, so that while Reason is breathing heavily there is Imagination capering lightly up the hill'.[31] William Blake declares 'I come in the grandeur of inspiration to abolish ratiocination.'[32]

Søren Kierkegaard offered an important corrective here, challenging the Romantic tendency to make an absolute out of the imagination, but also countering the Hegelian relegation of imagination to the realm of the trivial, divorced from conceptual truth.[33] Medawar aims for a similar middle path in his summary of the contemporary intellectual landscape which he sought to challenge: 'Our traditional views about imagination and criticism in literature and in science are based upon the literary propaganda of the Romantic poets and the erroneous opinions of inductivist philosophers.'[34] Paul Avis, though acknowledging the shortcomings of the Romantic approach, does not discount its value for a contemporary account of the imagination. 'To speak of the truth of the imagination is not to fall for the excesses of Romanticism, but to make a critical and discriminating appropriation of that tradition.'[35]

Interpretations are mixed, however, when it comes to just how much reason is denigrated in Romantic thought, and the imagination elevated. Midgley, contrary to other opinions discussed above, argues that Wordsworth and Coleridge 'went to great lengths to stress that the antithesis between thought and feeling was a false one'.[36] Imagination, rather than being the antithesis of reason, lies at the middle of a single whole incorporating both feeling and

[31] P. B. Medawar, 'Science and Literature', *Encounter* 32, no. 1 (1969), 16.
[32] As cited in Gerald Holton, *The Scientific Imagination: Case Studies* (Cambridge: Cambridge University Press, 1978), 88.
[33] Avis, *God and the Creative Imagination*, 30.
[34] Medawar, 'Science and Literature', 18.
[35] Avis, *God and the Creative Imagination*, 30.
[36] Midgley, *Science and Poetry*, 55.

thought.[37] Coleridge describes the imagination as 'that reconciling and mediating power' which incorporates both reason and the senses to produce truth-conducting symbols.[38] The faculty of reason is not the subject of ire, so much as the valuing of reason alone. Thus, Coleridge considers the rational instinct *in abstraction* to be the content of original temptation, essentially equating abstracted reason with original sin.[39] Cold reason (abstracted from other faculties) is associated by Coleridge with visionariness, moral indolence and hard-heartedness, and superstition in turn.[40] Neither does Wordsworth reject reason; rather, he describes the imagination as 'reason, in her most exalted mood'.[41]

Nor is the imagination treated as a monolithic entity by the Romantics. Coleridge distinguishes between allegories (phantom proxies of insubstantial principles) and symbols. A symbol is characterized by 'the translucence of the eternal through and in the temporal ... it always partakes in the reality which it renders intelligible'.[42] For Coleridge and Wordsworth, the truth-recognising capacity of the imagination is bound up with religious belief. The believer, using their imagination, is able to see objects in the secular world as they appear to everyone, but additionally 'as conductors or symbols of another dimension of reality'.[43]

---

37 *Ibid.*, 55.
38 Samuel Taylor Coleridge, *Collected Works: Lay Sermons*, ed. R. J. White, vol. VI. (London: Routledge, 1972), 29.
39 Samuel Taylor Coleridge, 'The Statesman's Manual', in *Political Tracts of Wordsworth, Coleridge and Shelley*, ed. R. J. White (Cambridge: Cambridge University Press, 1953), 32.
40 *Ibid.*, 32–33.
41 *The Prelude*, 14:193.
42 Coleridge, 'The Statesman's Manual', 25. Though not a Romantic writer, Le Guin makes a similar point, distinguishing between the 'dead equivalence' of allegory and the 'living meaning' of symbol. A symbol 'is not a sign of something known, but an indicator of something not known and not expressible otherwise than symbolically' Ursula Le Guin, 'Myth and Archetype in Science Fiction', in *The Language of the Night: Essays on Fantasy and Science Fiction*, ed. Susan Wood, 73–81. (New York: Putnam, 1979), 76).
43 Douglas Hedley, *Living Forms of the Imagination* (London: T. & T. Clark, 2008), 26. Atheism thus becomes a failure of the imagination (*ibid.*, 27).

The Legacy of Rationalism

If Romantic thought represents an overemphasis on the imagination, and its epistemological worth, then rationalism lies at the other extreme. Medawar summarises the shift in the value of reason that occurred during the Enlightenment period.

The seventeenth-century doctrine of the *necessity* of reason was slowly giving way to a belief in the *sufficiency* of reason – so illustrating the tendencies of many powerful human beliefs to develop into an extreme or radical form before they lose their power to persuade us, and in doing so, create anew many of the evils for which at one time they professed to be the remedy.[44]

British historian and politician Lord Thomas Babington Macaulay represents such a view: 'We cannot unite the incompatible advantages of reality and deception, the clear discernment of truth and the exquisite enjoyment of fiction.'[45] Where reason is exalted, the imagination is pushed to the margins, or even excluded from epistemology. David Gouwens describes the inability of Enlightenment thought to account for the imagination: 'For rationalism, the imagination did not possess the clarity of rational ideas; for empiricism, the imagination seemed to lack the concreteness and vividness of sense-impressions.'[46]

Holton traces the defence of a narrow rationality through the Popperian school to the pre-Second World War logical positivists, who sought the restriction of philosophical discourse to empirically discernible statements. He considers Popper's view that 'the rationality of science presupposes a common language and a common set of assumptions which themselves are subject to conventional rational criticism' to be heavily influenced by the prewar positivist

---

44 Medawar, 'On the "Effecting of All Things Possible"', 113.
45 Thomas Macaulay, 'Milton', in *Lord Macauley's Essays* (London: Longman, Greens & Co., 1905), 3f.
46 Gouwens, *Kierkegaard's Dialectic of the Imagination*, 17.

movement.[47] Thus, Popper shows little interest in the creative context of scientific discovery, considering it 'irrelevant to the logical analysis of scientific knowledge'.[48] Instead, he proposes to make such creative action 'rationally understandable' by giving 'an idealized reconstruction of the problem situation in which the [scientific] agent found himself'.[49] Midgley links Popper with positivism as well, but sees in Popper a reaction to the influence of positivism and its legitimation of Marxism and Freudianism as scientific theories.[50] In dismantling the scientific classification of such schools of thought, however, Popper did not challenge positivism itself but merely portioned off all 'non-scientific' claims into the vague, nonsensical category of 'metaphysics'.[51]

Lakatos, according to Holton, took up Popper's proposal of rationalisation both vigorously and dogmatically.[52] In Lakatos' attitude towards the history of science we can detect a fear of irrationalism; he adopts a defensive stance to rescue the idea of scientific progress as a product of rational methodology.[53] Forrai agrees with Holton, firmly locating Lakatos alongside the logical positivists in the project he terms 'rationalism'.[54] Though Lakatos challenges the Enlightenment ahistorical notion of objectivity that is displayed in the works of both Popper and the logical positivists, a similar claim of objectivity creeps into his denouncing of scientific elitism.[55]

[47] Holton, *The Scientific Imagination*, 103.
[48] Karl Popper, *The Logic of Scientific Discovery* (New York: Harper, 1965), 31.
[49] Popper, *Objective Knowledge*, 179.
[50] Midgley, *Science and Poetry*, 149.
[51] *Ibid.*, 150.
[52] Holton, *The Scientific Imagination*, 105. Lakatos' approach to the rational reconstruction of history, and associated criticisms, is treated in Lorrimar, 'Scientific Research Programmes'.
[53] Holton, *The Scientific Imagination*, 107.
[54] Gábor Forrai, 'Lakatos, Reason and History', in *Appraising Lakatos: Mathematics, Methodology and the Man*, ed. George Kampis, Ladislav Kvasz and Michael Stöltzner (Dordrecht: Kluwer Academic Publishers, 2002), 73.
[55] *Ibid.*, 79.

Even the opponents of rationalism may have played their part in prolonging its legacy. Holton describes a conflict arising, post-Second World War, between some writers he terms 'the new Dionysians', and a group of philosophers he designates 'the new Apollonians'.[56] The 'intuitive' Dionysians are primarily social and cultural critics, espousing suspicion of rationality and scientific reductionism, while the 'logical-rational' Apollonians (in which group Holton includes Popper and Lakatos) would restrict rationality's meaning to 'objective' mathematics and logic, and scientific consensus.[57] As is often the case with antagonists, both groups reinforce each other's position, and 'the scientist is caught between a large anvil and a fearful hammer'.[58] Holton describes the consequences of this conflict for ongoing attempts to understand the process of scientific enquiry: 'Possibly the worst service the new Dionysians and the new Apollonians render is that their antithetical attacks continue to discredit the accommodation of the classically rationalistic with the sensualist components of knowledge.'[59]

Why the Imaginative Deficit in Hefner?

Without succumbing to the excesses of Romanticism, how might greater attention to the imagination expand the co-creation theology treated in this work? Before we turn to this question, though, we might ask why it has not received more attention in Hefner's cross-disciplinary approach. Exploring the intellectual traditions that have shaped Hefner's thought may yield possible reasons for his underdevelopment of the imaginative aspects of knowing.

---

56 Holton, The Scientific Imagination, 86–87. He uses these terms in the same sense as Nietzsche, rather than drawing directly on Greek mythology (ibid., 324n; cf. Friedrich Nietzsche, The Birth of Tragedy, trans. Douglas Smith. (Oxford: Oxford University Press, 2008)).

57 Holton, The Scientific Imagination, 86–87.

58 Holton, The Scientific Imagination, 86.

59 Ibid., 109–110.

Theological Heritage

While Hefner's understanding of science offers some insights into the imaginative deficit in his work, we might also seek explanations in his theological commitments. Apart from the imaginative discourse of Romanticism and German Idealism, we can trace a very different understanding of imagination through the modern period. In stark contrast to the value placed on imagination by Romantics and Idealists, other thinkers denied a place for imagination in epistemology entirely.

Green locates the turn away from the imagination with Ludwig Feuerbach, whom he credits with initiating the 'hermeneutics of suspicion' identified and named by Ricoeur.[60] Feuerbach is largely overlooked, argues Green; however, he influenced the recognised 'masters of suspicion' (Marx, Nietzsche and Freud) and his thought still shapes religious interpretation today.[61] Very much a positivist in his own epistemology, Feuerbach 'always takes for granted ... the axiom that *imagination* and *reality* comprise an unproblematic duality, that they are opposed and mutually exclusive terms'.[62] So when Feuerbach identified the imagination as the 'original organ of religion' and described religion as the product of the imagination, he thus connected suspicion with imagination.[63] Feuerbach takes Hegel's dialectic of *Vorstellung* and *Begriff*, but instead of seeking synthesis in a higher plane he separates imagination and reason entirely, associating the latter with reality and relegating the former to illusion.[64] Viladesau suggests that this move

[60] Garrett Green, *Theology, Hermeneutics, and Imagination: The Crisis of Interpretation at the End of Modernity* (Cambridge: Cambridge University Press, 2000), 84.
[61] *Ibid.*, 84.
[62] *Ibid.*, 92.
[63] *Ibid.*, 92–93.
[64] *Ibid.*, 94; cf. Ludwig Feuerbach, *The Essence of Christianity*, trans. George Eliot (New York: Harper & Row, 1957), 214. In fact, the original German reads 'Die Phantasie ist das ursprüngliche Organ und Wesen der Religion', thus Feuerbach identifies

of Feuerbach's set the stage for positivism in the Victorian era.[65] Describing the same move, Iain McGilchrist argues that Feuerbach and the other 'young Hegelians' destroyed the bridge between the realms of sensory experience and concepts or ideas, thus reducing complex experience to a material view of reality.[66] It is worth considering, therefore, how much these theological schools of thought contributed to Hefner's intellectual formation.

Process theology leaves clear footprints in Hefner's writing. His conception of human nature as 'endless becoming' in particular lends itself to this interpretation of his work. Hefner affirms many aspects of process theology, contending that the likes of Whitehead and Charles Hartshorne have 'established in a determinative manner how this world's processes can unfold within God without compromising his divinity'.[67]

Perhaps surprising, given he does not address the role of the imagination directly in co-creative activity, is the reference Hefner makes to the work of Ricoeur. The extent to which Hefner has read and engages with Ricoeur's wider thought is unclear, but he does adopt Ricoeur's view of religious myth and the interpretation of the human condition in biological categories.[68] He sympathises with and describes the theological task set by Ricoeur: 'to transport the original symbols, where they are important vessels of information for us, into the realm of contemporary, second-naiveté experience, and enable them to coalesce with our experience to provide genuine knowledge of reality'.[69] Ricoeur represents a very different

---

imagination as not only the organ of religion but also its essence (Ludwig Feuerbach, *Das Wesen des Christentums* (Leipzig: Wigand, 1841), 318).

[65] Richard Viladesau, *Theological Aesthetics: God in Imagination, Beauty, and Art* (New York: Oxford University Press, 1999), 62.

[66] Iain McGilchrist, *The Master and His Emissary: The Divided Brain and the Making of the Western World* (New Haven, CT: Yale University Press, 2009), 383.

[67] Hefner, 'The Foundations of Belonging', 169.

[68] Hefner, *THF*, 21, 123, 138; c.f. Paul Ricoeur, *The Symbolism of Evil* (New York: Beacon Press, 1967), 3–18.

[69] Hefner, *THF*, 142.

tradition to the logical positivist movement already discussed. He sees instead a 'surplus of meaning' and explores the idea of the productive imagination and its relationship to reality.[70] George Taylor, referring to unpublished lectures by Ricoeur on the imagination, suggests that the imagination is 'connected with an ontology' in Ricoeur's thought.[71]

Hefner attempts to unite two quite disparate approaches. On the one hand, he sets out to articulate theology within a scientific framework that purports to be highly rational according to its author and to other theologians who have adopted it. Though Hefner might not be considered a rationalist personally, denying as he does the capacity of reason to attain a completely objective view of the whole of reality,[72] his use of Lakatos at the very least encourages him to overlook the imagination's full value. There are strong rationalist artefacts in Hefner's work. Midgley, to give one example, argues that the moral contractual view of rationalism does not consider humans to owe any duties to the non-human world; which perhaps begins to explain the anthropocentrism inherent in Hefner's model.[73]

As discussed earlier, however, the epistemic value of Lakatos' model is contentious, and Lakatos' claim of epistemological realism is self-referential. Hefner describes himself as a 'hopeful' critical realist – hopeful because he does not believe there to be a conclusive philosophical argument in favour of critical realism.[74] In following Ricoeur's understanding of myth, he attempts to wed this problematic scientific realism with a linguistic coherentist position.

---

[70] Paul Ricoeur, 'The Function of Fiction in Shaping Reality', *Man and World* 12, no. 2 (1979), 128.

[71] George Taylor, 'Ricoeur's Philosophy of Imagination', *Journal of French Philosophy* 16, no. 1 (2006), 98.

[72] Hefner, *THF*, 79–80.

[73] Midgley, *Science and Poetry*, 171. It cannot tell the entire story, because Hefner does argue that human co-creation should serve all of nature. He does, however, privilege 'rational' humans as the only species capable of co-creation.

[74] Hefner, *THF*, 220.

The reasons offered here for the underdevelopment of the imagination in Hefner's work are largely speculative. It may simply be a result of Hefner giving little attention to epistemology and metaphysics overall that we see this gap in his work. He draws on vastly different schools of thought, and it is difficult to ascertain how critically he approaches each position, or how he reconciles them into a single coherent framework.

The Development of Science and Religion

Hefner's particular academic environment is another factor shaping his views on rationality and imagination, and one on which we might be less speculative in our analysis. The early shapers of the science and religion field were primarily scientists. David Tracy reminds us that in spite of the growth in 'postmodern' accounts of science among philosophers of science, a degree of positivism persisted among many scientists in the period contemporary to Hefner's work.[75] Taede Smedes, writing on the history of the contemporary science and religion field, takes issue with the scientific notions incorporated into the field's origins. Ian Barbour is recognised as the founder of science and religion as a formal area of study.[76] Barbour's quest to integrate science and religion, argues Smedes, 'echoes the logical positivist vision of unification and has a strong bias toward science as the sole source of rationality, which does not take theology seriously'.[77] Considering the objectives of Barbour's landmark *Issues in Science and Religion* (1966), Smedes suggests it had the dual purpose of: (1) providing a conceptual investigation of the parallels and differences between science and theology, and (2) offering an apologetic for religion within the

---

75 David Tracy, *The Analogical Imagination: Christian Theology and the Culture of Pluralism* (London: SCM Press, 1981), 343.

76 Taede Smedes, 'Beyond Barbour or Back to Basics? The Future of Science-and-Religion and the Quest for Unity', *Zygon* 43, no. 1 (2008), 235.

77 *Ibid.*, 237.

context of a modern, scientific culture.[78] The aim was to restore a sense of intellectual respectability to theology, something that had been in decline since the Enlightenment period.[79]

The decline of theology in the intellectual arena as a result of science's ascent has been well canvassed. John Caputo locates the original reconfiguration of academic enquiry with Kant's conception of philosophy:

> By setting philosophy up a notch, as a higher science that oversees science, setting its conditions and limits, [Kant] means to give philosophy a supervisory position, but he also effectively removes philosophy from the action, like a restaurant critic who doesn't cook! Philosophy concerns a higher level epistemological theory of science, but it has abandoned the real world to the sciences.[80]

Though Caputo is overly critical of Kant, as Kant was not reductionist in his approach to religion, Kant's distinction between the functions of reason did affect a disengagement of religion from scientific thought. The resultant change in cultural attitudes is described by a number of historians and philosophers. Historian Owen Chadwick argues for a diminished sense of providence on the part of religious people since the Renaissance; an accompanying shift in attitudes to humanity.[81] Smedes terms this phenomenon 'scientism as a cultural mode of thinking', defining it more fully as 'a tacit faith or basic trust in science, an incorporation and internalization of scientific modes of thinking in our everyday-life mode of thinking – or, alternatively, the accommodation of our everyday-life mode of thinking to a scientific mode of thinking.'[82]

[78] Ibid., 237–238.
[79] Ibid., 238.
[80] John Caputo, Philosophy and Theology (Nashville, TN: Abingdon Press, 2006), 29.
[81] Owen Chadwick, The Secularization of the European Mind in the Nineteenth Century: The Gifford Lectures in the University of Edinburgh for 1973–74. (Cambridge: Cambridge University Press, 1975), 258.
[82] Smedes, 'Beyond Barbour', 242.

This cultural scientism, according to Smedes, is deeply enmeshed in the quest to integrate science and religion as conceived by the likes of Barbour.[83] Though Barbour adopts a critical realist position that 'affirms the role of mental construction and imaginative activity in the formation of theories' in his early work,[84] he later takes a more assimilative approach to integrating religion and science that draws on process philosophy.[85] Thus, Barbour argues that religious language is 'noncognitive' and 'no explicit propositional assertions about reality are made' in its use.[86] Berg reads in this view an echo of logical positivism, at least in the relegation of religion and metaphysics to a noncognitive level.[87] Smedes also considers the cultural scientism inherent in the work of Barbour, as well as Arthur Peacocke and John Polkinghorne, to be a remnant of logical positivism. Before taking up theology, these scholars received scientific training 'in an era in which the influence of logical positivism upon science was strong'.[88]

[83] Ibid., 242. Barbour, in defence against this charge, contends that scientism can only be understood in a more specific sense i.e. a combination of both an epistemological claim concerning scientific enquiry and an ontological claim concerning the material nature of the universe ('Taking Science Seriously Without Scientism: A Response to Taede Smedes', Zygon 43, no. 1 (2008), 260). Perhaps Smedes' choice of terms is not entirely prudent or fair; however, Barbour's objection to the term does not automatically protect his work from the charges contained within Smedes' more broadly defined 'scientism'.

[84] Ian Barbour, Issues in Science and Religion (London: SCM Press, 1966), 172.

[85] Christian Berg, Theologie im technologischen Zeitalter: Das Werk Ian Barbours als Beitrag zur Verhältnisbestimmung von Theologie zu Naturwissenschaft und Technik (Stuttgart: Kohlhammer, 2002), 70.

[86] Ian Barbour, Religion and Science: Historical and Contemporary Issues (New York: HarperCollins, 1997), 158.

[87] Berg, Theologie im technologischen Zeitalte, 151f. Smedes also finds similarities between Barbour's approach and that of logical positivism; however, he differentiates the nature of the unity that each seeks, as well as approaches to language (Smedes, 'Beyond Barbour', 251–252).

[88] Ibid., 253.

Examining the negligible impact that the science–religion dialogue concerning divine action has had on the work of contemporary systematic theologians, Smedes contends that the answers offered by said dialogue are often too scientific.[89] While divine action serves as a test case for Smedes, he concludes that the entire field tends towards 'theological naturalism'. 'Science not only has become our sole heuristic instrument to tackle questions that relate to our world but has extended its reach to deal with theological questions.'[90] This constitutes a category error – 'confusing the logic implicit in speaking about the natural order with the logic implicit in talking about the order of the divine'.[91] As a result of this kind of confused logic, Smedes argues that the science and religion field has essentially reached a 'mid-life crisis' – neither theologians nor scientists outside the field are taking the dialogue seriously and it has become an end in itself.[92]

Given its origins, is not surprising that a number of thinkers in the science and religion field were drawn to the philosophy of Lakatos. We can observe the tendency to make theology conform to scientific patterns of thought and expression in the work of Hefner's particular intellectual mentors. His use of Lakatosian research frameworks is very much in the same vein as Murphy's major 1990 work, *Theology in the Age of Science*. It appears that Murphy and Hefner were developing their separate interests in adopting Lakatos' thought for theological explanation at the same time, with Murphy's dissertation on Lakatos completed only a year before Hefner's first article on the subject was published.[93] Murphy's early

---

[89] *Ibid.*, 245.
[90] Smedes, 'Beyond Barbour', 245.
[91] *Ibid.*, 246. Logical possibilities become collapsed into physical possibilities.
[92] *Ibid.*, 236.
[93] Nancey Murphy, 'Theology in the Age of Probable Reasoning (Catholic Modernist, Jeffrey Stout, Imre Lakatos)' (PhD diss., Graduate Theological Union, Berkeley, 1987); Hefner, 'Theology's Truth'.

work represents the more sustained engagement with Lakatos, however, and Hefner states that he follows her interpretation of Lakatos in his own monograph.[94] Murphy rejects critical realism, her focus instead on explanatory adequacy is in service of achieving equal epistemic status for theology and science 'without the questionable invocation of a questionable philosophical doctrine'.[95] Though she is unwilling to tether rationality to realism, as Lakatos appears to do, her emphasis on rationality in order to bring theology closer to science leaves little room for the imagination to operate in her epistemology.

Ralph Burhoe was a long-time intellectual mentor to Hefner. Like Hefner, Burhoe has a strong interest in sociobiology, promulgating the theory of biocultural evolution.[96] Hefner, writing in memoriam of Burhoe, describes Burhoe's work as 'a comprehensive explanation of how traditional religion could be translated into serious scientific theories'.[97] Burhoe's biographer, David Breed, traces Burhoe's particular philosophy of science back to the work of Rudolf Carnap, prominent member of the Vienna Circle and author of logical positivism. The Institute for the Unity of Science, founded in 1947, grew out of the Vienna Circle's work and developed a close association with the American Academy of Arts and Sciences during Burhoe's lengthy executive tenure period with the Academy.[98] Breed describes how 'Burhoe's theological ideas began to be characterized by [the Academy's] potent scientific and intellectual climate'.[99] Accordingly, Burhoe sought to translate traditional religious doctrine into scientific language, to

---

[94] Hefner, THF, 23.
[95] Murphy, 'Critical Realism', 288.
[96] Burhoe, 'Religion's Role in Human Evolution'.
[97] Philip Hefner, 'Ralph Burhoe: Reconsidering the Man and His Vision of Yoking Religion and Science', Zygon 49, no. 3 (2014), 636.
[98] David Breed, Yoking Science and Religion: The Life and Thought of Ralph Wendell Burhoe (Chicago, IL: Zygon Books, 1992), 17–18.
[99] Ibid., 13.

'interpret religion by using the methods and conceptual tools of the sciences'.[100]

Burhoe developed his 'yoking' model of science and religion in conversation with scientists such as E. O. Wilson and Donald Campbell, and we see the concerns of sociobiology reflected particularly in the centrality of trans-kin altruism in his work, a theme which Hefner also develops.[101] Hefner, too, expresses admiration for the work of sociobiologist E. O. Wilson. Though Wilson at times offers conflicting views of how science and religion interact, he strongly supports the scientific approach to knowledge: 'Scientific materialism is the only mythology that can manufacture great goals from the sustained pursuit of pure knowledge.'[102] This scientific account of reality 'has always, point for point in zones of conflict, defeated traditional religion'.[103] As Midgley reminds us, however, sociobiology is highly ideological (despite its claims to be scientific), tends to normalise contemporary lifestyles (such as individualism) rather than describe human universals rationally on the basis of empirical evidence and is generally guided by an atomistic world view.[104]

Retrieving the Imagination

Understanding why the imagination receives short shrift in Hefner's model of theological anthropology, why might we accord it greater significance in a theology of co-creation? Not only are

[100] *Ibid.*, 19; cf. Ralph Burhoe, 'The Concepts of "God" and "Soul" in a Scientific View of Human Purpose', *Zygon* 8 (1973), 438; Ralph Burhoe, 'The Human Prospect and the "Lord of History"', *Zygon* 10 (1975), 330.
[101] Ralph Burhoe, 'War, Peace and Religion's Biocultural Evolution', *Zygon* 21, no. 4 (1986).
[102] Wilson, *On Human Nature*, 207.
[103] *Ibid.*, 192.
[104] Midgley, *Science and Poetry*, 153, 199.

the visions of human enhancement that prompt this theological reflection highly imaginative, but we can point to a renewal of interest in the imagination's contribution to knowledge in contemporary scholarship. We see this retrieval in both science and theology as separate disciplines (which have advanced well beyond the specific field of science and religion in this area); a few examples are provided in the remainder of this chapter to support the introduction of a more imaginative understanding of human co-creation in the next.

Imagination and Theology

Douglas Hedley reminds us that while not all of the Romantic poets operated from a Christian point of view, faith was central to Coleridge's and Wordsworth's understanding of the imagination.[105] This connection between imagination, reality and religious belief has been taken up by theologians across a range of traditions. Malcolm Guite makes the bold assertion that 'Theology has recovered from an atomising, reductive, demythologising period and is beginning to look at the importance of imaginative shaping and symbolic apprehension in the discovery of meaning and theological truth.'[106] Challenging earlier views, Guite suggests that 'the imagination, far from being a merely subjective realm of fantasy, is, in fact, an essential instrument with which we grasp the truth'.[107]

Similarly, Avis contends that the greatest truths can be conveyed only through the imagination.[108] He contrasts this with what he considers to be a false picture of rationality. 'We see more profoundly into reality through the truth of imagination than we do when we pursue the illusion of precise, specifiable, purely objective, literal description.'[109] For Avis, the Christian faith is essentially

[105] Hedley, Living Forms of the Imagination, 2.
[106] Guite, Faith, Hope and Poetry, 1.
[107] Ibid., 145.
[108] Avis, God and the Creative Imagination, 8.
[109] Ibid., 11.

held 'hostage' by 'the truth-bearing capacity of metaphor, symbol and myth'.[110] He explores the way in which the symbols of spirit, light and love in the Scriptures act as 'windows on the transcendent' for conveying knowledge of God.[111] Although they are expressed as practical, almost concrete, symbols in the biblical text, they also function as metaphysical assertions concerning the nature of ultimate reality.[112]

This has implications for both how we *understand* and how we *communicate* that understanding. The imagination illuminates that which cannot be known through the senses. Hedley describes the imagination as 'the capacity to see the world as disclosing that which transcends the spatio-temporal'.[113] The creative imagination is connected with divine inspiration; it is the 'light and energy of the soul as it relishes truth: knowledge "wedded" to feeling'.[114] Milbank describes a form of 'magic idealism' in which we can, through imagination, 'share in divine creativity by awakening the world beyond itself to its own reality'.[115]

When it comes to understanding, Garrett Green identifies the imagination as the 'anthropological point of contact for divine revelation'.[116] It is the *Anknüpfungspunkt*, or 'point of contact' between divine revelation and human experience.[117] God 'gives himself to the world … by touching the human imagination', especially through scripture.[118] Hans Urs von Balthasar makes the similar argument that 'the biblical revelation occurs in the same formal anthropological locus where the mythopoeic imagination designed

---

[110] *Ibid.*, 52.
[111] *Ibid.*, 52.
[112] Avis, *God and the Creative Imagination*, 52.
[113] Hedley, *Living Forms of the Imagination*, 22.
[114] *Ibid.*, 52.
[115] Milbank, 'Apologetics and the Imagination', 44.
[116] Garrett Green, *Imagining God: Theology and the Religious Imagination* (San Francisco, CA: Harper & Row, 1989), 40.
[117] *Ibid.*, 5.
[118] Green, *Theology, Hermeneutics, and Imagination*, 185.

its images of the eternal'.[119] The symbol functions as a necessary element of Karl Rahner's *Vorgriff* – it is only through the use of the symbol that we are able to reach out beyond ourselves towards our true nature.[120] Viladesau explores Rahner's transcendental method, contending that the non-objective pre-apprehension of spiritual realities is synthesised by the imagination via symbols connected with sensible experience.[121]

The understanding of scripture as expressing truth through symbol enjoys a long heritage in Christian thought, even if its retrieval in theology is a more recent development. Augustine, according to Carol Harrison, saw scripture as requiring 'an intuitive, imaginative, symbolic, image-making apprehension of God's word', more akin to the expressions of a poet than to a philosopher.[122] Aquinas, too, highlights the use of bodily metaphors in scripture to convey spiritual knowledge.[123] The imagination is thus central for scriptural hermeneutics. 'For God has chosen to reveal himself not in transparent doctrines appealing to pure reason but in opaque symbols and narratives that appeal to the imagination.'[124]

The imagination's role is not restricted to the comprehension of theological understanding but carries over into the communication of theological ideas. Hoffman identifies a strong presence of the religious imagination in modern literature, 'because of the need to establish new formulations of the central theological metaphors'.[125] By its very nature, theological language is companion to the

119 Hans Urs von Balthasar, *The Glory of the Lord: A Theological Aesthetics*, vol. I
   Edinburgh: T. & T. Clark, 1982), 145.
120 Karl Rahner, *Hörer des Wortes* (Munich: Kössel-Verlag, 1963), 180n.
121 Viladesau, *Theological Aesthetics*, 82.
122 Carol Harrison, *Beauty and Revelation in the Thought of Saint Augustine* (Oxford:
   Clarendon Press, 1992), 82.
123 Aquinas, *Summa theologiae*, Ia.1.9, *Responsio*.
124 Green, *Theology, Hermeneutics, and Imagination*, 182.
125 Frederick Hoffman, *The Imagination's New Beginning: Theology and Modern
   Literature* (Notre Dame, IN: University of Notre Dame Press, 1967), 16.

lyrical and the dramatic.[126] Yet we must take care not to equate scripture with poetry generally here – Austin Farrer's account that '[biblical] inspiration stands midway between the free irresponsibility of poetical images, and the sober and critical analogies of metaphysical discourse' is helpful as we maintain this necessary distinction.[127]

Ricoeur delves further into the metaphysics of the imagination in his discussion of metaphor. Though he cautions against drawing uncritically from the Romantic tradition to develop a metaphysics of imagination,[128] he contends that we must follow Kant rather than Hume and 'look at the imagination as the place of nascent meanings and categories, rather than as the place of fading impressions'.[129]

We might add our voice to Green's call for theologians in postmodernity to 'acknowledge unapologetically' that all religion (though he addresses himself particularly to Christian theologians) depends upon the imagination in its language and must use the imagination to articulate this grammar.[130] 'For God has chosen to reveal himself in the world in a manner accessible only to imagination.'[131] McGrath expands on the importance of this exercise:

> Retrieving the imaginative dimensions of theology addresses one of
> its most worrying blind spots – a failure to recognize that the theo-
> logical landscape extends beyond the constrained and constraining

---

[126] Avis, *God and the Creative Imagination*, 69.
[127] Austin Farrer, *The Glass of Vision* (London: Dacre Press, 1948), 148.
[128] Paul Ricoeur, 'Creativity in Language', *Philosophy Today* 17, no. 2 (1973), 107.
[129] *Ibid.*, 109.
[130] Green, *Theology, Hermeneutics, and Imagination*, 205.
[131] *Ibid.*, 206. At the same time, Green cautions against the possible detrimental consequences of postmodernity for the imagination – though the imagination may emerge triumphant in the relativistic postmodern context, this triumph may be purchased at the cost of forfeiting the imagination's grip on reality (*ibid.*, 199).

domains of the cognitive and rational on the one hand, and the experiential and existential on the other.[132]

Imaginative Science

It is perhaps unsurprising that the role of the imagination in epistemology has been attended to by theologians, given the strong narrative element of religious belief. But what of science? Scientists are often reluctant to speak of the imagination with respect to the scientific process. Scientific research is considered to be a logical, unemotional activity in which 'even the exhilarating flights of intuitive imagination must be recast in deductive style to be respectable'.[133] The work of a scientist is often portrayed as purer than other endeavours, untainted by human emotions. Richard Hamer describes the physicist's soul as 'aloof from mortal strife'.[134] Mathematical physicist James Clerk Maxwell refers to:

> those illustrious men [of science] who by aspiring to noble ends, whether intellectual or practical, have risen above the region of storms into a clearer atmosphere, where there is no misrepresentation of opinion, nor ambiguity of expression, but where one mind comes into closest contact with another at the point where both approach nearest to the truth.[135]

Einstein similarly speaks of the inhabitants of the 'Temple of Science' – drawn to the 'silent, high mountains, where the eye ranges freely through the still, pure air and traces the calm contours that seem to be made for eternity'.[136] The language used by Maxwell

---

132 McGrath, Re-imagining Nature, 48.
133 Holton, The Scientific Imagination, 237.
134 Richard Hamer, 'The Romantic and Idealistic Appeal of Physics', Science 61, no. 1570 (1925), 109.
135 James Clerk Maxwell, inaugural lecture at Cambridge (1871), as cited in Holton, The Scientific Imagination, 232.
136 Albert Einstein, 'Motive des Forschens', in Ideas and Opinions of Albert Einstein, ed. Sonja Bargmanns, trans. Sonja Bargmann (New York: Crown Publishers, 1954). The

and Einstein has rather a Nietszchean air to it; their picture of the scientist bearing strong resemblance to the *Übermensch*.[137]

Yet the scientific method can be understood differently, its emphasis on rationality and freedom from subjective elements challenged. Echoing Coleridge's objection to abstract reason, mathematician and philosopher Alfred North Whitehead also criticised 'one-eyed reason, deficient in its vision of depth'.[138] When it comes to discerning appropriate human intervention into human nature, and questioning the limits, Medawar suggests that our answer is grounded in 'a certain natural sense of the fitness of things, a feeling that is shared by most kind and reasonable people even if we cannot define it in philosophically defensible or legally accountable terms'.[139] If we cannot articulate this sense by appeal to reason or logic, how do we access this knowledge?

Medawar, by way of an answer, first sketches out what he considers the prevailing perception of scientific enquiry – that scientific truths find their origins in unadorned sense evidence and unprejudiced observation, upon which 'a great mountain of natural law is slowly built'.[140] He challenges this position, contending that 'without imagination scientific thought is barren'.[141] He makes his case in part by highlighting the role played by the imagination in Popper's scientific methodology. Scientific understanding begins with imaginative preconceptions, the 'invention of a Possible World'.[142] Medawar urges scientists, and the thinking public,

translation used here is taken from Gerald Holton, *Thematic Origins of Scientific Thought: Kepler to Einstein* (Cambridge, MA: Harvard University Press, 1973), 376.

[137] Friedrich Nietzsche, *Thus Spoke Zarathustra*, trans. R. Hollingdale and E. Rieu (London: Penguin, 1961).

[138] Alfred North Whitehead, *Science and the Modern World* (New York: Free Press, 1967), 59.

[139] Medawar, 'Science and the Sanctity of Life', 88.

[140] P. B. Medawar, 'Hypothesis and Imagination', in *Pluto's Republic* (Oxford: Oxford University Press, 1982), 115.

[141] *Ibid.*, 116.

[142] Medawar, 'Science and Literature', 17. This is clearly a different interpretation of Popper's thought than that offered by Holton (see page 143). Holton suggests that

to view the scientific process as inspirational, not the outcome of a merely logical process.[143] The imaginative and critical voices are in dialogue in scientific reasoning. This is not to say that arriving at a scientific hypothesis is illogical, rather Medawar describes it as 'non-logical' (i.e. outside logic), though it can be subjected to criticism and experimentation once formed.[144] Max Planck, too, affirms the need for the scientist to possess a 'vivid intuitive imagination, for new ideas are not generated by deduction, but by an artistically creative imagination'.[145] Physicist and biologist Leo Szilard also highlights the inherent creativity of science, identifying commonalities between the scientist and the artist or poet.[146]

Hedley gives examples of how the creative imagination is at work in scientific discovery. He relates the development of relativity theory to Einstein's image of a rider with a mirror on a beam of light, the discovery of benzene's chemical structure to Kekulé's dream of an ouroboros, and Mendeléev's breakthrough with the arrangement of the periodic table to his dream involving the card game Solitaire.[147] Speaking of both the humanities and the sciences, Hedley argues that 'wonder can inspire the imagination both to operate creatively and to illuminate the structures of reality'.[148]

Mathematician and chemist Charles Coulson also sees the use of imagination as one of the commonalities between science and

Popper himself was ambiguous concerning his proposal to rationally reconstruct the creative aspect of scientific discovery, later declaring the more ambivalent aim to delineate 'a theory of understanding which aims at combining an intuitive understanding of reality with the objectivity of rational criticism'. (Holton, *The Scientific Imagination*, 328n; cf. Popper, *Objective Knowledge*, 190).

143 P. B. Medawar, 'Imagination and Hypothesis', *The Times Literary Supplement*, 850.
144 P. B. Medawar, *Induction and Intuition* (Philadelphia, PA: American Philosophical Society, 1969), 46.
145 Max Planck, *A Scientific Autobiography* (London: Williams & Norgate, 1950), 109.
146 As cited in Antonio Damasio, *Descartes' Error: Emotion, Reason, and the Human Brain* (New York: G. P. Putnam's Sons, 1994), 189.
147 Hedley, *Living Forms of the Imagination*, 67.
148 *Ibid.*, 67.

other disciplines, for the interpretation of facts is a creative act.[149] Scientists draw on metaphor in surprising ways, engaging the imagination in our understanding of scientific concepts. Mary Midgley gives the example of the discovery of DNA and the central dogma. The selection of the terms 'transcription' and 'translation' to denote the process of moving from DNA to RNA to protein has contributed to the understanding of genetic material as digital information and the notion of the gene as an all-powerful controller of biological nature.[150]

Even the perceived antagonism between the disciplines of theology and science, Midgley argues, can be traced back to imaginative beginnings, impacted substantially by the thought of Greek atomistic philosophers epitomised in Lucretius' poem *De rerum natura*.[151] Lucretius not only, or even primarily, conceived of atomism as an answer to scientific questions, but rather applied it in the sense of 'a moral crusade – the only way to free mankind from a crushing load of superstition by showing that natural causation was independent of the gods'.[152] Thus, Epicurean hostility towards religion was imported into the scientific attitude alongside the development of atomic theory.[153] The creative elements of science and their accoutrements appear to exert their influence beyond the process of scientific enquiry. The impact that using machine imagery to describe the world, following the invention of early complex machines such as clocks, has had on world view is immense, particularly as machines are under human control by their very definition, to give another example.[154] Science, according to Midgley,

---

[149] Charles Coulson, *Science and Christian Belief* (London: Oxford University Press, 1955), 49.
[150] Midgley, *Science and Poetry*, 4–5.
[151] *Ibid.*, 23.
[152] *Ibid.*, 23.
[153] *Ibid.*, 30.
[154] *Ibid.*, 25; cf. Julien Offray de la Mettrie, *Machine Man and Other Writings*, ed. Ann Thomson (Cambridge: Cambridge University Press, 1996).

cannot help but be affected by the imagination as scientific activity occurs within our larger world-pictures – the imagination pervades 'the whole shape of our thinking. To picture [science] as ... a solitary example of rational thinking, standing out alone against a background of formless emotion – is to lose sight of its organic connection with the rest of our life'.[155]

The picture of science as coldly rational, free from emotion and imagination, runs counter to many past perceptions of the character of science. Sir Benjamin Brody, addressing the Royal Society in 1859, described how 'physical investigation' (science) actually highlights the value of the imagination if properly employed, it is 'that wondrous faculty which ... properly controlled by experience and reflection, becomes the noblest attribute of man: the source of poetic genius, the instrument of discovery in Science'.[156] The kinship between science and poetry is attested in Coleridge's abiding interest in the natural sciences – some of his poetry was even inspired in collaboration with scientist friends.[157]

Physicist and historian of science Gerald Holton describes what he considers to be a more balanced approach to epistemology:

We should, rather, strive to acquire a clearer notion of how actual mortal beings, with all their frailties, have managed to use both these faculties [imagination and reason] to grasp the outlines of a unique and fundamentally simple universe, characterised by necessity and harmony. Such knowledge, we may hope, can be of practical use at a time when our species seems to depend on tapping all the resources of reason for the generation of new ideas that are both imaginative and effective.[158]

[155] Midgley, *Science and Poetry*, 24.
[156] As cited in John Tyndall, *Scientific Use of the Imagination and Other Essays* (London: Longman, Greens & Co., 1872), 2.
[157] Owen Barfield, *What Coleridge Thought* (Middletown, CT: Wesleyan University Press, 1971), 37.
[158] Holton, *The Scientific Imagination*, 110.

Lakatos and Imagination

Neil Calver describes Medawar's reading of Popper, and accompanying conception of the scientific process, as a liberating one – 'one that enlarged and was not diminished by the thought that any truth begins life as an imaginative preconception of what that truth might be'.[159] But does this extend to scientific methodologies beyond that described by Popper? Whereas Popper suggested that the process of arriving at new conjectures in scientific discovery cannot be analysed rationally, Lakatos argued for 'a rational and non psychologistic [sic] heuristic providing a guideline, a set of instructions, from the criticism of an old conjecture to the 'discovery' of a new, improved one'.[160] Motterlini makes a convincing case, however, that Lakatos oscillated in his thought between a Hegelian understanding of method as an objective surrogate for truth, and an appeal to Popperian fallibilism and rejection of the absolute 'cunning of reason'.[161] In the latter, at least, there is perhaps room to read Lakatos in a way that accommodates the operation of the imagination, as Medawar does with Popper. Writing to colleague Adolf Grünbaum, Lakatos concedes 'there is no ultimate proof that ... we have been heading towards the Truth. We can only (non-rationally) believe, or, rather hope, that we have been'.[162]

Hefner's account of humans as co-creators, expressed in the form of a Lakatosian framework, appears to be shaped more by

---

[159] Neil Calver, 'Sir Peter Medawar: Science, Creativity and the Popularization of Karl Popper', *Notes and Records: The Royal Society Journal of the History of Science* 67 (2013), 308.

[160] Matteo Motterlini, 'Professor Lakatos Between the Hegelian Devil and the Popperian Deep Blue Sea', in *Appraising Lakatos: Mathematics, Methodology, and the Man*, ed. George Kampis, Ladislav Kvasz and Michael Stöltzner (Dordrecht: Kluwer Academic Publishers, 2002), 27.

[161] *Ibid.*, 45.

[162] Imre Lakatos, 'Anomalies Versus "Crucial Experiments" (a Rejoinder to Professor Grünbaum)', in *Mathematics Science and Epistemology: Philosophical Papers*, ed. John Worrall and Gregory Currie, vol. II (Cambridge: Cambridge University Press, 1978), 223.

rationalist understandings of Lakatos than the more imaginative alternatives. A strong case can be made, however, for the importance of the imagination in both the world view underpinning the work of a scientist, and the inspiration phase of scientific enquiry. Williamson suggests that the imagination's role in science extends beyond the discovery phase, arguing that mathematicians often appeal to the imagination to justify their first principles.[163] While the imagination may have been implicated in exacerbating the conflict thesis of science and religion, it offers far greater resources for harmonising the two pursuits. Einstein was cited earlier, concerning the lofty pursuits undertaken in the 'Temple of Science'. Yet Einstein does not consider this rarefied mountain atmosphere the domain of scientists alone.

> Man seeks to form for himself, in whatever manner is suitable for him, a simplified and lucid image of the world, and so to overcome the world of experience by striving to replace it to some extent by this image. This is what the painter does, and the poet, the speculative philosopher, the natural scientist, each in his own way. Into this image and its formation, he places the center of gravity of his emotional life, in order to attain the peace and serenity that he cannot find within the narrow confines of a swirling, personal experience.[164]

Imagination vs Reason?

Is it possible to address the imaginative deficits of a model such as Hefner's while retaining its appeal to reason, and its commensurability with scientific enquiry? Moving beyond an antithetical model, Medawar posits that the imagination and reason are in fact synergistic.[165] Midgley concurs, stating that 'we use a haphazard mix of faculties which are not fully unified, but which give us

---

[163] Williamson, 'Knowing by Imagining', 122.
[164] Einstein, as cited in Holton, *Thematic Origins*, 378.
[165] Medawar, 'Science and Literature', 17.

various different sorts of useful light'.[166] She counters rationalist reductionism with the suggestion that different ways of thinking are not rival alternatives but operate harmoniously.[167] Hart cautions against treating the imagination as a faculty separable from the intellect (even if it is to exalt the imagination), avowing that 'it is virtually impossible to identify any human activity or capacity from which imagination is entirely absent'.[168]

The entanglement and complementarity of imagination and reason has been emphasised by a number of past and present thinkers. For Gottfried Wilhelm Leibniz, the imagination serves to reconcile antitheses and polarities, raising dichotomies to a higher dialectic plane of understanding. According to Engell, Leibniz was the first to address the issue of how reason and the imagination relate to one another if the imagination is given due credit: 'Imagination becomes the process, the dynamic or the dialectic, through which the truths of reason may be obtained and understood. Reason is thus more static; it is a "higher" power than imagination but one fulfilled only through the active working and forms of the imagination.'[169] Tyndall speaks of 'that creative power in which reason and imagination are united' in his treatment of conical refraction.[170] 'Nourished by knowledge patiently won; bounded and conditioned by cooperant Reason, Imagination becomes the mightiest instrument of the physical discoverer.'[171] Eighteenth-century poet Leonard Welsted further expressed some of the complexities of the relationship of imagination and reason: 'imagination is as much a part of reason as is memory or judgment, or rather a more bright emanation from it, as to paint and to throw light on ideas is a finer act of the understanding than simply to separate or compare

---

[166] Midgley, *Science and Poetry*, 121. Midgley's use of the term 'faculty' here is slightly problematic, as a faculty psychology model is largely rejected today.
[167] *Ibid.*, 127.
[168] Hart, 'The Glory of Imagination', 229.
[169] Engell, *The Creative Imagination*, 30.
[170] Tyndall, *Scientific Use of the Imagination*, 10.
[171] *Ibid.*, 6.

them'.[172] And, more recently, in the encyclical *Laudato si'*, Pope Francis also calls for a broader context for reason:

> It cannot be maintained that empirical science provides a complete explanation of life, the interplay of all creatures and the whole of reality. If we reason only within the confines of the latter, little room would be left for aesthetic sensibility, poetry, or even reason's ability to grasp the ultimate meaning and purpose of things.[173]

Holton's objective to essentially unite imagination and reason for practical benefit is even more appropriate today as we consider the place of human enhancement technologies in the human future.[174] The postmodern period has arguably seen a turn back to the imagination, a greater emphasis on the alternative Romantic trajectory of thought without succumbing to its excesses. As surveyed in this chapter, contemporary thinkers in both theology and philosophy of science are according a greater role to the imagination in epistemology. Holton, examining the thought of Newton and Einstein, suggested that they 'were not satisfied with any primarily 'scientific' world construction but yearned for a still grander synthesis'.[175] An understanding of the human place in ongoing evolution (and creation) requires a synthesis of knowledge from both the sciences and the humanities, and the imagination has a vital role to play in both theological reflection and communication of matters concerning human enhancement. Avis sums it up in his conclusion that 'science, poetry and religion are all energised by the imagination and all tell us something about reality, appropriate to their various methods'.[176]

---

[172] Leonard Welsted, *Title Epistles, Odes, Written on Several Subjects: With a Translation of Longinus's Treatise on the Sublime* (London: J. Walthoe & J. Peele, 1724), xxii.

[173] Francis, *Laudato si'* (Rome: Vatican, 2015).

[174] See Holton, *The Scientific Imagination*, 110.

[175] *Ibid.*, 151.

[176] Avis, *God and the Creative Imagination*, 17.

Conclusion

Filling in the historical context to the role of the imagination in epistemology is helpful for understanding contemporary theological responses to the possibility of human enhancement. We currently inhabit a time where confidence in human malleability is higher than ever (see Chapter 2), while the imagination (in some fields of scholarship at least) receives little attention in approaches to truth and knowing. It should be stressed that these two historical trends described – the increase in human malleability and the overlooking of the imagination – are not represented here as causally linked, or even correlates with one another (though a study of how both relate to the development of modern science would perhaps be illuminating). For the present purposes, however, they are two separate strands of history that collide in the contemporary co-creation theology exemplified by Hefner. It has been demonstrated that such theologies privilege human rationality in the exercise of co-creative agency, resulting in a diminished sense of limits to human creativity, and a somewhat vague treatment of human discernment.

We may read in these contemporary theologies of co-creation a continuation of the modernist elevation of empirical reasoning, rather than the alternative Romantic and Idealist conception of imagination. It has been shown already how Hefner depends on a Lakatosian understanding of science in the explication of his theology, a framework which has been widely and convincingly critiqued for overstating the capacity of rationality. Yet we see also, in these thinkers an acknowledgement that the imagination has something to offer, that it represents an important resource in the development of their ideas. The historical context of the present chapter offers one explanation for the friction between the intuitions of key science and religion thinkers in favour of imagination and their stated objectives to present theology in scientifically commensurate ways. Their work is undergirded by epistemological assumptions that leave little room for the imagination in robust intellectual discourse. Their sense of imagination's importance cannot gain purchase in the science and religion dialogue model that they have inherited and therefore it remains underdeveloped in their work.

This chapter has indicated that an alternative reading of Lakatos might be possible – one that makes room for the imagination in the process of scientific enquiry. If we approach Hefner's appropriation of Lakatosian research programmes with this in view, then the theological claims he sketches out need not be subjected to rationality as the final arbiter. The strictures of empirical falsification might be relaxed with respect to theological claims, without relinquishing the explanatory power of the research programme. This would in turn give Hefner the freedom to develop his account of the imagination in epistemology, present in embryonic form through his use of poetry for illustration and his Ricoeurian approach to myth.

A deficit of imagination is rooted in the larger field of science and religion. Hefner simply has not found adequate conceptual tools to answer the questions he has about human agency and responsibility in the context of evolutionary science. With science given heuristic priority over theology from the outset in the study of science and religion, Hefner has essentially inherited a number of category mistakes from his predecessors.

The central question of the present work is to consider how a greater focus on imagination might equip and expand current theological responses to the challenges of human enhancement. In the first chapters we saw how vital the imagination is for transhumanist visions of the future, inspiring both technological innovation and fictional explorations of technologically enhanced humanity. Might not according equal weight to the imagination yield fruitful responses to such visions? The following chapter will consider the potential contribution that J. R. R. Tolkien's notion of sub-creation might make to a theological treatment of human enhancement, emphasising as it does the role of the imagination for guiding creative activity. Following this analysis, approaches to epistemology that accord sufficient attention to both the imagination and reason, and present an integrated account of cognition and understanding, will be explored as part of a broader theological anthropology that can engage human enhancement debates.

5 | Humans as 'Sub-creators'

Despite his preference for rationalist philosophies of science over imaginative traditions, Hefner does acknowledge the need for storytellers and poets as we ponder the future. Evolution may have entered the 'phase of poetry', in which 'imaginative frameworks of meaning' will further nature's project.[1] Though this notion is essentially an addendum to his created co-creator anthropology, we might develop his thought along the lines that he signals here by turning to the potential role of imagination and narrative in a theology of co-creation.

As a storyteller concerned with ideas of co-creation, J. R. R. Tolkien is a natural place to begin. Trevor Hart frames Tolkien's entire corpus as a sustained effort to answer a question that is also of central concern to us here: 'if human artistry is creative and powerful, what relationship does it have to that other "creativity" which Christian faith ascribes properly to God alone?'[2] Might Tolkien's notion of artistry and sub-creation be expanded to incorporate technological development and thus inform theological reflection on human enhancement?[3]

---

[1] Hefner, 'A Fuller Concept of Evolution', 307.

[2] Trevor Hart, 'Tolkien, Creation, and Creativity', in *Tree of Tales: Tolkien Literature and Theology*, ed. Trevor Hart and Ivan Khovacs (Waco, TX: Baylor University Press, 2007), 40. Tolkien acknowledges as much himself, writing that his *Legendarium* is 'fundamentally concerned with the relation of Art (and Sub-creation) and Primary Reality' and 'Creation to making and sub-creation' (*Letters*, 145n, 188).

[3] 'Sub-creation' will be used throughout instead of 'subcreation' to respect Tolkien's original use. Tolkien often divided words to draw attention to their compound nature and their etymology.

Tolkien's Sub-creation

Tolkien's proposal of sub-creation is not articulated with anywhere near the amount of detail that scaffolds Hefner's created co-creator and is primarily concerned with the production of art (particularly the writing of fiction) and the relationship of this type of creativity to divine creation. Tolkien's ideas of sub-creation are expressed most clearly in his essay 'On Fairy-Stories', and in the poem 'Myth-opoeia', and are illustrated in the short story 'Leaf by Niggle' and Tolkien's fictional creation myth, the 'Ainulindalë', which opens *The Silmarillion*. Indeed, all of Tolkien's fictional *Legendarium* may be viewed as the practical demonstration of Tolkien's sub-creation theory.[4]

The lecture 'On Fairy-Stories' is a defence of fantasy against particular literary theories of the time. The term 'sub-creation' first arises in a discussion of the invention of the adjective, and the attendant capacity this afforded the imagination.

> When we can take green from grass, blue from heaven, and red from blood, we have already an enchanter's power – upon one plane; and the desire to wield that power in the world external to our minds awakes ... We may put a deadly green upon a man's face and produce a horror; we may make the rare and terrible blue moon to shine; or we may cause woods to spring with silver leaves and rams to wear fleeces of gold, and put hot fire into the belly of the cold worm. But in such 'fantasy', as it is called, new form is made; Faërie begins; Man becomes a sub-creator.[5]

Sub-creation in this first instance of its use describes the imaginative application of language to devise new forms, which can be presented to the imagination of others in writing. Later, Tolkien describes the work of a successful sub-creator: 'He makes

---

4 *Letters*, 188.
5 *OFS*, 23.

a Secondary World which your mind can enter. Inside it, what he relates is "true", it accords with the laws of that world.'[6] Sub-creation is the product of art and the imagination to give the 'inner consistency of reality', i.e. to command secondary belief.[7]

Sub-creation is elevated from mere imaginative fancy by its connection to divine creation. Biographer Humphrey Carpenter captures a key aspect of what sub-creation means for Tolkien in his account of Tolkien and Lewis' well-known conversation concerning the truth of myth, recounting Tolkien's claim that 'not only the abstract thoughts of man but also his imaginative inventions must originate with God, and must in consequence reflect something of original truth'.[8] Tolkien uses several metaphors that are helpful for understanding his views on how sub-creation relates to God's creation. One example is his metaphor of refracted light, used in the poem 'Mythopoeia'.

> Man, Sub-creator, the refracted light
> through whom is splintered from a single White
> to many hues, and endlessly combined
> in living shapes that move from mind to mind.[9]

We humans act as crystals – we do not generate light on our own but instead draw upon God's light. Yet from that light we are able to produce something new after a fashion, a particular hue that would not exist apart from us. Flieger interprets the metaphor of 'splintering light to many hues' as 'splintering original perception into many concepts and words'.[10] In this way, the imagination is used to 'particularize and make manifest fragments of original truth'.[11] The splintering of light to many hues refers to the use of

---

[6] *Ibid.*, 37.

[7] *Ibid.*, 47.

[8] Humphrey Carpenter, *The Inklings* (London: Allen & Unwin, 1978), 43.

[9] 'Mythopoeia', in *Tree and Leaf* (London: HarperCollins, 2001), 87.

[10] Verlyn Flieger, *Splintered Light: Logos and Language in Tolkien's World* (Kent, OH: Kent State University Press, 2002), 47.

[11] *Ibid.*, 47.

words imaginatively in the making of secondary worlds, and in the process 'expressing some fragment of divine truth through fantasy'.[12] The very act of inventing stories orients us towards the 'true harbour' found in God, as Carpenter summarises the 'splintered light' metaphor, though our myths will inevitably contain error.[13]

Tolkien uses a similar metaphor in 'On Fairy-Stories' when he refers to the 'effoliation of creation'.[14] The hints around this particular metaphor of how sub-creation might correspond to our own world will be considered later; however, Tolkien returns frequently to language of trees and leaves in his idea that human creativity elaborates on what God has made. Both of these metaphors thus convey something essential to Tolkien's position: human creativity derives from, and builds on, divine creation. 'We make still by the law in which we're made', he writes in 'Mythopoeia'.[15]

Exploring the notion of sub-creation and its relation to divine creation further, we might ask whether human creating is genuinely 'creative', or simply mimetic?[16] Hart takes care that we do not claim too much novelty for sub-creation, describing its depiction in the *Silmarillion* as 'the participation in God's creative activity by angelic beings whose own mode of creativity is decisively marked by the fact that they are, in their turn, God's creatures rather than his divine counterparts'.[17]

There is a sense, however that sub-creation involves the making of something new. Greene argues that Tolkien 'felt that he was contributing to the effoliation of Creation by making things that were possible to God but not actually made by him'.[18] Hart

[12] Verlyn Flieger, 'Barfield's "Poetic Diction" and Splintered Light', *Studies in the Literary Imagination* 14, no. 2 (1981), 52.

[13] Humphrey Carpenter, *J. R. R. Tolkien: A Biography* (London: Allen & Unwin, 1977), 147.

[14] *OFS*, 73.

[15] 'Mythopoeia', 87.

[16] Hart, 'Tolkien, Creation, and Creativity', 40.

[17] *Ibid.*, 48.

[18] Deirdre Greene, '"Higher Argument": Tolkien and the Tradition of Vision, Epic, and Prophecy', *Mythlore* 21 (1996), 48–49.

also agrees, suggesting that when the Ainur join in with Ilúvatar's melody, 'each is invited to bring into existence something that has hitherto enjoyed no existence, and thereby to enhance the overall sound of the music'.[19] Randel Helms makes an even stronger case for the high value and originality of human creativity in Tolkien's work. Placing him in the company of Coleridge and Blake, Helms argues that all three saw human creativity as more than merely an imitation of divine creativity, but rather equivalent to it in some sense.[20] Clarifying the originality of human creativity, given how Coleridge's Primary and Secondary Imaginations are often understood, Helms argues that 'it is not that the human products of imagination are imitations of God's works, but that the human creative power itself is a repetition of, a small example of, the divine power'.[21]

Whether sub-creation produces something new hinges on how we understand 'new'. Tolkien appears to avoid any interpretation of sub-creation as creation *ex nihilo* in his emphasis on the organic growth of fantasy out of the soils of tradition – summed up by his image of the 'Tree of Tales'.[22] He differentiates between our creating and God's creation on this basis. While we cannot design a new leaf entirely, he writes, 'each leaf ... is a unique embodiment of the pattern' and 'Spring is, of course, not really less beautiful because we have seen or heard of other like events.'[23] Sub-creation is rather the fulfillment of latent possibilities, present from the first creation.[24] Sub-creation is also linked to a regaining of knowledge,

---

[19] Hart, 'Tolkien, Creation, and Creativity', 46.

[20] Randall Helms, 'All Tales Need Not Come True', *Studies in the Literary Imagination* 14, no. 2 (1981), 40.

[21] Helms, 'All Tales Need Not Come True', 41.

[22] Joanny Moulin, 'J. R. R. Tolkien's "Eucatastrophe" or Fantasy as a Modern Recovery of Faith' in *Re-embroidering the Robe: Faith Myth and Literary Creation Since 1850*, ed. Suzanne Bray, Adrienne Gavin and Peter Merchant (Newcastle: Cambridge Scholars Publishing, 2008), 78.

[23] J. R. R. Tolkien, 'On Fairy-Stories', in *Tree and Leaf* (London: HarperCollins, 2001), 56–57.

[24] Hart, 'Tolkien, Creation, and Creativity', 52.

a 'recollection of what we have always known but have forgotten how to see'.[25]

Of course, Tolkien's views on sub-creation must fall within a broader doctrine of creation. Donald Williams suggests that Tolkien grounds a resistance to reductionism into the very *createdness* of the world and of humans.[26] Williams draws on Francis Schaeffer to make a connection explicit that he believes that Tolkien would affirm: 'we are such irrepressible inventors and expressors of ourselves because we are made in the image of the Creator'.[27]

Sub-creation in Tolkien's Narrative

Perhaps one of the greatest differences between Tolkien's sub-creation and Hefner's co-creation is Tolkien's extensive use of narrative to convey his understanding of creativity. The Ainulindalë myth tells the story of Ilúvatar (the one sovereign god) and his creation of the Ainur (demi-gods) within his creation of Middle-earth.[28] Using the metaphor of making music, Tolkien sketches a participatory model of creativity, with Ilúvatar inviting the Ainur to add their own artistic efforts in adornment to his major music theme. The resultant harmony is a development of Ilúvatar's original theme, i.e. the Ainur do not create in the same way as Ilúvatar but rather ornament his creation.[29] Nevertheless, the Ainur are able to make a distinct contribution to Ilúvatar's creation and are given both freedom and responsibility to do so.[30] In Tolkien's mythology,

[25] Flieger, *Splintered Light*, 25.
[26] Donald Williams, *Mere Humanity: G. K. Chesterton C. S. Lewis, and J. R. R. Tolkien on the Human Condition* (Nashville, TN: B. & H. Publishing, 2006), 44.
[27] Williams, *Mere Humanity*, 44; cf. Francis Schaeffer, *Art and the Bible* (Downers Grove, IL: InterVarsity Press, 1973), 34–35. Certainly, Tolkien makes this claim with respect to Fantasy (*OFS*, 56). Here there are resonances with the theological analogies between human and divine creativity offered by Maritain and Sayers, near contemporaries of Tolkien, as described in Chapter 2.
[28] *Silmarillion*, 15–22.
[29] Hart, 'Tolkien, Creation, and Creativity', 44.
[30] *Ibid.*, 51.

however, humans are granted further creative responsibility even than the Ainur.

'but to Men I [Ilúvatar] will appoint a task and give a great gift'. And he devised that they should have free will and the power of fashioning and designing beyond the original music of the Ainu, that by reason of their operations all things shall in shape and deed be fulfilled, and the world that comes of the music of the Ainu be completed unto the last and smallest.[31]

Flieger contends that Tolkien envisioned a clear 'apotheosis in which the discord of the original Music would be harmonized in the Second Music, which explicitly includes Men in its performance'.[32] Tolkien wrote that the making of elves and humans in his creation myth was intended 'partly to redress the evil of the rebel Melkor, partly for the completion of all'.[33] While the myth is told from the elves' point of view, and does not concern itself with human activity, the creativity of the Ainur remains subordinate to that of Ilúvatar. They require his endorsement of their efforts and his speaking them into existence; until Ilúvatar pronounces '*Eä!* Let these things Be!' the Ainur's inventions exist only in their imaginations.[34]

The neatest illustration of sub-creation is given in *Leaf by Niggle*, usually interpreted as a biographical allegory.[35] Niggle is a

---

[31] This is the earliest version of Tolkien's myth, found in J. R. R. Tolkien, *The Book of Lost Tales Part I*, ed. Christopher Tolkien (London: Houghton Mifflin, 1986), 61. Hart demonstrates that the original drafts of the Ainulindulë represented the contribution of creaturely artistry and creation to God's world in stronger terms (Hart, 'Tolkien, Creation, and Creativity', 50).

[32] Verlyn Flieger, 'The Music and The Task: Fate and Free Will in Middle-Earth', in *Green Suns and Faerie: Essays on J. R. R. Tolkien* (Kent, OH: Kent State University Press, 2012), 36.

[33] *Letters*, 147.

[34] *Silmarillion*, 20.

[35] Tom Shippey, *J. R. R. Tolkien: Author of the Century* (Boston, MA: Houghton Mifflin, 2002), 266–277. Shippey interprets it as an expression of Tolkien's guilt over neglecting his academic writing and publishing for his writings on Middle-earth, as

painter, absorbed with an ever-expanding vision for his artwork, and resentful of the mundane intrusions on his time by visitors and necessary errands. From the very beginning we know that he is soon to depart on a long journey (death), and his garden remains neglected even as he despairs of finishing his painting. One particular painting becomes all-consuming, though he does divert his attention (albeit reluctantly) to fulfil his neighbourly obligations. When Niggle finally, belatedly, embarks on his required journey, he finds his meagre attempts at art realised in glorious actuality, made all the better by the collaborative efforts of his gardener neighbour. Yet the painting he made during his life is credited as a true glimpse of the ultimate splendour that was to come.[36] We see, therefore, a correspondence between sub-creation and a type of continuing creation (the phrase 'effoliation of creation' seems particularly apt in this context) that perhaps hints at Tolkien's hope for his own earthly projects.

The Limits of Sub-creation

We can also best understand the *limits* of sub-creation by reference to Tolkien's stories. Shippey points out that, for Tolkien, creative urges run along a spectrum from Melkor's entirely self-centred impulse (which Tolkien equates with the work of a 'magician') to wholly legitimate avenues (fantasy and sub-creation).[37] These are not easily distinguished and can shade into each other.[38] Hart terms both ends of the spectrum as sub-creation, which can take the form:

> both of a responsible and respectful creativity – making music in accord with Ilúvatar's own design and the fruitful possibilities pregnant within it – in which creaturely vocation is, as it were, fulfilled;

well as both his fears and hopes for the fantasy that so occupied his time (*ibid.*, 272–273).

[36] LBN, 115.
[37] Shippey, *J. R. R. Tolkien*, 241.
[38] *Ibid.*, 241.

and an irresponsible and disrespectful (insubordinate) 'creativity' that, in its pursuit of autonomy and self-glorification, succeeds only in a temporary spoiling of what Ilúvatar has made.[39]

Melkor, one of the Ainur, most clearly represents the perils of sub-creation if misused. After describing the musical harmony created by Ilúvatar together with the Ainur, Tolkien continues: 'But as the theme progressed, it came into the heart of Melkor to interweave matters of his own imagining that were not in accord with the theme of Ilúvatar; for he sought therein to increase the power and glory of the part assigned to himself.'[40] Ilúvatar and Melkor engage in a duel of sorts, Melkor weaving discord into the melody and Ilúvatar responding with new themes that restore harmony, incorporating the 'most triumphant notes' of Melkor into Ilúvatar's own solemn pattern.[41] Ilúvatar is able to redeem Melkor's attempts at disharmony using his own superior skills and the music ceases in abrupt victory. Melkor oversteps the bounds in aspiring to a 'creativity like unto Ilúvatar's own'.[42]

In *The Lord of the Rings*, it is Saruman who offers the clearest example of sub-creation gone awry. His domain, Isengard, is described thus:

A strong place and wonderful was Isengard ... But Saruman had slowly shaped it to his shifting purposes, and made it better, as he thought, being deceived – for all those arts and subtle devices for which he forsook his former wisdom, and which fondly he imagined were his own, came but from Mordor; so that what he made was naught, only a little copy, a child's model or a slave's flattery, of that vast fortress, armoury prison, furnace of great power, Barad-dûr, The Dark Tower, which suffered no rival, and laughed

---

[39] Hart, 'Tolkien, Creation, and Creativity', 46–47.
[40] *Silmarillion*, 16.
[41] *Ibid.*
[42] Hart, 'Tolkien, Creation, and Creativity', 47.

at flattery, biding its time, secure in its pride and its immeasurable strength.[43]

We see here the impulse to dominate present in corrupted co-creative activity; there are echoes of Heidegger in Tolkien's warning that will be explored later in this chapter.

We can also learn about these limits from Samwise Gamgee, as he resists the temptation to claim the Ring, and all the power it would afford him, for his own.

> In that hour of trial it was the love of his master that helped most to hold him firm; but also deep down in him lived still unconquered his plain hobbit-sense: he knew in the core of his heart that he was not large enough to bear such a burden ... The one small garden of a free gardener was all his need and due, not a garden swollen to a realm; his own hands to use, not the hands of others to command.[44]

His response requires two things: a greater love and a knowledge of his own limitations. He knows who he is and thus can reject the Ring's power.[45] Humility is clearly a virtue that guides proper sub-creation, and Sam recognises the rightful proportions of his creative domain in his modest efforts in the Shire.

In examining these instances of sub-creation used and misused, we can see that the notion of sub-creation immediately asserts some boundaries that are not as evident in other co-creation theologies. The sub-creator cannot create *ex nihilo*, rather 'each shall choose forever from the all'.[46] Sub-creation is a mimetic art that can only reshape or reform existing material. Even in sub-creation, Tolkien believed it was necessary to preserve certain fundamentals, such

---

[43] *TT*, 160–161.

[44] *RK*, 177.

[45] Eric Katz, 'The Rings of Tolkien and Plato: Lessons in Power, Choice, and Morality', in *The Lord of the Rings and Philosophy: One Book to Rule Them All*, ed. Gregory Bassham and Eric Bronson (Chicago, IL: Open Court, 2003), 18.

[46] 'Mythopoeia', 90.

as divine sovereignty and the goodness of creation.[47] For all must be under the will of God, 'in every world on every plane'.[48] In the Ainulindulë, Hart contends that 'our creaturely creativity' is set in 'proper theological perspective'.[49] After redirecting and overcoming Melkor's discordant efforts, Ilúvatar reiterates that 'no theme may be played that hath not its uttermost source in me'.[50]

Sub-creation and Reality

Before we turn to the challenge of how sub-creation might inform contemporary reflection on human enhancement, Tolkien's championing of the imagination in the way we construct and are compelled by particular visions of human existence bears closer examining. Tolkien was notoriously resistant to the classification of his works as allegory;[51] reviewer Roger Lancelyn Green appeals against allegorising the work too with his assertion that 'To seek for the meaning is to cut open the ball in search of its bounce'.[52]

Hopefully without destroying the bounce, we now turn to the real-world implications of sub-creation. It is clear through reading Tolkien that his theory of sub-creation was primarily developed with respect to the creation of *imaginary* worlds in literature. But is sub-creation restricted to the realm of fiction? Robley Evans contends the opposite: 'Tolkien tells us [in *OFS*] that the vital creative act is that of the imagination which perceives ultimate truth. Its vehicle is Secondary Creation, the fantastic breaking through the limitations of preconceived response, and revealing an essentially sacred reality.'[53] Tolkien argues that 'fairy-story has its own mode

---

47 Hart, 'Tolkien, Creation, and Creativity', 43.
48 *Letters*, 191.
49 Hart, 'Tolkien, Creation, and Creativity', 44, emphasis original.
50 *Silmarillion*, 17.
51 *Letters*, 144.
52 As cited in *Letters*, 388.
53 Robley Evans, 'Tolkien's World-Creation: Degenerative Recurrence', *Mythlore* 14, no. 1 (1987), 5.

of reflecting "truth"', a mode more powerful than simple allegory or realism.[54] 'Myth and fairy-story must, as all art, reflect and contain in solution elements of moral and religious truth (or error) but not explicit, not in the known form of the primary "real" world.'[55] Certain aspects of truth can *only* be received through the mediums of legend and myth.[56] Tolkien claims a moral objective too, pursuing 'the elucidation of truth, and the encouragement of good morals in this real world, by the ancient device of exemplifying them in unfamiliar embodiments, that may tend to "bring them home"'.[57]

Fiction is able to bypass the 'dissecting intellect' to reach imagination and intuition.[58] Duriez sees fiction as a medium for communicating religious ideas that would appeal more directly to the imagination. 'Tolkien was the master of the allusive story, relying on his deep faith in a natural theology of the imagination, in which the insights incarnate in the tale would be a vehicle of God's grace to the reader.'[59] Kevin Pask traces how the 'fairy way of writing' (i.e. fantasy) became the natural forum for expressing religious belief by Tolkien's time, highlighting predecessor George MacDonald's work as a prime example.[60] Nagy suggests that for Tolkien myth itself can be salvific – employed appropriately, myth is a device that expresses truth in continuity with tradition.[61] Jeffrey

[54] *Letters*, 233.
[55] *Ibid.*, 144.
[56] J. R. R. Tolkien, *The Silmarillion*, 1st edn, ed. by Christopher Tolkien (London: HarperCollins, 1999), xv.
[57] *Letters*, 194.
[58] Flieger, *Splintered Light*, 10.
[59] Colin Duriez, 'The Fairy Story: J. R. R. Tolkien and C. S. Lewis', in *Tree of Tales: Tolkien Literature and Theology*, ed. Trevor Hart and Ivan Khovacs (Waco, TX: Baylor University Press, 2007), 16.
[60] Kevin Pask, *The Fairy Way of Writing: Shakespeare to Tolkien* (Baltimore, MD: Johns Hopkins University Press, 2013), 123.
[61] Gergely Nagy, 'Saving the Myths: The Re-Creation of Mythology in Plato and Tolkien', in *Tolkien and the Invention of Myth: A Reader*, ed. Jane Chance (Lexington, KY: University of Kentucky Press, 2004), 95–96.

applauds Tolkien's work as a refutation to critical claims that grand narratives no longer exist.[62] Rather, literature offers 'shareable truth', which in turn sustains its social authority.[63] While Jeffrey would accord the ability to fully nourish the moral character to the 'Greater Book' alone (his approbation of Tolkien stems from the fact that he drew on the 'common treasure' of the scriptures), he asserts 'the power of literature to enable our will to truth'.[64]

Ursula Le Guin defends the ability of fantasy fiction to convey truths about the human condition, suggesting that 'realism is perhaps the least adequate means of understanding or portraying the incredible realities of our existence'.[65] Iris Murdoch, speaking of artistic production more generally, argues that it 'pierces the veil and gives sense to the notion of reality which lies beyond appearance'.[66] Gaiman describes the motivation for his move away from journalism to writing fiction as the desire 'to be able to tell the truth without ever needing to worry about the facts'.[67] In fact, Gaiman articulates specifically with respect to Tolkien (along with Lewis and Chesterton) that he learned from fiction 'that the best way to show people true things is from a direction that they had not imagined the truth coming'.[68] This confidence is not restricted to fiction writers either – David Sloan Wilson considers scientific and literary wisdom to be mutually reinforcing, rather than in competition, contending that 'the human mind, individually and

---

[62] David Lyle Jeffrey, 'Tolkien and the Future of Literary Studies', in *Tree of Tales: Tolkien Literature and Theology*, ed. Trevor Hart and Ivan Khovacs (Waco, TX: Baylor University Press, 2007), 65.

[63] Jeffrey, 'Tolkien and the Future of Literary Studies', 68.

[64] *Ibid.*, 70.

[65] Ursula Le Guin, 'National Book Award Acceptance Speech', in *Riverside Anthology of Children's Literature*, 6th edn, ed. Judith Saltman (Boston, MA: Houghton Mifflin, 1985), 58.

[66] Iris Murdoch, *The Sovereignty of Good* (London: Routledge, 1970), 86.

[67] Neil Gaiman, *The View from the Cheap Seats: Selected Non-Fiction* (London: Headline Publishing, 2016), 1.

[68] Neil Gaiman, 'Three Authors: On Lewis, Tolkien and Chesterton', in *The View from the Cheap Seats: Selected Non-Fiction* (London: Headline Publishing, 2016), 38.

collectively in the form of culture, is impressively adapted to derive conviction without [scientific] proof'.[69]

Flieger gives reasons for why the fantasy genre is best suited for conveying certain truths – it is the natural vehicle of a mythic mode of thought that no longer prevails, it allows a 're-creation of that original participation of man with his world which Barfield postulated'.[70] Le Guin uses the same language in speaking of imagination and play in the context of science fiction and fantasy writing, defining play as 'recreation, re-creation, the recombination of what is known into what is new'.[71] Furthermore, 'distancing, the pulling back from "reality" in order to see it better, is perhaps the essential gesture of SF. It is by distancing that SF achieves aesthetic joy, tragic tension, and moral cogency.'[72]

Flieger argues that even the fantastic elements of Tolkien's work are strongly reminiscent of reality, of the Primary World, to use Tolkien's vocabulary. Considering *LOTR*, she suggests elves and hobbits are familiar in their humanity, that orcs behave like soldiers in every culture, and that even the Ring, which seems the most fantastic at first glance, is not so fantastic as it might appear. Rather, the Ring is 'a direct reference to the Primary World, a sign pointing to and standing for an inescapable, underlying reality or truth, a hard recognition of the human condition'.[73] It represents the way that people in reality are subject to power, swayed by greed or envy, vulnerable to injury.[74]

---

[69] In introduction to Jonathan Gottschall and David Sloan Wilson, eds., *The Literary Animal: Evolution and the Nature of Narrative* (Evanston, IL: Northwestern University Press, 2005), xxii.

[70] Flieger, 'Barfield's "Poetic Diction" and Splintered Light', 55.

[71] Ursula Le Guin, 'Why Are Americans Afraid of Dragons?' in *The Language of the Night: Essays on Fantasy and Science Fiction*, ed. Susan Wood (New York: Putnam, 1979), 41.

[72] Ursula Le Guin, 'On Norman Spinrad's "The Iron Dream"', *Science Fiction Studies* 1, no. 1 (1973), 43–44.

[73] Verlyn Flieger, *Green Suns and Faerie: Essays on J. R. R. Tolkien* (Kent, OH: Kent State University Press, 2012), 13.

[74] *Ibid.*, 12.

In its capacity to illuminate the Primary World, fantasy is a medium of revelation.[75] Even within *LOTR* the ability of story to impart truth and increase understanding is attested, as the hobbits learn more of their world and their place within it through the stories told by Tom Bombadil, and at Rivendell.[76] Lore-masters are highly honoured, preserving knowledge important for the Quest.[77] Kirstin Johnson alerts us to the way in which brothers Boromir and Faramir are contrasted in Tolkien's epic: Boromir 'care[d] little for lore, save the tales of old battles' while Faramir was 'otherwise in mind ... a lover of lore and of music'.[78] This is connected to their respective wisdom and ability to resist the Ring's corrupting pull.

Sandner gives a helpful account of how fantasy and its emphasis on *Faërie* connect with reality in Tolkien's thought: 'The promise of *Faërie* for Tolkien is a return to the world from which we have become estranged. Fantasy expresses a yearning for the world itself, in all its lost (or missing or exiled) fullness.'[79]

Despite the value he places on the imagination, Tolkien does not fall into the Romantic tendency to denigrate reason. He suggested that 'the keener and the clearer is the reason, the better fantasy will it make',[80] and that fantasy 'does not destroy or even insult Reason' but instead enhances scientific verity.[81] He represents this in his mythology in his description of the Light of Valinor (from which the sources of light in Middle-earth – the Silmarils, the phial

---

75 Kirstin Johnson, 'Tolkien's Mythopoesis', in *Tree of Tales: Tolkien Literature and Theology*, ed. Trevor Hart and Ivan Khovacs (Waco, TX: Baylor University Press, 2007), 33.

76 Johnson, 'Tolkien's Mythopoesis', 34.

77 Johnson gives the example of an 'old wives' tale' told to Gandalf in Gondor teaching him of the healing properties of the *kingsfoil* herb, enabling him to save the lives of Faramir, Eowyn and Merry (*ibid.*, 35).

78 *Ibid.*, 35; *RK*, Appendix A, 337.

79 David Sandner, '"Joy Beyond the Walls of the World": The Secondary WorldMaking of J. R. R. Tolkien and C. S. Lewis', in *J. R. R. Tolkien and His Literary Resonances*, ed. George Clark and Daniel Timmons (Westport, CT: Greenwood Press, 2000), 137.

80 *OFS*, 55.

81 *Ibid.*

of Galadrial, the sun, moon and stars – originate) as 'The light of art undivorced from reason, that sees things both scientifically (or philosophically) and imaginatively (or subcreatively) and says that they are good'.[82]

Yet there is a sense of knowing, according to Tolkien, that bypasses reason. He describes the experience of 'eucatastrophe' as a certainty of knowing something, yet

> I could not reproduce any argument that had led to this, though the sensation was the same as having been convinced by *reason* (if without reasoning). And I have since thought that one of the reasons why one can't recapture the wonderful argument or secret when one wakes up is simply because there was not one: but there was (often maybe) a direct appreciation by the mind (sc. Reason) but without the chain of argument we know in our time-serial life.[83]

Richards suggests that at times Tolkien's use of the imagination strongly resembled the *lectio divina* method of mediaeval monasticism.[84] The imaginative reaching towards truth is not always activity; rather, Tolkien articulated a sense of receptivity; waiting patiently on the insights of the imagination in the writing process.

> I daresay something had been going on in the 'unconscious' for some time, and that accounts for my feeling throughout, especially when stuck, that I was not inventing but reporting (imperfectly) and had at times to wait till 'what really happened' came through.[85]

This experience of Tolkien's illustrates the importance of discipline in the exercise of the imagination – he had schooled his mind to wait, to reflect. He speaks of the 'leaf-mould of the mind', from

[82] *Letters*, 148n.
[83] *Ibid.*, 101.
[84] Darielle Richards, 'The Creative Process of J. R. R. Tolkien and the Tradition of the Magus' (PhD diss., Pacifica Graduate Institute, 2005), 23.
[85] *Letters*, 211.

which stories grow 'out of all that has been seen or thought or read'.[86]

Tolkien cautiously claimed truth for his Secondary Worlds. Writers hope to be drawing on reality.[87] He describes the 'joy' of successful fantasy as 'a sudden glimpse of the underlying reality or truth'.[88] Yet in the *eucatastrophe* of the fantasy tale, Tolkien hesitantly claims more – that we may see a 'far-off gleam or echo of *evangelium* in the real world'.[89] The gospel stories for Tolkien are the ultimate instance of sub-creation; in crossing over into the primary world 'the desire and aspiration of sub-creation has been raised to the fulfilment of Creation'.[90] It is because of this 'Great Eucatastrophe' that Christians hope for the redemption of their own sub-creation, and the possibility that they 'may actually assist in the effoliation and multiple enrichment of creation'.[91] Tolkien believed this for his own work, claiming that in his writing he 'had the sense of recording what was already "there" ... not of "inventing"'.[92]

Nils Ivar Agöy explores Tolkien's hope that the fruits of human creativity would finally be redeemed in the new creation.[93] We see this hope expressed most fully perhaps in *Leaf by Niggle*. Niggle's painting, dismissed by many in the tale as amateur daubing, a distraction from Niggle's duties, appears in the next world in full splendour, dazzlingly real. The story is particularly meaningful when we understand that Tolkien wrote it while having difficulties with the writing of *LOTR* – we can read the character of Niggle as conveying Tolkien's own worries over never completing his

---

[86] As quoted in Carpenter, *J. R. R. Tolkien*, 237–238.
[87] *OFS*, 71.
[88] *Ibid.*
[89] *Ibid.*
[90] *Ibid.*, 72.
[91] *Ibid.*, 73.
[92] *Letters*, 145.
[93] Nils Ivar Agöy, '*Quid Hinieldus cum Christo?* New Perspectives on Tolkien's Theological Dilemma and His Sub-creation Theory', *Mythlore* 21 (1996), 34.

art, and the constant need to perfect each piece rather than move on, and the plot as revealing Tolkien's hopes that his creativity is connected to the real world in some way.

Certainly, this hope was based on Tolkien's Christian conviction, his belief that stories are hallowed by the 'Evangelium'.[94] Williams identifies in Tolkien's work 'a wholeness of vision that increasingly eludes us', drawing on a humanity that remained unfragmented by reductionist philosophies.[95] This wholeness is made possible because 'body and spirit, history and myth, imagination and reason all found their unity, as indeed all reality does, in the creative and incarnated Logos which is also the ultimate paradigm of humanity'.[96]

Given the hopes that Tolkien harboured for the real-world implications of sub-creation, it may well be that his account of creativity is able to remedy some of the deficits in Hefner's model. Before we consider the specific questions that arise from applying Tolkien's thought to the subject of human enhancement, a short excursus into the connections between narrative, literature and our understanding of the good life will highlight the potential offerings of Tolkien's approach.

Narrative

Transhumanist Anders Sandberg argues that the scholarly debate over enhancement issues has largely ignored questions concerning flourishing and the meaning of life, 'perhaps because of the reluctance of postmodern academia to engage with "great stories" that provide an overarching explanation of life or give universal moral principles'.[97] This leads us quite naturally into a crucial resource for both reflecting on and shaping visions of a good life (which is obviously integral to the kinds of enhancements desired). Our

[94] OFS, 73.
[95] Williams, *Mere Humanity*, 133–134.
[96] *Ibid.*, 134.
[97] Sandberg, 'Transhumanism and the Meaning of Life', 8.

ability to reason about things, including technology, is determined by the framing we give a particular situation, by the metaphorical concepts that we use to categorise it.[98] And metaphor, in turn, is associated with and partially incorporated into another category that is central to the moral imagination: narrative.

Charles Taylor connects the communal aspect of defining human flourishing with narrative, which he sees as an 'inescapable' part of decision-making regarding the good life.[99] James K. A. Smith similarly locates the power of communicating visions of the good life in story and myth: 'Because we are affective before we are cognitive ..., visions of the good get inscribed in us by means that are commensurate with our primarily affective, imaginative nature.'[100] Furthermore,

> A particular vision of the good life becomes embedded in our dispositions or 'adaptive unconscious' by being *pictured* in concrete, alluring ways that attract us at a noncognitive level ... Such pictures appeal to our adaptive unconscious because they traffic in the stuff of embodiment and affectivity. Stories seep into us – and stay there and haunt us – more than a report on the facts.[101]

Liturgies, according to Smith, inculcate in us particular visions of the good life precisely because they are *story*-laden practices, which over time 'conscript us into the story they "tell" by showing'.[102]

Symbol and metaphor, as Alexander Lucie-Smith points out, are the 'stuff of story' – though human constructs, 'they represent our deepest appropriation of reality'.[103] Tolkien recognised the

---

[98] Mark Johnson, *Moral Imagination: Implications of Cognitive Science for Ethics* (Chicago, IL: University of Chicago Press, 1993), 2.

[99] Charles Taylor, *Sources of the Self: The Making of the Modern Identity* (Cambridge, MA: Harvard University Press, 1989), 51.

[100] Smith, *Desiring the Kingdom*, 53.

[101] *Ibid.*, 58.

[102] Smith, *Imagining the Kingdom*, 109.

[103] Alexander Lucie-Smith, *Narrative Theology and Moral Theology: The Infinite Horizon* (Aldershot: Ashgate, 2007), 2.

centrality of narrative to human existence, arguing that 'to ask what is the origin of stories, is to ask what is the origin of the mind, and of language'.[104] Understanding theology in narrative terms does not diminish God in any way, but rather 'may represent our most profound understanding of God' and divine revelation.[105] It is thus 'a mistake to assume too stark a polarity between the particularity of narrative and the universal import of abstract rationality'.[106]

Like metaphor, narrative has enjoyed recent attention in the evolutionary and cognitive sciences. A prototypical story maps well onto one of the most fundamental metaphors with which we conceive of human action: the 'source-path-goal' schema or 'journey' understanding.[107] David Sloan Wilson hypothesises that human adaptation to particular environments is partly accomplished through narrative construction.[108] Hefner also attests to the evolutionary significance of myth and story, citing a range of scientific resources that support the biological underpinnings of our capacity to construct contextualising narratives.

Stanley Hauerwas and L. Gregory Jones raised pertinent questions concerning the growing academic interest in narrative nearly thirty years ago. Though they recognise the significant contributions a narrative approach can bring to theology and ethics, they caution against an overly general appeal to 'narrative' that renders the notion unhelpful, as well as the tendency to apply it uncritically as part of a passing fad.[109] Appeals to narratives are not simply because we find 'stories' to be significant in some way,

---

[104] OFS, 17.
[105] Lucie-Smith, *Narrative Theology*, 2.
[106] *Ibid.*, 11.
[107] Johnson, *Moral Imagination*, 168.
[108] David Sloan Wilson, 'Evolutionary Social Constructivism', in *The Literary Animal: Evolution and the Nature of Narrative*, ed. Jonathan Gottschall and David Sloan Wilson (Evanston, IL: Northwestern University Press, 2005), 21.
[109] Stanley Hauerwas and L. Gregory Jones, 'Introduction: Why Narrative?' in *Why Narrative? Readings in Narrative Theology*, ed. Stanley Hauerwas and L. Gregory Jones (Grand Rapids, MI: Eerdmans, 1989), 1–2.

rather rationality, argumentation and historical understanding are fundamentally narrative in form.[110]

Lucie-Smith postulates that common precultural elements might exist in all stories – a shared structure that might point us towards some kind of universal truth.[111] While Lucie-Smith focuses mainly on developing a biblical hermeneutic,[112] an emphasis on narrative is often accompanied by an attention to the moral life. Though he eschews categorisation as a virtue ethicist,[113] Hauerwas immediately comes to mind as a thinker at the intersection of story and virtue.[114] Take, for example, his claim that 'The moral life is not simply a matter of decision governed by publicly defensible principles and rules; we can only act in the world we see, a seeing partially determined by the kind of beings we have become through the stories we have learned and embodied in our life plan.'[115]

Narrative is bound up with character, community and witness in Hauerwas' ecclesiology, which sees the imitation of God as the primary vocation of the church.[116] By attending to the narrative of Jesus' life we learn perfection from him, a learning process that Hauerwas argues can only be done as part of a community that practises virtues. As the 'historical Jesus' is impossible to know abstracted from the response of his followers, Hauerwas argues

---

[110] Hauerwas and Jones, 'Introduction', 4.

[111] Lucie-Smith, Narrative Theology, 74.

[112] Thus the examples he gives in the final chapter both involve interpreting specific scriptural passages (ibid., 199–206).

[113] While it is beyond the scope here to consider the category of virtue ethics more generally, Jennifer Herdt offers a helpful analysis of the reasons behind Hauerwas' aversion to the category ('Hauerwas Among the Virtues', Journal of Religious Ethics 40, no. 2 (2012), 212–213).

[114] Surveying the development of Hauerwas' engagement with the virtues, however, Herdt makes the convincing argument that his early focus on character and moral agency are replaced over time with the categories of community, tradition and narrative (ibid., 210).

[115] Stanley Hauerwas, 'The Self as Story: A Reconsideration of the Relation of Religion and Morality from the Agent's Perspective', Journal of Religious Ethics 1 (1973), 74.

[116] Stanley Hauerwas, The Peaceable Kingdom: A Primer in Christian Ethics (Notre Dame, IN: University of Notre Dame Press, 1983), 76–86.

that we ought instead to pay more attention to the narrative of Jesus' life recounted in the gospels. Though Hauerwas does not use the term imagination, surely his linking of moral action to a story-shaped perception of the world depends on the imaginative faculty.

Hauerwas' own emphasis on narrative brings to mind the work of Alasdair MacIntyre, who identifies humans as 'story-telling animals'. 'I can only answer the question "What am I to do?" if I can answer the prior question "Of what story or stories do I find myself a part?"'[117] Our ability to reason morally is developed within the context of our social relationships and early dependencies on others.[118] Johnson connects MacIntyre's ideas of narrative to a fuller theory of imagination, arguing that 'whatever human rationality consists in, it is certainly tied up with narrative structure and the question for narrative unity'.[119]

We also see narrative at work theologically (more accurately, from the perspective of analytical philosophy) in the defence Stump presents for God's allowing of suffering. Stump contends that 'narrative has a role to play in the discussion of certain philosophical issues, and what it contributes is not reducible to non-narrative philosophical explanation or expressible in non-narrative

---

[117] Alisdair MacIntyre, *After Virtue*, 2nd edn (Notre Dame, IN: University of Notre Dame Press, 1984), 216. A similar position is presented in Charles Taylor, *The Language Animal: The Full Shape of the Human Linguistic Capacity* (Cambridge, MA: Belknap Press, 2016). Hauerwas was already focused on narrative theology before the publication of MacIntyre's major works on the subject, so there is unlikely to be a direct correspondence. Hauerwas acknowledges the significant influence of MacIntyre for his work on virtue and politics, however, though his reading is broad and he is at least as indebted to John Howard Yoder, Iris Murdoch and Aquinas, among others (Stanley Hauerwas, *Hannah's Child: A Theologian's Memoir* (Grand Rapids, MI: Eerdmans, 2012), 68, 86, 160).

[118] Alisdair MacIntyre, *Dependent Rational Animals: Why Human Beings Need the Virtues* (London: Duckworth, 1999), 81–83.

[119] Mark Johnson, *The Body in the Mind: The Bodily Basis of Meaning Imagination and Reason* (Chicago, IL: University of Chicago Press, 1987), 172.

philosophical prose'.[120] Stump uses a selection of biblical narratives to illustrate a possible defence for the presence of suffering in a world created by God.

This all suggests that Hefner might find more helpful resources to articulate his theological anthropology were he to follow Nancey Murphy's epistemological lead away from Lakatos in the direction of MacIntyre. While MacIntyre's tradition-dependent rationality is not without its problems, he at least accords due significance to narrative and seeks to preserve some kind of truth-claim within that framework.[121] Additionally, though the broader field of bioethics has been approached previously from a narrative theological perspective,[122] human enhancement specifically has not been considered in the discourse.

The fundamental quality of storytelling and story comprehension as a human trait is driven home when we consider how poorly AI has been able to 'understand' narratives thus far. Hubert Dreyfus contends that AI researchers have laboured under a false cognitivist paradigm, thus overlooking the important point that processing facts is very different from comprehending stories.[123]

---

[120] Eleanore Stump, *Wandering in Darkness: Narrative and the Problem of Suffering* (Oxford: Oxford University Press, 2010), 22.

[121] We see this in Macintyre's discussion of the requirements narrative must fulfil in order to resolve epistemological crises (*Whose Justice? Which Rationality?* (London: Duckworth, 1988), 362).

[122] Greek Orthodox theologian Tristan Engelhardt, confronting what he describes as the 'irremedial plurality of postmodernity', rejects any claim to rationality in his grounding of Christian bioethics in liturgy (H. Tristan Engelhardt Jr, *The Foundations of Bioethics*, 2nd edn (New York: Oxford University Press, 1996), 9, 103–104, 167). For Engelhardt, meaning is conveyed in a 'content-full moral context' which appears to equate to the narratives operating in a particular tradition or community (*ibid.*, 277).

[123] Hubert Dreyfus, 'Overcoming the Myth of the Mental: How Philosophers Can Profit from the Phenomenology of Everyday Expertise', *Proceedings and Addresses of the American Philosophical Association* 79, no. 2 (2005), 48.

The Moral Value of Literature

The narrative structure of our own lives and cognitive processes is what gives fiction such power in developing our moral sensitivity.[124] 'Fictional narratives provide us rich, humanly realistic experimental settings in which we can make our own moral explorations.'[125] Science fiction in particular may be the 'ideal vehicle for a critique of science and technology'.[126] In Chapter 1 of this work, the purposes and functions of science fiction were briefly discussed. In his exploration of Mary Shelley's *Frankenstein* and its ongoing relevance to how we think about science and technology, van der Laan writes that 'the meditative thinking of literature as exemplified in *Frankenstein* offers an alternative and counterbalance, maybe even an antidote, to the calculative thinking of science and technology, possibly even a rescue from its dangers'.[127]

Treating speculative fiction as a serious subject of study is a step in the right direction. According to van der Laan, we must push back against the subordination of literature below the scientific-technological world view, exemplified in C. P. Snow's famous 'Two Cultures' speech.[128] Robinson, too, challenges the naturalistic model that rejects historical thinking, religious and theological, about the meaning of human existence, highlighting the degradation of the moral imagination that comes with such neglect.[129]

Imagination, literature and virtue have been more closely associated in the past. Brian Stock draws attention to the way the ancients read texts, giving careful contemplation to the vision presented by

---

[124] Johnson, *Moral Imagination*, 197.

[125] *Ibid.*, 198.

[126] van der Laan, 'Editor's Notes', 233.

[127] J. M. van der Laan, 'Frankenstein as Science Fiction and Fact', *Bulletin of Science Technology & Society* 30, no. 4 (2010), 303.

[128] van der Laan, 'Editor's Notes', 233; cf. C. P. Snow, *The Two Cultures* (Cambridge: Cambridge University Press, 1998).

[129] Marilynne Robinson, *Absence of Mind: The Dispelling of Inwardness from the Modern Myth of the Self* (New Haven, CT: Yale University Press, 2011), 32.

a text as a way to grow in the virtues.[130] Bieber Lake demonstrates the significance of the moral narrative for today in conveying larger visions by setting two narrative accounts alongside one another. Lee Silver and Flannery O'Connor both describe encounters with circus 'freaks', but whereas Silver draws on the experience to bolster a scientific naturalist rejection of the soul and 'spiritualist' interpretations of human being, O'Connor's similar encounter increases the imaginative possibilities of what it means to be human.[131]

Narrative and imagination are also connected to ethics – the imagination facilitates an emotional engagement with a particular narrative. According to Ward, this complements arguments put forward by Hauerwas and others that 'wish to show how narrative can function both as a form of rationality and as a shaper of character'.[132] Trevor Hart writes of the relationship between literature and ethics so that 'The imaginary cannot finally escape its genesis in the world of our actual experience, no matter how far the flights of analogical fancy may carry us, and like it or intend it or not, therefore, the artist is in some sense his ethical brother's keeper after all.'[133] This is demonstrated more fully by Steve Walker, who argues that Tolkien's main achievement in creating Middle-earth is the encouragement the reader receives to participate in the sub-creation.[134] We accept Tolkien's world as a vision of larger reality.[135] 'Experiencing the subcreations of Middle-earth makes us more capable of this-worldly creation, compounds our capacity for seeing the infinite potential not only in fiction but

[130] Brian Stock, 'Ethics and the Humanities: Some Lessons of Historical Experience', *New Literary History: A Journal of Theory and Interpretation* 36, no. 1 (2005), 11.

[131] Lake, *Prophets of the Posthuman*, 34–40.

[132] Graham Ward, 'Narrative and Ethics: The Structures of Believing and the Practices of Hope', *Literature and Theology* 20, no. 4 (2006), 455.

[133] Trevor Hart, 'Creative Imagination and Moral Identity', *Studies in Christian Ethics* 16, no. 1 (2003), 13.

[134] Steve Walker, *The Power of Tolkien's Prose: Middle-Earth's Magical Style* (New York: Palgrave Macmillan, 2009), 7.

[135] Walker, *The Power of Tolkien's Prose*, 25.

in life.'[136] Le Guin similarly upholds the power of narrative to shape virtue, writing that 'ethics flourishes in the timeless soil of Fantasy, where ideologies wither on the vine'.[137] Great fantasies often contain a moral dialectic, points out Le Guin, a motif of Light vs Darkness.[138] This is because 'fantasy is the natural, the appropriate, language for the recounting of the spiritual journey and the struggle of good and evil in the soul'.[139] Thus, Le Guin heralds science fiction author Philip K. Dick as a prophet, not because of his technological prescience, but rather because of the clarity of his moral vision.[140]

Beyond the more obviously imaginative capacity of fantasy literature, Martha Nussbaum describes the impact a tragedy may have for moral philosophy: 'it lays open to view the complexity, the indeterminacy, the sheer difficulty of actual human deliberation ... A tragedy does not display the dilemmas of its characters as pre-articulated; it shows them searching for the morally salient; and it forces us, as interpreters, to be similarly active.'[141] Nussbaum holds up the novel as particularly illuminating for enquiries into the human good, describing the narrative and emotional structures of novels as 'forms of Aristotelian ethical thinking'.[142]

---

[136] *Ibid.*, 173.

[137] Ursula Le Guin, 'European SF: Rottensteiner's Anthology, the Strugatskys, and Lem', *Science Fiction Studies* 1, no. 3 (1974), 183.

[138] Ursula Le Guin, 'The Child and the Shadow', in *The Language of the Night: Essays on Fantasy and Science Fiction*, ed. Susan Wood (New York: Putnam, 1979), 65.

[139] *Ibid.*, 68.

[140] Ursula Le Guin, 'The Modest One', in *The Language of the Night: Essays on Fantasy and Science Fiction*, ed. Susan Wood (New York: Putnam, 1979), 178.

[141] Martha Nussbaum, *The Fragility of Goodness: Luck and Ethics in Greek Tragedy and Philosophy* (Cambridge: Cambridge University Press, 1986), 14.

[142] Martha Nussbaum, 'Transcending Humanity', in *Love's Knowledge: Essays on Philosophy and Literature* (New York: Oxford University Press, 1990), 390–391. The relationship between literature and moral formation is a prominent theme throughout this collection of Nussbaum's essays. In another essay, Nussbaum declares that 'the novel is itself a moral achievement, and the well-lived life is a work of literary art' (Martha Nussbaum, '"Finely Aware and Richly Responsible": Literature and the Moral Imagination', in *Love's Knowledge: Essays on Philosophy and*

Within the context of medical ethics, P. Anne Scott argues that the moral imagination that is essential for practising medicine can be stimulated and nurtured through the 'serious reading of literature'.[143] Only by attending to this moral imagination, which Scott suggests is a composite faculty akin to an Aristotelian intellectual virtue, can practitioners develop the understanding and compassion required to treat their patients properly as persons.[144] She therefore calls for literature to be incorporated into medical and nursing curricula.[145] Shippey, in the parallels he draws between fictional explorations of evil offered by writers as diverse as Le Guin, Kurt Vonnegut, George Orwell and Tolkien, summarises the common way in which they reflect on personal experience through fiction. They are 'trying to explain something at once deeply felt and rationally inexplicable, something furthermore felt to be entirely novel and not adequately answered by the moralities of earlier ages'.[146] The writing and reading of fiction functions as a type of moral activity in these instances. Hart makes an even stronger case, suggesting that 'a training in the "art of understanding" ought always to incorporate engagement with imaginative literature of one sort or another as a means to the cultivation of a disciplined imagination'.[147]

Literature (New York: Oxford University Press, 1990), 148). She identifies in the work of the novelist Henry James an analogy between the creative imagination of the fiction writer, and the moral imagination if the person seeking to live an ethical life (*ibid.*). The attention is a significant element to this analogy – fictional texts that narrate positive moral commitments and experiences contribute to the moral development of readers who attend to them (*ibid.*, 149).

[143] P. Anne Scott, 'Imagination in Practice', *Journal of Medical Ethics* 23, no. 1 (1997), 49.

[144] *Ibid.*, 47.

[145] *Ibid.*, 50. Of course, she acknowledges the practical barriers to introducing more content into already crowded curricula.

[146] Shippey, *J. R. R. Tolkien*, 120.

[147] Trevor Hart, 'Imagination and Responsible Reading', in *Renewing Biblical Interpretation*, ed. Craig Bartholomew, Colin Greene and Karl Möller (Carlisle: Paternoster Press, 2000), 316.

What Is the Good Life?

It is all very well to talk of disciplining the imagination, but to what end? Discourse surrounding human enhancement technologies rarely asks the question: what constitutes a good life?[148] Will the use of enhancement technologies promote human flourishing? Graham suggests that emerging cybernetic, digital and genetic technologies 'call into question the deepest assumptions underlying our notions of normative and exemplary humanity'.[149] Probes into these underlying assumptions have tended to focus on the status of human nature (i.e. determined or plastic),[150] rather than the more abstract questions concerning human flourishing.[151]

Given the proliferation of human enhancement technologies and advocacy, addressing this neglect can only enrich contemporary discourse both on the good life and on the ethics of enhancement. Responses to human enhancement technology are derived from, and therefore may illuminate, underlying notions of what human flourishing ought to look like, and thus it is worth considering whether technology is compatible with human flourishing.

Technology itself is not necessarily in opposition to human flourishing. As Christina Bieber Lake points out, reflecting on the lessons from Nathaniel Hawthorne's short story 'The Birth-mark', 'it is thinking scientifically and technologically *first* about solving human problems that can do the greatest damage to persons

---

[148] Lake, *Prophets of the Posthuman*, 9.

[149] Graham, 'Bioethics After Posthumanism', 179.

[150] E.g. see Gerald McKenny, 'Biotechnology and the Normative Significance of Human Nature: A Contribution from Theological Anthropology', *Studies in Christian Ethics* 26, no. 1 (2013).

[151] Exceptions include Michael Burdett and Victoria Lorrimar, 'Creatures Bound for Glory: Biotechnological Enhancement and Visions of Human Flourishing', *Studies in Christian Ethics* 32, no. 2 (2019); Miriam Eilers, Katrin Grüber and Christoph Rehmann-Sutter, eds., *The Human Enhancement Debate and Disability: New Bodies for a Better Life* (Basingstoke: Palgrave Macmillan, 2014); Jonathan Cahill, 'Freedom for Life: Karl Barth, Transhumanism and Human Flourishing', *Ethics and Medicine: An International Journal of Bioethics* 30, no. 2 (2014), 81–95.

as persons within relationships'.[152] Turning to technology first to solve problems circumvents the cultivation of virtue, but this does not deny a place for technology in promoting human flourishing. In 1960, looking ahead to the potential of technology to address social ills, Charles Coulson warned that positive changes as a result of technology 'are possible only if we have a worthy view of man'.[153] Without such a view, technology may produce 'infinite harm', with it 'it may become a tool in the shaping of the Kingdom of Heaven on earth'.[154]

However, Bieber Lake ultimately finds transhumanism wanting because of its inadequate vision of human flourishing: 'transhumanism offers a false path to the good life. Transhumanism is wrong not because it promotes change, but because it promotes a dangerously thin definition of the good life, as if to be healthier, have a longer life, or experience less suffering will necessarily amount to a better life.'[155] The ends to which technology is employed in transhumanist thought are essentially 'a rejection of thousands of years of philosophical and theological thinking about what constitutes the highest and best life available to human beings'.[156]

Bieber Lake goes on to identify narrative as the only place in which we can flesh out what a good life ought to look like, for both humans and 'posthumans'.[157] She is not ruling out human enhancement in a rejection of transhumanism, simply countering the technological paradigm in which transhumanists operate, and the resultant understanding of (or lack of) the good life. It is interesting that Sandberg explicitly connects the lack of reflection on greater questions of human flourishing that surround enhancement issues

---

[152] Lake, *Prophets of the Posthuman*, 54, emphasis original.
[153] Charles Coulson, *Science Technology and the Christian* (London: Epsworth Press, 1960), 103.
[154] *Ibid.*, 103.
[155] Lake, *Prophets of the Posthuman*, 172.
[156] *Ibid.*, xii.
[157] *Ibid.*, 172.

with a lack of engagement with 'great stories',[158] a suggestion that narrative and imaginative approaches have an important role to play.

Sub-creation as a Response to Human Enhancement Issues

Tolkien as a writer did not shy away from these 'great stories' as a way of exploring and expressing truths of the human condition. As Hart reminds us, the Ainulindulë myth, though a fictional representation of angelic creativity, does convey how Tolkien thinks about human artistry.[159] Tolkien certainly harboured hope that his idea of sub-creation applied in the real world as well as the secondary world he created, but we are venturing into speculative territory by acknowledging such a possibility. We must not read Tolkien's writings as directly corresponding to a Christian world view (e.g. by equating the Ainulindulë with the creation account in Genesis, and thus reading a dualistic or polytheistic interpretation into Tolkien's theology).[160] It is more helpful to recognise the sacramental character of Tolkien's faith, its value of art and beauty for their own sake, and the freedom these affirmations gave him to imagine and inhabit worlds of his own invention.

The remainder of this chapter, therefore, explores how Tolkien's sub-creation proposal might inform real-world activity in theological perspective, all the while remembering that this goes beyond what Tolkien claimed with any assuredness. Going forward, Flieger's description of Tolkien's vision for the redemption of his Secondary World is taken as a starting point for thinking about human creativity in our own world:

> In a flawed and faulty Creation it is the task appointed for flawed and faulty human beings – struggling with the world around them,

---

[158] Sandberg, 'Transhumanism and the Meaning of Life', 8.
[159] Hart, 'Tolkien, Creation, and Creativity', 49.
[160] *Ibid.*, 43.

sometimes making false starts, often following twisting paths of which they themselves cannot always see the ends – to lead themselves and that world out of error and into light.[161]

Tolkien's Sub-creation vs. Hefner's Co-creation

As Hefner very clearly *does* claim the created co-creator designation as applicable to human activity in our world, we might begin by comparing the two approaches. Few scholars have set Hefner's co-creation and Tolkien's sub-creation against one another in even the briefest of comparisons. Peterson argues that sub-creation and co-creation have similar theological connotations, but differ in a slight but significant way:

> To sub-create is to imitate or to work on what has already been thought out. It may imply initiative on the local level, but it reminds us that the master task always belongs to God. The implication of co-creator, however, is radically different, for it suggests that we are as much in control or responsible for creation as God is. It suggests that there is no blueprint for the future; the future is open, not determined.[162]

Peterson may claim more for human creativity than Hefner intends in his interpretation; however, this is a common criticism of the created co-creator.[163] Both Hefner's co-creation and Tolkien's sub-creation acknowledge that human creativity is contingent on and derivative of God's creative activity.[164] Hefner's choice of terminology emphasises the fact that humans are created beings, even as they are creators. Tolkien wishes to highlight this also, noting that 'we make in our measure and our derivative mode, because we are made: and not only made, but made in the image

---

[161] Flieger, 'The Music and The Task', 40.
[162] Peterson, 'The Created Co-creator', 829.
[163] Case-Winters, 'Rethinking the Image of God', 821.
[164] Hefner, *THF*, 39.

and likeness of a Maker'.[165] Hefner explicitly identifies the capacity of humans to co-create with the *imago Dei*;[166] Tolkien seems to be making the same point.[167]

Yet sub-creation does not merely offer a terminological refinement of alternative co-creation theologies. What does Tolkien's proposal contribute that is not sufficiently supplied by Hefner's thought? Where sub-creation departs from co-creation is in its emphasis on the existence of divine norms, or templates, to human creativity. Charles Birch provides a helpful analogy: 'A note on a tuning fork elicits a response from a piano because the piano already has in it a string tuned to the same note. The individual entities of creation have within their subjective nature "strings" tuned to the persuasive influence of God for their immediate future.'[168]

The work of sub-creation respects the true nature of the subject, even while developing it towards its imagined purpose. 'By the forging of Gram cold iron was revealed; by the making of Pegasus horses were ennobled.'[169] Thus bad sub-creation is a perversion of an essence; Orcs, for example, are described as 'rational incarnate creatures, though horribly corrupted' by Melkor.[170]

Hart, speculating over the revisions Tolkien made to the Ainulindalë, suggests that he was especially sensitive to claiming too much for human creativity. He reads Tolkien's adjustments as a desire to avoid 'an unacceptable blurring of the boundaries between divine and creaturely prerogatives' (i.e. the very sin of Melkor).[171]

---

[165] *OFS*, 56.
[166] Hefner, 'Biocultural Evolution', 347.
[167] Greene, 'Higher Argument', 48–49.
[168] Charles Birch, 'Neo-Darwinism, Self-Organization, and Divine Action in Evolution', in *Evolutionary and Molecular Biology: Scientific Perspectives on Divine Action*, ed. Robert J. Russell, William R. Stoeger and Francisco J. Ayala (Vatican City State and Berkeley, CA: Vatican Observatory & CTNS, 1998), 244.
[169] *OFS*, 59.
[170] *Letters*, 190.
[171] Hart, 'Tolkien, Creation, and Creativity', 51.

As discussed previously, Tolkien was acutely aware of the potential for 'creative desire' to be corrupted. Sub-creation 'may become possessive, clinging to the things made as "its own", the sub-creator wishes to be the lord and God of his private creation'.[172]

Finally, Tolkien's notion of sub-creation does full justice to the role of the imagination in human co-creativity. Tolkien rejects the constraints of a scientific anthropology that limits Hefner's approach and does not shy away from claiming certain knowledge that cannot be explained through reason alone. In his refusal to set reason and the imagination against one another, there is room in his epistemology to consider aspects of human creativity, particularly in relation to divine creativity, that cannot be articulated in scientific terms.

Tolkien and Technology

Where Hefner may have the advantage over Tolkien is in his general openness to technology. At first glance, Tolkien is an unlikely interlocutor when it comes to the role of technology in human creative activity. Many of Tolkien's writings express his concerns over developments in technology during his own lifetime. Carpenter offers the amusing anecdote of how Tolkien, towards the end of his life, scrawled 'Not a penny for Concorde' emphatically across one of his tax cheques.[173]

Though Tolkien believed that fantasy and science were mutually enriching, he likely also shared fellow Inkling Owen Barfield's concerns that the scientific approach was encroaching on the imaginative sphere: 'first they insist on cutting out awe and reverence and wisdom and substituting sophistication as the goal of knowledge; and then they talk about this method with reverence and

---

[172] *Letters*, 145.
[173] Carpenter, *J. R. R. Tolkien*, 244.

awe'.[174] In one of his letters, he equates the modern manifestation of the 'evil spirit' in the world with mechanism and 'scientific' materialism.[175]

Towards some of the aims of transhumanism in particular, Tolkien might have been especially critical. Wood suggests that 'in the Sauronic temptation to live longer but not better, Tolkien is offering his own critical commentary on our death-fearing, life-worshipping culture.'[176] Catherine Madsen reminds us of how prominent loss and a sense of fading is in Tolkien's work. *LOTR* is a story not only of how the Ring is unmade but also of how the Elves disappeared from Middle-earth, making way for the Dominion of Men.[177] This sense of finitude, and even of tragedy, does not seem at all compatible with a transhumanist perspective.

It would be easy to discount Tolkien as opposed to technology in the way that older generations are often suspicious of new developments; however, Tolkien appears to have been quite reflective on the matter. How Tolkien primarily views technology is seen in his definition of the 'Machine' as 'all use of external plans or devices (apparatus) instead of development of the inherent inner properties or talents – or even the use of these talents with the corrupted motive of dominating: bulldozing the real world, or coercing other wills.'[178] Furthermore, this 'Machine' is the end result of the desire for Power that stems from possessive and hubristic sub-creation.[179] The misuses and abuses of technology are insidious, and often spring from good intentions.

---

[174] Owen Barfield, *Worlds Apart: A Dialogue of the 1960's* (Middletown, CT: Wesleyan University Press, 1964), 21–22.

[175] *Letters*, 110.

[176] Ralph Wood, 'Tolkien's Augustinian Understanding of Good and Evil: Why *The Lord of the Rings* Is Not Manichean', in *Tree of Tales: Tolkien Literature and Theology*, ed. Trevor Hart and Ivan Khovacs (Waco, TX: Baylor University Press, 2007), 90.

[177] Catherine Madsen, '"Light from an Invisible Lamp": Natural Religion in *The Lord of the Rings*', in *Tolkien and the Invention of Myth: A Reader*, ed. Jane Chance (Lexington, KY: University of Kentucky Press, 2004), 42.

[178] *Letters*, 145–146.

[179] *Ibid.*, 145.

The Enemy in successive forms is always 'naturally' concerned rather with sheer Domination, and so the Lord of magic and machines; but the problem: that this frightful evil can and does arise from an apparently good root, the desire to benefit the world and others – speedily and according to the benefactor's own plans – is a recurrent motive.[180]

Saruman was mentioned earlier as an example of corrupted sub-creation at work. In an etymological analysis of the name 'Saruman', Tom Shippey suggests it conveys more than just the notion of 'cunning man', but a kind of mechanical ingenuity, a 'smithcraft developed into engineering'.[181] Saruman represents the extreme manifestation of a sickness also present in Sandyman, the miller in the Shire. This disease, according to Shippey, 'starts as an intellectual curiosity, develops as engineering skill, turns into greed and the desire to dominate, corrupts further into a hatred and contempt of the natural world which goes beyond any rational desire to use it'.[182]

Part of the disenchantment Tolkien accorded to technology (specifically in the context of war), argues Garth, is the notion that effort is rendered meaningless by failure. Worth was no longer intrinsic – instinctive and inspirational values that required upholding – rather it was attached to end results.[183] For Tolkien, the dangerous human preoccupation with technology 'sticks out so plainly and is so horrifyingly exhibited in our time, with its even worse menace for the future, that it seems an almost world-wide mental disease that only a tiny minority perceive it'.[184] The Hobbit lifestyle is depicted as ideal – the Shire abounds in gardens, trees, and farms cultivated without the use of machinery.

---

[180] Ibid., 146.
[181] Shippey, J. R. R. Tolkien, 170.
[182] Ibid., 171.
[183] John Garth, Tolkien and the Great War: The Threshold of Middle-Earth (London: HarperCollins, 2003), 303.
[184] Letters, 88.

Its residents enjoy the simple pleasures of good plain food and a pipe.[185] It is for this reason that Hobbits were chosen to bear the Ring – they alone could resist its power because ambition was not a part of their nature.[186] In *LOTR*, the replacement of the water-mill in the Shire with its industrial equivalent, seen by Sam in the Mirror of Galadriel, is described as 'devilry'.[187] It is no coincidence that Sam is the gardener of the tale. The gardening metaphor is used throughout Tolkien's works to illustrate his understanding of sub-creation. Even more illuminating, perhaps, is the fact that Tolkien regarded Samwise as the true hero of *LOTR*.[188] Alun Morgan highlights Sam as the exemplar for the virtue of stewardship in the tale, connecting his role as gardener with a heightened appreciation of human solidarity with the natural world.[189]

Joshua Hren identifies in Tolkien's work a diagnosis of the same 'technocratic paradigm' that Pope Francis critiques in the 2015 encyclical *Laudato si'*.[190] In such a paradigm, the scientific method is the primary methodology, and the goal is control, mastery and manipulation.[191] In Tolkien's writings, this approach to technology is represented as the 'Machine', described above. The Ring itself symbolises for Tolkien 'the will to mere power, seeking to make itself objective by physical force and mechanism, and so inevitably by lies'.[192] Hren detects an echo of Heidegger's analysis of modern technology – the use of the Ring to impose force over others

---

[185] Tolkien identifies himself as a Hobbit, finding enjoyment in the same pleasures (*Letters*, 288–289).
[186] *Ibid.*, 158.
[187] *FR*, 278.
[188] *Letters*, 161.
[189] Alun, Morgan, 'The Lord of the Rings: A Mythos Applicable in Unsustainable Times?' *Environmental Education Research* 16, nos. 3–4 (2010), 396.
[190] Joshua Hren, 'Tolkien and the Technocratic Paradigm' *New Blackfriars* 99, no. 1079 (2018), 97.
[191] *Ibid.*, 97.
[192] *Letters*, 160.

(and objects) results in the treatment of these others and objects as a 'standing reserve'.[193] In our increasing dependence on machines and technology, our wills become 'standing reserve' in much the same way that the Ring draws to itself and masters the wills that use it.

Also drawing parallels between Tolkien and Heidegger, Simon Malpas argues that the two scholars shared a common struggle to understand community in the context of rapid industrialisation and technological growth.[194] Heidegger's famous notion of the 'standing reserve' (*Bestand*),[195] in which everything (including nature) is construed and conscripted for technological use, would likely have met with Tolkien's approbation.

Heidegger points us to the etymology of *technê*. *Technê* concerned not only the practical crafts in the early Greek context but also the arts. '*Techne* belongs to bringing-forth, to *poiesis*; it is something poietic.'[196] Heidegger additionally connects this to the Greek word *alētheia*, or 'truth', arguing that technology is a means of revealing truth.[197] While *technê* and *poiesis* have a traditional connection in meaning, modern technology has diverged from poetry away from 'revealing' and towards 'challenging-forth' (*Herausfordern*).[198] Modern technology 'puts to nature the unreasonable demand that it supply energy that can be extracted and stored as such'.[199]

Tolkien grasped this same important truth that technology itself is not neutral. He illustrates this point in Boromir's arguments

[193] Hren, 'Tolkien and the Technocratic Paradigm', 102.
[194] Simon Malpas, 'Home', in *Reading The Lord of the Rings: New Writings on Tolkien's Trilogy*, ed. Robert Eaglestone (London: Continuum, 2005), 86.
[195] Martin Heidegger, 'The Question Concerning Technology', in *The Question Concerning Technology and Other Essays*, trans. William Lovitt (New York: Harper Perennial, 1977), 19.
[196] *Ibid.*, 13.
[197] *Ibid.*, 13. Although it should be noted that Heidegger later, in *Being and Time*, corrected the linking of *alētheia* with truth, speaking instead in terms of 'disclosing'.
[198] *Ibid.*, 14.
[199] *Ibid.*, 14.

concerning the Ring, when he argues against its destruction and instead implores: 'Why should we not think that the Great Ring has come into our hands to serve us in the very hour of need? Wielding it the Free Lords of the Free may surely defeat the Enemy.'[200] Gandalf and Galadriel, however, both refused to use, or even possess, the Ring, recognising that it would eventually corrupt them despite their good intentions. Even Elrond would not take the Ring to hide it, saying that 'the very desire of it corrupts the heart'.[201] For the Ring is the Machine par excellence. Malpas suggests that it might even be equated with the technological imperative itself; to rid the world of this imperative is thus Frodo's quest.[202]

For Tolkien, technology is bound up with coercion, manifested most strongly in the wars of the twentieth century.[203] Shippey describes the modern vice detested by Tolkien as 'a kind of restless ingenuity, skill without purpose, bulldozing for the sake of change'.[204] Thus, Tolkien declares in 'Mythopoeia'

> I will not walk with your progressive apes
> Erect and sapient. Before them gapes
> The dark abyss to which their progress tends

He further rejects the technological world view and makes his own stand.

> Your world immutable wherein no part
> The little maker has with maker's art

[200] FR, 280–281.

[201] Ibid., 281.

[202] Malpas, 'Home', 88. Note that Malpas critiques a simplistic reading of LOTR as a victory over development, highlighting the tale's more ambivalent conclusion (ibid., 88).

[203] Ralph Wood, 'Tolkien and Postmodernism', in Tolkien Among the Moderns, ed. Ralph Wood (Notre Dame, IN: University of Notre Dame Press, 2015), 261.

[204] Shippey, J. R. R. Tolkien, 171. Despite his caution against allegorical reading, Shippey argues for a connection in The Hobbit between the goblins and the agents of technological advancement in human history (ibid., 187).

I bow not yet before the Iron Crown,
Nor cast my own small golden sceptre down.[205]

Sauron and Saruman offer obvious parables for the power of technology to possess and corrupt the will; yet a more subtle critique is offered through the character of Denethor. Denethor represents the relinquishment of hope, resignation in the face of technological enslavement. 'The West has failed', is Denethor's mantra.[206] It is perhaps not coincidental, however, that Denethor is also portrayed as vainglorious, angered by Gandalf's reminder of his position as Steward, not Lord, of Gondor.[207]

So how are we to respond to an increasingly technological world, if not with the resignation of Denethor? As Malpas points out, Tolkien does not advocate a return to a pre-technological past; this is sentimental impossibility.[208] Shippey reads into Tolkien's inclusion of rabbits, potatoes and tobacco in Middle-earth, despite their anachronistic nature as much later imports into the Northern archaic culture that pervades much of his work, an admission by Tolkien that some products of modernity are acceptable in an ideal world.[209] Yet there does seem to be a lingering nostalgia for Eden in Tolkien's thought. Bronislaw Szerszynski describes a particular view that is fitting:

From the late eighteenth century nature started to be seen in various ways as the unspoilt, as an Edenic arena of goodness and innocence, unsullied by the artifice, alienation and corruption of modern life

[205] 'Mythopoeia', 89.
[206] *RK*, 128.
[207] *Ibid.*, 130.
[208] Malpas, 'Home', 89.
[209] Tom Shippey, 'Creation from Philology', in *J. R. R. Tolkien Scholar and Storyteller: Essays in Memoriam*, ed. Mary Salu and Robert Farrell (Ithaca, NY: Cornell University Press, 1979), 296.

... nature came to take on new sacral meanings, as a counterpoint to the increased technologisation of society.[210]

Tolkien does avow that 'certainly there was an Eden on this very unhappy earth. We all long for it, and we are constantly glimpsing it: our whole nature at its best and least corrupted, its gentlest and most humane, is still soaked with the sense of "exile".'[211] Flieger explores the complicated (and arguably contradictory) stance Tolkien took towards nature. In *LOTR*, she argues, the characters of Old Man Willow and Treebeard both act in similar ways and with similar motivations, striking out against those who would destroy parts of their forests.[212] The orcs' felling of trees in Fangorn Forest, and the hobbits' chopping of the Old Forest at the border of the Shire are more similar than many readers might acknowledge.[213] Even Lórien, represented as the ideal and aesthetically pleasing forest, is a *cultivated* forest, civilised rather than wild.[214] This leads to a paradox in Tolkien's writings: 'civilization and nature are at undeclared war with one another. To make a place for itself, humankind will tame a wilderness whose destruction, and eventual eradication, however gradual, is at once an inevitable consequence and an irreparable loss.'[215] Lórien is exceptional, for the most part Tolkien sets human activity and technology against idyllic nature. Much of Tolkien's concerns about technology are inextricable from questions of power. Whether technology can be incorporated into Tolkien's sub-creation in any sense depends on how we understand technology, its relationship to us and to the world. If we can conceive of technology's essence as something other than Heidegger's *Gestell*,

---

[210] Bronislaw Szerszynski, *Nature, Technology and the Sacred* (Oxford: Blackwell Publishing, 2005), 102.

[211] *Letters*, 110.

[212] Verlyn Flieger, 'Taking the Part of Trees: Eco-Conflict in Middle-Earth', in *J. R. R. Tolkien and His Literary Resonances*, ed. George Clark and Daniel Timmons (Westport, CT: Greenwood Press, 2000), 156.

[213] *Ibid.*, 156.

[214] *Ibid.*, 155.

[215] *Ibid.*, 155–156.

as Heidegger himself calls on us to do,[216] this project may be advanced.

Theology and the Moral Imagination

What does this mean for our objective of developing a *theological* perspective for reflection on human enhancement? We have seen in Chapter 4 how theologians have understood the importance of the imagination and narrative for their own work. In the present chapter we have considered more particularly how the imagination and Christian truth-claims are connected in fiction, and have explored the value of literature in shaping the moral imagination (which in turn shapes our response to particular concerns such as human enhancement). These threads are now brought together, in asking what place might theology occupy in a broader understanding of the moral imagination?

The theological symbols discussed in earlier chapters are not peculiar to theology. Avis, following the work of Jung, reminds us that 'doctrines have their symbolic equivalents in the repertoire of humanity's symbolic inheritance'.[217] This is of immense importance if theologians are to enter into public dialogue, as is necessary when it comes to human enhancement. As Avis points out, even apart from theistic commitments regarding the imagination's ultimate source, the imagination nevertheless derives the power to inspire and motivate people in a transcendent sense from a long history of invocation in the aspirations of earlier generations.[218] The imagination's appeal and efficacy is not restricted to particular traditions of belief in the way that propositional accounts of truth often are.

For Tolkien, myth conveys meaning in its bringing together of many minds, all contemplating great human questions. Thus, he

---

[216] Heidegger, 'The Question Concerning Technology', 35.
[217] Avis, *God and the Creative Imagination*, 112.
[218] *Ibid.*, 46.

has Ramer, a character in 'The Notion Club Papers', point out to his colleagues:

> I don't think you realize, I don't think any of us realize, the force, the daimonic force that the great myths and legends have. From the profundity of the emotions and perceptions that begot them, and from the multiplication of them in many minds – and each mind, mark you, an engine of obscure but unmeasured energy.[219]

Clyde Kilby locates the power of *LOTR* in its recounting of 'the sadness of a paradise lost and the glory of one that can be regained'.[220] We do not need to understand this in religious terms; Madsen cautions against making 'an independent imagination a means to a religious end'.[221] Scott Moore, in an exploration of Tolkien's impact on the novelist Iris Murdoch, argues that for Murdoch the consolation of the ending of *LOTR* was 'devoid of explicit religion'.[222] An atheist, albeit one attracted to mysticism, Murdoch was nevertheless able to recognise Tolkien's work as the embodiment of true moral vision.[223] Wood, similarly, suggests that the *LOTR*'s success demonstrates that Christians are able to enter the 'tournament of narratives', a phrase used by theologian James McClendon to describe the postmodern milieu.[224]

Donald Williams is more explicit when it comes to the linking of narrative and Christian truth. Referring to Tolkien's brief mention

---

[219] J. R. R. Tolkien, *Sauron Defeated: The End of the Third Age, The Notion Club Papers and the Drowning of Anadûné*, ed. Christopher Tolkien, The History of Middle-Earth, vol. 9 (London: HarperCollins, 1992), 228.

[220] Clyde S. Kilby, 'Mythic and Christian Elements in Tolkien', in *Myth Allegory and Gospel: An Interpretation of J. R. R. Tolkien, C. S. Lewis, G. K. Chesterton, Charles Williams*, ed. John Montgomery (Minneapolis, MN: Bethany Fellowship, 1974), 143.

[221] Madsen, 'Light from an Invisible Lamp', 36.

[222] Scott Moore, 'The Consolations of Fantasy: J. R. R. Tolkien and Iris Murdoch', in *Tolkien Among the Moderns*, ed. Ralph Wood (Notre Dame, IN: University of Notre Dame Press, 2015), 214.

[223] *Ibid.*, 215.

[224] Wood, 'Tolkien and Postmodernism', 273; James McClendon, *Systematic Theology: Ethics* (Nashville, TN: Abingdon Press, 1986), 143.

of the gospels at the close of 'On Fairy-stories' Williams emphasises that the incarnation, sacrifice and resurrection of Christ fulfil
not only prophecies in the Hebrew scriptures, but also the plots
of all great myths and fairy stories throughout human history.[225]
Humans could be redeemed *only* through story, argues Williams,
as humans are storytellers by nature.[226]

In his discussion of how people convert by breaking out of the
'immanent frame' to acknowledge an open system of reality, Taylor emphasises the appeal to the senses and feeling in response
to the 'cross-pressure' of the transcendent.[227] Engaging Taylor's
A Secular Age, Smith suggests that the elasticity conferred on
language as it came to be understood as generative rather than
representative in the late eighteenth century 'creates just enough
openness to potentially rupture the closed take on the immanent
frame'.[228] Imaginative writing can challenge and inform contemporary social imaginaries without containing explicitly theological
content.

This is not to exclude the necessity of genuine theological discourse as well. Brent Waters speaks articulately of the need for
Christians to present a counter narrative to that of 'technoscience'
when it comes to the human future.

> This task need not be premised on the belief that Christians have a
> corner on truth and goodness, only that whatever they know about
> these qualities they know as Christians, however partial and imper-
> fect that knowledge may be. Moreover, in telling this story with the
> vocabulary and grammar of this counter discourse, they may also
> endeavor to tell it in a way that enables, rather than disables, other

---

225 Williams, *Mere Humanity*, 50.
226 *Ibid.*, 50.
227 Charles Taylor, *A Secular Age* (Cambridge, MA: Harvard University Press, 2007),
   729.
228 James K. A. Smith, *How (Not) to Be Secular: Reading Charles Taylor* (Grand Rapids,
   MI: Eerdmans, 2014), 136; cf. Taylor, *A Secular Age*, 756–758.

quests for the good and the true undertaken by those who do not share their faith.[229]

Thus, Hefner's call for the development of 'imaginative frameworks of meaning' might be connected more strongly with theological claims about human and non-human nature.[230] Combined with Tolkien's much greater appreciation for the ability of story to express deep truths about reality (without resorting to heavy-handed propositional statements of theology), a vision of co-creation that derives from theological truth-claims might be articulated imaginatively as part of a broader response to human enhancement questions.

Conclusion

Tolkien's theory of sub-creation, though primarily about constructing imaginary worlds, has the potential to inform our real-world understanding of human creativity. This implication of Tolkien's thought is somewhat underdeveloped; however, it may offer a more nuanced understanding of the divine limits to co-creation that is lacking in other proposals, such as Hefner's created co-creator. Furthermore, Tolkien's understanding of sub-creation and its relation to mythopoesis may correct the imaginative deficit identified in existing accounts of co-creation, permitting us more epistemological latitude as we seek to articulate a theological response to the questions surrounding human enhancement. Tolkien's wariness of technology is not easily dismissed, however, in bringing his thought into contemporary discourse. The next chapter will consider how Tolkien's (in conjunction with Hefner's) ideas might be challenged or supplemented by other relevant sources if it is to be of any value in thinking through theological perspectives on enhancing human traits with technology.

---

[229] Waters, *From Human to Posthuman*, xi.
[230] See Hefner, 'A Fuller Concept of Evolution', 307.

Part III | Seeking a Synthesis

Earlier chapters have concentrated on a deeper analysis of two specific approaches to co-creation theology, assessing their potential for dialogue with human enhancement questions. There are strengths to both Hefner's and Tolkien's conceptions of human creativity, and together these analyses have laid the foundation for further development. This final part presents a preliminary constructive proposal for co-creation theology, incorporating several new dialogue partners to locate this work's proposals with respect to pertinent contemporary discourses. Several markers of a more robust theological anthropology are outlined for constructive dialogue surrounding human enhancement questions, and the proposed anthropology is applied to a number of human enhancement scenarios.

6 | Engaging Human Enhancement Theologically
A New Model of Human Creativity

The co-creation theologies examined in Part II of this work may be enriched by contemporary threads of scholarship. Iain McGilchrist's work on the influence of brain lateralisation on the cultural and philosophical history of the West, George Lakoff and Mark Johnson's studies on metaphor, and the French phenomenological tradition on which both draw are potential resources to overcome the dichotomies of thought raised in the previous analysis of co-creation accounts. Emphasising the embodied dimension of 'knowing' is underscored in this challenging of binary approaches and posthumanist discourse is also introduced for its similar ability to break down thought dichotomies.

If a theology of humans as co-creators is to contribute to reflection on human enhancement technologies, it must be embedded within a context that also attends to virtue. Technological enhancement can only be accommodated within this theological understanding of the human future if technology itself can be conceived of in a way that does not erode virtue, as Tolkien feared. We therefore turn our attention to the shaping of the moral imagination, to consider whether greater attention to the imaginaries in which technology is developed and implemented might suggest a way forward. If the stories and myths that feed our visions of the future are carefully cultivated, there may be room for certain 'enhancing' technologies within a theologically orthodox conception of both human involvement in continuing creation and the eschatological future in which it hopes.

Overcoming Dichotomies of Thought in Co-creation Theologies

How useful are co-creation theologies in responding theologically to the challenges of human enhancement technology? Hefner's created co-creator model engages evolutionary science in its construction and adopts a generally positive stance towards the human use of technology in a God-given mandate to co-create. However, it does not attend sufficiently to the role of the imagination in our discernment regarding co-creation or develop a robust account of virtue formation that can support such discernment. J. R. R. Tolkien's alternative of sub-creation is underpinned by a strong sense of the imagination's value in human creativity, yet he engages little with science and has a largely negative view of technology, representing it as a threat to virtue.

The analyses of Hefner and Tolkien have revealed certain dichotomies relevant to the present consideration of human enhancement. Rationality and imagination are continually set against one another, as are technological development and human morality. A sufficient model of co-creation must be able to reconcile or overcome these dualisms if it is to serve us in reflecting on the possibilities of human enhancement.

Humans have a tendency to construct dichotomies that do not entirely map onto the real world. The duality in the way that we approach the world is well-described in Iain McGilchrist's acclaimed *The Master and His Emissary*.[1] McGilchrist offers a grand narrative that locates the present tension between analytical and rational perspectives and 'big-picture' syntheses in a reversal of particular hemispheric brain operations and their relationship with one another. According to McGilchrist, there are two 'fundamentally opposed realities' or modes of experiencing the world that are rooted in separate hemispheres of the brain, and which have been

---

[1] McGilchrist, *The Master and His Emissary*.

locked in a 'power struggle' key to understanding contemporary Western culture.[2]

McGilchrist characterises the left hemisphere approach to the world as: 'verbal and analytic, requiring abstracted, decontextualised, disembodied thinking, dealing in categories, concerning itself with the nature of the general rather than the particular, and adopting a sequential, linear approach to truth, building the edifice of knowledge from the parts, brick by brick'.[3] The right hemisphere, in contrast, 'sees the whole' and recognises patterns.[4] It 'sees each thing in its context, as standing in a qualifying relationship with all that surrounds it, rather than taking it as a single isolated entity'.[5]

Drawing on a fable that he attributes to Nietzsche, in which an emissary gradually comes to see himself in the role of the wise master he represents, McGilchrist suggests that in our contemporary experience the 'emissary' (left hemisphere) has also apparently usurped the place of the 'master' (right hemisphere). The result is: 'An increasingly mechanistic, fragmented, decontextualised world, marked by unwarranted optimism mixed with paranoia and a feeling of emptiness, has come about, reflecting · · · the unopposed action of a dysfunctional left hemisphere.'[6] While Enlightenment philosophy and the modern world view feature prominently in McGilchrist's account of this usurpation, he also highlights the Reformation as 'the first great expression of the search for certainty in modern times',[7] with its shift away from religious imagery in favour of the word.[8] McGilchrist cites the Cromwellian Revolution, the French Revolution and the rise of scientific materialism

---

[2] *Ibid.*, 3.
[3] *Ibid.*, 137.
[4] *Ibid.*, 47–48.
[5] *Ibid.*, 49.
[6] *Ibid.*, 6.
[7] *Ibid.*, 315. Here, McGilchrist applies 'modern' in the sense of 'recent', rather than in reference to the modern period.
[8] *Ibid.*, 315.

as examples of the left hemisphere's ongoing 'assault' on the right hemisphere's world.[9] However, it is in the Industrial Revolution, and particularly the increasing prevalence of *technology*, he argues, that 'the innate structures of the left hemisphere' are 'being incarnated in the world it has come to dominate'.[10]

Though McGilchrist overreaches with respect to some of the scientific claims he makes, implying that neurological phenomena are *driving* complex social and intellectual changes,[11] his general description of Western culture in thrall to a mechanistic and decontextualised rationality resonates. The metaphor of the master and the emissary, even untethered from specific claims concerning changes in brain lateralisation, is illuminating.[12] In terms of the interlocutors considered in the current project, we can certainly identify in Hefner's methodology the tendency towards the reductive 'brick-by-brick' approach that McGilchrist classifies as left-hemisphere thinking. In the germ of imaginative insights in his thought, which remain underdeveloped and constrained by the scientific methodology he adopts, we see the dichotomy of rationality and imagination reified by Hefner.

McGilchrist attests to the impossibility, identified earlier, of articulating an alternative 'truth' from the analytical using the tools of philosophy, restricted as they are by the particular limitations

---

[9] *Ibid.*, 386.

[10] *Ibid.*, 387.

[11] Kenan Malik points to McGilchrist's problematic attribution of agency to each brain hemisphere, when it is only at the level of the whole person that awareness can be spoken of meaningfully (Kenan Malik and Iain McGilchrist, 'Split Brain, Split Views: Debating Iain McGilchrist', *Pandaemonium*, February 2013, https://kenanmalik.wordpress.com/2013/02/24/split-brain-split-views-debating-iain-mcgilchrist/.

[12] To be fair, McGilchrist closes his book with an acknowledgement that the neurological specifics of his argument may prove unnecessary to an account of the history of human culture and philosophy, and that he would be content if his description of brain hemispheres were to serve only as a metaphor for the dichotomies we experience (*The Master and His Emissary*, 461–462).

of philosophical discourse's terms of reference and epistemology.[13] Yet the very attempt to do so, contends McGilchrist, witnesses powerfully to the reality of an alternate way of construing the world.[14] He cites the phenomenological tradition as an example, reading in Edmund Husserl's notion of intersubjectivity, which challenges the dualism between the objective and the subjective, an assertion of 'the essential role that the right hemisphere plays in constituting the world in which we live'.[15]

It is in such an alternative that McGilchrist locates the potential for overcoming dichotomous thinking. Western philosophy has been given over to a left-hemisphere version of the world, he argues, and thus is dependent on a naturalising dichotomising approach, which sees the world in terms of 'either/or'. The chief governing principle of the left hemisphere is division, after all.[16] Yet these dichotomies 'may cease to be problematic in the world delivered by the right hemisphere, where what appears to the left hemisphere to be divided is unified, where concepts are not separate from experience, and where the grounding role of "betweenness" in constituting reality is apparent'.[17]

James K. A. Smith is another thinker who challenges contemporary dichotomies, including that between reason and the imagination. In the third volume of his cultural liturgies trilogy, he envisions a public theology that rejects the perceived antithesis of church and state.[18] Indeed, his larger project of identifying secular liturgies repudiates sharp distinctions between sacred and

---

[13] *Ibid.*, 135. Eleanore Stump makes a similar point with her contrast of 'Dominican' (propositional) and 'Franciscan' (intuitive) approaches to knowledge, arguing that it is not fruitful to 'attempt to show the philosophical importance of Franciscan knowledge by Dominican means' (*Wandering in Darkness*, 60).

[14] McGilchrist, *The Master and His Emissary*, 135.

[15] *Ibid.*, 144.

[16] *Ibid.*, 137.

[17] *Ibid.*

[18] James K. A. Smith, *Awaiting the King: Reforming Public Theology* (Grand Rapids, MI: Baker Academic, 2017), xiii.

secular.[19] Like McGilchrist, Smith draws on the phenomenological tradition, referring to Maurice Merleau-Ponty's notion of 'preconscious knowledge', which in turn borrows much from Heidegger's 'being-in-the-world'.[20] This attests the 'hybridity' of human being, challenging both Cartesian and animalist dichotomies of mind and body.[21]

Affirming that our intellectual reflection is preceded by preconscious, bodily perceptions of the world, Smith then turns to the work of Pierre Bourdieu to consider how we might recruit the imagination in service of particular reflection. A sociologist and anthropologist, Bourdieu's work is mainly concerned with embodiment and practices in the establishment of *habitus*, dispositions he defines as 'embodied history, internalized as a second nature'.[22] He also tackles dichotomies, particularly what Smith identifies as the tension between intellectualism and voluntarism.[23]

Smith, too, is clear that the way out of dichotomy will not be expressed using philosophical discourse.[24] Bourdieu names a 'prelogical logic of practice' in his critique of theoretical reason and highlights the difference between this concept and a more objective notion of logic: that 'which is inherent in intellectual activity and the intellectual condition [] is no doubt what intellectual discourse has least chance of accurately expressing'.[25] Nevertheless, a 'logic of practice' moves past the intellectualism/voluntarism divide by rejecting both: against the former it asserts that a practitioner's

[19] Smith, *Desiring the Kingdom*, 25.
[20] Smith, *Imagining the Kingdom*, 43–44; cf. Maurice Merleau-Ponty, *Phenomenology of Perception* (London: Routledge, 1962), 92. Smith also connects this idea explicitly to McGilchrist's 'right brain' sense of 'betweenness' (Smith, *Imagining the Kingdom*, 44).
[21] Smith, *Imagining the Kingdom*, 43.
[22] Pierre Bourdieu, *The Logic of Practice*, trans. Richard Nice (Stanford, CA: Stanford University Press, 1990), 56.
[23] Bourdieu terms these 'obectivism' and 'subjectivism'; however, Smith adjusts the terms for clarity (Smith, *Imagining the Kingdom*, 77).
[24] *Ibid.*, 76.
[25] Bourdieu, *The Logic of Practice*, 19.

relationship to practice cannot be reduced to theory, and against the latter it refuses to accord radical autonomy to a 'rational' subject in decision-making.[26]

Indeed, language is a major contributor to the problem of dichotomy. Smith highlights the dualistic and reductionistic character of our lexicon in philosophical anthropology. The likes of Bourdieu and Merleau-Ponty, in attempting to honour 'the messy complexity of our being-in-the-world that is *between* all these [linguistic dichotomies]', struggle to find sufficient language to describe what they mean by a *betweenness*.[27] Recognising the insufficiency of language and philosophical arguments to overcome our tendency to think in dichotomous terms, the remainder of this chapter offers some markers of a theological anthropology that builds on Hefner's and Tolkien's understanding of human creativity as a starting point for engaging human technological enhancement.

But first, another dualism relevant to the present analysis bears mentioning. While Tolkien pushes against the imagination–rationality dichotomy to a certain extent in his affirmation of imagination's truths, he succumbs to a different dichotomy, one that is more subtle and does not concern human nature internally so much as how we understand the world. Technology stands in fundamental opposition to nature in Tolkien's thought, it is represented as the destroyer of everything natural, beautiful and good. To consider whether there might be middle ground between Hefner's and Tolkien's view of human creating is essentially to ask whether virtue can be sustained in an increasingly technological world. If Tolkien's chief concern about technology was that it eroded virtue, then his vision of sub-creation stands in opposition to technological 'progress'. If it is possible to maintain

---

[26] Smith, *Imagining the Kingdom*, 79.
[27] Thus Bourdieu resorts to the archaic term *habitus*, to be discussed in the next section (Smith, *Imagining the Kingdom*, 85).

(or even enhance) virtue alongside technological development, however, then perhaps Tolkien's vision can be expanded to include our technological future.

We might sum up the difference between Hefner and Tolkien in terms of their understanding of human creativity in relation to divine, a connection established in Chapter 2 of this work. If human creativity/artistry is understood in relation to God as the master craftsman, then Hefner does not give sufficient epistemic worth to the imagination in his understanding of creativity, while Tolkien fails to identify technology as a legitimate exercise of artistry. A sufficient account of theological anthropology will need to correct these imbalances in order to engage human technological enhancement.

A Vision of Moral Co-creation

Having explored several resources that assist us in moving beyond the problematic dichotomies identified in existing approaches to co-creation, we may now begin sketching out a new proposal that unites the strengths of its predecessors and overcomes some of their limitations. The difficulty of articulating a sufficient account of the imagination by means of theoretical discourse has already been raised; however, a more fruitful model of human creativity (or 'co-creation') for engaging human enhancement challenges will feature the following commitments.

1. Humans are products of a creative 'evolutionary' process.

This is Hefner's starting point. Acknowledging the evolutionary origins of humanity has often required theologians to reconceptualise particular ideas and doctrines, from the *imago Dei* to the nature of the soul and whether or not God knows the future. Anything we might say theologically about human traits must not run counter to what we know scientifically about the evolution of *Homo*

sapiens and non-human animals (though such theological statements need not be completely explained by scientific observation
either).

Agustín Fuentes connects the imagination to the evolutionary
process from which humans arose, arguing that the imagination's
deployment in religious experience is an outcome of niche construction.[28] While many who offer evolutionary explanations for
religion employ such explanations to discount the existence of
the supernatural, Fuentes provides a more synthetic account. For
Fuentes, evolutionary processes may act within a process of revelation, and 'the assumption of a supernatural engagement as part of
the emergence of the symbolic in the human evolutionary record
makes a lot of sense'.[29]

Fuentes' approach resonates with Hefner's own attempts to
understand theological ideas in light of our evolutionary history.
Whereas Hefner reaches for earlier sociobiological accounts, somewhat problematic in their ideological commitments, to reconcile
a theological understanding of human being with an evolutionary
perspective,[30] Fuentes is less concerned to fit a notion of revelation
neatly into a natural account. This perhaps has more to do with
an underlying approach to integrating theological and scientific

---

[28] Agustin Fuentes, *The Creative Spark: How Imagination Made Humans Exceptional*
(New York: Dutton Penguin Random House, 2017), 215. Graham Ward more
recently has traced the evolutionary origins of the imagination, highlighting the
moment when 'wandering becomes wondering' as the imagination unfolds from a
growing consciousness of the inconceivable (*Unimaginable: What We Imagine and
What We Can't* (London: I. B. Tauris, 2018), 39–40). The evolution of the
imagination has attracted attention in recent cultural anthropological scholarship
(e.g. Stephen Asma, *The Evolution of Imagination* (Chicago, IL: University of
Chicago Press, 2017); Robert Wilson and Lucia Foglia, 'Embodied Cognition',
Stanford Encyclopedia of Philosophy,
https://plato.stanford.edu/archives/spr2017/entries/embodied-cognition/).
[29] Fuentes, *The Creative Spark*, 216.
[30] See 'The Development of Science and Religion' beginning on p. 149.

knowledge, a challenge addressed in some detail in Chapter 3 of this work.

2. Creativity is central to human agency and responsibility.

This is the core thesis of Fuentes' recent work in anthropology *The Creative Spark*.[31] We might also return to the notion of the *imago Dei*. Though Hefner and others connect technological development, and co-creation more broadly, with the affirmation that humans are created in the divine image; we might go further and speak particularly of the imagination. 'We are makers of images because we are in the image *of*.'[32] This brings to mind Coleridge's description of the imagination as an echo in the finite of the infinite 'I am'.[33] Imagination is fundamental to our experience of human being.

A consideration of creativity and imagination, particularly within the context of human agency and responsibility, needs to be embedded within a sufficient recognition of fallenness. Humans are *not* entirely free, and this is a tension that must underpin reflections on discernment and ethics. Hefner's portrayal of sin as little more than a friction between our biological drives and our more civilised cultural selves is inadequate when it comes to accounting for the noetic limitations of human fallenness.[34] While sin is a distinctly theological category, scientific insights from psychology and epigenetics offer a consistent picture of human choice as constrained by our formative experiences and our biological heritage (going back a number of generations). We therefore need to find an adequate way of talking about responsibility within a context of limitation; moving beyond Hefner's dialectic of freedom and determinism.[35]

---

[31] Fuentes, *The Creative Spark*.

[32] Ward, *Unbelievable*, 207, emphasis original.

[33] Coleridge, *Biographia Literaria*, 167.

[34] Hefner does speak of sin in theological terms, and the dangers that our fallenness poses for our co-creative work at a later stage ('The Animal that Aspires', 165).

[35] Tolkien seems to imply a degree of both freedom and responsibility in his sub-creation, though this is less developed.

We might therefore ask whether an emphasis on the imagination accords due weight to human fallenness. As Hedley writes, 'Whereas much theology of the last century emphasized the gap between humankind and God, the imagination is evidence of a high estimate of human potential.'[36] Is this estimate too high? The call for a greater focus on the imagination must be tempered with this recognition of an uneasy tension. Acknowledging that the imagination must be subject to the same noetic limitations of sin as other aspects of cognition offers a check against untrammelled enthusiasm for and confidence in the technological futures we might dream up, without discouraging us from exercising creativity to the extent that we are able.[37]

The question of freedom and the constraints of sin returns us again to certain dichotomies of speech and thought. We cannot help but conceive of freedom and determinism, or responsibility, in dialectical terms. Here, we may recall Bourdieu's 'logic of practice' discussed earlier in this chapter as a challenge to the intellectualism/voluntarism divide. Similarly, Bourdieu's conception of *habitus* becomes 'a way to break out of false dichotomies between freedom and determinism, intellect and instinct'.[38] Thus Bourdieu is able to summarise the expansiveness of *habitus* as follows:

This infinite yet strictly limited generative capacity is difficult to understand only so long as one remains locked in the usual antinomies – which the concept of the *habitus* aims to transcend – of determinism and freedom, conditioning and creativity, consciousness and the unconscious, or the individual and society. Because the *habitus* is an infinite capacity for generating products – thoughts, perceptions, expressions and actions – whose limits are set by the

---

[36] Hedley, *Living Forms of the Imagination*, 29.
[37] A full consideration of the noetic limitations of the imagination is beyond the present scope – and perhaps ultimately unknowable; however, this point is raised as a reminder of the fallibility of all aspects of human cognition.
[38] Smith, *Imagining the Kingdom*, 85.

historically and socially situated conditions of production, the conditioned and conditional freedom it provides is as remote from creation of unpredictable novelty as it is from simple mechanical reproduction of the original conditioning.[39]

The language here, particularly with respect to freedom and determinism, recalls aspects of Hefner's anthropology. Whereas Hefner tries to assert both the freedom and the determinism that constitutes human being in the world,[40] attempting to resist dualisms as he does so, his dialectic construction falls short of the goal. Listening to the kind of approach set out by Bourdieu and other phenomenologists might give Hefner the resources he needs to overcome this dualism, without being forced into dichotomous language.

3. Human creativity is modelled on divine creativity.

Acknowledging the complicating matter of fallenness, the centrality of creativity to theological anthropology is supported by a connection between God's creative work and human making. This work began with the premise that human creativity belongs properly within a doctrine of creation. Hart's treatment of human artistry as a legitimate aspect of creation, as well as the theological works of Sayers and Maritain and insights from the field of creativity studies, laid the foundation for a treatment of technology along the same lines.

Hefner attempts to articulate the derivative character of human creating in his application of the prefix 'co' – although the ambiguity of the 'created co-creator' construction and its diverse interpretation has already been noted. The relationship of human creating

---

[39] Bourdieu, *The Logic of Practice*, 55.
[40] See 'Core Element 2' beginning on p. 84.

to divine is more clearly stated in Tolkien's sub-creation, as he intu-
its the presence of divine norms that guide our co-creating.[41] In
relating human creativity to divine creativity, however, we should
not exaggerate the contrast so much that we underestimate the
human capacity for novelty in creation. To give one example, technological advances in synthetic biology have allowed us to generate
new organisms.[42]

Ward describes an analogy between divine creation as the 'writing' of God (through the Logos) and the act of creation by authors
through the use of *logoi*.[43] Hart locates the meaningfulness of our
freedom to create in the fact that it is exercised within given boundaries.[44] Although human creativity imitates the divine, this does
not diminish its creative character – McGilchrist reminds us that
imitation requires us to imaginatively inhabit the other.[45] David
Jones speaks to the joyfulness of art in particular as an imitation of
divine creating, writing that 'there is a sense in which [the] grat-
uitousness in the operations of the Creator is reflected in the art
of the creature'.[46] The value ascribed to the imagination by scientists, poets, artists and theologians alike attests to its importance for
creativity generally, and implies the breadth of human activity that
may be treated under the rubric of creation. The cross-disciplinary
applicability of an understanding of human creativity in connection with divine creation is treated further in the fifth hallmark of
this proposed theological anthropology.[47]

[41] This seems implied in the line 'we make still by the law in which we're made' from
'Mythopoeia'.
[42] See, for example, Julius Fredens et al., 'Total Synthesis of *Escherichia coli* with a
Recoded Genome', *Nature* 569 (2019).
[43] Ward, *Unbelievable*, 204–205.
[44] Trevor Hart, 'Through the Arts: Hearing, Seeing and Touching the Truth', in
Beholding the Glory: Incarnation Through the Arts, ed. Jeremy Begbie (London:
Darton, Longman & Todd, 2000), 18.
[45] McGilchrist, *The Master and His Emissary*, 249.
[46] David Jones, 'Art and Sacrament', in *Epoch and Artist: Selected Writings*, ed. Harman
Grisewood (London: Faber & Faber, 1959), 153.
[47] See pp. 231ff.

4. Scientific insights should be respected and incorporated into an understanding and description of what it means to be human, without reducing theological and philosophical claims to scientific ones.

There is a degree of overlap here with the first marker identified, as a robust treatment of anthropology in the context of humanity's evolutionary beginnings necessitates an engagement with scientific discourse. The relationship of science to theology is an inexhaustible question; a field of research unto its own.

Cognitive science research supporting the role of metaphor and the importance of the imagination for how we make sense of the world is a good example of how science can inform our theological anthropology.[48] Similarly, Hefner's understanding of the genetic similarities among diverse species informs his assertion that humans are embedded within broader natural processes.[49] Some of the creativity studies literature outlined in Chapter 2 is presented from a scientific outlook and may also contribute to our theological understanding of how human creativity resembles the creative work of God.[50]

Nevertheless, in seeking a sufficient model of relating science and theology we must avoid reducing theological ideas to scientific statements. Hefner's approach to the science and religion dialogue is essentially to express theological claims in scientific terms; the evaluation in Chapter 3 concluded that he is not entirely successful at doing so. Additionally, he appears to affirm theological ideas and instincts that do not fit neatly within the constraints of his chosen scientific methodology. Tolkien, on the other hand, shies away from any explicit connection of his ideas on human creativity to scientific knowledge.

---

[48] Lakoff and Johnson, *Metaphors We Live By*, 257.
[49] See 'Hypothesis 2' on p. 80.
[50] E.g. Chirico et al., 'Awe Enhances Creative Thinking'.

Instead, we might envision an approach to theological anthropology that is able to incorporate scientific insights into its construction, yet acknowledges that certain theological content remains in the domain of faith and relies on special revelation. Such an approach is somewhat along the lines of the broader 'natural theology' recently drawn out by McGrath, outlining a coherence to the natural world and the science that explores it when understood through the lens of a Christian faith.[51]

5. Technology is a legitimate exercise of human co-creativity.

Scott Midson describes the need to develop a 'worldly ethic that is not distracted by Eden'.[52] Romanticised notions of Eden can lead to critique of human-built environments contrasted with the 'givenness' of the world not created by humans.[53] 'Where Eden is presented as a utopian part of our past, our nature, there will be understandable aims to return to it.'[54] Richard Sennett describes the paralysis that produces this type of escapism:

> So great are the changes required to alter humankind's dealings with the physical world that only this sense of self-displacement and estrangement can drive the actual practices of change and reduce our consuming desires; the dream of dwelling in equilibrium and at peace with the world risks, in my view, leading us to seek escape in an idealized Nature, rather than confronting the self-destructive territory we have actually made.[55]

Contemporary philosopher of technology Mark Coeckelbergh helps us to unpack this dichotomy in his own discussion of technology with respect to the Romantic movement, with which

---

[51] McGrath, Re-imagining Nature.
[52] Midson, Cyborg Theology, 10.
[53] Norman Wirzba, From Nature to Creation: A Christian Vision for Understanding and Loving Our World (Grand Rapids, MI: Baker Academic, 2015), 68.
[54] Midson, Cyborg Theology, 63.
[55] Richard Sennett, The Craftsman (New Haven, CT: Yale University Press, 2008), 13.

Tolkien is somewhat aligned. Technology is often seen as hostile to Romanticism, orienting us away from the natural and the sublime to the mechanical and informational. Coeckelbergh describes the current uses of information and communications technologies as a 'surprising marriage of Enlightenment rationalism and Romanticism'.[56] For Coeckelbergh, the notion that Romanticism is antithetical to technology is the result of a false definition of Romanticism, or perhaps a false assumption embedded within Romanticism itself.[57] The romantic dialectic is deterministic for both Romantic critiques of technology and rejections of these critiques. 'Romantic thinking is not only nostalgic and against the machine; it also looks forward to a future *with* the machine.'[58] Even those contemporary philosophies of technology that claim to reject the pessimism and Romanticism of earlier critics such as Weber and Heidegger have 'uncritically borrowed the same dichotomy' between Romanticism and technology, contends Coeckelbergh.[59] McGilchrist disagrees with Coeckelbergh here, however, instead construing Romanticism as attempting to transcend dichotomies rather than perpetuate them – he describes the Romantic goal using his brain structure metaphor as the 'reintegration of the left hemisphere's realm into that of the right'.[60]

Coeckelbergh lays significant blame at the feet of Romanticism: it has 'given us the conceptual tools to create a gap between science and religion, between technology and spontaneity, between machines and humanity'.[61] At the same time, however, Romanticism was a shaping influence in nineteenth-century science and technology, animating desire to discover more of 'mysterious

---

[56] Coeckelbergh, *New Romantic Cyborgs*, 3.
[57] *Ibid.*, 11.
[58] *Ibid.*, 13, emphasis original.
[59] *Ibid.*, 71.
[60] McGilchrist, *The Master and His Emissary*, 351.
[61] Coeckelbergh, *New Romantic Cyborgs*, 74.

Nature'.[62] Technology became the instrument of Romanticism.[63] John Tresch also identifies certain historical strands of Romanticism that 'were compatible with an embrace – an ambivalent, cautious embrace – of science and technology'.[64] Some have described science fiction in this vein of Romanticism embracing technology – for instance, Fred Botting labels Gibson's *Neuromancer* as a 'Gothic romance', highlighting its dark settings, its preoccupation with death and its confusion as to the borders of the self.[65] Coeckelbergh's critique of Romanticism appears a little overblown on balance – while some aspects of the movement do set technology in opposition to nature, humanity and virtue, there is overall a degree of ambiguity when it comes to the advantages and disadvantages of technological development.

All of this suggests that one aspect of Tolkien's approach to human creating at least, the centrality of the imagination, need not stand in opposition to technological development. Coeckelbergh asks whether techno-romanticism can be redeemed today and identifies a number of 'conceptual building blocks' that Romanticism offers in spite of its shortcomings. These include a protection of space for reflection and contemplation, an acknowledgement that we are not in control of our own destiny, a more complicated view of the self and of reality, and the refusal to set political action in dichotomy with utopian dreams.[66] McGilchrist, too, finds much of value in Romantic thought, viewing it as the right hemisphere's way of looking at the world reasserting its rightful dominance over the left.[67] Coeckelbergh's own answer, however, is not to redeem a particularly Romantic approach to thinking about technology,

---

[62] *Ibid.*, 98–99.

[63] *Ibid.*, 101. See also John Tresch, *The Romantic Machine: Utopian Science and Technology After Napoleon* (Chicago, IL: University of Chicago Press, 2012).

[64] Coeckelbergh, *New Romantic Cyborgs*, 311.

[65] Fred Botting, 'Virtual Romanticism', In *Romanticism and Postmodernism*, ed. Edward Larrissy (Cambridge: Cambridge University Press, 1999), 110–112.

[66] Coeckelbergh, *New Romantic Cyborgs*, 250.

[67] McGilchrist, *The Master and His Emissary*, 354.

but rather to move beyond the Romantic thought model and its dualisms.[68] He proposes a focus on skilled engagement, craftsmanship and narrative to escape the technology–human binary (which he identifies as Romantic) and birth the 'non machine.'[69] Coeckelbergh concedes that he cannot clearly envision a narrative that escapes this binary yet, but believes it to be possible if we bring a collective imagination to the task.[70] Coeckelbergh leaves us with a critique of dualistic thinking and a desire to escape binaries, but little in the way of constructive proposals for how to do so.

One way forward might be to re-examine the relationship between technology and virtue. Is the exercise of technology even compatible with virtue? Lewis expresses a strong negative, drawing a contrast between the pre-technological and technological mindsets.

> There is something which unites magic and applied science while separating both from the 'wisdom' of earlier ages. For the wise men of old the cardinal problem had been how to conform the soul to reality, and the solution had been knowledge, self-discipline, and virtue. For magic and applied science alike the problem is how to subdue reality to the wishes of men: the solution is a technique; and both, in the practice of this technique, are ready to do things hitherto regarded as disgusting and impious.[71]

Ellul identifies a key feature of a society governed absolutely by technique as the inability to consider technology in light of the ends that it serves, focusing instead on performance.[72] These

---

[68] Coeckelbergh, *New Romantic Cyborgs*, 252.

[69] *Ibid.*, 274–275.

[70] *Ibid* 278.

[71] C. S. Lewis, *Perelandra* (London: Simon & Schuster, 1996), 83–84. Note that 'applied science' is Lewis' term for technology.

[72] Jacques Ellul, *The Technological Society*, trans John Wilkinson (New York: Knopf, 1964), 302.

characterisations certainly are not promising for a moral technological future.

Can we tell a story in which technology is not a threat to virtue? James K. A. Smith points out that it is not as simple as rewriting the story of existing technologies. While the intent of the user matters to a certain degree, Smith contends that 'cultural phenomena and systems can be laden with an implicit vision of the good life that is inscribed in [their] very structure'.[73] Therefore it is not only the social imaginary of the users and decision-makers that requires attention, but that of the technology *makers*.[74] This shift must occur at a level beyond the discerning individual. We must consider how imaginations are recruited, which stories are compelling when it comes to the possibilities for enhancing humans with technology.

In exploring Brent Water's critique of posthumanism, Midson suggests that technology and nature are dichotomised in terms of sinfulness and Edenic innocence, respectively.[75] Possibly we can see Tolkien's views on technology in a similar light and draw further connections to the influence of Romanticism on his thought. Hefner, on the other hand, rejects the fall 'except in a decisively figurative manner, since we cannot accept that humans ever existed in a prior state of perfection',[76] and this may factor into his more open stance towards technology. Perhaps an 'alternative articulation of Eden in terms of non-innocence' might be a way through the difficulties that both Edenic paradise and alternative utopian origin myths produce,[77] and would additionally be more compatible with an evolutionary account of origins.

[73] Smith, *Imagining the Kingdom*, 144.
[74] Hannah Arendt shows how engineers and technologists necessarily receive guidance from politics, speaking of the 'political integration of technical power' ('The Threat of Conformism'), in *Essays in Understanding 1930–1954: Formation Exile, and Totalitarianism*, ed. Jerome Kohn (New York: Schocken Books, 2005), 427.
[75] Midson, *Cyborg Theology*, 171.
[76] Hefner, *THF*, 274.
[77] Midson, *Cyborg Theology*, 173.

Another dichotomy that ought to be addressed is the tendency to see *technê* and art as antithetical. In the same way that Tolkien sets virtue and technology in opposition, he also makes a clear distinction between art and technology. He did not see any synthesis between what he understood as two very distinct creative impulses, with entirely separate ends. He explains how the two diverge, represented in his narrative by the 'magic' of the Elves. '[Elf] magic is Art, delivered from its many human limitations: more effortless, more quick, more complete (product, and vision in unflawed correspondence). And its object is Art not Power, sub-creation not domination and tyrannous re-forming of Creation.'[78]

Indeed, with all the limitations of human fallenness, even what Tolkien designates as 'Art' can slide into all of the perils of a technological outlook.

> This desire [to create Art] is at once wedded to a passionate love of the real primary world, and hence filled with the sense of mortality, and yet unsatisfied by it. It has various opportunities of 'Fall'. It may become possessive, clinging to the things made as 'its own', the sub-creator wishes to be the Lord and God of his private creation. He will rebel against the laws of the Creator – especially against mortality. Both of these (alone or together) will lead to the desire for Power, for making the will more quickly effective, – and so to the Machine (or Magic).[79]

But what if it were possible for the devices and processes that we currently think of as technology to be brought closer to Tolkien's conception of Art? It is not so easy as resolving to create technology for good ends, however. Tolkien's very definition of technology (or magic, as he closely equates the two) suggests an inevitable corruptibility. The 'evil' of domination Tolkien describes very often

---

[78] *Letters*, 146.
[79] *Ibid.*, 145.

grows out of good intentions to benefit the world,[80] a point Tolkien illustrates in the reasons behind Gandalf, Elrond and Galadriel all refusing to take the Ring. Hart summarises the role of art as he understands it in Tolkien's thought:

> artistic making, therefore, departs freely, properly, and often from the constraints of whatever appears to be given in the world; but when it does so its end is never selfish, always being rooted in a delight in the world for its own sake and desiring nothing more than the world's own good, its enhancement, and the fulfilment of possibilities latent within it.[81]

Yet, as Hart describes art as participation in God's creativity,[82] might we not think of technology in the same way? Heidegger, as highlighted in the previous chapter, called for a greater incorporation of poetic vision into the modern technological orientation towards the world.[83] Richard Sennett develops a related thesis in his work, arguing that technology and technical understanding should be understood in the vein of a skilled craft, beginning as a bodily practice and developing through the power of the imagination.[84] This aligns with Hart's analysis of how our understanding of art has shifted over time, moving further away from the 'craftmanship' notion of operating within a divinely ordered 'workshop' to the idea that artists, by their own ingenuity, are themselves responsible for ordering chaos.[85]

In a critique of Bronislaw Szerszynski's *Nature, Technology, and the Sacred*, Michael DeLashmutt laments the omission of 'any reference to the significant power of both myth and imagination in

---

80 *Ibid.*, 146.

81 Hart, 'Tolkien, Creation, and Creativity', 52.

82 Hart, 'Through the Arts', 16.

83 Heidegger, 'The Question Concerning Technology', 34–35.

84 Sennett, *The Craftsman*.

85 Hart, *Making Good*, 197. Certainly, Tolkien's own understanding of art aligns more with the early notion, rather than its more audacious development.

the postmodern sacred world', arguing that reflections of technology would be enriched by attending to such neglect.[86] Bohm, too, identifies a similar deficiency when exploring technology from a creativity studies perspective, arguing that 'fundamentally, the wrong order of human action that is responsible for our basic difficulties is due to the fact that we tend to be mechanical when what is called for is creativity.'[87] Mary Midgley calls for a reintegration of the vision of artists and philosophers with that of scientists.[88] They come together, she argues, via a greater use of the imagination.

> We need to compare those visions, to articulate them more clearly, to be aware of changes in them, to think them through so as to see what they commit us to. This is not itself scientific business, though of course scientists need to engage in it. It is necessarily philosophic business (whoever does it) because it involves analysing concepts and attending to the wider structures in which those concepts get their meaning. It starts with the fuller articulation of imaginative visions and moves on later to all kinds of more detailed thought, including scientific thought.[89]

This kind of attention to the visions of the world that we construct will also improve our capacity to discern how we ought to act. 'A clearer, more realistic imaginative vision of the world is bound to make for a clearer sense of priorities.'[90]

Ellul describes art in technological society as 'at once the positive reflection of the freedom conferred by technology and a compensation for the fatality of technological growth'.[91] Yet the many

---

[86] Michael DeLashmutt, 'The Technological Imaginary: Bringing Myth and Imagination into Dialogue with Bronislaw Szerzynski's *Nature, Technology and the Sacred*, *Zygon* 41, no. 4 (2006), 804.

[87] Bohm, *On Creativity*, 19.

[88] Midgley, *Science and Poetry*, 38.

[89] *Ibid.*, 36.

[90] *Ibid.*, 205.

[91] Jacques Ellul, 'Remarks on Technology and Art', *Bulletin of Science, Technology & Society* 21 (2001), 36.

qualities of art surely spring from more than just a technology-enabled freedom. In a more integrated approach described by Midgley, art may be allowed to critique technology (without setting the two in complete opposition). Van der Laan raises the 'inherent contradiction of technofix answers for a technologically caused ecological degradation'.[92] An awareness of the shortcomings of technology, and possible mitigations, is unlikely to come from technologists alone. Bieber Lake offers an analysis of Margaret Atwood's *Oryx and Crake*, demonstrating how it satirises a society in which the arts are eclipsed and language is diminished by the dominance of technique.[93] In an article decrying the decline and devaluing of the humanities in the university, author Marilynne Robinson points out that both the Massachusetts Institute of Technology and Rensselaer Polytechnic Institute invest substantially in the arts. 'These schools might know something about nurturing the technical mind.'[94]

In some respects, science fiction is the perfect bridge between *technê* and art as they are presently conceived. Le Guin describes proper science fiction as 'ethically responsible art' – it brims with potential for 'playing games with and making sense and beauty out of our fearfully enlarged world of knowledge and perception'.[95] In a similar vein, Bohm reminds us that the artist (or in this case, the fiction writer) can learn a lot from scientists in terms of coherency – artistic beauty and scientific truth are 'inseparable' and thus scientific insights may guide the use of the imagination in fiction.[96] Bohm's notion of 'fittingness' as applicable to the whole of life

---

92 Laan, 'Editor's Notes', 238.

93 Lake, *Prophets of the Posthuman*, 118–119; cf. Margaret Atwood, *Oryx and Crake: A Novel* (New York: Random House, 2003).

94 Marilynne Robinson, 'What Are We Doing Here?' in *What Are We Doing Here?: Essays* (London: Virago, 2018), 29.

95 Ursula Le Guin, 'Escape Routes', in *The Language of the Night: Essays on Fantasy and Science Fiction*, ed. Susan Wood (New York: Putnam, 1979), 206.

96 Bohm, *On Creativity*, 46.

means that we 'have to be both creative artists and skilled artisans', and this extends into the moral realm.[97]

Hefner's entire created co-creator construction is premised on the idea that technology is intrinsic to human being (he extends the category of technology to include transhumanist impulses).[98] Recognising that humans have always engaged with technology in some form, that it is instrumental in the way that we have related to our environment, reorients the discourse. Technology ceases to be a monolithic entity that represents the antithesis of all that is natural and good. Brian Brock offers further resources for how to orient ourselves theologically to technology's ubiquity. Rather than eschew technology generally (or perhaps even enhancement technologies specifically) as necessarily representing a threat to the created order, Christians must familiarise themselves with the decision-making processes currently surrounding technology.[99] Technological artefacts represent the collective judgement of a society on what is meaningful, argues Brock, and therefore reflecting on these technologies offers resources to both understand and critique broader social values.[100] Though Brock denounces what he considers to have been moral theology's 'embrace' of prevailing methods of technology assessment as 'an unwarranted capitulation to the spirit of the age', he nevertheless argues for a middle path between wholesale rejection of technology and the uncritical adoption of the 'progress' narrative.[101] He 'aim(s) to locate modern technology within the dynamics of sin as self-assertion against God and good works as service, so offering Christian theology better purchase on the landscape within which all human action is set in a technological age.'[102]

---

[97] Ibid., 1–6.
[98] Philip Hefner, 'The Evolutionary Epic', Zygon 44, no. 1 (2009), 163.
[99] Brian Brock, Christian Ethics in a Technological Age (Grand Rapids, MI: Eerdmans, 2010), 3.
[100] Ibid., 11.
[101] Ibid., 20, 191.
[102] Ibid., 191.

By using the language of sin in his situating of technology, and our decision-making surrounding technology, Brock leaves room for enhancement technologies to be approached like any other ethical challenge. They are not categorically different from other technologies, in that they can be employed for either good or evil purposes. While theology is tasked with 'desacralising' technology, questioning the power it reinforces, whether it embodies love and how it impacts our relationships with one another and with the rest of creation,[103] it is with the help of other resources explored here (imagination and story) that these tasks are undertaken.

6. Humans are storytellers and myth makers at their core, with narrative central to the way in which we understand the world.

Again, this is a conclusion that is supported by findings in cognitive science. Not only do many metaphors appear to be universal across cultures, and constitutive of how we conceptualise the world, rather than merely operative at the level of language,[104] but myths are ubiquitous in human societies. Our ideas of what is good are inscribed in us by stories, or storied practices such as liturgy.

Here, the calls of Hefner and Cole-Turner for more stories and liturgies that can shape our reflection on human enhancement questions (though their philosophy of the imagination is not sufficiently developed to follow through on these claims) are justified and strengthened. A narrative approach to the task of theology and ethical reflection resonates most with the way that we naturally make sense of our world, supporting the conclusions made in this work surrounding the moral imagination.

Given literature's crucial role in moral reasoning, how might it engage with the specific moral challenges raised by human

---

[103] Ibid., 225–235.
[104] George Lakoff and Mark Johnson, *Metaphors We Live By* (Chicago, IL: University of Chicago Press, 2003).

enhancements? Farah Mendlesohn contends that 'in a genre predicated on the thought experiment, theological discourse comes naturally'.[105] If science fiction is such a focal point in 'non-fiction' futurist literature, then it makes sense to use it in our theological reflection on the same questions. The directing of the imagination towards questions of future human being, and of technological possibilities, not only shapes popular hopes and expectations, but might also help with discernment. The medium of fiction allows us to probe our own values – in science fiction it can serve to expose the metaphysical commitments of technologists who may otherwise claim a neutral or objective position for their research. Burdett summarises the value of science fiction as a corrective to transhumanist philosophies, because 'it is unabashed about the mythic status of its narratives and the inherent religious undertones it seeks to explore'.[106]

Recent scholarship indicates theologians and religious scholars are beginning to recognise this potential. The 2019 American Academy of Religion annual meeting included a panel that explored the modelling of sociotechnological futures in science fiction in conjunction with theological ideas, premised on the claim that 'exploring the technological determinations of a possible future always creates the conditions for imagining or reimagining human life and its significance under those conditions.'[107] But can we go further than this in linking fiction and the real technological future?

Arguably we can – as well as a resource for reflecting on these issues, fiction may also provide a helpful medium for *expressing* these theological reflections on human enhancement. Given how

[105] Farah Mendlesohn, 'Religion and Science Fiction', in *The Cambridge Companion to Science Fiction*, ed. Edward James (Cambridge: Cambridge University Press, 2003), 274–275. Paul Ricoeur makes this point concerning literature more generally (*Oneself as Another* (Chicago, IL: University of Chicago Press, 1992), 148).
[106] Burdett, *Eschatology and the Technological Future*, 69.
[107] Emmanuel Burton, 'The Nuts and Bolts of Transformation', *Zygon* 55, no. 3 (2020), 712. This guest editorial introduces the panel and its published papers.

vital the imagination is for transhumanist visions of the future, a greater focus on imagination might also equip and expand current theological responses to the challenges of human enhancement. Exploring the imaginative capacity of humans suggests that we *should* apply our creativity and ingenuity to improve human nature if possible, though we need to think carefully about limits and discernment. At the very least, a theological response to human enhancement that engages the imagination will go further in the public sphere than outlining a set of theological propositions and doctrines which many do not affirm. How might science fiction be a resource for theological discourse with respect to human enhancement and the human future?

Fiction is much more forgiving when it comes to the complexities surrounding the human enhancement debate, it can tease out some of the advantages and disadvantages of particular technologies yet resists the urge to provide an ethical 'checklist' against which each new technology ought to be evaluated. Some examples of fiction that allow us to engage human technological enhancement fruitfully will be offered in the final chapter.

7. The formation of the moral imagination requires our attention, including the diversity of stories which shape our moral imaginary.

The imagination has taken central place in our reflection on epistemology, and on the co-creative aspect of human action. McGilchrist identifies the work of the imagination as crucial to breaking out of the left hemisphere's deadening view of the world and restoring balance, according to his metaphor of hemispheric struggle.[108] As the imagination cannot be properly exercised apart from the moral life, so, Percy Bysshe Shelley contends, is the imagination 'the great instrument of moral good'.[109] He blames

---

[108] McGilchrist, *The Master and His Emissary*, 374.
[109] Shelley, 'A Defense of Poetry', 202.

'the cultivation of the mechanical arts in a degree disproportioned to the presence of the creative faculty' for the contemporary inequalities and abuses he observed.[110]

Philosopher Mark Johnson has highlighted the importance of the imagination in our ethical decision-making.

> We human beings are imaginative creatures, from our most mundane, automatic acts of perception all the way up to our most abstract conceptualization and reasoning. Consequently, our moral understanding depends in large measure on structures of imagination, such as images, image schemas, metaphors, narratives, and so forth. Moral reasoning is thus basically an imaginative activity, because it uses imaginatively structured concepts and requires imagination to discern what is morally relevant in situations, to understand empathetically how others experience things, and to envision the full range of possibilities open to us in a particular case.[111]

Ricoeur identifies the imagination as crucial for social action, for challenging the status quo.[112] Iris Murdoch places it at the centre of our moral vision, writing that 'I can only choose within the world I can see, in the moral sense of "see" which implies that clear vision is a result of moral imagination and moral effort.'[113] In attempting to articulate a framework that describes the imaginative dimensions of moral experience, Johnson argues that it is necessary to discard traditional conceptual dichotomies (those between intellect and feeling, imagination and reason, mind and body).[114] As he

---

[110] *Ibid.*, 205.

[111] Johnson, *Moral Imagination*, ix–x.

[112] Paul Ricoeur, 'Imagination in Discourse and in Action', in *The Human Being in Action: The Irreducible Element in Man, Part II Investigations at the Intersection of Philosophy and Psychiatry*, ed. Anna-Teresa Tymieniecka (Dordrecht: Springer, 1978).

[113] Iris Murdoch, 'Vision and Choice in Morality', *Proceedings of the Aristotelian Society* Supplementary vol. 30 (1956), 36–37.

[114] Johnson, *Moral Imagination*, x.

proceeds, he suggests that what we know of the imagination and its role in reasoning is inconsistent with certain aspects of a culturally inherited view of morality.[115]

To begin with, an affirmation of humans as fundamentally imaginative refutes any received views of morality that would seek out universal moral principles in an absolutist fashion. Such approaches depend on views of reasoning and conceptionalisation that have been demonstrated to be false by developments in the cognitive sciences.[116] Moral absolutism and moral relativism are both rejected for misconstruing the relationship between reason and imagination (regarding the latter as entirely subjective and unconstrained).[117] Johnson also challenges notions of moral objectivity as only secured through universal laws.[118] Instead, 'a new view is emerging of concepts as grounded in structures of our bodily interaction and as irreducibly imaginative in character', undermining the assumptions of traditional moral law theories which depend on a mind/body dualistic understanding of human nature.[119] Johnson problematises a moral law approach by demonstrating how its foundational concepts are metaphorically defined, which in turn can only be understood in embodied ways.[120]

The outcome of Johnson's analysis is a call for revisioning traditional conceptions of ethics, and the proffering of a constructive alternative, though he acknowledges that much of the revisioning

---

[115] *Ibid.*, x. Of course, this is not to suggest that the link between imagination and morality is a novel one. Interpreting the work of Mark Akenside, Engell describes 'the power of the imagination as the hinge connecting experience and perception with moral judgment'. Disordered imagination 'becomes the primary source of evil', whereas 'when guided properly, [the imagination] gives a sense of the cosmos as created by God and existing in harmony with man' (Engell, *The Creative Imagination*, 42).

[116] Johnson, *Moral Imagination*, 1.

[117] *Ibid.*, 3.

[118] *Ibid.*, 218.

[119] *Ibid.*, 6.

[120] *Ibid.*, 42.

of an imaginative morality remains to be accomplished.[121] An attentiveness to the moral imagination, however, gives us insight into the way that prototype concepts operate in our moral deliberation, the kinds of frames we apply to situations and the underlying metaphors that are definitive to our basic moral concepts and values.[122] We might probe the possibility of changing certain metaphors, and what this might do to our moral reasoning.[123] We can explore with empathy the experiences of others.[124] This level of reflection will at least promote a humility when it comes to our own moral claims, and a recognition that there can be a variety of moral options.[125] Johnson argues for a firmer imperative, however: 'We must cultivate moral imagination by sharpening our powers of discrimination, exercising our capacity for envisioning new possibilities, and imaginatively tracing out the implications of our metaphors, prototypes and narratives.'[126] Similarly, McGilchrist identifies art and religion as possible means for escaping the 'hall of mirrors' of the left hemisphere, allowing the right hemisphere to 'make a comeback'.[127]

When it comes to the use of the imagination in morality, Johnson argues for a notion of 'human objectivity' that can assess competing moral philosophies according to shared dimensions of human life (biological, cognitive, social and ecological) without purporting to achieve a 'God's-eye-view' form of objectivity.[128] Steven Winter offers a similar account of 'transperspectivity', in which the imagination allows us to perceive our own constructions

---

[121] Ibid., xi.
[122] Ibid., 189–194.
[123] Ibid., 194.
[124] Ibid., 242.
[125] Ibid., 195
[126] Ibid., 198. The importance of narrative will be examined more closely later in this chapter.
[127] McGilchrist, The Master and His Emissary, 388.
[128] Johnson, Moral Imagination, 240.

of the world and consider alternatives.[129] Lakoff and Johnson argue furthermore that 'we are not free to think just anything', rather learned conceptual systems become instantiated in our brains neurally and thus guide even our imagination.[130]

Despite the work of these champions of the imagination, James K. A. Smith contends that we mainly operate with flawed models of Christian formation that focus on 'convincing the intellect rather than recruiting the imagination'.[131] This echoes Johnson's warning that we need to move away from formulating moral laws in favour of cultivating the moral imagination.[132] Thinking about how we might recruit the imagination (of both Christians and the broader public) to moral reflection on human enhancement will surely enrich any understanding of co-creation in this domain.

Literature plays a major role in the shaping of the moral imagination. In his consideration of imaginative apologetics, Andrew Davison draws attention to the dearth of contemporary fiction engaging in apologetics through appeal to the imagination.[133] Perhaps one answer to the questions raised here is simply to produce more works of fiction that engage the challenges posed by human enhancement imaginatively.

In thinking through the impact of narrative generally and literature more particularly on our moral reflection, we are prompted to ask: *which* stories are shaping our beliefs and our moral imagination? For it is very easy for beliefs to become habits of mind to the extent that we view them as truths, as Ward points out with respect

---

[129] Steven Winter, '*Bull Durham* and the Uses of Theory', *Stanford Law Review* 42 (1990), 685–686.

[130] George Lakoff and Mark Johnson. *Philosophy in the Flesh: The Embodied Mind and Its Challenge to Western Thought* (New York: Basic Books, 2003), 4–5.

[131] Smith, *Imagining the Kingdom*, 39.

[132] Johnson, *Moral Imagination*, xii.

[133] Andrew Davison, ed., *Imaginative Apologetics: Theology, Philosophy and the Catholic Tradition* (London: SCM Press, 2011), 59. This comment comes in the introduction to Ward's essay 'The Good Serves the Better and Both the Best: C. S. Lewis on Imagination and Reason in Apologetics'.

to ideas of ethnicity and gender.[134] It is important not to overlook those stories that do not align with the dominant narratives of our broader cultural context.

A major critique of current human enhancement proposals is that they are only likely to increase existing inequalities.[135] Much is at stake in determining the ideals towards which humans ought to be enhanced: what should a human become? The potential for inequality can be challenged if a diversity of stories are actively sought and incorporated into a social imaginary within which the human future is reflected upon.

Some of these stories might involve a retelling of history, drawing attention to alternative accounts. Edward Said's *Orientalism*, for example, has led the field of postcolonial studies and in particular has challenged Western cultural representations of the Orient.[136] Kwok Pui-lan offers a postcolonial feminist theology, sketching a vision of theological practice that foregrounds gender and sexuality in a transnational approach.[137] She points out that postcolonial critics often resist construing the world in dichotomous terms, thus giving another reason for listening to non-Western accounts that hold myth and reason together without difficulty.[138] An analysis of the theological symbols operative in the colonial period, and their reappropriation in postcolonial discourse, offers new perspectives for a global theology.[139] The gospel has always accommodated the culture it inhabits in some way, and non-Western cultures represent additional dialogue partners as theology continues to find renewed expression in every age.[140] Thus, Kwok outlines the goal

---

[134] Ward, *Unbelievable*, 113.
[135] Tom Shakespeare, in foreword to Eilers et al., *The Human Enhancement Debate and Disability*, xii.
[136] Edward Said, *Orientalism* (New York: Vintage, 1979).
[137] Kwok Pui-lan, *Postcolonial Imagination and Feminist Theology* (London: SCM Press, 2005).
[138] *Ibid.*, 73.
[139] *Ibid.*, 144.
[140] *Ibid.*, 161.

of postcolonial critiques to offer 'a reading strategy and discursive practice that seek to unmask colonial epistemological frameworks, unravel Eurocentric logics, and interrogate stereotypical cultural representations'.[141]

In contrast to transhumanist arguments that justice requires the enhancement of human capabilities,[142] disability studies aim to expose the misconstruing of disabled bodies. Tobin Siebers describes the field:

> Disability studies does not treat disease or disability, hoping to cure or avoid them; it studies the social meanings, symbols, and stigmas attached to disability identity and asks how they relate to enforced systems of exclusion and oppression, attacking the widespread belief that having an able body and mind determines whether one is a quality human being.[143]

Siebers further argues that disability 'often comes to stand for the precariousness of the human condition, for the fact that individual human beings are susceptible to change, decline over time, and die'.[144] This is entirely opposed to the transhumanist endeavour, and thus, disability accounts are an important check to particular visions of the technological future. While some within the disability community welcome 'enhancement', others see it as a misguided solution.[145] Many with first-hand experience of particular conditions that would be targeted for eradication with biotechnology attest to the value of the 'impairments', arguing that human experience overall would be diminished without these atypical experiences. Dan Goodley and Katherine Runswick-Cole call

---

[141] *Ibid.*, 2.

[142] Julian Savulescu, 'Justice, Fairness, and Enhancement', *Annals of the New York Academy of Sciences* 2006; James Hughes, *Citizen Cyborg: Why Democratic Societies Must Respond to the Redesigned Human of the Future* (Cambridge, MA: Westview Press, 2004).

[143] Tobin Siebers, *Disability Theory* (Ann Arbor, MI: University of Michigan Press, 2008), 3–4.

[144] *Ibid.*, 5.

[145] Shakespeare, in Eilers et al., *The Human Enhancement Debate and Disability*, ix.

out the way in which many 'disabled' people have not been permitted to occupy the position of the 'modern human subject'.[146] In addition to challenging certain ideals of enhancement, disability studies offer bioethics a more concrete engagement with varied embodiment, rather than relying only on abstract thought.[147]

Other stories that ought to be listened to are fictional. The short story collection *Outlaw Bodies* explores from a number of perspectives the ways in which future bodies might be controlled through enhancements and modifications, and the implications for gender and sexual identity, and disability.[148] Kathryn Allan has edited a volume of essays that explore disability in science fiction, challenging the dominant presentation of technology as cure.[149] Ato Quayson focuses on frames applied to disability in Nobel Prize-winning literature, arguing that literature helps to 'refract these multivalent attitudes towards disability'.[150]

Afrofuturism is a movement that blends science fiction with African culture. 'Can a community whose past has been deliberately rubbed out, and whose energies have subsequently been consumed by the search for legible traces of its history, imagine possible futures?', asks major proponent Mark Dery.[151] Ytasha Womack shows that the answer is a resounding 'yes', giving a

---

[146] Dan Goodley and Katherine Runswick-Cole. 'Becoming Dishuman: Thinking About the Human Through Dis/ability', *Discourse: Studies in the Cultural Politics of Education* 37, no. 1 (2016), 3.

[147] Miriam Eilers, Katrin Grüber and Christoph Rehmann-Sutter, 'Refocusing the Enhancement Debate', in *The Human Enhancement Debate and Disability*, ed. Eilers et al., 15.

[148] Lori Selke and Djibril al-Ayad, eds., *Outlaw Bodies: A Speculative Fiction Anthology* (United States: Futurefire.net Publishing, 2012).

[149] Kathryn Allan, ed., *Disability in Science Fiction: Representations of Technology as Cure* (New York: Palgrave Macmillan, 2013).

[150] Ato Quayson, *Aesthetic Nervousness: Disability and the Crisis of Representation* (New York: Columbia University Press, 2007), 36.

[151] Mark Dery, 'Black to the Future: Interviews with Samuel R. Delany, Greg Tate, and Tricia Rose', *The South Atlantic Quarterly* 92, no. 4 (1993). Dery first coined the term 'Afrofuturism'.

clear introduction to Afrofuturist thought that reimagines the technological future through a Black cultural lens.[152]

In terms of a broader theological anthropology, Thweatt-Bates highlights the connections between the 'hybridity' of the cyborg and aspects of hybridity in feminist, disability, postcolonial and queer theologies.[153] Narratives of disability and bodily suffering challenge normative ideas of the human body. The way in which ideal 'types' of the human are encoded in the technologies we develop must be examined critically.[154] To do this critique justice requires much more space than we have here; however, the necessity of listening to diverse stories requires more than just lip service in reflecting on questions of human enhancement. Hart describes how 'the capacity to picture and to speak of the world otherwise than in accordance with the currently favoured social construct is itself a capacity to change reality', and this is the task before us.[155]

The concept of moral imagination and the more particular roles of narrative and literature described here connect in important ways to the notion of social imaginaries. Although we have arrived at similar ideas through the alternative routes of metaphor studies and phenomenology, the structure of the social imaginary has silently scaffolded much of these reflections. The social imaginary was first described in full by social theorist Cornelius Castoriadis with his publication of *L'institution imaginaire de la société* in 1975.[156] Castoriadis wrote of a creative force from which novelty emerges as a rupture in history; the instituting society forming

---

[152] Ytasha Womack, *Afrofuturism: The World of Black Sci-Fi and Fantasy Culture* (Chicago, IL: Chicago Review Press, 2013).

[153] Thweatt-Bates, *Cyborg Selves*, 142.

[154] Midson, *Cyborg Theology*, 193.

[155] Hart, 'The Glory of Imagination', 233. Here, Hart engages the utopian imagination explored in George Steiner, *After Babel: Aspects of Language and Translation* (Oxford: Oxford University Press, 1998).

[156] Of course, the term 'imaginary' is not original to Castoriadis (though he applies it in novel ways), and we may find it in both Sartre's *L'Imaginaire: Psychologie phénoménologique de l'imagination* (1940) and Lacan's *Le séminaire. Livre XI. Les quatre concepts fondamentaux de la psychanalyse* (1973). Note that the original French

worlds and bestowing meaning on them.[157] The 'imaginary' is the 'originary structuring component' which orients institutional systems and determines what is important for a society.[158] Symbol, myth and legend are the media by which social imaginaries are created.[159]

Dilip Parameshwar Gaonkar, in reference to Charles Taylor's use of the social imaginary, provides a helpful description:

> the way a given people imagine their collective social life. Within the folds of a social imaginary, we see ourselves as agents who traverse a social space and inhabit a temporal horizon, entertain certain beliefs and norms, engage in and make sense of our practices in terms of purpose, timing, and appropriateness, and exist among other agents.[160]

Taylor frames his secularisation narrative in terms of social imaginaries, arguing that we have shifted from imagining the world as an ordered 'cosmos' to a colder, lesser known 'universe'.[161] The sense of the sublime, so important in Romantic thought, replaces genuine transcendence within the immanent frame, provoking in us a tension that pushes back against the closed circle of materialism that constitutes the modern social imaginary.[162] The present social imaginary of 'expressive individualism' emphasises freedom of choice and tolerance as people seek authenticity in the way they

publications are mentioned here to give an accurate timeline of influence, but later English translations were read for this work.

[157] Corneliusm Castoriadis, *The Imaginary Institution of Society*, trans. Kathleen Blamey (Cambridge, MA: MIT Press, 1987), 184.

[158] *Ibid.*, 145.

[159] Thus Dilip Parameshwar Gaonkar draws parallels between Castoriadis and Ricoeur when it comes to language ('Toward New Imaginaries: An Introduction', *Public Culture* 14, no. 1 (2002), 8).

[160] *Ibid.*, 10. It should be noted that Taylor himself draws more on the prior work of Benedict Anderson than Castoriadis (Charles Taylor, 'Modern Social Imaginaries', *Public Culture* 14, no. 1 (2002), 92).

[161] Taylor, *A Secular Age*, 325–327.

[162] *Ibid.*, 339.

live out their humanity.[163] Furthermore, Taylor makes the case that a particular *moral* vision has come to shape the social imaginary of Western modernity, one that derives from seventeenth-century theories of natural law.[164] In this picture of society, people form a political entity against pre-existing notions of natural rights, and a version of the social contract emerges.[165] The modern moral order centres around mutual respect and benefit, and function and form are instrumentalised to the preservation of members as 'free agents', whereas the pre-modern moral order was directed towards excellence of virtue.[166]

Ward focuses on the power structures at work in creating social imaginaries, the political nature of the '*making* of a belief believable'.[167] This is a domain that depends on the work of the imagination; in creating belief in others 'there is a reaching down into levels of human being that are profound, rooted in evolutionary development, neurological substrates, and somatic and affected conditions'.[168] In his exploration of the architecture of belief, Ward draws together the offerings of Lakoff and Johnson, and McGilchrist among others to paint a picture of belief (and 'unbelief') as a relational and affective mode of cognition.[169] Belief is strongly associated with imagination, and further galvanised by literature.[170] Myths are operative within social imaginaries, they invoke the imagination 'to make us believe that this is the society in which we live or in which we should aspire to live'.[171] These mythic resonances can impact public reasoning in both good and evil ways, again highlighting the dangers that can be associated with

---

[163] Ibid., 478, 486.
[164] Taylor, 'Modern Social Imaginaries', 92.
[165] Taylor, *Modern Social Imaginaries*, 3–4.
[166] Ibid., 12–13.
[167] Ward, *Unbelievable*, 18–19.
[168] Ibid., 19.
[169] Ibid., 76.
[170] Ibid., 77, 136.
[171] Ibid., 164.

the imagination.[172] Ward's focus on the power dynamics at play in the creation of belief and social imaginaries leads us back to the necessity of listening to a diversity of stories.

We see a turn to the imagination in relation to our social conscience and questions of justice in the recent philosophical dialogue between philosopher Mary Zournazi and theologian Rowan Williams.[173] Their central concern is how to imagine a just world in the face of present violence and economic injustice, and they identify the training of the imagination as a crucial part of this moral task.[174]

8. Embodiment is crucial for imagination and understanding.

N. Katherine Hayles recounts the story of 'how information lost its body, that is, how it came to be conceptualized as an entity separate from the material forms in which it is thought to be embedded'.[175] As the previous chapter demonstrated, however, attending to the embodied dimension of knowing assists us in overcoming certain entrenched dichotomies. Lakoff and Johnson remind us that 'our common embodiment allows for common, stable truths', mediated through the imagination.[176]

We might also draw connections between Bourdieu's emphasis on the embodied dimension of 'knowing', the limitations of language, and Lakoff and Johnson's extensive research into the neuroscience of metaphor. In their 2003 afterword to the original 1980 text of *Metaphors We Live By*, they demonstrate from a range of research perspectives that metaphors operate unconsciously, at the level of concept rather than just language, and are

---

[172] Ward, *Unimaginable*, 224–225.

[173] Mary Zournazi and Rowan Williams, *Justice and Love: A Philosophical Dialogue* (London: Bloomsbury Academic, 2020).

[174] *Ibid.*, 158.

[175] Hayles, *How We Became Posthuman*, 2, emphasis original. Note that Hayles uses the term posthumanism; however, Thweatt-Bates critiques this as a conflation of posthumanist and transhumanist discourse, and considers Hayles' characterisation more relevant to the latter (Thweatt-Bates, *Cyborg Selves*, 68).

[176] Lakoff and Johnson, *Philosophy in the Flesh*, 6.

fundamentally embodied. They summarise one aspect of metaphor in understanding that resists linguistic articulation: 'our metaphors will reflect our commonplace experiences in the world. Inevitably, many primary metaphors are universal because everybody has basically the same kinds of bodies and brains and lives in basically the same kinds of environments'.[177]

McGilchrist, too, highlights the embodiment and foundational nature of metaphor, as 'the *only* way in which understanding can reach outside the system of signs to life itself'.[178] 'Everything has to be expressed in terms of something else, and those something elses eventually have to come back to the body.'[179] McGilchrist also reminds us that the gap that metaphor is able to carry us across is not experiential, but artificially created by language.[180] Not only is metaphor a remnant of previous understanding, but it can generate novel understanding.[181]

Johnson goes further in another work, strongly connecting both reason and the imagination with the body in an examination of the structure of rationality.[182] Challenging 'objectivist' approaches, in which 'the structure of rationality is regarded as transcending structures of bodily existence',[183] Johnson calls for a radical re-orientation towards the *embodiment* of human understanding.[184] He resists entrenched epistemological and ontological dichotomies in Western thought that he argues have resulted in the idea that 'imagination seems to exist in a no-man's land between the clearly demarcated territories of reason and sensation'.[185] At the same time, he also avoids the pitfalls of an outdated faculty psychology

---

[177] Lakoff and Johnson, *Metaphors We Live By*, 257.
[178] McGilchrist, *The Master and His Emissary*, 115, emphasis original.
[179] *Ibid.*, 116.
[180] *Ibid.*, 116.
[181] *Ibid.*, 179.
[182] Johnson, *The Body in the Mind*.
[183] *Ibid.*, x.
[184] *Ibid.*, xiii.
[185] *Ibid.*, xxix.

approach to cognition.[186] Building on Kant's work, Johnson thus concludes that 'All meaningful experience and all understanding involves the activity of imagination which orders our representations (the reproductive function) and constitutes the temporal unity of our consciousness (the productive function).'[187]

This approach to cognition furthermore resists the tendency, identified earlier in this work, to set reason and imagination in opposition with one another. In parallel to McGilchrist's and Smith's comments on the inadequacies of philosophical discourse for bridging binary thought, Marcel Proust attests to the more general difficulty of speaking theoretically about aspects of understanding and cognition apart from the rational. 'If intellect does not deserve the crown of crowns, only intellect is able to award it. And if intellect only ranks second in the hierarchy of values, intellect alone is able to proclaim that the first place must be given to instinct.'[188]

Posthumanist scholarship is another area that foregrounds the embodied dimension of our existence. Though the focus of this work has been on responding theologically to human enhancement questions that are most concentrated within transhumanist philosophies, the alternative proposals of posthuman discourse offer additional resources.[189]

---

[186] *Ibid.*, 139–140. John Coulson, too, warns against the tendency to view the imagination as a distinct mental faculty, separated entirely from reason (*Religion and Imagination: In Aid of a Grammar of Assent* (Oxford: Clarendon Press, 1981), 6–7). This error appears on both sides of the debate over rationalism, as Charles Frankel points out: 'The Irrationalist's theory of human nature is steeped in the tradition of the dualistic psychology it condemns. It talks about "reason" as though it were a department of human nature in conflict with "emotions". But "reason", considered as a psychological process, is not a special faculty, and it is not separate from the emotions; it simply the process of reorganising the emotions' ('The Nature and Sources of Irrationalism', *Science* 180 (1973), 930).

[187] Johnson, *The Body in the Mind*, 157.

[188] Marcel Proust, *On Art and Literature*, trans. Sylvia Townsend Warner (New York: Carroll & Graf, 1997), 25–26.

[189] The difference between posthumanism and transhumanism is discussed in footnote 1, p. 11.

Donna Haraway is a leading representative of posthumanist thought, particularly known for her 'cyborg manifesto'. Cyborgs are not foreign entities, argues Haraway; *we* are cyborgs.

A cyborg body is not innocent; it was not born in a garden; it does not seek unitary identity and so generate antagonistic dualisms without end (or until the world ends); it takes irony for granted. One is too few, and two is only one possibility. Intense pleasure in skill, machine skill, ceases to be a sin, but an aspect of embodiment. The machine is not an it to be animated, worshipped, and dominated. The machine is us, our processes, an aspect of our embodiment.[190]

Haraway arrives at the notion of the cyborg via a critique of feminist essentialism; all claims that would locate human identity in nature are challenged as importing patriarchal or colonial assumptions. Though addressing the technological dimension of human being, Haraway's proposals have little in common with the visions of transhumanists. Cary Wolfe contrasts the Renaissance and Enlightenment ideals of perfectability, rationality and agency inherent in transhumanism with Haraway's suspicion of reason, for example.[191] Thweatt-Bates sets the cyborg against the transhumanist vision of mind-uploading, in particular, arguing that the two represent a bifurcation in the possibility of posthuman existence.[192]

Thus, Haraway also challenges dichotomies, in this case between nature and technology.[193] In many respects, this is an answer to Coeckelbergh's search for the 'nonmachine' that can overcome the

---

190 Donna Haraway, 'A Cyborg Manifesto: Science, Technology, and Socialist-Feminism in the Late Twentieth Century', in *Simians Cyborgs and Women: The Reinvention of Nature* (New York: Routledge, 1991), 180.

191 Cary Wolfe, *What Is Posthumanism?* (Minneapolis, MN: University of Minnesota Press, 2010), xiii.

192 Thweatt-Bates, *Cyborg Selves*, 15.

193 See also Anne Kull, 'Mutations of Nature, Technology, and the Western Sacred', *Zygon* 41, no. 4 (2006).

technology–human binary. Thweatt-Bates points out that trans-humanist proposals tend to reinforce the nature/culture dichotomy through which posthumanism offers a way forward.[194] It is important to note that the hybridity of humans is not a new development. Andy Clark and David Chalmers, to give one example, argue for the externalisation of cognition, using technology to extend the mind into the environment outside the body.[195] This kind of hybridisation problematises Tolkien's wariness of technology – our experiences of the world have always been entwined with technology in some way.

9. Technology must not instrumentalise non-human nature.

This point echoes Heidegger's critique of the 'standing reserve'.[196] Tolkien's concerns around the impact of technology on the natural world were not unfounded, indeed the years since his death have seen even greater destruction than the industrial havoc which so dismayed him. As Hefner reminds us, we live in the 'technological civilization', the era in which all natural systems are affected by human decision.[197]

Christian theology has been charged with a tendency towards anthropocentrism at least since the publication of Lynn White's well-known exposition of the ecological crisis.[198] Here we can point to and learn from theologies that have sought to correct particular aspects of anthropocentrism. David Clough and Christopher Southgate both explore theologies that attend to the redemption of non-human animals, challenging notions of human exceptionalism.[199] It is also not surprising that we should find multiple concerns coming together in theological critique: thus feminist

[194] Thweatt-Bates, *Cyborg Selves*, 56.
[195] Andy Clark and David Chalmers. 'The Extended Mind', *Analysis* 58, no. 1 (1998).
[196] Heidegger, 'The Question Concerning Technology', 19.
[197] Hefner, *THF*, 48.
[198] Lynn White, 'The Historical Roots of our Ecologic Crisis', *Science* 155 (1967).
[199] David Clough, *On Animals* (London: Bloomsbury Publishing, 2013); Southgate, *The Groaning of Creation: God, Evolution and the Problem of Evil* (Louisville, KY: Westminster John Knox Press, 2008).

theology often finds common ground with ecological critiques and liberation theology. Ivone Gebara's *Longing for Running Water*, for example, is an ecofeminist work from a Latin American perspective, calling for a biocentric view of salvation. Speaking of Jesus, she reminds us that 'He comes from here, from this earth, this body, this flesh, from the evolutionary process that is present both yesterday and today in this Sacred Body within which love resides. It continues in him beyond that, and it is turned into passion for life, into mercy and justice.'[200]

Hefner offers a rather anthropocentric understanding of co-creation, not entirely surprising given his focus on theological anthropology. While he challenges instrumental views of non-human nature, he still preserves a special status for humans among the creation.[201] He does acknowledge those who would reject the created co-creator concept as too anthropocentric, yet articulates his own position as follows:

> Fundamentally, to suggest that the ecosystem is defining itself decisively in *Homo sapiens* is to suggest that the human species stands in special relationship to God – a relationship that I designate as 'co-creator'. To interpret the current situation as I have, with human beings poised as individuals, groups, and as a species on spaceship earth, bearing responsibility for discovering what 'it is all about', and acting upon that discovery – this is to suggest that the human species has become an agent in the creative process in a way that cannot be attributed to any other species – either in quality or quantity.[202]

Others, however, would go further than Hefner does and extend this co-creative agency to non-human animals. Roberts contends that

---

[200] Ivone Gebara, *Longing for Running Water: Ecofeminism and Liberation* (Minneapolis, MN: Fortress Press, 1999), 190.

[201] Hefner, *THF*, 230.

[202] Hefner, 'The Foundations of Belonging', 175.

the shared evolutionary history of all living species makes them all created co-creators to some extent and makes interspecies relationships constitutive of the image of God. While the divine image may be borne by human beings in distinct ways, it is shared with the rest of creation in at least this sense.[203]

Even the doctrine of the *imago Dei* does not have to be understood in terms of human exceptionalism. Andrew Linzey, for example, promotes a creation-centric view of stewardship in his own functional interpretation of the *imago Dei*.[204] Herzfeld highlights relational interpretations of the *imago Dei* as obviating the essentialism that pervades substantive (and usually functional) approaches.[205] Attempts to understand the image of God often move quickly through ideas of human uniqueness to ideas of human superiority, but this need not be the case.

We can also listen to anthropologies that are distinctly non-theological. Midson adapts Haraway's 'cyborgology', which heavily critiques theology for anthropocentrism, ultimately disagreeing with Haraway in his argument that 'theology is to be recognised as *part of* a problematic legacy insofar as its dominant anthropological perspective has lent itself well to humanocentric notions of human dominance, but it is also *part of* the way that we must rethink our understandings.'[206]

Midson lists a number of dichotomies that the cyborg may subvert because of its critical distance for reflection: 'givenness and constructedness; Eden and Fall; paradise and sin; angels and beasts'.[207] Elaine Graham draws attention to a lingering dualism

---

[203] Roberts, 'Fill and Subdue?', 52.
[204] Andrew Linzey, *Animal Theology* (Champaign, IL: University of Illinois Press, 1994), 144–146.
[205] Noreen Herzfeld, *In Our Image: Artificial Intelligence and the Human Spirit* (Minneapolis, MN: Augsburg Fortress, 2002), 90.
[206] Midson, *Cyborg Theology*, 24.
[207] *Ibid.*, 69, 86. Haraway herself lists an even more extensive number of dualisms overcome by the cyborg, including mind/body and God/man (Haraway, 'A Cyborg Manifesto', 177).

in Haraway's work, however – that between immanence and transcendence, or sacred and secular.[208] While Graham sees the sacramentalism inherent in Haraway's cyborg construction as incongruous, an artefact of her socialist-feminist rejection of religion, Thweatt-Bates more generously affirms a latent spirituality in Haraway that invites theological engagement.[209]

Thweatt-Bates does acknowledge the challenges of bringing Haraway's cyborg into theological discourse, noting the rejection of the Christian tradition embedded into the construct.[210] However, she develops the notion of 'hybridity' in a more theologically conducive direction, primarily by countering Haraway's assertion that cyborgs have never belonged to Eden in her understanding of Adam and Eve themselves as cyborg figures.[211]

Other theologians have engaged with the idea of the cyborg in conjunction with ideas of human exceptionalism. Despite critiques, Graham suggests that the cyborg might serve as a heuristic tool – it rejects 'solutions of either denial or mastery in favour of a post/human ethic grounded in complicity with, not mastery over, non-human nature, animals and machines'.[212] Hefner's interest in the idea of the cyborg was noted earlier.[213] Thweatt-Bates suggests that 'the hybrid embodiment of the cyborg serves as a symbol for the ontological kinship of the human with the non-human'.[214] This challenges the anthropocentrism inherent in much

---

208 Elaine Graham 'Nietzsche Gets a Modem: Transhumanism and the Technological Sublime', *Literature and Theology* 16, no. 1 (2002), 211.

209 Thweatt-Bates, *Cyborg Selves*, 83.

210 *Ibid.*, 12; cf. Haraway, 'A Cyborg Manifesto', 162.

211 Thweatt-Bates, *Cyborg Selves*, 172.

212 Graham, 'Nietzsche Gets a Modem', 228.

213 See p. 108. We may also find parallels here with van Huyssteen's scientifically engaged theological anthropology, contending as he does that humans are in continuity with non-human nature and that the *imago Dei* emerges from nature itself (Wentzel van Huyssteen, *Alone in the World? Human Uniqueness in Science and Theology* (Grand Rapids, MI: Eerdmans, 2006), 322).

214 Thweatt-Bates, *Cyborg Selves*, 5. This also accounts for Haraway's more recent scholarly focus on companion species (*ibid.*, 104).

of transhumanism, and thus the figure of the cyborg presents itself as a more natural ally for Hefner's hypothesis that the human purpose is to serve the entire natural order within which it is embedded.[215] Like Haraway, Hefner resists a nature/technology dichotomy at times: 'Now that we have broken down the walls that separate humans from both nature and technology, now that we are crossing the boundaries between these domains, we see that humans and their technology are a set of nature's possibilities.'[216]

However, Midson reasonably contends that Hefner misappropriates the cyborg in a more humanocentric way, locating 'the specifically technological within the specifically human'.[217] Midson highlights another important difference in the way Hefner interprets Haraway's cyborg: whereas Haraway jettisons the notion that we can somehow define human being, Hefner maintains some sense of normalisation.[218] Incorporating these critiques into a theological anthropology is a step in the right direction when it comes to envisioning a technological future that does not instrumentalise non-human creation for human interests.

We may, therefore, draw together several attempts to escape the restrictions of entrenched dichotomies in the way we understand ourselves and the world. From a variety of different starting points, scholars are highlighting the interconnectedness of nature and culture, and the embodied nature of mind and cognition, and recognising that this troubles historical dualisms in Western philosophy. Though Bourdieu, for example, is concerned with slightly different

[215] See 'Hypothesis 2' on p. 80.
[216] Hefner, *Technology and Human Becoming*, 77. While Hefner does challenge some aspects of human exceptionalism, he still accords 'much more worth' to humans over their 'lower kin' (Hefner, *THF*, 85).
[217] Midson, *Cyborg Theology*, 142. Hefner himself confirms the anthropocentrism in his proposals (Hefner, *Technology and Human Becoming*, 76–77).
[218] Midson, *Cyborg Theology*, 139. In sympathy with the analysis of Hefner presented earlier in this work, Midson attributes this difference to Hefner's greater certainty when it comes to metaphysics (*ibid.*, 140).

dichotomies from those identified here as operative in co-creation theologies, his articulation of the *betweenness* of *habitus* may offer some tools for how we conceive of imagination and its relationship to reason and epistemology more generally. Metaphor is not *either* conceptual *or* linguistic, but *both*, and draws on bodily relationships to the world to generate meaning. The intellect and affect are both embodied as well, relying on the imagination and unable to be disentangled from the imagination. Dichotomies break down as we try unsuccessfully to examine each faculty in isolation and distinguish an independent function. Following along this line of enquiry that acknowledges a 'betweenness' or a sense of 'hybridity' with respect to traditional dichotomies, resisting the tendency to construe the imagination as opposed to reason, or technology as antithetical to nature and virtue, may open up new ways of conceiving of human activity and responsibility from a theological perspective as we are confronted with questions of human enhancement.

10. Elements of the visions of transcendence inherent in transhumanist thought can be reclaimed as central to a Christian imagination.

Challenging dichotomies in this fashion restores the imagination to a central place in a response to transhumanism. As raised earlier, there are a number of common elements between transhumanist visions of the future and Christian eschatology.[219] The language of transhumanism is replete with references to gods, salvation, heaven and the like. Presented in ways that 'recruit' the imagination (as Smith puts it), the visions of transcendence and glorification proclaimed so confidently in transhumanist literature are ripe for reclamation by Christian theologians, philosophers, writers and artists. We might respond with a fuller vision of the

---

[219] See 'Transhumanism as a Religious Narrative' beginning on p. 23.

human future, a greater hope to set alongside the imaginings of transhumanists and techno-utopians.[220]

Whereas technology itself tends to occupy many of the classic roles of a deity in the present technological paradigm, theologians are able to expose the 'pretensions to self-love' inherent in certain technological mindsets.[221] A Christian account of hope declares that in conceiving, assessing and implementing technologies, we bear neither the burden of correctly envisioning or accomplishing redemption for ourselves nor the risk and dread of complete failure. Technology occupies its proper place within the work of a gracious God who allows creation to participate in bringing the creation towards glorious fulfillment.

In this respect, by setting imaginative portrayals of Christian hope alongside transhumanist projections of the future we might think of theology as entering the 'tournament of narratives', to return to McClendon's phrase.[222] A theological anthropology that is robust and resilient, engaging the challenges of the day, is well-resourced to compete for people's imagination in the present pluralistic context.

It should be clear at this point that an emphasis on moral imagination is not going to offer directives in specific ethical cases, including those relevant to human enhancement (apart from those which pose a threat to embodiment perhaps). Moral theories (or even laws) can only ever provide clear guidance for the most straightforward of cases.[223] Johnson summarises the outcome of a shift towards the moral imagination. 'We will reflect and act differently, because we see the importance of moral perception and discernment, of imaginatively taking up the part of others, and

---

[220] Justin Ariel Bailey has recently argued for an apologetics which engages the imagination that could serve as a helpful foundation, though he does not tackle the subject of human technological enhancement (*Reimagining Apologetics: The Beauty of Faith in a Secular Age* (Downers Grove, IL: InterVarsity Press, 2020)).

[221] Brock, *Christian Ethics in a Technological Age*, 376–379.

[222] McClendon, *Systematic Theology: Ethics*, 143.

[223] Johnson, *Moral Imagination*, 187.

of envisioning alternative possibilities for composing situations in ways that contribute to human flourishing.'[224]

Obviously, the fact that we can imagine something about the future does not mean it will or should come true. Much of the distrust of the imagination stems from the fact that its realm is so large. If we can imagine the wildly fantastic, what use is it to us as we try to say anything real about the present or future? John Tyndall, addressing the Royal Society in 1870, suggested that 'There are tories [sic] in science who regard Imagination as a faculty to be avoided rather than employed. They observe its action in weak vessels and are unduly impressed by its disasters. But they might with equal justice point to exploded boilers as an argument against the use of steam.'[225] Let us not explode the boiler of imagination by treating science fiction as straight-up prophecy. But let us not underestimate the value of the imagination as a resource for both theological reflection and communication either. Kevin Vanhoozer makes a similar point, arguing that the existence of vain imaginings 'no more disqualifies the imagination from serving theology than the existence of logical fallacies disqualifies reason'.[226] By thinking about enhancement technologies within the context of the moral imagination, however, we are freed from the requirement or impulse to develop a prescriptive, propositional approach to technological assessment. Brock reminds us that the Christian gospel 'reveals as good news human ingenuity and the richness of creation's given material order, insisting that the two can come together in the creation of good and beneficial techniques and mechanical artefacts'.[227] In making this statement, he affirms two basic claims: that human collaboration with God's work can compete

---

[224] *Ibid.*, 215.

[225] Tyndall, *Scientific Use of the Imagination*, 6.

[226] Kevin Vanhoozer, 'Imagination in Theology', in *New Dictionary of Theology: Historical and Systematic*, 2nd edn, ed. Martin Davie et al. (London: InterVarsity Press, 2016), 442.

[227] Brock, *Christian Ethics in a Technological Age*, 381.

with mixed motives in a world that is still being redeemed, but also that we are freed from 'the burden of ensuring that God triumphs over the powers of this age'.[228]

Conclusion

The theological anthropology gestured towards here combines Hefner's interest in the technological future and the biocultural nature of humans with Tolkien's affinity for the imagination, both literary and moral. This type of synthesis requires additional resources to challenge existing dichotomies of thought between imagination and reason, nature and technology, and mind and body. Incorporating wide-ranging threads of the phenomenological tradition, cognitive sciences and metaphor, and posthuman discourse, Hefner's and Tolkien's articulations of human creativity are brought together, promising a fruitful engagement with proposals for human technological enhancement.

[228] *Ibid.*, 380–381.

7 | Engaging Human Enhancement Theologically
A Productive Approach

The novelty of the co-creation theology articulated in the previous chapter lies partly in its ability to engage contemporary debates around hybridity and embodiment. It retains the strengths of a scientifically oriented anthropology, while also overcoming the constraints of earlier models that sought to integrate science and theology. The co-creation theology sketched out here is unapologetically *theological* in its starting point. It operates within a Christian world view, yet seeks to understand human being in terms that are also compatible (though not synonymous) with what we can know from scientific enquiry. This approach is likely to gain more traction now that the science and religion field is maturing, moving on from the need to justify theological claims through translation into scientifically verifiable proposals.[1]

At the same time, the imaginative and artistic dimensions of co-creativity are fleshed out – brought to the fore even. Resisting sharp distinctions between different types of 'making' such as art and technology permits a more integrated vision of human creativity. We have tended to be more comfortable with the idea that art forms can mirror divine creativity in some way, perhaps because we can more easily classify art as beautiful, but expanding the territory of the creative imitation of the divine (imitation, of course, reminds us of the boundaries) into the realm of technology gives us new vantage points from which we can reflect on moral implications.

---

[1] For a discussion of this maturation, see the articles discussing Joshua Reeve's *Against Methodology in Science and Religion* (2018) in *Zygon* 55, no. 3 (2020).

This also intersects with contemporary accounts that ground our thinking about technology within more traditional understandings of what it means to practise a craft well, in dialogue with historical understandings of *technê* and its relation to virtue and the good life.[2] Of course, this issues a number of challenges for how we think about technology today, suggesting a move away from the contemporary emphasis on self-expression and individuality in design towards a more reflective practice of craftsmanship.

The contemporary contrast between the artist and the engineer is not all that helpful when it comes to technologically enhancing human characteristics and abilities. We may not be able to return to the earlier aesthetic spirit that animated scientific discovery and technological innovation in bygone eras, but perhaps we can find a new expression of creativity in technology that pushes back against more clinical, instrumentalising methodologies. Heidegger continues to resonate in such undertakings.

The critique of technology offered by Tolkien is representative of his historical location, understandable against the backdrop of his wartime experiences and the rapid industrialisation of the English countryside. In that particular historical moment, critics played a vital role in countering the overly optimistic narrative of technological progress. Tolkien's work also represents a key challenge to the atomising, reductive tendencies of his time. At the same time, more contemporary discourse has revealed the fallacies present in distinguishing too neatly between nature and culture or nature and technology – not only is technology somewhat inchoate a concept, but in reality it is entangled with our existence in ways that Tolkien simply does not do justice to in his own treatment of the subject. For the most part, his wariness of technology prompted him into imaginative forays that were nostalgic, and perhaps escapist, in the sense that they avoid attempting to envision a more positive future that is at the same time technological. We may retain his

[2] See, for example, Sennett, *The Craftsman*.

268

capacity for *mythopoesis* and his intuitive understanding that narrative can communicate and inspire commitment to grand visions, while simultaneously engaging the present technological landscape in a more pragmatic fashion.

The proposed approach is thus fruitful in that it understands narrative accounts to do important work, recruiting imaginations in their articulation of a particular way of being. It encourages engagement with both the sciences and the arts and humanities as valuable for understanding the human condition and reflecting on future possibility. It also acknowledges the particularity of story, and the need for visions of what a good life ought to look like (and the associated goals of enhancement) to be formed by a plurality of stories, located in particular times, places, cultures and bodies.

With a greater blurring of boundaries between nature, culture, technology and the embodied mind, this enriched iteration of previous theological anthropologies is far better resourced to address questions of human enhancement, which inherently confound these traditional boundaries, than Tolkien's stark contrasts. While Hefner comes closer to the mark in his understanding of humans as biocultural organisms, this model additionally avoids his tendency to collapse culture into evolutionary science, and to define it in strongly anthropocentric terms.

Thus, a constellation of contemporary discourses is identified within which the proposed approach to human creativity as it impinges on human enhancement debates might operate and flourish. As scholarship continues to pursue a more integrated approach to understanding human being and relationship with the non-human world in all its complexity, it will continue refining a theological anthropology that can support ongoing ethical deliberation over how and what we create.

While this framework for co-creation does not produce quick or easy answers to the forms of enhancement we might devise, it does solidify a few guidelines. Enhancements that radically alter the human body, or eradicate biological existence entirely, require careful assessment as to how drastic changes to our present embodied existence might impact our common metaphorical understanding, mediated through our bodily experience of the world.

Though enhancements that threaten to eradicate a physical body entirely have been cautioned against, other potential enhancements may be more benign. For the most part, potential enhancements can be framed as warranting ethical deliberation over their use in much the same way as any other kind of technology. If a pill improves our concentration in prayer, should we take it? Do we lose something in forgoing the process of disciplining our minds and wills in favour of a technological solution, or does the end result justify this kind of approach? These are not new quandaries, though the technological means itself might be novel.

Thus, greater attention to the moral imagination, and the way it is being formed, is the appropriate anchor to which reflection on co-creation through human enhancement technologies ought to be tethered. So where might this approach to human creativity be productive? The remainder of this chapter will return to some of the specific examples of human technological enhancement introduced in the first chapter of this work, to consider how the model proposed in the previous chapter might inform a theological engagement with these particular scenarios.

Applying the Proposal

In Chapter 1, four domains of human technological enhancement were briefly surveyed to give an idea of the human future envisioned by many enhancement advocates: radical life extension, mind-uploading, hedonic recalibration and moral enhancement. These are now revisited in light of the approach to human creativity sketched out in the previous chapter, proffered as a starting point for theological engagement. The hallmarks identified are not treated sequentially, and some are discussed generally at the end rather than applied to each individual scenario; the intent is to outline the potential of this framework rather than complete an exhaustive analysis.

Radical Life Extension

Understanding the creative evolutionary process as the context in which human life has arisen, we are able to resist the tendency to designate narrow biological parameters as normative in our theological understanding of what makes us human. While there are some religious critiques of radical life extension that fall back on the idea that 'three-score and ten' (i.e. 70 years) is the proper duration of a human lifespan,[3] it is evident that the average lifespan is increasing for a number of reasons.[4] We observe a trajectory towards greater longevity in human evolutionary history; at the same time scientific research into ageing directs us towards particular physiological processes (e.g. telomere shortening and oxidative stress) that need to be halted or reversed if we are to 'transcend' apparent upper limits to the human lifespan. By incorporating scientific insights and being aware of evolutionary origins we are freed from ascribing normativity to any quantifiable lifespans in scripture (understanding these not to be prescriptive) but also understand that mortality, a feature of creaturehood, is attested for biological reasons as well.

In itself, this does not mean we are prohibited from employing technology to extend lifespans if possible; to overcome some of these physical limitations. Technology is, after all, a legitimate exercise of our creative capacities. When we account for the proper

---

3 This comes from Psalms 90:10, but ironically the same verse mentions an 80-year lifespan as a possibility for the strong, and Genesis 6:3 refers to 120 years as the limit placed by God on a human lifespan.

4 This is generally true, although health and economic issues have led to a recent decline in average lifespan in the United States (Steven Woolf and Heidi Schoomaker, 'Life Expectancy and Mortality Rates in the United States, 1959–2017', *JAMA* 322, no. 20 (2019)).

relationship between human and divine creativity, however, we are given some firmer guidance. In particular, the distinction highlighted in Chapter 2 between the two modes of divine creation – *bārā'* and *yatsar* – is significant. Given that all material creation is finite, and only God the creator is infinite, we might reserve certain attributes to *bārā'* creation alone. Increasing longevity by itself through technological means might be considered appropriate human activity (*yatsar* creation), but where the goal of radical life extension is ultimately immortality (as is often the case), we may say this has crossed over into the type of creation that belongs to God alone.

In attending to the nature of human creativity, most akin to the notion of craftsmanship, the ends to which putative radical life extension technologies are directed come into focus. Hart reminds us that the authority to exercise freedom, creativity and 'originality' is hard-won in the context of craftsmanship,[5] and even this authority is accountable to community and collective wisdom in a way that little resembles the autonomy and creative latitude claimed by the majority of contemporary artists and technological innovators alike.

We may also turn to imaginative explorations of radical longevity and its implications. *The Price of Life* (1987) and *In Time* (2011) are both science fiction films with a similar premise: that ageing can be controlled and time therefore becomes a currency. Both films explore the social inequalities that rapidly spring up between a short-lived working class and the near immortal elite. Johann Roduit, Tobias Eichinger and Walter Glannon demonstrate how fiction can be used to engage the ethical concerns around radical life extension from a philosophical perspective, analysing its potential consequences as portrayed in *In Time*.[6] They raise many

---

[5] Hart, *Making Good*, 27.

[6] Johann Roduit, Tobias Eichinger and Walter Glannon. 'Science Fiction and Human Enhancement: Radical Life-Extension in the Movie "In Time" (2011)', *Medicine Healthcare and Philosophy* 21 (2018).

of the same questions that theologians might put to the prospect of 'engineering negligible senescence' – the justice of inequitable distribution and regulation, the boredom or heightened fear of death and risk avoidance that would likely characterise the lives of the negligibly senescent, and the issue of overpopulation (which may be translated into issues of procreation).[7]

Zhange Ni explores the contemporary Chinese subgenre of immortality cultivation fiction for a different perspective to the dominant transhumanist vision of radical life extension. Though transhumanism is largely associated with 'white bourgeoisie males', Ni focuses on a non-white iteration of transhumanism that 'strives to rebel against rather than replicate' colonial depictions of the ideal human.[8] In contrast to most Western visions of technological immortality, the enhancement project described in these Chinese works of immortality cultivation 'builds a public cultivation/education system open to all, promotes cooperation rather than competition, and writes into its constitution the social obligations of accomplished cultivators to care for the less powerful and disenfranchised'.[9]

The appeal to fictional portrayals reminds us that technology itself does not address underlying issues of justice and equality but is likely to exacerbate them unless radical redress is an explicit motivation. Rather than denounce the project of radically extending life with theological condemnations of 'playing God', or declarations concerning the sanctity of created human life in static terms, we might instead address the public imagination, asking people to reflect on how 'more' of our present existence is likely to look. Science fiction resources this reflection with its

---

[7] Ibid., 289–291.

[8] Zhange Ni, 'Reimagining Daoist Alchemy, Decolonizing Transhumanism: The Fantasy of Immortality Cultivation in Twenty-First Century China', Zygon 55, no. 3 (2020); cf. Syed Mustafa Ali, ' "White Crisis" and/as "Existential Risk", or the Entangled Apocalypticism of Artificial Intelligence', Zygon 54, no. 1 (2019).

[9] Ni, 'Reimagining Daoist Alchemy', 764.

overwhelmingly dystopic nature, exploring the consequences of present social realities if they are allowed to extend into the future without radical transformation.

This imaginative exercise then provides the opportunity of presenting an alternative vision. Instead of 'more of the same', the Christian anticipates a future that actually *is* radically different from the present. More will be said about this in the next section, as mind-uploading goes further than radical life extension in its vision of digital immortality.

Mind-Uploading

Extending our biological lifespan is not the only way to create more time. Some transhumanists envision the uploading of our minds to a digital substrate, trading our dependence on frail, degenerating 'meat' bodies for the immortality of software existence.[10]

This is one point at which we might give a more concrete response to a particular type of technological enhancement. Given that our capacity to 'know' is bound up in our embodied existence, the more radical proposal of 'mind-uploading' is extremely problematic.[11] What would jettisoning the body do to our ability to make sense of our world? Husserl's 'intersubjectivity', the 'preconscious knowing' of Merleau-Ponty and the *habitus* of Bourdieu all depend on a bodily experience that is somewhat shared. This also raises questions as to how a radical morphological freedom and diversity as a result of enhancing technologies might impact our present ability to comprehend the world and the other.

Some advocates of mind-uploading have recognised these concerns. Kurzweil thus argues that 'a reinstantiated mind will need a body, since so much of our thinking is directed toward physical needs and desires' and imagines a virtual human body 'version

---

[10] In fact, for many the goal of increasing biological longevity is viewed as an intermediate measure until mind-uploading technology is developed.

[11] Thweatt-Bates, *Cyborg Selves*, 139.

2.0'.[12] Bostrom makes a similar case for the use of simulated bodies that would permit uploads to experience the same sensations as a 'regular' human body via virtual reality.[13] The notion of 'extended cognition' already operates as we augment our minds with tools and other devices, and the plasticity of the brain and its relationship with the body which allows for the possibility of new forms of embodiment.[14] Andy Clark's view of the human self as 'a constantly negotiable collection of resources easily able to straddle and crisscross the boundaries between biology and artifact' comes close to the hybrid existence recognised in posthuman discourse.[15] The agent/world boundary is reconfigurable; human–machine interfaces are the outworking of a biological plasticity that humans have always enjoyed.[16]

Respecting and incorporating scientific information into our theological reflections, as the model proposes, reveals a certain ambiguity over the value of the body. While some transhumanism advocates (but not all, as mentioned above) are looking to escape embodiment via a mind-uploading process, it is ironic that many of their otherwise close allies in AI research are turning emphatically *towards* the body in their work. AI researchers are recognising the centrality of embodiment for cognition, and accounting for this in their technological development. In fact, AI is one of the strands of enquiry that feeds into the broader field of embodied cognition. Matej Hoffman and Rolf Pfeifer, for example, have experimented with embodied AI, demonstrating a greater ability to process information in robots able to interact with the environment through

---

[12] Kurzweil, *The Singularity Is Near*, 199.
[13] Bostrom, 'The Transhumanist FAQ'.
[14] Andy Clark, 'Re-inventing Ourselves: The Plasticity of Embodiment, Sensing, and Mind', in *The Transhumanist Reader: Classical and Contemporary Essays on the Science, Technology and Philosophy of the Human Future*, ed. Max More and Natasha Vita-Moore (Oxford: Wiley & Sons, 2013), 120.
[15] *Ibid.*, 124.
[16] *Ibid.*, 125.

movement and sensors.[17] Embodiment was a key priority in MIT researcher Rodney Brook's AI development.[18] Noel Sharkey and Tom Ziemke question whether robot embodiment might produce the sought-after 'strong' AI (though they answer in the negative, their question reveals the priority of the body in their research).[19] These scientific explorations lend weight to a theological appraisal of mind-uploading proposals and their consequences for embodiment.

The type of AI possible is only one of a number of scientific questions prompted by reflection on the relationship between 'intelligence' and the body. Essentially, these questions centre around what happens to bodies as we pursue the hypothetical scenarios of both the uploading of our own minds (which presumably will not remain restricted to our current 'processing' capacities) or the development of general AI. We might ask whether 'artificial' intelligence is aimed at simulating *human* intelligence. Although human intelligence has tended to be the starting template in AI research, notions of general AI have acknowledged a plurality to the concept of intelligence. Could non-embodied intelligence be better than our present embodied experience? This is mainly speculation at this stage and depends upon subjective evaluations of different forms of intelligence. We do need to consider what we might lose if we move further away from our present bodily relation to the world outside of us, what happens to our intuitive ability, our shared language and understanding, etc. But on the flip side, new ways of occupying the physical world may enrich our metaphorical understanding and thought processes in unforeseen ways.

---

[17] Matej Hoffman and Rolf Pfeifer, 'The Implications of Embodiment for Behavior and Cognition: Animal and Robotic Case Studies', in *The Implications of Embodiment: Cognition and Communication*, ed. Wolfgang Tschacher and Claudia Bergomi (Exeter: Imprint Academic, 2012).

[18] A helpful analysis of the Cog and Kismet project is offered by Anne Foerst, 'Cog, a Humanoid Robot, and the Question of the Image of God', *Zygon* 33 (1998).

[19] Noel Sharkey and Tom Ziemke, 'Mechanistic Versus Phenomenal Embodiment: Can Robot Embodiment Lead to Strong AI?', *Cognitive Systems Research* 2, no. 4 (2001).

Can there be adequate communication between embodied and non-embodied intelligence?[20] Can minds enmeshed in biological systems and bodies find a common way of communicating and understanding with minds embedded in other material, or even disembodied, given they inhabit the same world in very different physical configurations? The mind-uploading project tends to be focused on whether a computer can either simulate or possess a *human mind*. Whatever kind of mind a computer might lay claim to, it cannot really be a *human* mind, because human minds come in human bodies. All the subtleties of human-to-human communication, many of which operate at intuitive and instinctive levels, are at the very least complicated by an increase in alternative morphologies or non-physical existence. It is a much bigger communication gap than those presently in place due to language or cultural barriers.

In fact, the reality of our imaginations being tethered to our bodily relations with the world means we may not even be capable of meaningfully imagining an entirely disembodied uploaded existence. It is perhaps not trivial that fictional uploaded minds tend to still adopt virtual bodies of some sort. To give one example, we might direct people to Charles Stross' excellent novel *Glasshouse*. Stross imagines a post-Singularity existence in which everyone exists as an uploaded mind, and highlights the dangers of censorship, memory preservation and identity theft. Large swaths of history have been expunged, vulnerable to viruses developed with malevolent intent. The freedom of morphological and psychological expression and identity (and the ability to change these at will) is represented as a vast improvement over the constrained sexual relationships of the past (especially as biological reproduction is no longer relevant), yet a controlled experiment attempting to recover knowledge of twentieth-century social practices ultimately challenges some of these assumptions. Stross is

---

[20] Note that this question has implications for AI research as well as mind-uploading.

able to simultaneously critique present social realities and imagined future ideals.

Or we might consider the recent work *Lock In*, by John Scalzi, in which neural network implants and virtual reality technologies are used to enhance the quality of life and freedom of individuals suffering from total paralysis in their physical bodies. They are able to control robotic personal transport units, and can therefore pursue 'normal' activities in their daily lives. These imaginings open up a possibility for such technologies that theologians may not have considered: where medicine may continue to fail in healing paralysis, other technologies may step in to restore a fuller experience of human flourishing that could otherwise by denied to particular individuals. Of course, the difficulty of distinguishing enhancement from therapy comes into play here, but fictional explorations assist our theological reflection on such technologies. Perhaps an uploaded mind controlling an artificial body of a sort may restore dignity in some cases and reduce inequalities around physical access and mobility issues.

Listening to the diversity of human experience yields the insight that we do not share one common bodily experience even now. Studies in gender or disability already challenge us to consider how different bodies shape different perspectives and produce different realities. They can expose the ways in which particular types of bodies are treated as normative, as well as the dominant representation of technological 'cure'. The way in which ideal 'types' of the humans are encoded in the technologies we develop must be examined critically.[21] We still have a lot to learn when it comes to present embodiment, but these discourses at the margins offer a more concrete engagement with varied embodiment than the abstraction of much of cognitive science and AI research.

This is not to say that uploading human minds is prohibited by a theological understanding of what it means to be human,

---

[21] Midson, *Cyborg Theology*, 193.

or that a proper theological anthropology will necessarily exclude these alternative beings from its understanding of what constitutes humanity. Karen O'Donnell, drawing on performative accounts of the *imago Dei*, argues that AI may well have the capacity to learn to image God.[22] This is a good example of the way in which theological enquiry needs to engage with and respond to emerging technologies and their implications for human being.

Our understanding of what it means to be human is not only shaped by specific embodiment experiences; a particular conception of human has coalesced and been reified in exclusionary discourse. Sylvia Wynters traces the emergence of the 'ethnoclass Man', a male, Euro-centric religious form of human that exists in antagonistic relation to various subhuman 'others'.[23] Her analysis is magisterial, yielding too many insights to do it justice here, but reminds us of the need to interrogate the source of our assumptions about human being, to consider *who* decides what ought to be preserved and prioritised in attempts to extend 'human' existence via technological means.

A theological engagement with the prospect of mind-uploading will be substantially enriched by the final aspect of this work's proposal: a reclamation of Christian ideas about hope and flourishing. Mind-uploading and radical life extension both desire more *time*. In the social imaginary terms associated with Charles Taylor, they are very much confined within the immanent frame. In the language of eschatology, they see the future only as an extension of the past and present, something they can extend indefinitely – there is no room in their thinking for a future that breaks in unexpectedly and transforms time. Jürgen Moltmann first drew attention

[22] Karen O'Donnell, 'Performing the imago Dei: Human Enhancement, Artificial Intelligence and Optative Image-Bearing', *International Journal for the Study of the Christian Church*, 2018, 2.

[23] Sylvia Wynter, 'Unsettling the Coloniality of Being/Power/Truth/Freedom: Towards the Human, After Man, Its Overrepresentation – An Argument', *CR: The New Centennial Review* 3, no. 3 (2003).

to the difference between *futurum* (the future is a continuation of the present) and *adventus* (the future arises from outside of time and space as a fulfillment of divine promise).[24] The end to which transhumanism is directed is *futurum*, with humans the agent of a technological redemption.[25] Here, Christian hope may expose these enhancement proposals not as unreasonable, or nonsensical, or even hubristic (even if they are true adjectives, these hardly lend themselves to constructive dialogue) but rather as insufficiently imaginative, or ambitious, by comparison. Richard Bauckham and Trevor Hart go as far to argue that the failure of both modernity and postmodernity in sustaining hope creates room for the renewed expression of Christian hope – while these failures do not demonstrate the truthfulness of Christianity they allow its vision of the future to be heard.[26]

A full theology of the resurrection is beyond the present scope, but the bodily resurrection that occupied the centre of eschatological hope for much of Christian history is a powerful image of future being when set alongside a disembodied 'shadow' existence. In Romans 8:23, Paul speaks of 'the redemption of our bodies'. N. T. Wright traces the way that hope in the bodily resurrection has been relegated to the margins in contemporary Christian thought, but contends that a renewal of the biblical vision for resurrection hope re-establishes the drive for 'lively and creative Christian work in the present world'.[27] The particulars of the incorruptible, immortal resurrection body described in I Corinthians 15 are beyond description here, beyond our powers to imagine fully at all perhaps, but even

[24] Jürgen Moltmann, *The Coming of God: Christian Eschatology*, trans. Margaret Kohl (Minneapolis, MN: Fortress Press, 2004), 25–26.
[25] Michael Burdett develops this thesis extensively in *Eschatology and the Technological Future*.
[26] Richard Bauckham and Trevor Hart, 'The Shape of Time', in *The Future as God's Gift: Explorations in Christian Eschatology*, ed, David Fergusson and Marcel Sarot (Edinburgh: T. & T. Clark, 2000), 68.
[27] N. T. Wright, *Surprised by Hope: Rethinking Heaven the Resurrection and the Mission of the Church* (New York: HarperOne, 2008), 148.

attempts to imagine this aspect of Christian hope (C. S. Lewis' *The Great Divorce* is a wonderful place to start) are far more thrilling than the techno-immortality envisioned by transhumanists.

Moral Enhancement

Historically, the idea of moral enhancement has generally been uncontroversial; one of the objectives of education, formation and participation in spiritual activities. In terms of *technological* enhancement, however, the aim is to act directly on specific neurological states or functions to bring about particular moral improvements.[28] The focus in this work is not on the feasibility of such technologies per se, but it is worth noting that the lack of a unified cognitive system for moral judgement and the complex interplay of emotion and reason in moral discernment are formidable obstacles that putative technologies must overcome.[29]

Harris Wiseman critiques moral bioenhancement discourse on intellectual grounds, arguing that it construes evil and character as biological problems.[30] Many theologians would likely dismiss the notion that morality can be engineered in any way; the idea of moral enhancement leads us naturally back to the question of sin and fallenness. If we take scientific insights seriously, however, hamartiology becomes significantly complicated by a commitment to the evolutionary origins of human beings, and traditional accounts of the fall require some revision. If we account for the embodied nature of cognition, and the complex interplay between affect, intellect and imagination, we cannot avoid the conclusion that sin itself is bound up in biological and psychological

---

[28] Brian Earp, Thomas Douglas and Julian Savulescu, 'Moral Neuroenhancement', in *The Routledge Handbook of Neuroethics*, ed. L. Syd Johnson and Karen Rommelfanger (New York: Routledge, 2018), 166.

[29] John Shook, 'Neuroethics and the Possible Types of Moral Enhancement', *American Journal of Bioethics: Neuroscience* 3, no. 4 (2012), 6.

[30] Harris Wiseman, 'The Sins of Moral Enhancement Discourse', *Royal Institute of Philosophy Supplement* 83 (2018), 35.

processes.[31] Given that we are able to alter some of these processes by means of technology, it seems that moral biotechnological
enhancement is not out of the question.[32]

In terms of imaginative treatments, Michelle Marvin explores
a related proposal, memory-altering technology, considering its
theological implications in dialogue with its representation in the
science fiction television series *Westworld*.[33] The removal of trau-
matic memories by technological means would appear to improve
overall happiness, yet Marvin argues that it places constraints on an
individual's capacity for forgiveness, thus impeding both their healing and their moral reasoning.[34] Through an analysis of the way in
which memories are erased, manipulated or falsely implanted in
the fictional series, Marvin uses the imagination as a resource to
examine the relational aspects of memory and invites viewers 'to
contemplate the potential disastrous moral outcomes initiated by
memory manipulation'.[35] Marvin questions whether memory alteration technologies might even be the enemy of individual moral
agency'.[36] and uses this imaginative appeal as an entry point for
engaging with Miroslav Volf's theology of 'remembering rightly'
and forgiveness.[37] It exemplifies a mode of theological reflection
via science fiction.

Greg Egan's short story was already mentioned in Chapter 1;
reflecting imaginatively on the way that moral engineering might

[31] Simeon Zahl, *The Holy Spirit and Christian Experience* (Oxford: Oxford University
Press, 2020), 240.
[32] Simeon Zahl, 'Engineering Desire: Biotechnological Enhancement as Theological
Problem', *Studies in Christian Ethics* 32, no. 2 (2019).
[33] Michelle Marvin, 'Memory Altering Technologies and the Capacity to Forgive:
Westworld and Volf in Dialogue', *Zygon* 55, no. 3 (2020).
[34] *Ibid.*, 714.
[35] *Ibid.*, 715.
[36] *Ibid.*, 714.
[37] See Miroslav Volf, *Exclusion and Embrace: A Theological Exploration of Identity
Otherness and Reconciliation* (Nashville, TN: Abingdon Press, 1996); Miroslav Volf,
The End of Memory: Remembering Rightly in a Violent World (Grand Rapids, MI:
Eerdmans, 2006).

be employed to amoral ends, in this case the overriding of a natural moral aversion to killing.[38] While the potential to abuse any given technology is not an argument against its development (all technology is subject to misuse and abuse), in the case of moral enhancement it reveals a more fundamental issue. How can morally ambiguous individuals (and research communities) develop a technology that genuinely enhances morality?

One of the problems when it comes to moral enhancement is determining what precisely is moral. Thomas Douglas advocates for moral enhancement yet states his intention to 'avoid committing [himself] to any particular view about what determines the moral goodness of a motive'.[39] He does, however, make the argument that the attenuation of several 'counter-moral' emotions would 'sometimes' constitute a moral enhancement.[40] Asking the question of 'what is moral?' in conjunction with so-called 'moral' enhancements may well demonstrate that 'behavioural engineering' is a more appropriate term. This would have knock on consequences for authority, enforcement and control that require further exploration.

A Christian vision of moral formation will not necessarily oppose specific technologies that promise to enhance aspects of human morality – curbing anti-social impulses, increasing concentration, etc.[41] But it will situate these technologies within their proper context, offering a picture of communities in which ethics are formed over a lifetime, primarily through relationships. Any proposed technological solutions make sense only against this backdrop; within this context, however, technology may indeed contribute to our moral development, particularly as it operates on

[38] Egan, 'Axiomatic'.
[39] Thomas Douglas, 'Moral Enhancement', in *Enhancing Human Capacities*, ed. Julian Savulescu, Ruud ter Meulen and Guy Kahane (Chichester: Wiley-Blackwell, 2011), 468.
[40] *Ibid.*, 470.
[41] As previously mentioned, we already employ pharmaceutical therapies to treat these impulses where they are deficient.

those biological and psychological processes that contribute to a broader picture of sin.

When it comes to these biological and psychological processes, a scientific understanding does not have to reduce to a naturalistic understanding. Simeon Zahl demonstrates this compellingly in his correlation of the psychological phenomenon of 'cruel optimism' (problematic attachments) with the experiential aspects of the doctrine of sin. His analysis is not simply one of identification, however; he explains how the theological understanding provides a potential way out (gospel hope) that is not offered by scientific explanation alone.[42] The model proposed in this work invites a parallel synthesis of scientific knowledge concerning the processes that influence both moral reasoning and theological understandings of sin, sanctification and moral formation.[43] It goes further, however, proposing that alternatives to technological enhancement as a means to increase morality (or even eradicate immorality) need to be presented imaginatively. Existing imaginative explorations around moral enhancement are overwhelmingly dystopic, showing how quickly these technologies may become instruments of control. *Westworld* provides just one example of how attempts to engineer mood through memory alteration can negatively impact moral formation – there would be real value in a constructive portrayal of how community and relationship can engender true healing and shape morality for the better in less theologically explicit terms than Volf employs in his work on memory and reconciliation.[44]

---

[42] Zahl, *The Holy Spirit and Christian Experience*, 172–175.

[43] To do this in the same register as Zahl's treatment of experience and pneumatology would constitute an entire project in its own right.

[44] This would align with Volf's more recent work on joy together with Justin Crisp; he argues for an interfaith approach to human flourishing that may become normative in ways that an explicit theological description of the good life is incapable of accomplishing (Miroslav Volf, 'The Crown of the Good Life: A Hypothesis', in *Joy and Human Flourishing: Essays on Theology, Culture and the Good Life*, ed. Miroslav Volf and Justin Crisp (Minneapolis, MN: Fortress Press, 2015)); cf. (Charles

Hedonic Recalibration

Many of the reflections on moral enhancement apply to mood enhancement as well so will not be repeated here, e.g. memory alteration technologies can be applied in an attempt to increase happiness (by removing painful memories), and mood and emotion are both entangled in our moral awareness. In Chapter 1 we already considered the representation of mood enhancement technologies in the novels of Aldous Huxley and Philip K. Dick. Both authors portray hedonic recalibration in a negative light; subjects of these 'enhancements' are less authentic and free, they raise no objections to being controlled. In contrast, the characters who reject these technologies are presented as heroic, independent thinkers.

Rather than zero in on particular examples of fiction here, we might engage the issue of mood enhancement by reflecting on fiction more generally. Our propensity to make sense of the world, and to understand ourselves, by telling stories has already been traversed.[45] In fact, fiction is itself used as a kind of mood enhancement, e.g. bibliotherapy has been demonstrated to alleviate symptoms of depression.[46]

While the point is admittedly somewhat trite, it is backed up by the real-life experience of many individuals who have taken mood-altering substances. While a minority may pursue a drug-induced 'high' undiminished by side effects, or withdrawal, the greater population of people taking prescription medication to treat mood disorders more often reveal a frustration at being unable to experience 'normal' emotions properly, both the lows and

---

Mathewes, 'Towards a Theology of Joy', in *Joy and Human Flourishing*, ed. Volf and Crisp, 64).

[45] See 'Narrative' beginning on p. 193.

[46] Ramona Moldovan, Oana Cobeanu and Daniel David, 'Cognitive Bibliotherapy for Mild Depressive Symptomatology: Randomized Clinical Trial of Efficacy and Mechanisms of Change', *Clinical Psychology and Psychotherapy* 20, no. 6 (2013).

the highs.[47] People may seek to treat extremely painful emotions, and ameliorate acute suffering, but there is also a sense of loss at being unable to experience appropriate sadness, or grief.

The idyllic state described by hedonic recalibration advocates Pearce and Bostrom appears nonsensical in this light.[48] The only way for that state of perennial bliss to be experienced as positively as they represent it is if the external reality aligned to the perception. This is not to say that positive outlook does not impact perception of reality, but even deeply contented and optimistic individuals experience appropriate 'negative' emotions when circumstances warrant. Listening to the stories of those who have been impaired in their ability to respond appropriately to events on an emotional level should provoke empathy, e.g. we need to *imagine* a future in which our emotional state is artificially divorced from our experience. It is not an appealing future to many, and again will go further than any explicit religious prohibition.

Eternal bliss properly aligns with paradise, which returns us to the territory of Christian hope discussed earlier. We arrive at a similar position to other enhancement technologies – particular mood enhancement technologies may have a place (we already pursue a range of strategies related to self-help and well-being) but the more extreme transhumanist goal of eradicating suffering altogether, so long as it seeks to address our *response* to circumstances, rather than the *nature* of those circumstances, should be exposed as insufficiently ambitious. It is mere *futurum*, and our imagination reveals its poverty against an *adventus* future in which suffering is wiped out at its source, not the effects.

---

[47] Guy Goodwin et al., 'Emotional Blunting with Antidepressant Treatments: A Survey Among Depressed Patients', *Journal of Affective Disorders* 221 (2017). Of course, pharmaceutical therapies for mood disorders are becoming increasingly sophisticated, and their intention is not to 'flatten' affect – the stigma of older medications such as Valium still influence opinion towards anti-depressant medications.

[48] See 'Hedonic Recalibration' beginning on p. 15.

Engineering Wakefulness

Finally, to test the versatility of this model, let us apply the same type of approach to a scenario that is less of a present focus in transhumanism, but conceivably could present as a popular enhancement possibility in the not-too-distant future. We may, perhaps, imagine a scenario in which technological means reduce our dependency on sleep without the host of negative consequences that presently accompany sleep deprivation. 'Sleep engineers' may develop a way to maintain the neurological advantages of sleep while increasing periods of wakefulness and reducing overall sleep duration. At the very least, the effect of our existing circadian rhythm in producing a mid-afternoon trough in alertness, a phenomenon attended to in our past through biphasic sleep patterns but now vastly out of sync with many contemporary cultural practices,[49] might be mitigated against as a form of human enhancement.

Theologically, we might consider the importance of sleep generally as a correlate of creaturely finitude, and within an appreciation of 'rest'. Sleep reminds us daily that we are not God, that our capacities can be exhausted, that we require ongoing sustenance. Our biological need for rest and renewal has its spiritual counterpart, whether people turn to prayer and meditation or other recreational practices. Even without a physical dependency, life without periodic rest is likely to be experienced as a burden. At the same time, the Christian practice of vigil shows us that abstaining from sleep is beneficial in some circumstances. We understand the failure of Jesus' disciples to remain awake in the garden of Gethsemane to be essentially a moral lapse, for example.

Before turning to the imagination, our reflection on the potential enhancement of sleep ought to be informed by scientific research

---

49 Charles Nunn, David Samson and Andrew Krystal, 'Shining Evolutionary Light on Human Sleep and Sleep Disorders', *Evolution Medicine and Public Health* 2016, no. 1 (2016).

as well. Though sleep researchers are yet to reach consensus as to the essential function(s) of sleep, they are certainly united in their conclusion that sleep is crucial.[50] Perhaps our dependency on sleep therefore ought not to be engineered entirely away; the fact that evolution has not produced an entirely sleep-free existence in any other higher order species suggests that sleep retains vital functions.[51] The benefits of a rhythm of rest are attested scientifically.[52] The scientific support for retaining some amount of sleep (though the degree may be disputed) aligns with the theological and philosophical reflections on the advantages of sleep. Any reduction or eradication of sleep through technological means must match the benefits currently obtained through sleep, or provide some disproportionate advantage.

Richard Bauckham and Trevor Hart assert that 'imagination fuels the engines of our movement into the future'.[53] How might our imaginative facilities be brought to bear on this question? Like the majority of technologies (and therapies) that presently exist, a sleep enhancement would certainly allow for the possibility of abuse. The very fact that current research into sleep enhancement is overwhelmingly conducted in military settings, with visions of a 24-hour soldier, attests to the potential for misuse.[54] Several works of science fiction have centered around sleep, e.g. H. G. Bell's *Sleep Over* (2018) features the 'Longest Day', a horrifying account of a

[50] Shinichi Miyazaki, Chih-Yao Liu and Yu Hayashi, 'Sleep in Vertebrate and Invertebrate Animals, and Insights into the Function and Evolution of Sleep', *Neuroscience Research* 118 (2017); J. Krueger et al., 'Sleep Function: Toward Elucidating an Enigma', *Sleep Medical Review* 28 (2016).
[51] This is not to suggest that evolutionary limitations should dictate what we might accomplish with technology, of course, but it is a source of insight. In considering evolutionary significance, we must avoid dichotomising nature and culture/technology as previously discussed.
[52] Russell Foster and Katharina Wulff, 'The Rhythm of Rest and Excess', *Nature Reviews Neuroscience* 6 (2005).
[53] Bauckham and Hart, 'The Shape of Time', 67.
[54] E. Williams, 'Human Performance', March 2008, https://fas.org/irp/agency/dod/jason/human.pdf.

worldwide insomnia pandemic,[55] while Nancy Kress imagines a malevolent genetically modified 'Sleepless' class in her *Beggars* trilogy (1993–1993). Engaging Kress' work, Deborah Steinberg demonstrates how the pursuit of a sleepless existence is entangled with neoliberal ideas of efficiency and economic utility.[56] Though Steinberg writes from a sociological perspective, her insights may be incorporated into a theological reflection on sleep engineering.

The majority of fiction featuring sleeplessness represents it in dystopian terms, yet we can imagine scenarios in which an ability to function without negative consequences on less or even no sleep (at least for short periods of time) could serve the good and express love for others, or work towards renewing the creation (as Brock and Cole-Turner both remind us is the rightful employment of technology).[57] In disaster relief scenarios, or being present with a loved one at the very end of life, for example, this kind of enhancement can perhaps be used lovingly and wisely. Neither of these scenarios, however, necessitates a permanent eradication of sleep.

Listening to a diversity of stories as well, we may seek out and amplify the experiences of those who already have atypical sleep behaviours. Insomniac Bill Haye's memoir *Sleep Demons* (2018) gives a first-hand account of sleeplessness; while many of his difficulties are due to negative consequences that enhancement technologies would seek to remove, even apart from the direct side effects, Hayes laments the loss of positive elements of sleep like respite, and relinquishment. While it is possible that sleep could be replaced with another restorative practice (meditation, for instance, is often proposed as an alternative to sleep), the goal of sleep engineering as a human enhancement would likely be primarily focused

55 Adrian Barnes' *Nod* (2013) and Kenneth Calhoun's *Black Moon* (2014) also feature insomnia plagues that trigger societal breakdown.
56 Deborah Steinberg, 'Reading Sleep Through Science Fiction: The Parable of Beggars and Choosers', *Body and Society* 14, no. 4 (2008), 25.
57 Brock, *Christian Ethics in a Technological Age*, 235; Cole-Turner, 'Religion, Genetics and the Future', 213.

on maximising productivity. This is where analyses like Steinberg's, in dialogue with imaginative works, can make a contribution.

Ultimately, an impulse to eradicate sleep would likely stem from the same motivation as the broader project of human technological enhancement: to take control of the human future and to engineer away the limitations of creaturehood. The more we consider individual enhancement scenarios, the more parallels we discover – there will always be the need for discernment on a case-by-case basis, but these reflections will be more robust if they are undertaken and communicated in creative ways.

Conclusion

One of the hallmarks of the theology of human creativity proposed in this work is a resistance to anthropocentrism. While none of these enhancement scenarios considered necessarily instrumentalise non-human creation in a direct sense, it may well be that particular technologies developed do. Certainly, the increasing technologisation of society is likely to increase the sense of human superiority that underpins much of the 'progress narrative' previously discussed, along with the corresponding Heideggerian critiques. This is again a matter where a simple theological assertion of the dignity of all creation, of the responsibility to care and to steward it, or other theological means of expressing the worth of non-human creation apart from its value to us, will not carry much weight with those who subscribe to a different anthropology. Critiques that appeal to the imagination will be more effective. To give one example, we might highlight works such as the philosophical novel *Ishmael*, by Daniel Quinn.[58] The book creatively reveals the myth that has captivated modern Western culture: *'the world was made for man, and man was made to rule it.'*[59]

---

[58] Daniel Quinn, *Ishmael: An Adventure of the Mind and Spirit* (New York: Bantam/Turner, 1992).

[59] *Ibid.*, 72, emphasis original.

Through a Socratic questioning process, a number of related myths concerning the status and role of humanity are exposed; while the novel undoubtedly challenges, even undermines, orthodox Christian teachings on sin, it may nevertheless assist in communicating the dangers of anthropocentrism.

This more practical exploration has been necessarily brief and tentative in nature; however, we can already see that 'enhancement' in itself need not threaten a theological understanding of humans, their place in the world, or the larger picture of God's work in salvation history. It becomes a matter for ethical deliberation like any other,[60] deliberation that takes place within an already formed but (hopefully) dynamic moral imaginary in which the imagination works to generate and deliberate over potential scenarios of use or abuse. Applying this framework to human enhancement proposals ultimately suggests that, though such endeavours are not prohibited, and may be relatively benign in many instances, they are often not the best investment of our creaturely resources and our creative agency. Where they are pursued, we should advocate for equality of access and protect freedom of choice for those who take them up or elect not to do so. These are not necessarily radical insights to the thoughtful Christian; however, the strength of this model lies not only in synthesising the input of scientific, theological and imaginative resources, but also in communicating through more effective means than the propositional approaches religious spokespersons have traditionally adopted. By presenting the distinction between Christian eschatology and the future that arises from human enhancement technology alone in

---

[60] The identification of human enhancement questions as the proper subject of ethical enquiry has already been affirmed by advocates such as Bostrom and Savulescu ('Human Enhancement Ethics: The State of the Debate', in *Human Enhancement*, ed. Nick Bostrom and Julian Savulescu (Oxford: Oxford University Press, 2009), 18); however, this recognition has not entirely penetrated alternative circles, including certain religious contexts.

an imaginatively compelling way, we do not reject these technologies as 'playing God' but instead reveal them to be insufficiently ambitious or hopeful in the vision of future being they project.

When it comes to imagining the future, and the claim that Christian hope exceeds that of transhumanism, we come up against the limitations of our own imagination. The apophatic tradition in Christian theology recognises this reality – when it comes to God, and to the eschatological future brought about mainly by God, it is much easier to say what they are not than what they are. For this reason, though we may speak boldly and extravagantly about the nature of the new creation, even our most creative efforts are unable to do it justice. If they are able to offer a glimpse, to peel back a corner of the veil, then Christian artists have succeeded. In the vein of *apophasis*, an imaginative response to human enhancement technologies by Christian thinkers will involve drawing on the plethora of dystopic renditions of the human future to demonstrate precisely what the new creation is *not* – leaving space for less tangible, but vastly more compelling attempts to express something of the Christian hope. Tolkien's 'Leaf by Niggle' is an excellent example of the type of imaginative work that can make a contribution here – perhaps more contemporary Christian writers might be persuaded to write equally hopeful, albeit speculative, fiction for our own age. The dystopic has its place, but are there instances of hope breaking in, of interrupting in unexpected ways that might capture some element of Christian eschatological hope? The novel *The Children of Men* (1992) by P. D. James and its 2006 film adaptation *Children of Men* is one example. Much of the tale is dystopic, depicting a bleak, lawless society experiencing a pervasive hopelessness. For an unexplored reason, the entire human species has lost the ability to reproduce, and no children have been born for eighteen years. There is no hope, because hope requires a future. Replete with Christian symbolism, the story takes an *adventus* turn when a child is miraculously born (to a woman from an underprivileged class, no less). The hope conveyed in this moment offers the type of entry point needed for productive conversations about the human future and technological visions of enhancement, representing a particular understanding of the future as not entirely continuous with the present.

Conclusion

Technologies that promise improvements to human abilities are continually being imagined, and a number of technological augmentations are beginning to be commercially available. Through film and print media, both fiction and journalistic, we are awash with visions of technologically enhanced human existence to the extent that some degree of enhancement appears inevitable.

This work begins with the pragmatic acknowledgement that technological 'progress' continues, usually more rapidly than the ethical reflection that would ideally accompany technological research and development. Considering the role of theological discourse when it comes to technological assessment, it concedes that a Christian world view no longer represents the dominant voice in the public sphere (at least in the West) and does not seek to recapture the authority it may have exercised in the past. Christianity must enter the 'tournament of narratives', offering a particular account of what it means to be human that is compelling when set alongside competing visions.

For many, the church is perceived as against the kinds of technologies that alter our biological makeup. The charge of 'playing God' is often used as a conversation-ender, a firm boundary around scientific enterprise across which humans are prohibited from trespassing. In search of resources within the Christian tradition that do not automatically recoil at the idea of human enhancement, theologies that represent humans as co-creators with God in some fashion were explored. Philip Hefner's anthropology of the 'created co-creator' was selected as particularly relevant, given its construction within the context of science and religion and his occasional direct engagement with technology and transhumanism.

A closer examination of Hefner's theological anthropology finds it to be a good starting point for engaging with human enhancement questions, as it locates human being and becoming within our evolutionary history and our connectedness with the non-human world. Hefner underscores creativity as fundamental to human nature and accords real agency, and responsibility, to us in employing our creativity to ensure a better future for all creation. His tendency to avoid theological concepts such as 'sin' in much of his work, coupled with his related methodology of translating theological content into scientific statements, means that he gives less attention to both the effects of fallenness on our ability to co-create and the ensuing need for discernment. The role of the imagination in knowing and discerning is also sidelined in his construction, though he does affirm its importance at times. With the prevalence of imaginatively rich epistemologies developed within science and theology as distinct disciplines, it is surprising that the imagination has received relatively little traction in the science and religion field. Is it possible to bring science and theology together in an account of co-creation, without diminishing both or reducing one to the other?

For this reason, Tolkien was brought into the conversation as a thinker who also views humans as creators in imitation of the Creator, and who locates the imagination at the centre of his anthropology of sub-creation. His general aversion to technology renders him a complicated dialogue partner when it comes to human enhancement concerns; however, his synthesis of imagination and reason, myth and reality in his vision of human creativity compensates for many of the shortcomings in Hefner's approach. He has a much stronger account of sin and its noetic effects, as well as the role of great stories in recruiting people's imaginations towards a particular vision and understanding of reality. Yet Tolkien attempts to neatly divide nature and technology into distinct entities, and looks to Edenic paradise with a simple nostalgia.

The present contribution thus seeks a middle ground, combining Hefner's understanding of humans as inherently technological and Tolkien's understanding of humans as fundamentally mythopoetic. Drawing on a wide range of scholarship (as surveyed in Chapter 6) that challenges dualisms between reason and the imagination, nature and technology and the mind and body, the contours of a contemporary theology of co-creation, situating human creativity firmly within a broader doctrine of creation, are mapped out. As described, the commitments of a fruitful approach will include:

1. Humans are products of a creative 'evolutionary' process.
2. Creativity is central to human agency and responsibility.
3. Human creativity is modelled on divine creativity.
4. Scientific insights should be respected and incorporated into an understanding and description of what it means to be human, without reducing theological and philosophical claims to scientific ones.
5. Technology is a legitimate exercise of human co-creativity.
6. Humans are storytellers and myth makers at their core, with narrative central to the way in which we understand the world.
7. The formation of the moral imagination requires our attention, including the diversity of stories which shape our moral imaginary.
8. Embodiment is crucial for imagination and understanding.
9. Technology must not instrumentalise non-human nature.
10. Elements of the visions of transcendence inherent in trans-humanist thought can be reclaimed as central to a Christian imagination.

This promise of this proposal for human creativity was demonstrated by applying it to several human enhancement domains: radical life extension, mind-uploading, moral enhancement, hedonic recalibration and sleep engineering. Though preliminary, the framework allowed for robust theological reflection that synthesises perspectives from multiple disciplines, and the imaginative focus provided a strong foundation for communicating these insights in the broader sphere.

Affirming humans as creators in imitation of and to the glory of our Creator while attending to the narratives that shape our technological imagination and use, we are able to locate the possibilities of human enhancement technology within a responsibility to create carefully, in ways that do not perpetuate inequality or instrumentalise non-human nature. The compelling visions of transhumanism that resonate with so many might be rehabilitated and recalibrated by the acknowledgement that we are not ultimately the agents of redemption, and the future glory in which we hope is not entirely of our own design.

Future Direction

The previous chapters indicate a number of directions for expanding or complementing the present study. For example, a greater attention to the competing visions of human flourishing that underpin attitudes towards human enhancement would be fruitful.[1] A Christian vision of the good life answers both the secular humanist respect for human finitude and the transhumanist hope for glorious transformation, thus may be presented as a vital dialogue partner in the enhancement debate. Gaymon Bennett's recent anthropology of the imagination and practice of human dignity over the past half-century, attending to the power structures at play in bioethics and biotechnology, exemplifies the approach required: it steps back from the particular technologies of the field and considers the assumptions, unstated beliefs and practices in which this

---

[1] This was explored briefly in 'What Is the Good Life?' beginning on p. 198.

technological innovation occurs.[2] Examining concepts of human flourishing operative in the same sphere would be fruitful for both understanding and evaluating competing attitudes towards human enhancement, and for future dialogue with innovators of enhancement technologies. Additionally, the articulation of a Christian vision of human flourishing that specifically addresses questions surrounding human enhancement will equip theologians and the church more generally as they are confronted with the emergence of such technologies.

The importance of listening to diverse portrayals of both present human experience and what an ideal human ought to be was raised earlier, with more work needed in this area. This connects with the previously identified task of interrogating visions of human flourishing, and theological reflection on what constitutes a good life will be more representative and just if it does not reinforce certain 'normative' accounts of human being.

This work has mainly focused on the role of literature in shaping our imagination of the future of human being. Other forms of art ought to be explored further as equally formative for our moral imagination. The discussion here is also very much at the conceptual level, a long way from any practical implementation that would see artistic sensibility and imagination brought explicitly into the realm of technological innovation. A more direct engagement with both technology developers and users that encourages a more reflective stance on technology is desirable, and future efforts should be oriented towards that goal.

The relationship between moral imagination, the arts and Christian faith has implications for apologetics too. Presented in ways that 'recruit' the imagination, the visions of transcendence and glorification proclaimed so confidently in transhumanist literature are ripe for reclamation by Christian theologians, philosophers,

---

[2] Gaymon Bennett, *Technicians of Human Dignity: Bodies Souls and the Making of Intrinsic Worth* (New York: Fordham University Press, 2016).

writers and artists. There are rich collaborative opportunities for presenting an imaginative account of the future, and technology's role in it, from a Christian perspective that offers neither a fearful response to technological innovation nor a wholehearted embrace of technological 'redemption'.

Although this work was unable to extend to a comprehensive doctrine of sin, questions around human responsibility and agency with respect to technology would benefit from further reflection on the extent to which our fallenness impacts them. In addressing questions that concern creation and redemption, the associated doctrine of providence would also be a crucial part of a more systematic approach.

The present research highlighted a number of thought dichotomies that were impacting many perspectives on human creativity today. Many of these concepts (e.g. imagination, reason, *technê*) have long pedigrees in the history of ideas, and an examination of their historical development would enrich the present discourse. A more historical approach would also connect with the focus on human flourishing outlined earlier. Both transhumanist and secular humanist ideals look to earlier humanisms as a part of their ideological heritage. A sustained study that compares these positions in greater depth, and considers the extent to which they draw on historical forms of humanism in their conceptions of the good life, would provide helpful context. Transhumanist roots are often located in Enlightenment thought, yet many transhumanists express their admiration for classical and mediaeval philosophies of humans forming themselves. Given the shared respect of secular humanists and transhumanists for thinkers such as Francis Bacon and Julian Huxley, it is worth exploring the points at which their notions of human flourishing diverge, and whether these are prescriptive for their perspectives on human enhancement.

We have seen how the question 'should humans enhance themselves?' dissolves with a little probing; clearly, we have always been in the business of enhancing ourselves. Overwhelmed by the

montage of neural implants, nootropic drugs, gene-editing precision, and do-it-yourself 'augmentations' in the form of magnetic
and RFID implants, that make up just a fraction of the more feas-
ible technologies accessible now or in the near future (not to
mention the vast array of 'enhancing' technologies that exist external to the body), we must resist categorising these prospects as
entirely novel or separate from other types of technology. Therefore, continuing to locate reflection on human enhancement within
developments in philosophy of technology and moral theology
more generally will curb the tendency to cordon off enhancement
debates as exceptional and broaden the pool of available resources
for ethical deliberation.

The final word goes to Hefner, who at once captures the expansiveness and fecundity of exploring questions of human becoming
at the nexus of theology and science, and the present unresolved,
and often uncomfortable, nature of these explorations.

> What is the significance of the fact that ... God has set up a system
> in which the creatures who transcend humans in the chain of evolu-
> tion may be creatures we have designed and created, so that their act
> of transcending us is at the same time our own act of transcending
> ourselves?[3]

---

[3] Hefner, *Technology and Human Becoming*, 80.

Bibliography

Abrams, M. H. *Natural Supernaturalism: Tradition and Revolution in Romantic Literature.* New York: W. W. Norton & Co., 1971.

Agøy, Nils Ivar. '*Quid Hinieldus cum Christo?* New Perspectives on Tolkien's Theological Dilemma and His Sub-creation Theory'. *Mythlore* 21 (1996): 31–38.

Ali, Syed Mustafa. '"White Crisis" and/as "Existential Risk", or the Entangled Apocalypticism of Artificial Intelligence'. *Zygon* 54, no. 1 (2019): 207–224.

Allan, Kathryn, ed. *Disability in Science Fiction: Representations of Technology as Cure.* New York: Palgrave Macmillan, 2013.

Amis, Kingsley. *New Maps of Hell: A Survey of Science Fiction.* New York: Arno Press, 1975.

Aquinas, Thomas. *Summa theologica.* Trans. Fathers of the English Dominican Province. Westminster, MD: Christian Classics, 1981.

Arendt, Hannah. 'The Threat of Conformism'. In *Essays in Understanding, 1930–1954: Formation, Exile, and Totalitarianism,* ed. Jerome Kohn, 423–427. New York: Schocken Books, 2005.

Asma, Stephen. *The Evolution of Imagination.* Chicago, IL: University of Chicago Press, 2017.

Atwood, Margaret. *Oryx and Crake: A Novel.* New York: Random House, 2003.

Atwood, Margaret. '*The Handmaid's Tale* and *Oryx and Crake* in Context'. *PMLA: Publications of the Modern Language Association of America* 119, no. 3 (2004): 513–517.

Avis, Paul. *God and the Creative Imagination: Metaphor, Symbol and Myth in Religion and Theology.* London: Routledge, 1999.

Backeljau, Thierry, Luc de Bruyn, Hans de Wolf, Kurt Jordaens, Stefan van Dongen, Ron Verhagen and Birgitta Winnepenninckx. 'Random Amplified Polymorphic DNA (RAPD) and Parsimony Methods'. *Cladistics* 11 (1995): 119–130.

Bacon, Francis. '*Novum Organon* 12.52'. In *The Works of Francis Bacon*, ed. James Spedding, Robert Ellis and Douglas Heath. London: Longman, 1858.

Bacon, Francis. 'Of the Dignity and Advancement of Learning'. In *The Works of Francis Bacon*, ed. James Spedding, Robert Ellis and Douglas Heath. New York: Garrett Press, 1860.

Bacon, Francis. 'The Masculine Birth of Time'. In *The Philosophy of Francis Bacon: An Essay on its Development from 1603–1609*, ed. Benjamin Farrington. Liverpool: Liverpool University Press, 1964.

Bailey, Justin Ariel. *Reimagining Apologetics: The Beauty of Faith in a Secular Age*. Downers Grove, IL: InterVarsity Press, 2020.

Balthasar, Hans Urs von. *The Glory of the Lord: A Theological Aesthetics*. Vol. I. Edinburgh: T. & T. Clark, 1982.

Banner, Michael. *Christian Ethics and Contemporary Moral Problems*. Cambridge: Cambridge University Press, 1999.

Barazzetti, Gaia, and Massimo Reichlin. 'Life Extension and Personal Identity'. In *Enhancing Human Capacities*, ed. Julian Savulescu, Ruud ter Meulen and Guy Kahane, 398–409. Chichester: Wiley-Blackwell, 2011.

Barbour, Ian. *Issues in Science and Religion*. London: SCM Press, 1966.

Barbour, Ian. *Religion and Science: Historical and Contemporary Issues*. New York: HarperCollins, 1997.

Barbour, Ian. 'Taking Science Seriously Without Scientism: A Response to Taede Smedes'. *Zygon* 43, no. 1 (2008): 259–269.

Barfield, Owen. *What Coleridge Thought*. Middletown, CT: Wesleyan University Press, 1971.

Barfield, Owen. *Worlds Apart: A Dialogue of the 1960's*. Middletown, CT: Wesleyan University Press, 1964.

Barkow, Jerome, Leda Cosmides and John Tooby. *The Adapted Mind: Evolutionary Psychology and the Generation of Culture*. Oxford: Oxford University Press, 1992.

Bauckham, Richard. *Living with Other Creatures: Green Exegesis and Theology*. Waco, TX: Baylor University Press, 2011.

Bauckham, Richard, and Trevor Hart. 'The Shape of Time'. In *The Future as God's Gift: Explorations in Christian Eschatology*, ed. David Fergusson and Marcel Sarot, 41–72. Edinburgh: T. & T. Clark, 2000.

Baudelaire, Charles. *Baudelaire as a Literary Critic*. Trans. Francis Hyslop Jnr. University Park, PA: Pennsylvania State University Press, 1964.

Beauchamp, Tom, and James Childress. *Principles of Biomedical Ethics*. New York: Oxford University Press, 2001.

Becker, Gerhold. 'Biotechnology: The New Ethical Frontier'. In *Changing Nature's Course: The Ethical Challenge of Biotechnology*, ed. Gerhold Becker, 1–14. Hong Kong: Hong Kong University Press, 1996.

Bennett, Gaymon. *Technicians of Human Dignity: Bodies, Souls, and the Making of Intrinsic Worth*. New York: Fordham University Press, 2016.

Berg, Christian. *Theologie im technologischen Zeitalter: Das Werk Ian Barbours als Beitrag zur Verhältnisbestimmung von Theologie zu Naturwissenschaft und Technik*. Stuttgart: Kohlhammer, 2002.

Bertranpetit, Jaume, and Francesc Calafell. 'Genome Views on Human Evolution'. In *Evolution: From Molecules to Ecosystems*, ed. Andrés Moya and Enrique Font, 260–271. Oxford: Oxford University Press, 2004.

Birch, Charles. 'Neo-Darwinism, Self-Organization, and Divine Action in Evolution'. In *Evolutionary and Molecular Biology: Scientific Perspectives on Divine Action*, ed. Robert J. Russell, William R. Stoeger and Francisco J. Ayala, 225–248. Vatican City State and Berkeley, CA: Vatican Observatory & CTNS, 1998.

Blackwell, B. C. *Christosis: Pauline Soteriology in Light of Deification in Irenaeus and Cyril of Alexandria*. Trans. J. E. Steely. Tübingen: Mohr Siebeck, 2011.

Bly, Robert. *The Science in Science Fiction: Eighty-Three SF Predictions That Became Scientific Reality*. Dallas, TX: BenBella, 2005.

Boden, Margaret. *The Creative Mind: Myths and Mechanisms*. London: Routledge, 2004.

Bohm, David. *On Creativity*. London: Routledge, 2003.

Booker, M. Keith, and Anne-Marie Thomas. *The Science Fiction Handbook*. Chichester: Wiley-Blackwell, 2009.

Bostrom, Nick. 'A History of Transhumanist Thought'. *Journal of Evolution and Technology* 14, no. 1 (2005): 1–27.

Bostrom, Nick. 'The Fable of the Dragon Tyrant'. *Journal of Medical Ethics* 31 (2005): 273–277.

Bostrom, Nick. 'The Transhumanist FAQ: A General Introduction (Version 2.1)'. *World Transhumanist Association*, 2003. www.nick-bostrom.com/views/transhumanist.pdf.

Bostrom, Nick, and Michael Depaul. 'Transhumanist Values'. *Journal of Philosophical Research* 30 (2005): 3–14.

Bostrom, Nick, and Julian Savulescu. 'Human Enhancement Ethics: The State of the Debate'. In *Human Enhancement*, ed. Nick Bostrom and Julian Savulescu, 1–24. Oxford: Oxford University Press, 2009.

Botting, Fred. 'Virtual Romanticism'. In *Romanticism and Postmodernism*, ed. Edward Larrissy, 98–112. Cambridge: Cambridge University Press, 1999.

Bourdieu, Pierre. *The Logic of Practice*. Trans. Richard Nice. Stanford, CA: Stanford University Press, 1990.

Brake, Mark, and Neil Hook. *Different Engines: How Science Drives Fiction and Fiction Drives Science*. London: Macmillan, 2008.

Brandt, Anthony, and David Eagleman. *The Runaway Species: How Human Creativity Remakes the World*. Edinburgh: Canongate Books, 2017.

Breed, David. *Yoking Science and Religion: The Life and Thought of Ralph Wendell Burhoe*. Chicago, IL: Zygon Books, 1992.

Brock, Brian. *Christian Ethics in a Technological Age*. Grand Rapids, MI: Eerdmans, 2010.

Bukatman, Scott. *Terminal Identity: The Virtual Subject in Post/Machine Science Fiction*. Durham, NC: Duke University Press, 1993.

Burdett, Michael. 'Assessing the Field of Science and Religion: Advice From the Next Generation'. *Zygon* 52, no. 3 (2017): 747–763.

Burdett, Michael. *Eschatology and the Technological Future*. New York: Routledge, 2015.

Burdett, Michael, and Victoria Lorrimar. 'Creatures Bound for Glory: Biotechnological Enhancement and Visions of Human Flourishing'. *Studies in Christian Ethics* 32, no. 2 (2019): 241–253.

Burhoe, Ralph. 'Religion's Role in Human Evolution: The Missing Link Between Ape-Man's Selfish Genes and Civilized Altruism'. *Zygon* 14 (1979): 135–162.

Burhoe, Ralph. 'The Concepts of "God" and "Soul" in a Scientific View of Human Purpose'. *Zygon* 8 (1973): 412–442.

Burhoe, Ralph. 'The Human Prospect and the "Lord of History"'. *Zygon* 10 (1975): 299–375.

Burhoe, Ralph. *Toward a Scientific Theology: Essays on the Relation of Science to Religion*. Belfast: Christian Journals, 1981.

Burhoe, Ralph. 'War, Peace and Religion's Biocultural Evolution'. *Zygon* 21, no. 4 (1986): 439–472.

Burton, Emmanuel. 'The Nuts and Bolts of Transformation'. *Zygon* 55, no. 3 (2020): 710–712.

Cahill, Jonathan. 'Freedom for Life: Karl Barth, Transhumanism and Human Flourishing'. *Ethics and Medicine: An International Journal of Bioethics* 30, no. 2 (2014): 81–95.

Calver, Neil. 'Sir Peter Medawar: Science, Creativity and the Popularization of Karl Popper'. *Notes and Records: The Royal Society Journal of the History of Science* 67 (2013): 301–314.

Calvin, William. *The Cerebral Symphony: Seashore Reflections on the Structure of Consciousness*. New York: Bantam Press, 1989.

Campbell, Donald. 'On the Conflicts Between Biological and Social Evolution and Between Psychology and Moral Tradition'. *Zygon* 11 (1976): 167–208.

Campbell, Donald. 'The Conflict Between Social and Biological Evolution and the Concept of Original Sin'. *Zygon* 10 (1975): 234–249.

Caputo, John. *Philosophy and Theology*. Nashville, TN: Abingdon Press, 2006.

Carpenter, Humphrey. *J. R. R. Tolkien: A Biography*. London: Allen & Unwin, 1977.

Carpenter, Humphrey. *The Inklings*. London: Allen & Unwin, 1978.

Case-Winters, Anna. 'Rethinking the Image of God'. *Zygon* 39, no. 4 (2004): 813–826.

Castoriadis, Cornelius. *The Imaginary Institution of Society*. Trans. Kathleen Blamey. Cambridge, MA: MIT Press, 1987.

Center for Science and the Imagination, Arizona State University. 'Project Hieroglyph'. Accessed 19 May 2017. http://csi.asu.edu/project-hieroglyph/page/2/.

Chadwick, Owen. *The Secularization of the European Mind in the Nineteenth Century: The Gifford Lectures in the University of Edinburgh for 1973–74*. Cambridge: Cambridge University Press, 1975.

Chirico, Alice, Vlad Glaveanu, Pietro Cipresso, Giuseppe Riva and Andrea Gaggiolo. 'Awe Enhances Creative Thinking: An Experimental Study'. *Creativity Research Journal* 30, no. 2 (2018): 123–131.

Clark, Andy. 'Re-inventing Ourselves: The Plasticity of Embodiment, Sensing, and Mind'. In *The Transhumanist Reader: Classical and Contemporary Essays on the Science, Technology, and Philosophy of the Human Future*, ed. Max More and Natasha Vita-Moore, 113–127. Oxford: Wiley & Sons, 2013.

Clark, Andy, and David Chalmers. 'The Extended Mind'. *Analysis* 58, no. 1 (1998): 7–19.

Clark, Timothy. *The Theory of Inspiration: Composition as a Crisis of Subjectivity in Romantic and Post-Romantic Writing*. Manchester: Manchester University Press, 1997.

Clarke, Arthur C. 'Extra-Terrestrial Relays: Can Rocket Stations Give WorldWide Radio Coverage?' *Wireless World*: 305–308.

Clayton, Philip. *Explanation from Physics to Theology: An Essay in Rationality and Religion*. New Haven CT: Yale University Press, 1989.

Clough, David. *On Animals*. London: Bloomsbury Publishing, 2013.

Cocking, J. M. *Imagination: A Study in the History of Ideas*. Ed. Penelope Murray. London: Routledge, 1991.

Coeckelbergh, Mark. *New Romantic Cyborgs: Romanticism, Information Technology, and the End of the Machine*. Cambridge, MA: MIT Press, 2017.

Cole-Turner, Ronald. 'Biotechnology and the Religion-Science Discussion'. In *The Oxford Handbook of Religion and Science*, ed. Philip Clayton, 929–944. Oxford: Oxford University Press, 2008.

Cole-Turner, Ronald. 'Going beyond the Human: Christians and Other Transhumanists'. *Theology and Science* 13, no. 2 (2015): 150–161.

Cole-Turner, Ronald. 'Human Limits: Theological Perspectives on Germ-Line Modification'. In *Designing Our Descendants: The Promises and Perils of Genetic Modifications*, ed. Audrey Chapman and Mark Frankel, 188–198. Baltimore, MD: John Hopkins University Press, 2003.

Cole-Turner, Ronald. 'Introduction: The Transhumanist Challenge'. In *Transhumanism and Transcendence: Christian Hope in an Age of Technological Enhancement*, ed. Ronald Cole-Turner, 1–18. Washington, DC: Georgetown University Press, 2011.

Cole-Turner, Ronald. 'Is Genetic Engineering Co-creation?' *Theology Today* 44, no. 3 (1987): 338–349.

Cole-Turner, Ronald. 'Religion and the Question of Human Germline Modification'. In *Design and Destiny: Jewish and Christian Perspectives on Human Germline Modification*, ed. Ronald Cole-Turner, 1–27. Cambridge, MA: MIT Press, 2008.

Cole-Turner, Ronald. 'Religion, Genetics and the Future'. In *Design and Destiny: Jewish and Christian Perspectives on Human Germline Modification*, ed. Ronald Cole-Turner, 201–223. Cambridge, MA: MIT Press, 2008.

Cole-Turner, Ronald. 'Science, Technology, and Mission'. In *The Local Church in a Global Era: Reflections for a New Century*, ed. Max L. Stackhouse, Tim Dearborn and Scott Paeth, 100–112. Grand Rapids, MI: Eerdmans, 2000.

Cole-Turner, Ronald. 'Synthetic Biology: Theological Questions about Biological Engineering'. In *Without Nature? A New Condition for Theology*, ed. David Albertson and Cabell King, 136–151. New York: Fordham University Press, 2010.

Cole-Turner, Ronald. *The New Genesis: Theology and the Genetic Revolution*. Louisville, KY: Westminster John Knox Press, 1993.

Cole-Turner, Ronald. 'The Singularity and the Rapture: Transhumanist and Popular Christian Views of the Future'. *Zygon* 47, no. 4 (2012): 777–796.

Cole-Turner, Ronald. 'Toward a Theology for the Age of Biotechnology'. In *Beyond Cloning: Religion and the Remaking of Humanity*, ed. Ronald Cole-Turner, 137–150. Harrisburg, PA: Trinity Press International, 2001.

Cole-Turner, Ronald, ed. *Transhumanism and Transcendence: Christian Hope in an Age of Technological Enhancement*. Washington, DC: Georgetown University Press, 2011.

Coleridge, Samuel Taylor. *Biographia Literaria*. Ed. George Watson. London: Dent, 1965.

Coleridge, Samuel Taylor. *Collected Works: Lay Sermons*. Ed. R. J. White. Vol. VI. London: Routledge, 1972.

Coleridge, Samuel Taylor. 'The Statesman's Manual'. In *Political Tracts of Wordsworth, Coleridge and Shelley*, ed. R. J. White, 1–53. Cambridge: Cambridge University Press, 1953.

Coulson, Charles. *Science and Christian Belief*. London: Oxford University Press, 1955.

Coulson, Charles. *Science, Technology and the Christian*. London: Epsworth Press, 1960.

Coulson, John. *Religion and Imagination: In Aid of a Grammar of Assent*. Oxford: Clarendon Press, 1981.

Csikszentmihalyi, Mihaly. *Tomorrow's Mind*. San Francisco, CA: Harper-Collins, 1993.

Damasio, Antonio. *Descartes' Error: Emotion, Reason, and the Human Brain*. New York: G. P. Putnam's Sons, 1994.

Davies, Paul. 'Putting the Science in Fiction'. *Cosmos*. https://cosmos magazine.com/the-future/putting-science-fiction.

Davison, Andrew, ed. *Imaginative Apologetics: Theology, Philosophy and the Catholic Tradition*. London: SCM Press, 2011.

Deacon, Terrence. 'Brain-Language Co-Evolution'. In *The Evolution of Human Languages*, ed. John Hawkins and Murray Gell-Mann, 49–83. Reading, MA: Addison-Wesley, 1992.

Deacon, Terrence. *Incomplete Nature: How Mind Emerged from Matter*. New York: Norton, 2012.

DeepMind. 'Agents that Imagine and Plan'. Accessed 28 March 2018. https://deepmind.com/blog/agents-imagine-and-plan/.

DeLashmutt, Michael. 'The Technological Imaginary: Bringing Myth and Imagination into Dialogue with Bronislaw Szerzynski's *Nature, Technology and the Sacred*'. *Zygon* 41, no. 4 (2006): 801–810.

Deleuze, Gilles, and Felix Guattari. *What Is Philosophy?* Trans. Graham Burchell and Hugh Tomlinson. London: Verso, 1994.

Dery, Mark. 'Black to the Future: Interviews with Samuel R. Delany, Greg Tate, and Tricia Rose'. *The South Atlantic Quarterly* 92, no. 4 (1993): 735–738.

Dery, Mark. *The Pyrotechnic Insanitarium: American Culture on the Brink*. New York: Grove Press, 1999.

Dick, Philip K. *Do Androids Dream of Electric Sheep?* New York: Ballantine Books, 1996.

Dillistone, Frederick. *Charles Raven: Naturalist, Historian, Theologian*. Grand Rapids, MI: Eerdmans, 1975.

Disch, Thomas. *The Dreams Our Stuff Is Made Of: How Science Fiction Conquered the World.* New York: Simon & Schuster, 1998.

Dobzhansky, Theodosius. *The Biological Basis of Human Freedom.* New York: Columbia University Press, 1956.

Doctorow, Cory. 'I've Created a Monster! (And So Can You)'. In *Frankenstein, or the Modern Prometheus: Annotated for Scientists, Engineers, and Creators of All Kinds,* ed. David Guston, Ed Finn and Jason Robert, 209–213. Cambridge, MA: MIT Press, 2017.

Douglas, Thomas. 'Moral Enhancement'. In *Enhancing Human Capacities,* ed. Julian Savulescu, Ruud ter Meulen and Guy Kahane, 467–485. Chichester: Wiley-Blackwell, 2011.

Drees, Willem. '"Playing God? Yes!" Religion in the Light of Technology'. *Zygon* 37, no. 3 (2002): 643–654.

Dreyfus, Hubert. 'Overcoming the Myth of the Mental: How Philosophers Can Profit from the Phenomenology of Everyday Expertise'. *Proceedings and Addresses of the American Philosophical Association* 79, no. 2 (2005): 47–65.

Duriez, Colin. 'The Fairy Story: J. R. R. Tolkien and C. S. Lewis'. In *Tree of Tales: Tolkien, Literature and Theology,* ed. Trevor Hart and Ivan Khovacs, 13–23. Waco, TX: Baylor University Press, 2007.

Dyson, Freeman. *Imagined Worlds.* Cambridge, MA: Harvard University Press, 1997.

Earp, Brian, Thomas Douglas and Julian Savulescu. 'Moral Neuroenhancement'. In *The Routledge Handbook of Neuroethics,* ed. L. Syd Johnson and Karen Rommelfanger, 166–184. New York: Routledge, 2018.

Egan, Greg. 'Axiomatic'. In *Axiomatic,* 119–136. London: Millennium, 1995.

Eilers, Miriam, Katrin Grüber and Christoph Rehmann-Sutter. 'Refocusing the Enhancement Debate'. In *The Human Enhancement Debate and Disability: New Bodies for a Better Life,* ed. Miriam Eilers, Katrin Grüber and Christoph Rehmann-Sutter, 1–20. Basingstoke: Palgrave Macmillan, 2014.

Eilers, Miriam, Katrin Grüber and Christoph Rehmann-Sutter, eds. *The Human Enhancement Debate and Disability: New Bodies for a Better Life.* Basingstoke: Palgrave Macmillan, 2014.

Einstein, Albert. 'Motive des Forschens'. In *Ideas and Opinions of Albert Einstein*, ed. Sonja Bargmanns, trans. Sonja Bargmann, 224–227. New York: Crown Publishers, 1954.

Ellul, Jacques. 'Remarks on Technology and Art'. *Bulletin of Science, Technology & Society* 21 (2001): 26–37.

Ellul, Jacques. *The Technological Society*. Trans. John Wilkinson. New York: Knopf, 1964.

Ellul, Jacques. *The Technological System*. Trans. J. Neugroschel. New York: Continuum, 1980.

Engelhardt, H. Tristan, Jr. *The Foundations of Bioethics*. 2nd edn. New York: Oxford University Press, 1996.

Engell, James. *The Creative Imagination: Enlightenment to Romanticism*. Cambridge, MA: Harvard University Press, 1981.

Eschrich, Joey. 'Hieroglyph Anthology Earns Futurist Award'. *Center for Science and the Imagination, ASU*. http://csi.asu.edu/press/news/hieroglyph-anthology-earns-futurist-award/.

Ettinger, Robert. 'The Penultimate Trump'. *Startling Stories* 17, no. 1 (1948): 104–115.

Ettinger, Robert. *The Prospect of Immortality*. New York: Doubleday, 1964.

Evans, Robley. 'Tolkien's World-Creation: Degenerative Recurrence'. *Mythlore* 14, no. 1 (1987): 5–8.

Farrer, Austin. *The Glass of Vision*. London: Dacre Press, 1948.

Feuerbach, Ludwig. *Das Wesen des Christentums*. Leipzig: Wigand, 1841.

Feuerbach, Ludwig. *The Essence of Christianity*. Trans. George Eliot. New York: Harper & Row, 1957.

Feyerabend, Paul, Robert Cohen and Marx Wartofsky, eds. *Essays in Memory of Imre Lakatos*. Dordrecht: D. Reidel Publishing, 1976.

Ficino, Marsilio. *Platonic Theology*. Ed. James Hankin and William Bowen. Trans. Michael Allen. Vol. IV. Cambridge, MA: Harvard University Press, 2004.

Flieger, Verlyn. 'Barfield's "Poetic Diction" and Splintered Light'. *Studies in the Literary Imagination* 14, no. 2 (1981): 47–66.

Flieger, Verlyn. *Green Suns and Faerie: Essays on J. R. R. Tolkien*. Kent, OH: Kent State University Press, 2012.

Flieger, Verlyn. *Splintered Light: Logos and Language in Tolkien's World.* Kent, OH: Kent State University Press, 2002.

Flieger, Verlyn. 'Taking the Part of Trees: Eco-Conflict in Middle-Earth'. In *J. R. R. Tolkien and His Literary Resonances*, ed. George Clark and Daniel Timmons, 147–158. Westport, CT: Greenwood Press, 2000.

Flieger, Verlyn. 'The Music and The Task: Fate and Free Will in Middle-Earth'. In *Green Suns and Faerie: Essays on J. R. R. Tolkien*, 14–40. Kent, OH: Kent State University Press, 2012.

Foerst, Anne. 'Cog, a Humanoid Robot, and the Question of the Image of God'. *Zygon* 33 (1998): 91–111.

Forrai, Gábor. 'Lakatos, Reason and History'. In *Appraising Lakatos: Mathematics, Methodology, and the Man*, ed. George Kampis, Ladislav Kvasz and Michael Stöltzner, 73–83. Dordrecht: Kluwer Academic Publishers, 2002.

Foster, Russell, and Katharina Wulff. 'The Rhythm of Rest and Excess'. *Nature Reviews Neuroscience* 6 (2005): 407–414.

Francis. *Laudato si'*. Rome: Vatican, Winter 2015.

Frankel, Charles. 'The Nature and Sources of Irrationalism'. *Science* 180 (1973): 927–931.

Fredens, Julius, Kaihang Wang, Daniel de la Torre, Louise F. H. Funke and Wesley E. Robertson. 'Total Synthesis of *Escherichia coli* with a Recoded Genome'. *Nature* 569 (2019): 514–518.

Fuentes, Agustin. *The Creative Spark: How Imagination Made Humans Exceptional.* New York: Dutton Penguin Random House, 2017.

Gaiman, Neil. 'The Pornography of Genre, or the Genre of Pornography'. In *The View from the Cheap Seats: Selected Non-Fiction*, 39–48. London: Headline Publishing, 2016.

Gaiman, Neil. *The View from the Cheap Seats: Selected Non-Fiction.* London: Headline Publishing, 2016.

Gaiman, Neil. 'Three Authors: On Lewis, Tolkien and Chesterton'. In *The View from the Cheap Seats: Selected Non-Fiction*, 33–38. London: Headline Publishing, 2016.

Gaonkar, Dilip Parameshwar. 'Toward New Imaginaries: An Introduction'. *Public Culture* 14, no. 1 (2002): 1–19.

Garner, Stephen. 'Christian Theology and Transhumanism: The "Created Co-creator" and Bioethical Principles'. In *Religion and Transhumanism: The Unknown Future of Human Enhancement*, ed. Calvin Mercer and Tracy Trothen, 229–245. Santa Barbara, CA: Praeger Publishers, 2015.

Garner, Stephen. 'Transhumanism and the *imago Dei*: Narratives of Apprehension and Hope'. PhD diss., University of Auckland, 2006.

Garth, John. *Tolkien and the Great War: The Threshold of Middle-Earth*. London: HarperCollins, 2003.

Gebara, Ivone. *Longing for Running Water: Ecofeminism and Liberation*. Minneapolis, MN: Fortress Press, 1999.

Geertz, Clifford. *The Interpretation of Cultures: Selected Essays*. New York: Basic Books, 1973.

Geraci, Robert. *Apocalyptic AI: Visions of Heaven in Robotics, Artificial Intelligence, and Virtual Reality*. New York: Oxford University Press, 2010.

Gerbault, Pascale, Anke Liebert, Yuval Itan, Adam Powell, Mathias Currat, Joachim Burger, Dallas Swallow and Mark Thomas. 'Evolution of Lactase Persistence: An Example of Human Niche Construction'. *Philosophical Transactions of the Royal Society B: Biological Sciences* 366 (2011): 863–877.

Gibson, William. *Neuromancer*. New York: Ace Books, 1984.

Goldsmith, Timothy. *The Biological Roots of Human Nature: Forging Links Between Evolution and Behavior*. New York: Oxford University Press, 1991.

Goodley, Dan, and Katherine Runswick-Cole. 'Becoming Dishuman: Thinking About the Human Through Dis/ability'. *Discourse: Studies in the Cultural Politics of Education* 37, no. 1 (2016): 1–15.

Goodwin, Guy, Jonathan Price, Christian de Bodinat and Judith Laredo. 'Emotional Blunting with Antidepressant Treatments: A Survey Among Depressed Patients'. *Journal of Affective Disorders* 221 (2017): 31–35.

Gottschall, Jonathan, and David Sloan Wilson, eds. *The Literary Animal: Evolution and the Nature of Narrative*. Evanston, IL: Northwestern University Press, 2005.

Gouwens, David. *Kierkegaard's Dialectic of the Imagination*. New York: Peter Lang, 1989.

Graham, Elaine. 'Bioethics after Posthumanism: Natural Law, Communicative Action and the Problem of Self-Design'. *Ecotheology* 9, no. 2 (2004): 178–198.

Graham, Elaine. 'Nietzsche Gets a Modem: Transhumanism and the Technological Sublime'. *Literature and Theology* 16, no. 1 (2002): 65–80.

Green, Garrett. *Imagining God: Theology and the Religious Imagination*. San Francisco, CA: Harper & Row, 1989.

Green, Garrett. *Theology, Hermeneutics, and Imagination: The Crisis of Interpretation at the End of Modernity*. Cambridge: Cambridge University Press, 2000.

Greene, Deirdre. '"Higher Argument": Tolkien and the Tradition of Vision, Epic, and Prophecy'. *Mythlore* 21 (1996): 45–52.

Grey, Aubrey de. 'Escape Velocity: Why the Prospect of Extreme Human Life Extension Matters Now'. *PLOS Biology* 2, nos. 723–726 (2004).

Grey, Aubrey de, Bruce Ames, Julie Andersen, Andrzej Bartke, Judith Campisi, Christopher Heward, Roger McCarter and Gregory Stock. 'Time to Talk SENS: Critiquing the Immutability of Human Aging'. *Annals of the New York Academy of Sciences* 959 (2002): 452–62.

Guite, Malcolm. *Faith, Hope and Poetry: Theology and the Poetic Imagination*. Farnham: Ashgate Publishing, 2012.

Gunn, Eileen. 'How America's Leading Science Fiction Authors Are Shaping Your Future'. *Smithsonian Magazine*. www.smithsonianmag .com/arts-culture/how-americas-leading-science-fiction-authors-are-shaping-your-future-180951169/.

Gunton, Colin. *The Triune Creator: A Historical and Systematic Study*. Grand Rapids, MI: Eerdmans., 1998.

Hacker, Peter. *Wittgenstein: Connections and Controversies*. New York: Oxford University Press, 2001.

Haidt, Jonathan. *The Righteous Mind: Why Good People Are Divided by Politics and Religion*. New York: Vintage Books, 2013.

Hamer, Richard. 'The Romantic and Idealistic Appeal of Physics'. *Science* 61, no. 1570 (1925): 109–110.

Hanson, Robin. 'Enhancing Our Truth Orientation'. In *Human Enhancement*, edited by Nick Bostrom and Julian Savulescu, 357–372. Oxford: Oxford University Press, 2009.

Haraway, Donna. 'A Cyborg Manifesto: Science, Technology, and Socialist-Feminism in the Late Twentieth Century'. In *Simians, Cyborgs and Women: The Reinvention of Nature*, 149–181. New York: Routledge, 1991.

Harrington, David. 'On the Usefulness of 'Value' in the Definition of Creativity: A Commentary'. *Creativity Research Journal* 30, no. 1 (2018): 118–121.

Harrison, Carol. *Beauty and Revelation in the Thought of Saint Augustine*. Oxford: Clarendon Press, 1992.

Hart, Trevor. 'Creative Imagination and Moral Identity'. *Studies in Christian Ethics* 16, no. 1 (2003): 1–13.

Hart, Trevor. 'Imagination and Responsible Reading'. In *Renewing Biblical Interpretation*, ed. Craig Bartholomew, Colin Greene and Karl Möller, 307–334. Carlisle: Paternoster Press, 2000.

Hart, Trevor. *Making Good: Creation, Creativity and Artistry*. Waco, TX: Baylor University Press, 2014.

Hart, Trevor. 'The Glory of Imagination and the Imagination of Glory'. In *Called to Hope: Perspectives on Life to Come*, ed. John Colwell, 226–239. Carlisle: Paternoster Press, 2000.

Hart, Trevor. 'Through the Arts: Hearing, Seeing and Touching the Truth'. In *Beholding the Glory: Incarnation Through the Arts*, ed. Jeremy Begbie, 1–26. London: Darton, Longman & Todd, 2000.

Hart, Trevor. 'Tolkien, Creation, and Creativity'. In *Tree of Tales: Tolkien, Literature and Theology*, ed. Trevor Hart and Ivan Khovacs, 39–53. Waco, TX: Baylor University Press, 2007.

Hauerwas, Stanley. *Hannah's Child: A Theologian's Memoir*. Grand Rapids, MI: Eerdmans, 2012.

Hauerwas, Stanley. 'In Defence of "Our Respectable Culture": Trying to Make Sense of John Howard Yoder's Sexual Abuse'. *ABC Religion and Ethics*. www.abc.net.au/religion/articles/2017/10/18/4751367.htm.

Hauerwas, Stanley. *The Peaceable Kingdom: A Primer in Christian Ethics*. Notre Dame, IN: University of Notre Dame Press, 1983.

Hauerwas, Stanley. 'The Self as Story: A Reconsideration of the Relation of Religion and Morality from the Agent's Perspective'. *Journal of Religious Ethics* 1 (1973): 73–86.

Hauerwas, Stanley, and L. Gregory Jones. 'Introduction: Why Narrative?' In *Why Narrative? Readings in Narrative Theology*, ed. Stanley Hauerwas and L. Gregory Jones, 1–18. Grand Rapids, MI: Eerdmans, 1989.

Hauskeller, Michael. *Better Humans? Understanding the Enhancement Project*. New York: Routledge, 2013.

Hayles, N. Katherine. *How We Became Posthuman: Virtual Bodies in Cybernetics, Literature, and Informatics*. Chicago, IL: University of Chicago Press, 1999.

Hedley, Douglas. 'Austin Farrer's Shaping Spirit of Imagination'. In *Scripture, Metaphysics, and Poetry: Austin Farrer's The Glass of Vision with Critical Commentary*, ed. Robert MacSwain, 195–210. London: Routledge, 2016.

Hedley, Douglas. *Living Forms of the Imagination*. London: T. & T. Clark, 2008.

Hefner, Philip. 'A Fuller Concept of Evolution – Big Bang to Spirit'. *Zygon* 47, no. 2 (2012): 298–307.

Hefner, Philip. 'Biocultural Evolution and the Created Co-creator'. In *Science and Theology: The New Consonance*, ed. Ted Peters, 174–188. Boulder, CO: Westview Press, 1998.

Hefner, Philip. 'Biocultural Evolution: A Clue to the Meaning of Nature'. In *Evolutionary and Molecular Biology: Scientific Perspectives on Divine Action*, ed. Robert J. Russell, William R. Stoeger and Francisco J. Ayala, 329–356. Vatican Observatory and Berkeley, CA: Vatican Observatory & CTNS, 1998.

Hefner, Philip. *Faith and the Vitalities of History*. New York: Harper & Row, 1966.

Hefner, Philip. 'Human Being: Questioning and Being Questioned'. *Zygon* 39, no. 4 (2004): 733–736.

Hefner, Philip. 'Life in Religion-and-Science'. *Theology and Science* 13, no. 1 (2015): 8–24.

Hefner, Philip. 'Nature, Mystery and God'. In *Our Bodies Are Selves*, ed. Philip Hefner, Ann Milliken Pederson and Susan Barreto, 136–154. Eugene, OR: Cascade Books, 2015.

Hefner, Philip. 'Ralph Burhoe: Reconsidering the Man and His Vision of Yoking Religion and Science'. *Zygon* 49, no. 3 (2014): 629–641.

Hefner, Philip. 'Sociobiology, Ethics and Theology'. *Zygon* 19 (1984): 185–207.

Hefner, Philip. 'Spiritual Transformation and Healing: An Encounter with the Sacred'. In *Spiritual Transformation and Healing: Anthropological, Theological, Neuroscientific, and Clinical Perspectives*, ed. Joan Koss-Chioino and Philip Hefner, 119–133. Oxford: Altamira Press, 2006.

Hefner, Philip. *Technology and Human Becoming*. Minneapolis, MN: Fortress Press, 2003.

Hefner, Philip. 'The Animal that Aspires to be an Angel: The Challenge of Transhumanism'. *Dialog* 48, no. 2 (2009): 158–167.

Hefner, Philip. 'The Created Co-creator Meets Cyborg'. Accessed 30 March 2016. www.metanexus.net/essay/created-co-creator-meets-cyborg.

Hefner, Philip. 'The Cultural Significance of Jesus' Death as Sacrifice'. *Journal of Religion* 60, no. 4 (1980): 411–439.

Hefner, Philip. 'The Evolutionary Epic'. *Zygon* 44, no. 1 (2009): 3–7.

Hefner, Philip. 'The Foundations of Belonging in a Christian Worldview'. In *Belonging and Alienation: Religious Foundations for the Human Future*, ed. Philip Hefner and Widick Schroeder, 161–180. Chicago, IL: Centre for the Scientific Study of Religion, 1976.

Hefner, Philip. *The Human Factor: Evolution, Culture, Religion*. Minneapolis, MN: Fortress Press, 1993.

Hefner, Philip. 'The Human Journey'. In *Our Bodies Are Selves*. ed. Philip Hefner, Ann Milliken Pederson and Susan Barreto, 122–135. Eugene, OR: Cascade Books, 2015.

Hefner, Philip. 'The Role of Science in Pannenberg's Theological Thinking'. *Zygon* 24, no. 2 (1989): 135–151.

Hefner, Philip. 'Theology's Truth and Scientific Formulation'. *Zygon* 23, no. 1 (1988): 263–279.

Heidegger, Martin. 'The Question Concerning Technology'. In *The Question Concerning Technology and Other Essays*, trans. William Lovitt, 3–35. New York: Harper Perennial, 1977.

Heinlein, Robert. *Methuselah's Children*. New York: Gnome Press, 1958.

Helms, Randall. 'All Tales Need Not Come True'. *Studies in the Literary Imagination* 14, no. 2 (1981): 31–45.

Herdt, Jennifer. 'Hauerwas Among the Virtues'. *Journal of Religious Ethics* 40, no. 2 (2012): 202–227.

Herzfeld, Noreen. *In Our Image: Artificial Intelligence and the Human Spirit.* Minneapolis, MN: Augsburg Fortress, 2002.

Hick, John. 'An Irenaean Theodicy'. In *Encountering Evil*, ed. Stephen Davis, 39–68. Atlanta, GA: John Knox, 1981.

Hoffman, Frederick. *The Imagination's New Beginning: Theology and Modern Literature.* Notre Dame, IN: University of Notre Dame Press, 1967.

Hoffman, Matej, and Rolf Pfeifer. 'The Implications of Embodiment for Behavior and Cognition: Animal and Robotic Case Studies'. In *The Implications of Embodiment: Cognition and Communication*, ed. Wolfgang Tschacher and Claudia Bergomi, 31–58. Exeter: Imprint Academic, 2012.

Hollinger, Veronica. 'Science Fiction and Postmodernism'. In *A Companion to Science Fiction*, ed. D. Seed, 232–247. Malden, MA: Blackwell, 2005.

Holmes, Rodney. 'Did *Homo Religiosus* Emerge from the Evolution of the Brain?' *Insights: The Magazine of the Chicago Centre for Religion and Science* 3 (1991): 10–14.

Holton, Gerald. *The Scientific Imagination: Case Studies.* Cambridge: Cambridge University Press, 1978.

Holton, Gerald. *Thematic Origins of Scientific Thought: Kepler to Einstein.* Cambridge, MA: Harvard University Press, 1973.

Horne, Brian. 'Art: A Trinitarian Imperative'. In *Trinitarian Theology Today: Essays on Divine Being and Act*, ed. Christoph Schwöbel, 80–91. Edinburgh: T. & T. Clark, 1995.

Houghton, John T. *Global Warming: The Complete Briefing.* Cambridge: Cambridge University Press, 2015.

Hren, Joshua. 'Tolkien and the Technocratic Paradigm'. *New Blackfriars* 99, no. 1079 (2018): 97–107.

Hughes, James. *Citizen Cyborg: Why Democratic Societies Must Respond to the Redesigned Human of the Future.* Cambridge, MA: Westview Press, 2004.

Hughes, James. 'The Big Questions: What Comes After Homo Sapiens?' Accessed 23 October 2017. www.newscientist.com/article/mg1922 5780-076-the-big-questions-what-comes-after-homo-sapiens/.

Hull, David. 'Philosophy and Biology'. In *Philosophy of Science: Contemporary Philosophy: A New Survey*, ed. Guttorm Fløistad, 280–316. The Hague: Nijhoff, 1982.

Hume, David. *A Treatise on Human Nature*. Ed. L. A. Selby-Bigge. Oxford: Clarendon Press, 1888.

Huxley, Julian. 'Transhumanism'. In *New Bottles for New Wine*, 13–17. London: Chatto & Windus, 1957.

Huyssteen, Wentzel van. *Alone in the World? Human Uniqueness in Science and Theology*. Grand Rapids, MI: Eerdmans, 2006.

Intergovernmental Panel on Climate Change. *Climate Change 2014: Impacts, Adaptation, and Vulnerability*. Cambridge: Cambridge University Press, 2014.

Irenaeus. 'Against Heresies'. In *Ante-Nicene Fathers*, ed. Alexander Roberts and James Donaldson, vol. I. Peabody, MA: Hendrickson Publishers, 2004.

Jaynes, Julian. *The Origin of Consciousness in the Breakdown of the Bicameral Mind*. Boston, MA: Houghton Mifflin, 1977.

Jeffrey, David Lyle. 'Tolkien and the Future of Literary Studies'. In *Tree of Tales: Tolkien, Literature and Theology*, ed. Trevor Hart and Ivan Khovacs, 55–70. Waco, TX: Baylor University Press, 2007.

Jersild, Paul. *Spirit Ethics: Scripture and the Moral Life*. Minneapolis, MN: Fortress Press, 2000.

John Paul II. *Laborem exercens*. Rome: Vatican, 1981.

Johnson, Kirstin. 'Tolkien's Mythopoesis'. In *Tree of Tales: Tolkien, Literature and Theology*, ed. Trevor Hart and Ivan Khovacs, 25–38. Waco, TX: Baylor University Press, 2007.

Johnson, Mark. *Moral Imagination: Implications of Cognitive Science for Ethics*. Chicago, IL: University of Chicago Press, 1993.

Johnson, Mark. *The Body in the Mind: The Bodily Basis of Meaning, Imagination, and Reason*. Chicago, IL: University of Chicago Press, 1987.

Jones, David. 'Art and Sacrament'. In *Epoch and Artist: Selected Writings*, ed. Harman Grisewood, 143–179. London: Faber & Faber, 1959.

Kass, Leon. 'Ageless Bodies, Happy Souls: Biotechnology and the Pursuit of Perfection'. *The New Atlantis* 1 (2003): 9–28.

Katz, Eric. 'The Rings of Tolkien and Plato: Lessons in Power, Choice, and Morality'. In *The Lord of the Rings and Philosophy: One Book to Rule Them All*, ed. Gregory Bassham and Eric Bronson, 5–20. Chicago, IL: Open Court, 2003.

Kaufman, James, and Ronald Beghetto. 'Beyond Big and Little: The Four C Model of Creativity'. *Review of General Psychology* 13, no. 1 (2009): 1–12.

Kearney, Richard. *Poetics of Imaginings: Modern to Postmodern*. Edinburgh: Edinburgh University Press, 1998.

Kearney, Richard. *The Wake of Imagination: Toward a Postmodern Culture*. London: Routledge, 1994.

Kilby, Clyde S. 'Mythic and Christian Elements in Tolkien'. In *Myth, Allegory, and Gospel: An Interpretation of J. R. R. Tolkien, C. S. Lewis, G. K. Chesterton, Charles Williams*, ed. John Montgomery, 119–143. Minneapolis, MN: Bethany Fellowship, 1974.

Kilby, Karen. 'Perichoresis and Projection: Problems with Social Doctrines of the Trinity'. *New Blackfriars* 81, no. 957 (2000): 432–445.

Kline, Stephen. 'What Is Technology?' *Bulletin of Science, Technology & Society* 5, no. 3 (1985): 215–218.

Koene, Randal. 'Uploading to Substrate-Independent Minds'. In *The Transhumanist Reader: Classical and Contemporary Essays on the Science, Technology, and Philosophy of the Human Future*, ed. Max More and Natasha Vita-More, 147–156. Oxford: Wiley & Sons, 2013.

Krogh, Anders, Björn Larsson, Gunnar von Heijne and Erik Sonnhammer. 'Predicting Transmembrane Protein Topology with a Hidden Markov Model: Application to Complete Genomes'. *Journal of Molecular Biology* 305 (2001): 567–580.

Krueger, J., M. Frank, J Wisor and S. Roy. 'Sleep Function: Toward Elucidating an Enigma'. *Sleep Medical Review* 28 (2016): 46–54.

Kuhn, Thomas. 'Logic of Discovery or Psychology of Research?' In *Criticism and the Growth of Knowledge*, ed. Imre Lakatos and Alan Musgrave, 1–24. Amsterdam: North-Holland Publishing Co., 1970.

Kull, Anne. 'Mutations of Nature, Technology, and the Western Sacred'. *Zygon* 41, no. 4 (2006): 785–792.

Kurzweil, Ray. *The Singularity Is Near: When Humans Transcend Biology.* London: Penguin Books, 2005.

Kwok, Pui-lan. *Postcolonial Imagination and Feminist Theology.* London: SCM Press, 2005

Laan, J. M. van der. 'Editor's Notes: Science, Technology, and Science Fiction'. *Bulletin of Science, Technology & Society* 30, no. 4 (2010): 233–239.

Laan, J. M. van der. 'Frankenstein as Science Fiction and Fact'. *Bulletin of Science, Technology & Society* 30, no. 4 (2010): 298–304.

Lacan, Jacques. *The Four Fundamental Concepts of Psychoanalysis.* Ed. Jacques-Alain Miller. Trans. Alan Sheridan. New York: W. W. Norton & Co., 1977.

Lakatos, Imre. 'Anomalies Versus "Crucial Experiments" (a Rejoinder to Professor Grünbaum)'. In *Mathematics, Science and Epistemology: Philosophical Papers*, ed. John Worrall and Gregory Currie, vol. II, 211–223. Cambridge: Cambridge University Press, 1978.

Lakatos, Imre. *The Methodology of Scientific Research Programmes.* Ed. John Worrall and Gregory Currie. Vol. I. Cambridge: Cambridge University Press, 1978.

Lake, Christina Bieber. *Prophets of the Posthuman: American Fiction, Biotechnology, and the Ethics of Personhood.* Notre Dame, IN: University of Notre Dame Press, 2013.

Lakoff, George, and Mark Johnson. *Metaphors We Live By.* Chicago, IL: University of Chicago Press, 2003.

Lakoff, George, and Mark Johnson. *Philosophy in the Flesh: The Embodied Mind and its Challenge to Western Thought.* New York: Basic Books, 2003.

Laland, Kevin, John Odling-Smee and Marcus Feldman. 'Niche Construction, Biological Evolution, and Cultural Change'. *Behavioral and Brain Sciences* 23 (2000): 131–175.

Laland, Kevin, John Odling-Smee and Sean Myles. 'How Culture Shaped the Human Genome: Bringing Genetics and the Human Sciences Together'. *Nature Reviews Genetics* 11 (2010): 137–148.

Laughlin, Charles, John McManus and Eugene d'Aquili. *Brain, Symbol and Experience: Toward a Neurophenomenology of Human Consciousness.* New York: Columbia University Press, 1990.

Le Guin, Ursula. 'Escape Routes'. In *The Language of the Night: Essays on Fantasy and Science Fiction*, ed. Susan Wood, 201–206. New York: Putnam, 1979.

Le Guin, Ursula. 'European SF: Rottensteiner's Anthology, the Strugatskys, and Lem'. *Science Fiction Studies* 1, no. 3 (1974): 181–185.

Le Guin, Ursula. 'Myth and Archetype in Science Fiction'. In *The Language of the Night: Essays on Fantasy and Science Fiction*, ed. Susan Wood, 73–81. New York: Putnam, 1979.

Le Guin, Ursula. 'National Book Award Acceptance Speech'. In *Riverside Anthology of Children's Literature*, 6th edn, ed. Judith Saltman. Boston, MA: Houghton Mifflin, 1985.

Le Guin, Ursula. 'On Norman Spinrad's "The Iron Dream"'. *Science Fiction Studies* 1, no. 1 (1973): 41–44.

Le Guin, Ursula. 'The Child and the Shadow'. In *The Language of the Night: Essays on Fantasy and Science Fiction*, ed. Susan Wood, 59–71. New York: Putnam, 1979.

Le Guin, Ursula. 'The Modest One'. In *The Language of the Night: Essays on Fantasy and Science Fiction*, ed. Susan Wood, 175–178. New York: Putnam, 1979.

Le Guin, Ursula. 'Why Are Americans Afraid of Dragons?' In *The Language of the Night: Essays on Fantasy and Science Fiction*, ed. Susan Wood, 39–45. New York: Putnam, 1979.

Lehman, Darrin R., Chi-yue Chiu and Mark Schaller. 'Psychology and Culture'. *Annual Review of Psychology* 55, no. 1 (2004): 689–714.

Lewis, C. S. *Perelandra*. London: Simon & Schuster, 1996.

Linzey, Andrew. *Animal Theology*. Champaign, IL: University of Illinois Press, 1994.

Lorrimar, Victoria. 'Are Scientific Research Programmes Applicable to Theology? On Philip Hefner's Use of Lakatos'. *Theology and Science* 15, no. 2 (2017): 188–202.

Lubart, Todd. 'Creativity Across Cultures'. In *Handbook of Creativity*, ed. Robert Sternberg, 339–350. Cambridge: Cambridge University Press, 1999.

Lucie-Smith, Alexander. *Narrative Theology and Moral Theology: The Infinite Horizon*. Aldershot: Ashgate, 2007.

Luisi, Pier Luigi. *The Emergence of Life: From Chemical Origins to Synthetic Biology.* Cambridge: Cambridge University Press, 2016.

Macaulay, Thomas. 'Milton'. In *Lord Macauley's Essays.* London: Longman, Greens & Co., 1905.

MacIntyre, Alasdair. *Whose Justice? Which Rationality?* London: Duckworth, 1988.

MacIntyre, Alisdair. *After Virtue.* 2nd edn. Notre Dame, IN: University of Notre Dame Press, 1984.

MacIntyre, Alisdair. *Dependent Rational Animals: Why Human Beings Need the Virtues.* London: Duckworth, 1999.

Madsen, Catherine. '"Light from an Invisible Lamp": Natural Religion in *The Lord of the Rings*'. In *Tolkien and the Invention of Myth: A Reader,* ed. Jane Chance, 35–47. Lexington, KY: University of Kentucky Press, 2004.

Malik, Kenan, and Iain McGilchrist. 'Split Brain, Split Views: Debating Iain McGilchrist'. *Pandaemonium,* February 2013. https://kenanmalik.wordpress.com/2013/02/24/split-brain-split-views-debating-iain-mcgilchrist/.

Malpas, Simon. 'Home'. In *Reading The Lord of the Rings: New Writings on Tolkien's Trilogy,* ed. Robert Eaglestone, 85–98. London: Continuum, 2005.

Manetti, Giannozzo. *De dignitate et excellentia hominis.* Ed. Elizabeth Leonard. Patavii: In Aedibus Antenoreis, 1974.

Maritain, Jacques. *Art and Scholasticism and the Frontiers of Poetry.* Trans. J. Evans. New York: C. Scribner's Sons, 1962.

Martin, Lee, and Nick Wilson. 'Defining Creativity with Discovery'. *Creativity Research Journal* 29, no. 4 (2017): 417–425.

Marvin, Michelle. 'Memory Altering Technologies and the Capacity to Forgive: Westworld and Volf in Dialogue'. *Zygon* 55, no. 3 (2020): 713–732.

Mathewes, Charles. 'Towards a Theology of Joy'. In *Joy and Human Flourishing: Essays on Theology, Culture and the Good Life,* ed. Miroslav Volf and Justin Crisp, 63–95. Minneapolis, MN: Fortress Press, 2015.

Maurice, F. D. *Subscription No Bondage, Or the Practical Advantages Afforded by the Thirty-Nine Articles as Guides in All the Branches of Academical Education.* Oxford: J. H. Parker, 1835.

McClendon, James. *Systematic Theology: Ethics*. Nashville, TN: Abingdon Press, 1986.

McDonough, Paul G. 'The Ethics of Somatic and Germline Gene Therapy'. *Annals of the New York Academy of Sciences* 816, no. 1 (1997): 378–382.

McGilchrist, Iain. *The Master and His Emissary: The Divided Brain and the Making of the Western World*. New Haven, CT: Yale University Press, 2009.

McGrath, Alister. *Re-imagining Nature: The Promise of a Christian Natural Theology*. Hoboken, NJ: Wiley-Blackwell, 2016.

McKenny, Gerald. 'Biotechnology and the Normative Significance of Human Nature: A Contribution from Theological Anthropology'. *Studies in Christian Ethics* 26, no. 1 (2013): 18–36.

McKibben, Bill. *Enough: Genetic Engineering and the End of Human Nature*. London: Bloomsbury Publishing, 2004.

Medawar, P. B. 'Hypothesis and Imagination'. In *Pluto's Republic*, 115–135. Oxford: Oxford University Press, 1982.

Medawar, P. B. 'Imagination and Hypothesis'. *The Times Literary Supplement*: 849–850.

Medawar, P. B. *Induction and Intuition*. Philadelphia, PA: American Philosophical Society, 1969.

Medawar, P. B. 'On "The Effecting of All Things Possible"'. In *The Hope of Progress*, 110–127. London: Methuen & Co., 1972.

Medawar, P. B. 'Science and Literature'. *Encounter* 32, no. 1 (1969): 15–23.

Medawar, P. B. 'Science and the Sanctity of Life'. In *The Hope of Progress*, 87–100. London: Methuen & Co., 1972.

Medawar, P. B. 'Technology and Evolution'. In *Pluto's Republic*, 184–190. Oxford: Oxford University Press, 1982.

Medawar, P. B. 'The Genetic Improvement of Man'. In *The Hope of Progress*, 69–76. London: Methuen & Co., 1972.

Meilaender, Gilbert. *Bioethics*. Grand Rapids, MI: Eerdmans, 2013.

Mendlesohn, Farah. 'Religion and Science Fiction'. In *The Cambridge Companion to Science Fiction*, ed. Edward James, 264–275. Cambridge: Cambridge University Press, 2003.

Merkle, Ralph. 'Uploading: Transferring Consciousness from Brain to Computer'. *Extropy: The Journal of Transhumanist Thought* 11 (1993): 5–8.

Merleau-Ponty, Maurice. *Phenomenology of Perception*. London: Routledge, 1962.

Midgley, Mary. *Science and Poetry*. London: Routledge, 2001.

Midson, Scott. *Cyborg Theology: Humans, Technology and God*. London: I. B. Taurus, 2018.

Milbank, Alison. 'Apologetics and the Imagination: Making Strange'. In *Imaginative Apologetics: Theology, Philosophy and the Catholic Tradition*, ed. Andrew Davison, 31–45. London: SCM Press, 2011.

Milburn, Colin. 'Modifiable Futures: Science Fiction at the Bench'. *Isis* 101 (2010): 560–569.

Milburn, Colin. 'Posthumanism'. In *The Oxford Handbook of Science Fiction*, ed. Rob Latham, 524–536. Oxford: Oxford University Press, 2014.

Miller, Clark, and Ira Bennett. 'Thinking Longer Term About Technology: Is There Value in Science Fiction-Inspired Approaches to Constructing Futures?' *Science and Public Policy* 35, no. 8 (2008): 597–606.

Miner, Robert. *Truth in the Making: Creativity Knowledge in Theology and Philosophy*. London: Routledge, 2013.

Miyazaki, Shinichi, Chih-Yao Liu and Yu Hayashi. 'Sleep in Vertebrate and Invertebrate Animals, and Insights into the Function and Evolution of Sleep'. *Neuroscience Research* 118 (2017): 3–12.

Moczek, Armin P., Sonia Sultan, Susan Foster, Cris Ledón-Rettig, Ian Dworkin, H Fred Nijhout, Ehab Abouheif, and David W Pfennig. 'The Role of Developmental Plasticity in Evolutionary Innovation'. *Proceedings of the Royal Society B: Biological Sciences* 278, no. 1719 (2011): 2705–2713.

Moldovan, Ramona, Oana Cobeanu and Daniel David. 'Cognitive Bibliotherapy for Mild Depressive Symptomatology: Randomized Clinical Trial of Efficacy and Mechanisms of Change'. *Clinical Psychology and Psychotherapy* 20, no. 6 (2013): 482–493.

Moltmann, Jürgen. *The Coming of God: Christian Eschatology*. Trans. Margaret Kohl. Minneapolis, MN: Fortress Press, 2004.

Monsma, Stephen V. *Responsible Technology: A Christian Perspective*. Grand Rapids, MI: Eerdmans, 1986.

Moore, Scott. 'The Consolations of Fantasy: J. R. R. Tolkien and Iris Murdoch'. In *Tolkien Among the Moderns*, ed. Ralph Wood, 195–218. Notre Dame, IN: University of Notre Dame Press, 2015.

Moravec, Hans. *Mind Children: The Future of Robot and Human Intelligence*. Cambridge, MA: Harvard University Press, 1988.

More, Max. 'The Extropian Principles 2.5'. *Extropy* 11 (1993).

Morgan, Alun. 'The Lord of the Rings: A Mythos Applicable in Unsustainable Times?"' *Environmental Education Research* 16, nos. 3–4 (2010): 383–399.

Motterlini, Matteo. 'Professor Lakatos Between the Hegelian Devil and the Popperian Deep Blue Sea'. In *Appraising Lakatos: Mathematics, Methodology, and the Man*, ed. George Kampis, Ladislav Kvasz and Michael Stöltzner, 23–52. Dordrecht: Kluwer Academic Publishers, 2002.

Moulin, Joanny. 'J. R. R. Tolkien's "Eucatastrophe", or Fantasy as a Modern Recovery of Faith'. In *Re-embroidering the Robe: Faith, Myth and Literary Creation Since 1850*, ed. Suzanne Bray, Adrienne Gavin and Peter Merchant, 77–86. Newcastle: Cambridge Scholars Publishing, 2008.

Murdoch, Iris. *The Sovereignty of Good*. London: Routledge, 1970.

Murdoch, Iris. 'Vision and Choice in Morality'. *Proceedings of the Aristotelian Society* Supplementary vol. 30 (1956): 32–58.

Murphy, Nancey. 'From Critical Realism to a Methodological Approach: Response to Robbins, Van Huyssteen, and Hefner'. *Zygon* 23, no. 3 (1988): 287–290.

Murphy, Nancey. *Theology in an Age of Scientific Reasoning*. Ithaca, NY: Cornell University Press, 1990.

Murphy, Nancey. 'Theology in the Age of Probable Reasoning (Catholic Modernist, Jeffrey Stout, Imre Lakatos)'. PhD diss., Graduate Theological Union, Berkeley, 1987.

Murphy, Nancey, and Warren Brown. *Did My Neurons Make Me Do It? Philosophical and Neurobiological Perspectives on Moral Responsibility and Free Will*. Oxford: Oxford University Press, 2007.

Nagy, Gergely. 'Saving the Myths: The Re-Creation of Mythology in Plato and Tolkien'. In *Tolkien and the Invention of Myth: A Reader*, ed.

Jane Chance, 81–100. Lexington, KY: University of Kentucky Press, 2004.

Neville, Graham. *Coleridge and Liberal Religious Thought: Romanticism, Science and Theological Tradition*. London: Tauris, 2010.

Ni, Zhange. 'Reimagining Daoist Alchemy, Decolonizing Transhumanism: The Fantasy of Immortality Cultivation in Twenty-First Century China'. *Zygon* 55, no. 3 (2020): 748–771.

Nietzsche, Friedrich. *The Birth of Tragedy*. Trans. Douglas Smith. Oxford: Oxford University Press, 2008.

Nietzsche, Friedrich. *Thus Spoke Zarathustra*. Trans. R. Hollingdale and E. Rieu. London: Penguin, 1961.

Niu, Weihua, and Robert Sternberg. 'Contemporary Studies on the Concept of Creativity: The East and the Western'. *Journal of Creative Behavior* 36 (2002): 269–288.

Norris Clarke, W. 'Technology and Man: A Christian Vision'. *Technology and Culture* 3, no. 4 (1962): 422–442.

Nunn, Charles, David Samson and Andrew Krystal. 'Shining Evolutionary Light on Human Sleep and Sleep Disorders'. *Evolution, Medicine, and Public Health* 2016, no. 1 (2016): 227–243.

Nussbaum, Martha. *The Fragility of Goodness: Luck and Ethics in Greek Tragedy and Philosophy*. Cambridge: Cambridge University Press, 1986.

Nussbaum, Martha. '"Finely Aware and Richly Responsible": Literature and the Moral Imagination'. In *Love's Knowledge: Essays on Philosophy and Literature*, 148–167. New York: Oxford University Press, 1990.

Nussbaum, Martha. 'Transcending Humanity'. In *Love's Knowledge: Essays on Philosophy and Literature*, 365–392. New York: Oxford University Press, 1990.

O'Donnell, Karen. 'Performing the imago Dei: Human Enhancement, Artificial Intelligence and Optative Image-Bearing'. *International Journal for the Study of the Christian Church*, 2018.

O'Gieblyn, Meghan. 'God in the Machine: My Strange Journey into Transhumanism'. *The Guardian*, www.theguardian.com/technology/2017/apr/18/god-in-the-machine-my-strange-journey-into-transhumanism.

Offray de la Mettrie, Julien. *Machine Man and Other Writings.* Ed. Ann Thomson. Cambridge: Cambridge University Press, 1996.

Otzen, B. 'Yatsar'. In *Theological Dictionary of the Old Testament,* ed. G. Johannes Botterweck and Helmer Ringgren, 258–259. Grand Rapids, MI: Eerdmans, 1990.

Pannenberg, Wolfhart. 'Theological Appropriation of Scientific Understandings: Response to Hefner, Wicken, Eaves, and Tipler'. *Zygon* 24, no. 2 (1989): 255–271.

Pask, Kevin. *The Fairy Way of Writing: Shakespeare to Tolkien.* Baltimore, MD: Johns Hopkins University Press, 2013.

Peacocke, Arthur. *Creation and the World of Science: The Bampton Lectures 1978.* Oxford: Clarendon Press, 1979.

Pearce, David. 'The Abolitionist Project', 2007. Accessed 18 May 2017. www.abolitionist.com/.

Persson, Ingmar, and Julian Savulescu. 'The Perils of Cognitive Enhancement and the Urgent Imperative to Enhance the Moral Character of Humanity'. *Journal of Applied Philosophy* 25, no. 3 (2008): 162–177.

Persson, Ingmar, and Julian Savulescu. *Unfit for the Future: The Need for Moral Enhancement.* Oxford: Oxford University Press, 2012.

Persson, Ingmar, and Julian Savulescu. 'Unfit for the Future? Human Nature, Scientific Progress, and the Need for Moral Enhancement'. In *Enhancing Human Capacities,* ed. Julian Savulescu, Ruud ter Meulen and Guy Kahane, 486–498. Chichester: Wiley-Blackwell, 2011.

Pesce, Mark. 'Magic Mirror: The Novel as a Software Development Platform'. *MIT Communications Forum.* http://web.mit.edu/comm-forum/papers/pesce.html.

Peters, Karl. 'Empirical Theology in Light of Science'. *Zygon* 27, no. 3 (1992): 297–325.

Peters, Karl. 'Humanity in Nature: Conserving Yet Creating'. *Zygon* 24 (1989): 469–485.

Peters, Karl. 'Religion and an Evolutionary Theory of Knowledge'. *Zygon* 17 (1982): 285–415.

Peters, Ted. 'CRISPR, the Precautionary Principle, and Bioethics'. *Theology and Science* 13, no. 3 (2015): 267–270.

Peters, Ted. *Playing God? Genetic Determinism and Human Freedom*. 2nd edn. New York: Routledge, 2003.

Peters, Ted. *Science, Theology and Ethics*. Aldershot: Ashgate Publishing, 2003.

Peterson, Gregory. 'The Created Co-creator: What It Is and What It Is Not'. *Zygon* 39, no. 4 (2004): 827–840.

Peterson, Gregory. 'The Scientific Status of Theology: Imre Lakatos, Method and Demarcation'. *Perspectives in Science and Christian Faith* 50 (1988): 22–31.

Peterson, James. *Genetic Turning Points: The Ethics of Human Genetic Intervention*. Grand Rapids, MI: Eerdmans, 2001.

Pew Research Center. 'U.S. Public Wary of Biomedical Technologies to "Enhance" Human Abilities'. July 2016.

Pfeiffer, John. *The Creative Explosion: An Enquiry into the Origins of Art and Religion*. Ithaca: Cornell University Press, 1982.

Pico della Mirandola, Giovanni. *Oration on the Dignity of Man*. Trans. A. Robert Caponigri. Chicago, IL: Henry Regnery Co., 1956.

Planck, Max. *A Scientific Autobiography*. London: Williams & Norgate, 1950.

Pope, Rob. *Creativity: Theory, History, Practice*. Abingdon: Routledge, 2005.

Popper, Karl. *Objective Knowledge: An Evolutionary Approach*. Oxford: Clarendon Press, 1972.

Popper, Karl. *The Logic of Scientific Discovery*. New York: Harper, 1965.

Proust, Marcel. *On Art and Literature*. Trans. Sylvia Townsend Warner. New York: Carroll & Graf, 1997.

Quayson, Ato. *Aesthetic Nervousness: Disability and the Crisis of Representation*. New York: Columbia University Press, 2007.

Quinn, Daniel. *Ishmael: An Adventure of the Mind and Spirit*. New York: Bantam/Turner, 1992.

Rahner, Karl. *Hören des Wortes*. Munich: Kössel-Verlag, 1963.

Ramsey, Paul. *Fabricated Man: The Ethics of Genetic Control*. New Haven, CT: Yale University Press, 1970.

Rapport, Nigel. '"Imagination Is the Barest Reality": On the Universal Human Imagining of the World'. In *Reflections on Imagination:*

Human Capacity and Ethnographic Method, ed. Mark Harris and Nigel Rapport, 3–22. Farnham: Ashgate, 2015.

Raulerson, Joshua. *Singularities: Technoculture, Transhumanism, and Science Fiction in the 21st Century*. Liverpool: Liverpool University Press, 2013.

Richards, Darielle. 'The Creative Process of J. R. R. Tolkien and the Tradition of the Magus'. PhD diss., Pacifica Graduate Institute, 2005.

Richards, Robert. *Darwin and the Emergence of Evolutionary Theories of Mind and Behavior*. Chicago, IL: University of Chicago Press, 1987.

Ricoeur, Paul. 'Creativity in Language'. *Philosophy Today* 17, no. 2 (1973): 97–111.

Ricoeur, Paul. 'Imagination in Discourse and in Action'. In *The Human Being in Action: The Irreducible Element in Man, Part II Investigations at the Intersection of Philosophy and Psychiatry*, ed. Anna-Teresa Tymieniecka, 3–22. Dordrecht: Springer, 1978.

Ricoeur, Paul. *Oneself as Another*. Chicago, IL: University of Chicago Press, 1992.

Ricoeur, Paul. 'The Function of Fiction in Shaping Reality'. *Man and World* 12, no. 2 (1979): 123–141.

Ricoeur, Paul. *The Symbolism of Evil*. New York: Beacon Press, 1967.

Ridley, Mark. *Evolution*. 3rd edn. Oxford: Blackwell Publishers, 2004.

Roberts, Adam. *The History of Science Fiction*. Basingstoke: Palgrave Macmillan, 2007.

Roberts, Jason. '"Fill and Subdue?" Imaging God in New Social and Ecological Contexts'. *Zygon* 50, no. 1 (2015): 42–63.

Robinson, Marilynne. *Absence of Mind: The Dispelling of Inwardnes from the Modern Myth of the Self*. New Haven, CT: Yale University Press, 2011.

Robinson, Marilynne. 'What Are We Doing Here?' In *What Are We Doing Here?: Essays*, 17–33. London: Virago, 2018.

Roduit, Johann, Tobias Eichinger and Walter Glannon. 'Science Fiction and Human Enhancement: Radical Life-Extension in the Movie "In Time" (2011)'. *Medicine, Healthcare and Philosophy* 21 (2018): 287–293.

Runco, Mark. *Creativity: Theories and Themes: Research, Development, and Practice*. London: Academic Press, 2014.

Runco, Mark, and Garrett Jaeger. 'The Standard Definition of Creativity'. *Creativity Research Journal* 24, no. 1 (2012): 92–96.

Russell, Robert. 'Cosmology from Alpha to Omega: Response to Reviews'. *Zygon* 45, no. 1 (2010): 237–250.

Russell, Robert. 'Ian Barbour's Methodological Breakthrough: Creating the "Bridge" Between Science and Theology'. *Theology and Science* 15, no. 1 (2017): 28–41.

Said, Edward. *Orientalism*. New York: Vintage, 1979.

Sandberg, Anders. 'Transhumanism and the Meaning of Life'. In *Religion and Transhumanism: The Unknown Future of Human Enhancement*, ed. Calvin Mercer and Tracy Trothen, 3–22. Santa Barbara, CA: Praeger Publishers, 2015.

Sandner, David. '"Joy Beyond the Walls of the World": The Secondary WorldMaking of J. R. R. Tolkien and C. S. Lewis'. In *J. R. R. Tolkien and His Literary Resonances*, ed. George Clark and Daniel Timmons, 133–145. Westport, CT: Greenwood Press, 2000.

Sartre, Jean-Paul. *The Imaginary: A Phenomenological Psychology of the Imagination*. Trans. Jonathan Webber. London: Routledge, 2004.

Savulescu, Julian. 'Justice, Fairness, and Enhancement'. *Annals of the New York Academy of Sciences*, 2006, 321–338.

Savulescu, Julian. 'Procreative Beneficence: Why We Should Select the Best Children'. *Bioethics* 15 (2001): 413–26.

Savulescu, Julian. 'The Maverick: "It's Our Duty to Have Designer Babies"'. Accessed 13 October 2016. www.readersdigest.co.uk/magazine/readers-digest-main/themaverick-its-our-duty-to-have-designer-babies.

Sawyer, Robert. *Mindscan*. New York: Tor, 2005.

Sayers, Dorothy. *Four Sacred Plays*. London: Victor Gollancz, 1948.

Sayers, Dorothy. *The Mind of the Maker*. New York: HarperCollins, 1987.

Sayers, Dorothy. 'Vocation in Work'. In *A Christian Basis for the Post-War World*, ed. A. E. Baker, 88–103. London: SCM Press, 1942.

Schaeffer, Francis. *Art and the Bible*. Downers Grove, IL: InterVarsity Press, 1973.

Scott, P. Anne. 'Imagination in Practice'. *Journal of Medical Ethics* 23, no. 1 (1997): 45–50.

Scott, Peter. 'The Technological Factor: Redemption, Nature, and the Image of God'. *Zygon* 35, no. 2 (2000): 371–384.

Selke, Lori, and Djibril al-Ayad, eds. *Outlaw Bodies: A Speculative Fiction Anthology*. United States: Futurefire.net Publishing, 2012.

Seltzer, Kimberley, and Tom Bentley. *The Creative Age: Knowledge and Skills for the New Economy*. Buckingham: Demos, 1999.

Sennett, Richard. *The Craftsman*. New Haven, CT: Yale University Press, 2008.

Sharkey, Noel, and Tom Ziemke. 'Mechanistic Versus Phenomenal Embodiment: Can Robot Embodiment Lead to Strong AI?' *Cognitive Systems Research* 2, no. 4 (2001): 251–262.

Shatner, William, and Chip Walter. *I'm Working on That: A Trek from Science Fiction to Science Fact*. New York: Pocket, 2002.

Shelley, Percy Bysshe. 'A Defense of Poetry'. In *Political Tracts of Wordsworth, Coleridge and Shelley*, ed. R. J. White, 195–206. Cambridge: Cambridge University Press, 1953.

Sher, Leo. 'Neuroimaging, Auditory Hallucinations, and the Bicameral Mind'. *Journal of Psychiatry and Neuroscience* 25, no. 3 (2000): 239–240.

Shippey, Tom. 'Creation from Philology'. In *J. R. R. Tolkien, Scholar and Storyteller: Essays in Memoriam*, ed. Mary Salu and Robert Farrell, 286–316. Ithaca, NY: Cornell University Press, 1979.

Shippey, Tom. *J. R. R. Tolkien: Author of the Century*. Boston, MA: Houghton Mifflin, 2002.

Shook, John. 'Neuroethics and the Possible Types of Moral Enhancement'. *American Journal of Bioethics: Neuroscience* 3, no. 4 (2012): 3–14.

Siebers, Tobin. *Disability Theory*. Ann Arbor, MI: University of Michigan Press, 2008.

Siegelbaum, Debbie. 'Project Hieroglyph: Fighting Society's Dystopian Future'. *BBC News*. www.bbc.co.uk/news/magazine-28974943.

Sim, Stuart. 'Posthumanism'. In *The Routledge Companion to Postmodernism*, ed. Stuart Sim, 283. London: Routledge, 2012.

Sittler, Joseph. 'The Sittler Speeches'. In *Center for the Study of Campus Ministry Yearbook*, ed. Phil Schroeder, 8–61. Valparaiso, IN: Valparaiso University Press, 1978.

Skinner, Michael. 'Environmental Epigenetics and a Unified Theory of the Molecular Aspects of Evolution: A Neo-Lamarckian Concept that Facilitates Neo-Darwinian Evolution'. *Genome Biology and Evolution* 7, no. 5 (2015): 1296–1302.

Smedes, Taede. 'Beyond Barbour or Back to Basics? The Future of Science-and-Religion and the Quest for Unity'. *Zygon* 43, no. 1 (2008): 235–258.

Smith, James K. A. *Awaiting the King: Reforming Public Theology*. Grand Rapids, MI: Baker Academic, 2017.

Smith, James K. A. *Desiring the Kingdom: Worship, Worldview, and Cultural Formation*. Grand Rapids, MI: Baker Academic, 2009.

Smith, James K. A. *How (Not) to Be Secular: Reading Charles Taylor*. Grand Rapids, MI: Eerdmans, 2014.

Smith, James K. A. *Imagining the Kingdom: How Worship Works*. Grand Rapids, MI: Baker Academic, 2013.

Snow, C. P. *The Two Cultures*. Cambridge: Cambridge University Press, 1998.

Solana, Michael. 'Stop Writing Dystopian Sci-Fi: It's Making Us All Fear Technology'. *Wired*. www.wired.com/2014/08/stop-writing-dystopian-sci-fiits-making-us-all-fear-technology/.

Southgate, Christopher. *The Groaning of Creation: God, Evolution and the Problem of Evil*. Louisville, KY: Westminster John Knox Press, 2008.

Stableford, Brian, John Clute and Peter Nicholls. 'History of SF'. In *The Encyclopedia of Science Fiction*. New York: St. Martin's Press, 1993.

Stallman, Richard. 'Made for You', 2012. Accessed 10 March 2018. https://ieet.org/index.php/IEET2/more/stallman20121228.

Steinberg, Deborah. 'Reading Sleep Through Science Fiction: The Parable of Beggars and Choosers'. *Body and Society* 14, no. 4 (2008): 115–135.

Steiner, George. *After Babel: Aspects of Language and Translation*. Oxford: Oxford University Press, 1998.

Stevens, Anthony. *Archetypes: A Natural History of the Self*. New York: Morrow, 1983.

Stivers, Richard. 'Our Brave New World Today'. *Bulletin of Science, Technology & Society* 30, no. 4 (2010): 247–251.

Stock, Brian. 'Ethics and the Humanities: Some Lessons of Historical Experience'. *New Literary History: A Journal of Theory and Interpretation* 36, no. 1 (2005): 1–17.

Stump, Eleanore. *Wandering in Darkness: Narrative and the Problem of Suffering*. Oxford: Oxford University Press, 2010.

Swingle, Mari. *I-Minds: How Cell Phones, Computers, Gaming, and Social Media are Changing Our Brains, Our Behavior and the Evolution of our Species*. Gabriola, BC: New Society Publishers, 2016.

Szerszynski, Bronislaw. *Nature, Technology and the Sacred*. Oxford: Blackwell Publishing, 2005.

Taylor, Charles. *A Secular Age*. Cambridge, MA: Harvard University Press, 2007.

Taylor, Charles. 'Modern Social Imaginaries'. *Public Culture* 14, no. 1 (2002): 91–124.

Taylor, Charles. *Modern Social Imaginaries*. Durham, NC: Duke University Press, 2004.

Taylor, Charles. *Sources of the Self: The Making of the Modern Identity*. Cambridge, MA: Harvard University Press, 1989.

Taylor, Charles. *The Language Animal: The Full Shape of the Human Linguistic Capacity*. Cambridge, MA: Belknap Press, 2016.

Taylor, George. 'Ricoeur's Philosophy of Imagination'. *Journal of French Philosophy* 16, no. 1 (2006): 93–104.

Teilhard de Chardin, Pierre. *Activation of Energy*. Trans. Renè Hague. London: Collins, 1970.

Teilhard de Chardin, Pierre. 'Mass on the World'. In *Hymn of the Universe*, trans. Gerald Vann, 9–31. New York: Harper & Row, 1965.

Teilhard de Chardin, Pierre. *The Future of Man*. Trans. Norman Denny. London: Collins, 1964.

Teilhard de Chardin, Pierre. *The Phenomenon of Man*. Trans. Bernard Wall. New York: Harper & Row, 1961.

Temkin, Larry. 'Is Living Longer Living Better?' In *Enhancing Human Capacities*, ed. Julian Savulescu, Ruud ter Meulen and Guy Kahane, 350–367. Chichester: Wiley-Blackwell, 2011.

Theissen, Gerd. *Biblical Faith: An Evolutionary Approach*. Philadelphia, PA: Fortress Press, 1985.

Thweatt-Bates, Jeanine. *Cyborg Selves: A Theological Anthropology of the Posthuman*. Surrey: Ashgate Publishing, 2012.

Tillich, Paul. *Systematic Theology*. Vol. I. Chicago, IL: University of Chicago Press, 1951.

Tillich, Paul. *Systematic Theology*. Vol. III. Welwyn: James Nisbet & Co., 1964.

Tillich, Paul. 'The Technological City as Symbol'. In *The Spiritual Situation in Our Technological Society*, ed. J. Mark Thomas and D. Ric Thomas, 179–184. Macon, GA: Mercer University Press, 1988.

Tiptree, James, Jr. 'The Girl Who Was Plugged In'. In *Her Smoke Rose Up Forever*, 43–78. San Francisco, CA: Tachyon Publications, 2004.

Tolkien, J. R. R. 'Leaf by Niggle'. In *Tree and Leaf*, 93–118. London: Harper-Collins, 2001.

Tolkien, J. R. R. 'Mythopoeia'. In *Tree and Leaf*, 83–90. London: Harper-Collins, 2001.

Tolkien, J. R. R. 'On Fairy-Stories'. In *Tree and Leaf*, 1–81. London: HarperCollins, 2001.

Tolkien, J. R. R. *Sauron Defeated: The End of the Third Age, The Notion Club Papers and the Drowning of Anadûné*, Ed. Christopher Tolkien. Vol. 9. The History of Middle-Earth, vol. 9 London: HarperCollins, 1992.

Tolkien, J. R. R. *The Book of Lost Tales, Part I*. Ed. Christopher Tolkien. London: Houghton Mifflin, 1986.

Tolkien, J. R. R. *The Fellowship of the Ring*. 2nd edn. London: Allen & Unwin, 1966.

Tolkien, J. R. R. *The Letters of J. R. R. Tolkien*. Ed. Humphrey Carpenter and Christopher Tolkien. London: Allen & Unwin, 1981.

Tolkien, J. R. R. *The Return of the King*. 2nd edn. London: Allen & Unwin, 1966.

Tolkien, J. R. R. *The Silmarillion*. 1st edn. Ed. Christopher Tolkien. London: Allen & Unwin, 1977.

Tolkien, J. R. R. *The Silmarillion*. 1st edn. Ed. by Christopher Tolkien. London: HarperCollins, 1999.

Tolkien, J. R. R. *The Two Towers*. 2nd edn. London: Allen & Unwin, 1966.

Tracy, David. *The Analogical Imagination: Christian Theology and the Culture of Pluralism*. London: SCM Press, 1981.

Tresch, John. *The Romantic Machine: Utopian Science and Technology After Napoleon*. Chicago, IL: University of Chicago Press, 2012.

Trinkaus, Charles. *In Our Image and Likeness: Humanity and Divinity in Italian Humanist Thought*. Notre Dame, IN: University of Notre Dame Press, 1995.

Tyndall, John. *Scientific Use of the Imagination and Other Essays*. London: Longman, Greens & Co., 1872.

United Nations Environment Program. *Global Environment Outlook 2000*. London: Earthscan, 2000.

Vanhoozer, Kevin. 'Imagination in Theology'. In *New Dictionary of Theology: Historical and Systematic*, 2nd edn, ed. Martin Davie, Tim Grass, Stephen Holmes, John McDowell and T. A. Noble, 441–443. London: InterVarsity Press, 2016.

Viladesau, Richard. *Theological Aesthetics: God in Imagination, Beauty, and Art*. New York: Oxford University Press, 1999.

Vint, Sherryl. *Bodies of Tomorrow: Technology, Subjectivity, Science Fiction*. Toronto: University of Toronto Press, 2007.

Volf, Miroslav. *Exclusion and Embrace: A Theological Exploration of Identity, Otherness, and Reconciliation*. Nashville, TN: Abingdon Press, 1996.

Volf, Miroslav. 'The Crown of the Good Life: A Hypothesis'. In *Joy and Human Flourishing: Essays on Theology, Culture and the Good Life*, ed. Miroslav Volf and Justin Crisp, 127–135. Minneapolis, MN: Fortress Press, 2015.

Volf, Miroslav. *The End of Memory: Remembering Rightly in a Violent World*. Grand Rapids, MI: Eerdmans, 2006.

Wadley, Greg. 'Mood-Enhancing Technology'. In *Proceedings of the 28th Australian Conference on Computer-Human Interaction*, 326–332. New York: ACM, 2016.

Walker, Steve. *The Power of Tolkien's Prose: Middle-Earth's Magical Style*. New York: Palgrave Macmillan, 2009.

Walton, Kendall. *Mimesis as Make-Believe: On the Foundation of the Representational Arts*. Cambridge, MA: Harvard University Press, 1990.

Ward, Graham. 'Narrative and Ethics: The Structures of Believing and the Practices of Hope'. *Literature and Theology* 20, no. 4 (2006): 438–461.

Ward, Graham. *Unbelievable: Why We Believe and Why We Don't*. London: I. B. Tauris, 2014.

Ward, Graham. *Unimaginable: What We Imagine and What We Can't*. London: I. B. Tauris, 2018.

Waters, Brent. *From Human to Posthuman: Christian Theology and Technology in a Postmodern World*. Aldershot: Ashgate Publishing, 2006.

Weber, Richard. 'Where No One Has Gone Before: When Science Fiction Inspires Technology'. *Journal of Financial Service Professionals* 70, no. 4 (2016): 43–46.

Weisberg, Robert. 'On the Usefulness of "Value" in the Definition of Creativity'. *Creativity Research Journal* 27 (2015): 111–124.

Welsted, Leonard. *Title Epistles, Odes, Written on Several Subjects: With a Translation of Longinus's Treatise on the Sublime*. London: J. Walthoe & J. Peele, 1724.

White, Lynn. 'The Historical Roots of our Ecological Crisis'. *Science* 155 (1967): 1203–1207.

Whitehead, Alfred North. *Science and the Modern World*. New York: Free Press, 1967.

Williams, Donald. *Mere Humanity: G. K. Chesterton, C. S. Lewis, and J. R. R. Tolkien on the Human Condition*. Nashville, TN: B. & H. Publishing, 2006.

Williams, E. 'Human Performance', March 2008. Accessed 2 February 2018. https://fas.org/irp/agency/dod/jason/human.pdf.

Williamson, Timothy. 'Knowing by Imagining'. In *Knowledge Through Imagination*, ed. Amy Kind and Peter Kung, 113–123. Oxford: Oxford University Press, 2016.

Wilson, David Sloan. 'Evolutionary Social Constructivism'. In *The Literary Animal: Evolution and the Nature of Narrative*, ed. Jonathan Gottschall and David Sloan Wilson, 20–37. Evanston, IL: Northwestern University Press, 2005.

Wilson, Edward O. *Half-Earth: Our Planet's Fight for Life*. New York: Liveright Publishing, 2016.

Wilson, Edward O. *On Human Nature*. Cambridge, MA: Harvard University Press, 1978.

Wilson, Robert, and Lucia Foglia. 'Embodied Cognition'. *Stanford Encyclopedia of Philosophy*. https://plato.stanford.edu/archives/spr2017/entries/embodied-cognition/.

Winter, Steven. '*Bull Durham* and the Uses of Theory'. *Stanford Law Review* 42 (1990): 639–93.

Wirzba, Norman. *From Nature to Creation: A Christian Vision for Understanding and Loving Our World*. Grand Rapids, MI: Baker Academic, 2015.

Wiseman, Harris. *The Myth of the Moral Brain: The Limits of Moral Enhancement*. Cambridge, MA: MIT Press, 2016.

Wiseman, Harris. 'The Sins of Moral Enhancement Discourse'. *Royal Institute of Philosophy Supplement* 83 (2018): 35–58.

Wolfe, Cary. *What Is Posthumanism?* Minneapolis, MN: University of Minnesota Press, 2010.

Womack, Ytasha. *Afrofuturism: The World of Black Sci-Fi and Fantasy Culture*. Chicago, IL: Chicago Review Press, 2013.

Wood, Ralph. 'Tolkien and Postmodernism'. In *Tolkien Among the Moderns*, ed. Ralph Wood, 247–278. Notre Dame, IN: University of Notre Dame Press, 2015.

Wood, Ralph. 'Tolkien's Augustinian Understanding of Good and Evil: Why *The Lord of the Rings* Is Not Manichean'. In *Tree of Tales: Tolkien, Literature and Theology*, ed. Trevor Hart and Ivan Khovacs, 85–102. Waco, TX: Baylor University Press, 2007.

Woolf, Steven, and Heidi Schoomaker. 'Life Expectancy and Mortality Rates in the United States, 1959-2017'. *JAMA* 322, no. 20 (2019): 1996–2016.

Wright, N. T. *Surprised by Hope: Rethinking Heaven, the Resurrection and the Mission of the Church*. New York: HarperOne, 2008. ISBN: 9780281056170.

Wynter, Sylvia. 'Unsettling the Coloniality of Being/Power/Truth/Freedom: Towards the Human, After Man, Its Overrepresentation

– An Argument'. *CR: The New Centennial Review* 3, no. 3 (2003): 257–337.

Zahl, Simeon. 'Engineering Desire: Biotechnological Enhancement as Theological Problem'. *Studies in Christian Ethics* 32, no. 2 (2019): 216–228.

Zahl, Simeon. *The Holy Spirit and Christian Experience.* Oxford: Oxford University Press, 2020.

Zardoya, Rafael, and Axel Meyer, 'Molecular Evidence on the Origin of and the Phylogenetic Relationships Among the Major Groups of Vertebrates'. In *Evolution: From Molecules to Ecosystems*, edited by Andrés Moya and Enrique Font, 209–217. Oxford: Oxford University Press, 2004.

Zhang, Feng, Yan Wen, and Xiong Guo. 'CRISPR/Cas9 for Genome Editing: Progress, Implications and Challenges'. *Human Molecular Genetics* 23 (2014): R40–46.

Zournazi, Mary, and Rowan Williams. *Justice and Love: A Philosophical Dialogue.* London: Bloomsbury Academic, 2020.

Zylstra, Sarah Eekhoff. 'Christians to Science: Leave Our Bodies How God Made Them', *Christianity Today*, 26 July 2016, https://www.christianitytoday.com/news/2016/july/christians-science-leave-bodies-alone-pew-human-enhancement.html.

Index

Afrofuturism, 250–251
anthropocentrism, 6, 77, 84, 148, 262,
    258–262
apocalypticism, 23
apologetics, 264, 299
artificial intelligence (AI), 33, 193,
    275–277, 279
Avis, Paul, 141, 155–156, 167, 211

Bacon, Francis, 48–49
Barbour, Ian, 149–151
Barfield, Owen, 203
bicameral mind, 95, 97
Bieber Lake, Christina, 199–200, 239
biocultural evolution, 88–91
Bostrom, Nick, 11, 15, 21
Bourdieu, Pierre, 222, 227–228
Brock, Brian, 240–241, 265
Burdett, Michael, 123, 242
Burhoe, Ralph, 88, 100–102, 153–154

climate crisis, 93
co-creation, 4, see also created co-creator;
    sub-creation
    and evolution, 61, 68, 224–225, see also
        biocultural evolution
    and science, 57–59
    importance of imagination, 154
Coeckelbergh, Mark, 21, 231–234
Cole-Turner, Ronald, 40, 42, 114–119,
    126–128, 132
Coleridge, Samuel Taylor, 140, 142
created co-creator, 4
    ambiguity as a metaphor, 122–123
    and ecology, 78, 93–94
    and Haraway's cyborg, 108, 262
    and human freedom, 76, 85, 87, 91

dialectic of freedom and
    determinism, 85
and human technological
    enhancement, 110, 114, 109–122
and technology, 93–95, 108, 112, 240
and the *imago Dei*, 91, 112
as a Lakatosian research programme,
    75–97
    Lakatosian evaluation of, 103–109
    scientific validity of, 78–84, 86–87,
        89–90, 92–93, 95–97
    theological coherency of, 97–103
in Hefner's theological task, 67–69
limitations on co-creativity, 124–129
meaning and purpose, 80–81
role of the imagination, 133, 129–148
versus Tolkien's sub-creation, 201–203
'wholesomeness' of human action, 81
within evolutionary context, 76, 85, see
    also biocultural evolution
creation, see also human creativity
    doctrine of creation, 3, 63
cultural scientism, 150–151
cyborgs (posthumanism), 251, 257,
    260–262

de Chardin, Teilhard, 3, 58, 111
de Grey, Aubrey, 13, 14
disability studies, 249–250

ecology, 78
Eden, 209, 210, 231, 235, 261
Ellul, Jacques, 27, 234, 238
environmental crisis, 93
epigenetics, 85, 90, 226
eschatology, 118, 279–281, 286, 291
evolution, see also biocultural evolution

and morality, 102
extropianism, *see* transhumanism

Feuerbach, Ludwig, 146–147
Ficino, Marsilio, 47
fiction, *see also* myth; science fiction
  and moral formation, 194–197,
    241–243, 247–248, 265–266, 292
  medium for communicating truth,
    182–185, 188, 187–214

Gaiman, Neil, 30, 183
grace, 83, 84, 91, 118
Graham, Elaine, 260, 261
Green, Garrett, 146

Haraway, Donna, 108, 257, 262
Hart, Trevor, 44–45, 49–50, 54, 166, 178,
    237, 251
Hauerwas, Stanley, 190–192
Hayles, N. Katherine, 2, 254
Hedley, Douglas, 139, 161, 227
hedonic recalibration, 15–16, 285–286
  in science fiction, 38
Hefner, Philip, 4, *see also* created
    co-creator, 301
  doctrine of God, 98–99
  understanding of sin and evil, 99–102
Heidegger, Martin, 180, 206–207, 232, 237
Holton, Gerald, 143, 167
Hughes, James, 12
human creativity, 3, 226–228, *see also*
    co-creation; sub-creation
  and fallenness, 61, 226–227
  and moral discernment, 128, 136
  creativity studies, 50–54
  epistemology of, 128, 131–132, *see also*
    imagination, epistemology of
  in Renaissance humanism, 46–47
  relationship to divine creativity, 43–50,
    119, 174, 175, 224, 228–229, 272
human dominion, 48, 58, *see also*
    anthropocentrism
human enhancement, *see* human
    technological enhancement
human exceptionalism, *see*
    anthropocentrism
human flourishing, 235

human germline modification, 41–43
human nature, malleability of, 22
human technological enhancement, *see*
    also transhumanism; created
    co-creator, and human technological
    enhancement; hedonic recalibration;
    mind-uploading; moral
    enhancement; radical life extension
  and embodiment, 250–251, 254–258,
    274–279
  and human flourishing, 198–200
  Christian opposition to, 40–43
  enhancement versus therapy, 43
  moral reflection on, 241–243
  novelty of, 20–22

imagination, 4–5, *see also* co-creation,
    importance of imagination; created
    co-creator, role of the imagination
  and embodiment, 137, 254–258
  definition, 136–137
  epistemology of, 136, 143, 163, 168, 203,
    211, 243, 255, *see also* human
    creativity, epistemology of
  in harmony with reason, 166–167, 203,
    238, 255–256
  in revelation and scripture, 156–157
  in Romanticism, 138–142
  in science, 159–165, 203
  legacy of the Enlightenment, 143–145
  moral imagination, 211–214, 244,
    243–248, 254, 265, 264–265
  and technology, 217
  truthfulness of, 139–142
  versus reason, 138–141, 218, 221

Jaynes, Julian, 95, 97
Johnson, Mark, 192, 244–247, 256,
    254–256

Kuhn, Thomas, 70
Kurzweil, Ray, 19, 274

Lakatos, Imre, 70, 144, 164
Lakatosian research programmes, 70–72
  adaptation by Hefner, 72–74
Lakoff, George, 247, 254–255
Le Guin, Ursula, 142, 183, 184, 239

literature, *see* fiction
logical positivism, 143, 149, 151, *see also* rationalism

MacIntyre, Alisdair, 192–193
malleability, of human nature, 3, 60, 168
Manetti, Giannozzo, 46
Maritain, Jacques, 55
Maurice, Merleau-Ponty, 222
Max More, 16
McGilchrist, Iain, 147, 218–221, 229, 243, 246, 255
Medawar, Peter, 21, 22, 141, 143, 160–161, 165
memory, alternation of, 282
metaphor studies, 254–255, *see also* narrative, cognitive science of
Midgley, Mary, 141, 154, 162–163, 166, 238
Midson, Scott, 35, 231, 235, 260–262
mind-uploading, 18–20, 274–281
  in science fiction, 37–38, 277–278
Moltmann, Jürgen, 279
mood enhancement, *see* hedonic recalibration
moral enhancement, 16–18, 281–284
  in science fiction, 38, 282
Moravec, Hans, 18–19
Murdoch, Iris, 183, 212
Murphy, Nancey, 72, 74, 152–153
myth, 95–97, 173, 182, 211, 237
mythopoesis, 96

narrative, 131, *see also* fiction; myth
  cognitive science of, 86, 190, 241
  in moral discernment, 86, 193, 241, 190–243
  visions of the good life, 189–190, 199
neuroscience, 86, 92
niche construction, 89

original sin, 99–100, 142

Peacocke, Arthur, 59
Pearce, David, 15
Peters, Ted, 122, 119–132
Peterson, Gregory, 74, 122, 124, 201
phenomenology, 221–223, 227–228

philosophy of science, *see* Lakatosian research programmes
Pico della Mirandola, Giovanni, 46
'playing God', *see* human technological enhancement, Christian opposition to
Popper, Karl, 70, 143, 164
postcolonialism, 248–249, 273
posthumanism, 256–257
process theology, 147
Prometheus, 3

radical life extension, 13–15, 271–274
  in science fiction, 36, 272–273
rationalism, 138, 143–145, 148, 168
Renaissance humanism, *see also* human creativity, in Renaissance humanism
resurrection, 279–281
Ricoeur, Paul, 95, 147–148, 158, 244
Romanticism, 138–142, 231–234

Sandberg, Anders, 12, 188
Savulescu, Julian, 17, 18
Sayers, Dorothy, 55
science and religion
  methodology, 106–108, 149–154, 230–231, *see also* Lakatosian research programmes
science fiction, 2, 250, 282, 288, *see also* hedonic recalibration, in science fiction; mind-uploading, in science fiction; moral enhancement, in science fiction; radical life extension, in science fiction
  and present anxieties, 27, 34
  and reflection on technology, 31, 34, 35, 242
  as laboratory for the future, 34, 35
  cyberpunk, 36–37
  definition and purpose, 25–27, 34
  relationship with technological innovation, 25, 27–33
Shelley, Percy Bysshe, 139, 243
sleep engineering, 287–290
Smedes, Taede, 149–152
Smith, James K. A., 137, 189, 221–223, 235, 247
social imaginary, 251–254
Stump, Eleanore, 192, 221

sub-creation
    and the Primary (real) world, 181–182,
        187–188
    definition, 172–176
    in 'Leaf by Niggle', 177–178, 187–188
    in 'Mythopoeia', 173, 174, 180
    in 'On Fairy-Stories', 172–174, 202
    in the 'Ainulindalë', 176–177
    in *The Lord of the Rings*, 179–180
    limits of, 178–181
    metaphors for, 173–174, 176, 206
    misuse of, 178–181
    novelty of, 174–176
    versus Hefner's co-creation, 201–203

Taylor, Charles, 189, 213, 252–253
technology, *see also* created co-creator,
        and technology
    and culture, 110
    and moral formation, 217, 234–235,
        240–241, 265–266
    and nature, 110, 209–210, 223, 231, 235,
        257, 262
    and Romanticism, 231–234
    as legitimate human creativity, 3, 57,
        60, 231, 237, 264
    definition of, 60, 111, 113
    technocratic paradigm, 206, 208, 210,
        236, 240, 264
    Tolkien's concern over, 203–209

teleology, 79–80
teleonomy, 77–80
Thweatt-Bates, Jeanine, 5, 251, 257, 261
Tolkien, J. R. R., 171–172, *see also*
        sub-creation
    Christian faith, 188, 200
    classification of works as allegory, 181
    concern about technology, 203–209,
        235–236
    view of nature, 209–210
    view of the imagination, 185–187, 203
transhumanism, 1, 109
    and religion, 23–25, 118
    conception of the good life, 13, 15, 16,
        188, 199, 249, 264
    definition, 11–12
    history of, 21–22
    representation of Enlightenment
        ideals, 13, 22
    versus posthumanism, 11, 257

Volf, Miroslav, 282

Ward, Graham, 5, 229, 253–254
Waters, Brent, 23, 213
Whitehead, Alfred North, 98, 160
Wilson, E. O., 94, 96, 154
Wordsworth, William, 141, 142

Zahl, Simeon, 284